MOON

PORTLAND

HOLLYANNA McCOLLOM

CONTENTS

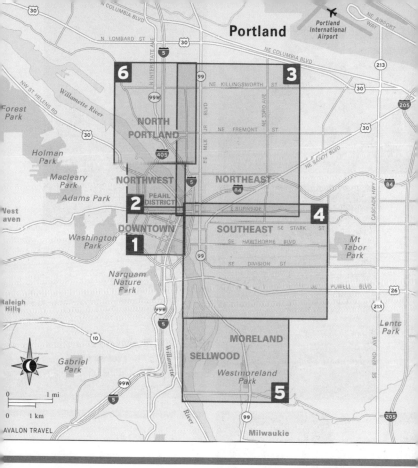

MAPS

1 Portland food cart

2 iconic Old Town stag sign

3 Portland Japanese Garden

4 mural created by Forest for the Trees

5 Paley's Place

6 downtown Portland

DISCOVER
PORTLAND

The rain may fall and the skies may be gray, but still they come to Portland. Every day the city swells in numbers thanks to the influx of people seeking an answer to the question, "Why is everyone so in love with Portland?"

The truth is that this place inspires passion because its creative lifestyle amid natural beauty is contagious. Collaborative energy and unbridled playfulness make for happier living. With its vibrant and hospitable personality, Portland has all the stimulation and excitement of a big city and all the charm of a small town. It's hard not to feel like a local when you visit.

Artists, playwrights, actors, and musicians have made Portland a bohemian playground, rich with color, opulence, and activity. The culinary scene continues to explode, with food lovers flocking to sample the flavors of the Pacific Northwest by chefs and master mix-

ologists who are finding their way onto the pages of the *New York Times, Travel + Leisure,* and *Bon Appétit.* Portland also has quite the backyard, perfectly nestled between green forests and snowcapped mountains, with a river running through it and in close proximity to the Pacific Ocean.

Whether you call it P-Town, Bridge City, the City of Roses, or Stumptown, Portland is what you make it. From the urban delights of the downtown Cultural District to the unspoiled wilderness of Forest Park, each corner of this DIY-centric city is bursting with that distinctive Portland spirit. From the coffee shops and thrift stores of Hawthorne to the lounges and boutiques of the Pearl District, each neighborhood possesses its own voice, part of the whimsical carnival choir of this dynamic city.

8 TOP
EXPERIENCES

1 **Wander Green Spaces:** Portland is a lush urban paradise with great escapes right in the city, like **Oaks Bottom Wildlife Refuge** (page 32), **Washington Park** (page 35), and **Forest Park** (page 159).

2 **Browse Powell's City of Books:** Bibliotourists, rejoice! More than one million books occupy an entire square block of the city (page 25).

3 **Drink Craft Beer:** Portland is known as Beervana. You'll understand why once you taste some of its many local brews (page 13).

4 **Bike:** Portland has ample bike paths, a city bike share program, and celebrates its love of cycling with bike-centered events like **Pedalpalooza**—including the **World Naked Bike Ride**—and **Bridge Pedal** (page 152).

^
^
^

5 **Enjoy Nearby Adventures:** Portland has quite the backyard. Drive the **Oregon Coast,** hike the **Columbia River Gorge,** go wine tasting in the **Willamette Valley,** and ski on **Mount Hood** (page 208).

6 Experience Live Music: Portland is a favorite stop for touring indie bands thanks to unique spots such as the **Crystal Ballroom** (page 95) and hip, intimate venues like the **Aladdin Theater, Doug Fir,** and **Revolution Hall** (page 111).

<<<

7 Take an Art Walk: Celebrate art at **First Thursday in the Pearl** and **Last Thursday on Alberta,** when galleries and shops serve beer and wine and street vendors show off their wares (page 127).

>>>

8 Fulfill Your Foodie Dreams: From pizza and poutine at **food carts** (page 76) to fine dining on **Pacific Northwest cuisine** (page 55), Portland sates your cravings.

<<<

EXPLORE
PORTLAND

THE THREE-DAY BEST OF PORTLAND

Portland has a lot to offer, and it can be hard to pack all of the city's charms into a weekend. Stick to one area a day and you can save money by skipping a rental car—you can access most of these places using public transportation or your own two feet.

DAY 1

Start your day with a hearty brunch downtown at **Tasty n Alder** to prepare yourself for some walking. Fill up on French toast, charcuterie, and Bloody Marys, and don't forget to try the chocolate potato doughnuts.

When you've had your fill, head to **Pioneer Courthouse Square**, where you can meet up with the **Best of Portland Walking Tour** to learn about the city. Continue your education at the **Oregon Historical Society**, where you can see the very penny that decided the fate of Portland's name. Or pop over to the **Portland Art Museum**, which is just steps away and the home of more than 240,000 square feet of art.

For a quick lunch, head over to the **food cart "pod"** at SW Alder Street between 9th and 10th Avenues,

a bird's-eye view of the city at dawn

YEAST MEETS WEST: PORTLAND'S BEST BREWERIES

Nicknamed Beervana, Portland is widely recognized as a destination for craft beer lovers. Each year, Oregon harvests over 12 million pounds of hops, many of which stay right here in the region and become part of the IPAs so popular among Portlanders. There are about 70 breweries in the city proper, and over 100 in the metro area. More continue to pop up every day because we just can't get enough.

BRIDGEPORT BREWING COMPANY
Bridgeport has been brewing for over 30 years, and its IPA is a regular award-winner (page 96).

ALAMEDA BREWHOUSE
This award-winning brewery started small, but now its ales are for sale in pubs across the state (page 100).

LAURELWOOD BREWING CO.
Certified-organic brewery Laurelwood has been making beer for over 17 years and produces popular brews like the Free Range Red and Tree Hugger Porter (page 101).

BASE CAMP BREWING
This outdoorsy-themed brewing company has concocted some bold beers, including the S'more Stout, served with a toasted marshmallow (page 105).

HOPWORKS URBAN BREWERY
Hopworks made a name for itself by using locally sourced, organic, salmon-safe hops and now produces nearly 14,000 barrels of beer each year (page 106).

where you'll find a variety of delicious options.

Then it's time for **Powell's City of Books,** where you can easily lose an afternoon (and a family member) exploring the one million books on-site.

If you're hungry for more culture, pick up theater tickets from the **Portland Center Stage** box office in the Brewery Blocks. Or you might enjoy a pint at nearby **Deschutes Brewery and Public House.**

For a post-show nightcap and snacks, walk a few blocks to **Pepe Le Moko** for a stylish Manhattan and some oysters with champagne mignonette and horseradish.

Powell's City of Books

DAY 2
Head to North Portland today to spend a leisurely day hanging out on **Mississippi Avenue.** Grab a spot in the line for brunch at **Gravy,** where you can nosh on a fried egg sandwich and a special blend of coffee made just for the diner.

Once fortified, while away the day wandering the small but bustling street and soaking up its indie vibe. Go to **Land Gallery,** where you can check out the latest exhibit and find some unique products made by local artists. Head to **The Meadow,** where you can learn about Himalayan salt blocks and maybe pick up some tasty gifts. **Bridge City Comics** has offerings from major publishers as well as small local presses. Or stop over at **Paxton Gate** and marvel at some weird taxidermied critters and a kaleidoscope of butterflies in frames.

When you're ready for a break, head to **Mississippi Studios.** Previously a church and now an intimate live music venue, it's a great spot to catch a show; check out the calendar to see if there's a band you're interested in seeing later. Then head out back to the venue's huge outdoor patio bar, Bar Bar, a pleasant place for a drink.

When your hunger kicks in again and the sun begins to go down, it's time for **Mississippi Pizza.** You can order a pizza—for instance a fresh pie with pesto, roasted red pepper, spinach, and sheep's feta—in the eatery or its back area, the Atlantis Lounge. Then stick around for a cocktail or maybe catch some pub trivia or comedy in the typically happening space.

Next walk about 10 minutes northwest of Mississippi to **The Alibi** for karaoke, where you can top the night off by belting out songs in this classic tiki bar.

DAY 3

Head across the river today to Southeast Portland and start your day with a hearty breakfast from **Bertie Lou's** in Sellwood, where the scrambles come with a side of sass.

Then get in a morning hike at nearby **Oaks Bottom Wildlife Refuge,** where you might spot an egret, a heron, or a beaver.

From here grab a rideshare or hop on the TriMet 70 bus from SE 13th Avenue and Lambert Street to

BEST VIEWS

PITTOCK MANSION
With its stunning architecture, this historic home is a pretty remarkable sight on its own, but from high up on the hill on which it's perched you also get great views of the city as well as the surrounding forests and Mount Hood (page 35).

INTERNATIONAL ROSE TEST GARDEN
More than 10,000 rose bushes are in this garden, but even when not in bloom this is a beautiful park to visit, with its panoramic views of the city down below (page 37).

PORTLAND AERIAL TRAM
If you really want to get a look at the city, there's no better way than to take to the sky in one of these glass bubbles that float 500 feet above the ground (page 38).

PORTLAND CITY GRILL
Atop a big pink tower in the heart of downtown, this 30th-floor restaurant offers one of the highest public vantage points in the city, with lovely views of town and the Cascades (page 45).

REVOLUTION HALL
Head to the rooftop bar at this renovated high school for panoramic views across the river to the city skyline and the West Hills (page 111).

MOUNT TABOR
This dormant volcano in southeast Portland is a popular spot for picnics and hikes and, thanks to its views of the city, a local favorite for stargazing or fireworks (page 161).

SE 12th Avenue and Clay Street, and walk one block north for **Hawthorne Boulevard.** Catch some lunch first at **OK Omens**—its signature burger is made with smoked beef fat remoulade—and then make your way slowly east down the lively street, stopping in some of the many shops along the way (or one of the many eateries and

BEST PEOPLE-WATCHING

PIONEER COURTHOUSE SQUARE
Dubbed "Portland's living room," this city square has amphitheater-style seating overlooking a main plaza, where office workers, hacky sack and chess players, and countless travelers convene (page 20).

POWELL'S CITY OF BOOKS
The iconic bookstore occupies an entire city block, with multiple levels and plenty of places to tuck in, including just inside both entrances, where you'll find large, open gathering areas perfect for browsing and observing (page 25).

COLONEL SUMMERS PARK
Come here on a sunny weekend or weekday evening to see gatherings of hipsters, hula hoopers, busking musicians, and fire dancers (page 157)

HAWTHORNE BOULEVARD
Ditch the downtown scene and head to Southeast Portland's bustling Hawthorne Boulevard, where you'll find restaurants, bars, and coffee shops with large street-side windows and outdoor seating, giving you a front-row seat to the action (page 166).

PORTLAND SATURDAY MARKET
With its many arts and crafts vendors, live music, and food carts, this open-air market draws in an estimated one million tourists and locals each year, making it a prime place to people-watch, especially near the live music stage and Skidmore Fountain (page 167).

Oaks Bottom Wildlife Refuge

food carts if you couldn't bear the line at OK Omens). Take a break at the **Bagdad Theater & Pub**, where you can sip a beer while watching a movie in a gorgeous setting.

Walk about 20 minutes northwest for dinner to another lively thoroughfare, SE 28th Avenue, where you can enjoy hand-tossed, wood-fired pizzas at **Ken's Artisan Pizza**.

To cap off the night, catch a drink or show or both at **Revolution Hall**, a renovated high school auditorium that books headliner comics and big musical acts. The venue also has a rooftop bar that's open to the public and boasts great views of the city skyline.

NEIGHBORHOODS

Portland's an easily navigable city. Its east and west sides are divided by the Willamette River; its north and south sides by Burnside Street. Northeast Portland is separated from North Portland by Williams Avenue.

DOWNTOWN

Many of Portland's galleries and performing arts venues are in the heart of downtown, in an area known as the Cultural District. To the south is Portland's oldest neighborhood, Old Town, home to a number of great nightclubs and restaurants, as well as Chinatown and the beautiful Lan Su Chinese Garden.

NORTHWEST AND THE PEARL DISTRICT

Whether you're in the Pearl District or strolling NW 23rd, the northwest side of Portland is a shopper's paradise and the city's most fashionable spot for galleries, restaurants, boutiques, and urban living. Farther north, you'll find the area interchangeably known as Nob Hill or the Alphabet District, an immensely walkable area that is home to a number of Portland's most chic boutiques and trendy restaurants.

NORTHEAST

In the midst of modern condos snuggled nicely with historic Victorian homes is the Alberta Arts District, where there are blocks of art galleries, studios, and restaurants. The Irvington District is where you'll find the Rose Garden Arena and Oregon

Old Town

Convention Center. To the north is the **Hollywood District,** with an iconic Byzantine-style movie theater, several burger shops, and international restaurants.

Pearl District

SOUTHEAST

The southeast is a vibrant and **wildly diverse** sector, with numerous thoroughfares paralleling each other. **Hawthorne Boulevard** and its sister, **Belmont Street,** are chock-full of restaurants, bars, and shops that are off the beaten path. **Division Street** also houses a remarkably large number of locally favored stops. Each street's offerings tend to crescendo around avenues in the mid-SE 30th range. **Clinton Street** is home to a shorter six-block section of charming businesses, converging around SE 26th Avenue.

SELLWOOD AND MORELAND

Rounding out the farthest edges of Southeast Portland and extending up to the area known as Woodstock,

Sellwood and Moreland are two smaller areas collectively known as **Antique Row,** thanks to the large concentration of **vintage and antiques shops** that inhabit them. There are some lovely walking areas through the neighborhoods of **swank houses,** and you can easily spend a day strolling down some of the main streets—like **13th Avenue**—visiting **quaint shops** and nibbling on food from **homey cafés** and casual but chic eateries.

NORTH PORTLAND

The newest P-Town darling, NoPo is the affordable, **eclectic** home to many of Portland's imaginative newcomers. The influx of artistic energy has made for some remarkable transformations in the area, bringing **fun brewpubs,** unique dining options, and several **popular bars.** Young and artsy **Mississippi Avenue** is one of Portland's best-kept secrets, with shops and cute cafés galore.

GREATER PORTLAND

The city of Portland spans **five quadrants,** but the greater Portland metro area includes a number of suburbs, neighborhoods, and outright cities that are as easy to get to as the other side of town. The hills of Southwest Portland house a number of driveworthy **restaurants, parks, and natural retreats;** and a little jaunt down the freeway in any direction from the city proper can take you to some stops that perhaps even a few seasoned locals may not have discovered yet.

SIGHTS

Locals are accustomed to a life alongside the lush and colorful backdrop of trees, flowers, and rolling rivers, and many will tell you that one of the reasons they love this city so much is its proximity to some of the nation's most beautiful scenery. So perhaps it's easy to understand why so many of Portland's sights involve greenery.

In this bustling little city, respite is never far. Portland is home to wildlife areas like Oaks Bottom Wildlife Refuge, sprawling Washington Park—which encompasses museums, the Oregon Zoo, and International Rose Test Garden—as well as numerous other tranquil botanical and cultural gardens.

International Rose Test Garden in Washington Park

Portlanders are also known for their scrappy, do-it-yourself culture, and this is reflected throughout the city in its integration of art, nature, architecture, and urban planning. The Vera Katz Esplanade grew out of a need to beautify and utilize the east waterfront area. The Park Blocks were developed because early planners felt the city needed a "cathedral of trees with a simple floor of grass." The Zoobomb Monument turned what was once an oddity, and to some an eyesore—precariously stacked bikes in the center of town—into art.

HIGHLIGHTS

Lan Su Chinese Garden

✪ **BEST PLACE TO GET LOST:** If heaven were an independent book store, it would look a lot like **Powell's City of Books** (page 25).

✪ **BEST PLACE TO FIND A ZEN MOMENT:** Right in the middle of Old Town, the **Lan Su Chinese Garden** is an oasis of quiet beauty influenced by the famous classical gardens in Suzhou, China (page 25).

✪ **BEST PLACE TO COMMUNE WITH THE DEAD:** More park than graveyard, **Lone Fir Cemetery** is a quiet, ethereal spot where more than 25,000 of Portland's dead have been laid to rest (page 30).

✪ **BEST PLACE TO SPOT A BLUE HERON:** Hawks, ducks, woodpeckers, and kestrels are just some of the wildlife that inhabit **Oaks Bottom Wildlife Refuge,** a 140-acre floodplain wetland (page 32).

✪ **BEST PLACE TO SEE IT ALL: Washington Park** encompasses some of the city's top attractions, including the International Rose Test Garden, Portland Japanese Garden, Oregon Zoo, and Portland Children's Museum, among others (page 35).

✪ **BEST PLACE TO DEVELOP HOUSE ENVY:** The beautiful and stately **Pittock Mansion** is an amazing French Renaissance chateau in the west hills of the city (page 35).

✪ **BEST PLACE TO TAKE A TODDLER: Portland Children's Museum** is fun for all ages, but especially the very little ones who will love playing with the water cannon and helping build Bridgetown (page 36).

✪ **BEST PORTLAND CRASH COURSE:** In just a few hours, the **Best of Portland Walking Tour** will have you eating and talking like a local (page 40).

SIGHTS

DOWNTOWN

Pioneer Courthouse Square

The true heart of Portland is the area affectionately known as "Portland's living room." Occupying 40,000 square feet of the downtown Cultural District, Pioneer Square is the nucleus of performance and function. It's a fashionable spot for locals on lunch breaks, who can grab a bite from the popular food carts, do some people-watching, or just unwind with a book.

The square is home to art pieces like the iconic P-Town statue *Allow Me*, featuring a well-dressed gentleman extending his hand to you while holding an umbrella, and the *Weather Machine*, which opens each day at noon to announce the weather amid trumpet fanfare and flashing lights.

Chess games often crop up on the three bronze chessboards atop what appear to be fallen columns on the Morrison corner, built in 2003 by Soderstrom Architects. In the summer, chess clubs and game enthusiasts meet here (instead of at pubs and coffeehouses) for alfresco matches. It's not uncommon for crowds to gather as they wait for the nearby MAX train.

Whether you're catching a concert, attending a festival, or just hanging out with locals at play, be sure to check out one of the lesser-known novelties here: the **echo chamber** on the western side facing Morrison. In this tiny circular amphitheater, if you stand on the small center circle (the Sweet Spot) and speak, your voice will reverberate back to you as if amplified to a massive stadium. Remarkably, the sound

Pioneer Courthouse Square, "Portland's living room"

of your voice remains unchanged to anyone except you.

MAP 1: City block bounded by SW Morrison St., SW 6th Ave., SW Yamhill St., and SW Broadway, 503/223-1613, www.thesquarepdx.org; daily 5am-midnight; free

Central Library

This Georgian Revival landmark was built in 1903 by A. E. Doyle and bears the names of famous historians, philosophers, scientists, and artists etched along its outer walls and benches, and the interior is no less impressive. Renovated in the mid-1990s, the library boasts a number of awe-inspiring elements, such as lofty, arched ceilings and windows and the grand, intricately etched black granite staircase. The Beverly Cleary Children's Library, named for the author who wrote her beloved Ramona books about growing up on Portland's Klickitat Street, houses a 14-foot bronze *Tree of Knowledge* sculpture by artists Dana Lynn Lewis and Barbara Eiswerth. Its trunk is a menagerie of toys, animals, storybook characters, and musical instruments that both children and adults love to explore while enjoying a little structured (or unstructured) story time. Climb the sweeping staircase to the third floor and you'll find the Collins Gallery, which hosts regular recitals, poetry readings, community events, and frequent educational and artistic exhibits.

True to its Oregonian style, however, the library is not only committed to preserving history, but also to protecting the environment. In 2008, the Central Library became the first library in Oregon to construct an "eco-roof" in response to the growing need for green spaces amid urban growth. Besides extending the overall life of the roof and providing a habitat for wildlife, the eco-roof reduces rain run-off by 70 percent.

MAP 1: 801 SW 10th Ave., 503/988-5123, www.multcolib.org; Mon. 10am-8pm, Tues.-Wed. noon-8pm, Thurs.-Sat. 10am-6pm, Sun. 10am-5pm; free

North and South Park Blocks

In the midst of Portland's downtown Cultural District are the 18 collective blocks that make up the North and South Park Blocks. The area is sprinkled with some of Portland's most interesting pieces of public art, like the 12-foot-tall father-and-son elephant statue that honors a piece from the late Shang Dynasty (circa 1200-1100 BC) and the 18-foot-tall representation of Rough Rider Teddy Roosevelt.

The land to the south was donated to the public in 1852 by Daniel H. Lownsdale, who hoped that it would become a promenade, a "cathedral of trees with a simple grass floor." Nowadays, the area is a popular gathering place for Portland State University students or the downtown workers who wish to eat their lunch under the 100-plus Lombardy poplars and elms. It is also the home of one of the city's popular farmers markets on Saturday.

To the north, you'll find six blocks lined with bigleaf maples, black locusts, and American elms. A popular place for both rest and recreation, the North Park Blocks contain a playground, basketball court, and bocce ball area, as well as a popular fountain, the *Portland Dog Bowl,* designed by famed Weimaraner photographer William Wegman.

MAP 1: SW Park Ave. from SW Salmon St. to SW Jackson St., and NW Park Ave. from SW Ankeny St. to NW Glisan St., www.portlandoregon.gov/parks; daily 5am-9pm; free

The Old Church

The Calvary Presbyterian Church was erected in 1883, thanks to the help of architect Warren H. Williams, who donated his designs for the Victorian-style Carpenter Gothic building. It cost a total of $36,000 to build and included a number of elegant touches, like the ornate window traceries, archways, chimneys, buttresses, and spires. Key features are the "wedding ring," which is nestled on the bell tower, and the recently rebuilt porte cochere at the Clay Street entrance. Nowadays, the building is referred to simply as the Old Church, and it serves as a secular place for meetings, weddings, concerts, and events. The building is open weekdays for self-guided tours, and each Wednesday there's a free lunchtime concert, which is a great time to check out the cast-iron Corinthian columns, hand-carved fir pews, and elaborate stained-glass windows.

MAP 1: 1422 SW 11th Ave., 503/222-2031, www.theoldchurch.org; Tues.-Fri. 11am-3pm; free

Portlandia

Like a sentinel over the city, *Portlandia* sits as inconspicuously as a 35-foot-tall woman can. Based on the city seal of Portland, which bears a woman as a representation of commerce, *Portlandia* was designed by sculptor Raymond Kaskey and is thought to be the second-largest repoussé statue in the United States (after the Statue of Liberty). *Portlandia* can seem both menacing and welcoming in different light, and although she is an iconic figure for the city, her image belongs to the sculptor. So, while you will not see keychains and miniatures of her as you will of Lady Liberty, you can catch a quick glimpse of her in the opening of the IFC show that bears her name, *Portlandia*.

MAP 1: 1120 SW 5th Ave.; daily 24 hours; free

Ira Keller Fountain

Just outside the Civic Auditorium is an enormous fountain built in honor of Ira C. Keller, a Portland civic leader and the first chairperson of the Portland Development Commission (PDC), who is credited with pushing through much of the urban renewal work that happened during his time on the PDC. The grand two-level fountain is designed to mimic the falls and cataracts of the Cascade Range and provide a peaceful white noise to diminish the sounds of the city. It's a popular spot for afternoon business traffic, where people go to unwind or just cool off.

MAP 1: Keller Fountain Park, SW 3rd Ave. and SW Clay St.; daily 5am-9pm; free

Tom McCall Waterfront Park

Tom McCall Waterfront Park

On the west bank of the Willamette River, stretching the length of most of downtown, is Tom McCall Waterfront Park, named for Oregon governor Tom

McCall. After a seawall was installed in 1920 to protect the downtown area from rising winter waters, city planners began to reexamine ways to provide access to the riverbanks and green spaces and constructed walkways and open park spaces along the river, which gained particular popularity in the mid-1980s, when McCall was governor.

Between NW Davis and SW Naito Parkway, you'll find the Japanese American Historical Plaza, built to honor citizens deported to internment camps during World War II. In the spring, cherry blossoms line the riverbank here.

At the intersection where Salmon Street meets the park, the Salmon Street Springs is a popular fountain for children (of all ages) to cool off in the summer heat. Tom McCall Waterfront Park is also the base for a number of festivals and events in the summertime.

MAP 1: SW Naito Pkwy. between SW Harrison St. and NW Glisan St.; daily 5am-midnight; free

Salmon Street Springs

This centerpiece of the Tom McCall Waterfront Park cycles through an impressive 4,924 gallons of water per minute at full capacity, pushing (recycled) water through as many as 137 jets at one time. It is regulated by an underground computer, which switches between the three phases of the fountain. In the first setting, a light mist covers the center of the fountain, as if luring unsuspecting kids into the fray and thus setting them up for disaster. The second setting involves three circles of water, shooting up to resemble a wedding cake. The final setting is by far the most amusing and most dangerous, as water jets around the perimeter

of the fountain activate and shoot inwards, creating a huge shower of water in the middle. It's this setting that tends to catch passersby and parents with cameras off guard, soaking them and knocking children to the ground.

MAP 1: SW Naito Pkwy. at SW Salmon St., Tom McCall Waterfront Park; daily 5am-midnight; free

Mill Ends Park, smallest park in the world

Mill Ends Park

There are more than 9,000 acres of park space in the Portland metropolitan area—and some areas are so big you can forget that you are in the city. Mill Ends Park could be that kind of escape—providing you're the size of an ant. Noted in the *Guinness Book of World Records* as the world's smallest park, Mill Ends occupies only 452 square inches (yes, inches) and measures just two feet across. As the story goes, Dick Fagan, a columnist for the now-defunct *Oregon Journal*, spotted a leprechaun from his window, which overlooked what is now Naito Parkway. He raced out to capture the creature and, upon doing so, wished for a park of his own. The clever leprechaun granted the wish, but since Fagan had been unspecific as to the size of park he wanted, he was given the small patch of dirt upon which the capture had taken place.

Fairy tales aside, Mill Ends Park was named an official park on St. Patrick's Day in 1971. Over the years, a number of curious "contributions" have shown up, such as a tiny swimming pool (complete with diving board), a Ferris wheel, and several miniature statues.

MAP 1: SW Naito Pkwy. and SW Taylor St., www.portlandoregon.gov/parks; daily 24 hours; free

Ankeny Plaza

Before Pioneer Courthouse Square became "Portland's living room," Ankeny Plaza was considered the heart of Portland commerce. Built by Captain Alexander Ankeny after an 1872 fire devastated the region, Ankeny Plaza (also known as Ankeny Square) has housed a number of retail businesses, public marketplaces, and performance spaces over the years. When first opened, it was known as the New Market Theater. The area is a popular spot for photographers hoping to capture some of Portland's most historical facades, thanks to its ornate pilasters, pediments, and cornices. In fact, the Victorian Italianate masonry and grand cast-iron columns that surround the equally iconic Skidmore Fountain are considered to be the largest and best-preserved group of such architecture in the American West.

MAP 1: SW Ankeny St. and SW Naito Pkwy., 503/823-2223, www.portlandoregon.gov/parks; 24 hours daily; free

Zoobomb Monument

Zoobomb is a weekly bicycling event that has become an integral part of Portland's culture. Every Sunday, cyclists meet up and take a wild ride down the city's west hills. It bears mentioning that most of these riders are not riding mountain bikes. No, the preference for most Zoobombers is a mini bike or child's bike. It's a wild bunch, but they're also some of the nicest and most city-conscious people you'll meet.

It used to be that bombers would chain a pile of these child-sized bikes (mostly spare bikes to use as loaners) to a bike rack outside of Powell's, but back in 2009, the Zoobombers were given their own official sculpture upon which to perch their bikes. Once you spot the giant pile of bikes, look up and gaze at the golden bike, an homage to the city's lively Zoobombers.

MAP 1: SW 13th Ave. and SW Harvey Milk St.; daily 24 hours; free

Northwest and the Pearl District

Map 2

SIGHTS

NORTHWEST AND THE PEARL DISTRICT

✪ Powell's City of Books

They don't call it a city of books for nothing. Occupying a full city block, Powell's is the largest independently owned new and used bookstore in the world. Within the walls of this bibliophile's dream, you can find a million new, used, rare, and out-of-print books. Grab a map as you enter or ask an employee to help you navigate the labyrinth of color-coded rooms. Grab a couple of locally produced zines or small-press books and head to the on-site café for a cup of coffee. Whatever your preference, it is easy to lose hours exploring the shelves, listening to guest authors speak in the Pearl Room, or simply people-watching. Since Powell's buys over 3,000 used books every day, they are almost guaranteed to have everything you are looking for and several things you didn't even know you wanted. The rare book room is especially inviting, with its soft lighting, antique furniture, and dark wood shelves housing thousands of first editions, odd volumes, and books far older than Portland itself—some dating as far back as the 1400s. **MAP 2:** 1005 W. Burnside St., 503/228-4651, www.powells.com; daily 9am-11pm; free

Lan Su Chinese Garden

✪ Lan Su Chinese Garden

Envisioned in 1988 when Portland and Suzhou, China, became sister cities, this Ming Dynasty scholar's garden opened in September 2000 and has since become an oasis for tranquility right in the heart of Old Town/Chinatown. A sanctuary devoted to the "five elements" (rock, water, flora, architecture, and words), the garden is an extraordinary landscape of blossoms, sculpture, and poetry that seems worlds away from the city. The majority of plants and materials contained within the garden's stone walls originated in China, including indigenous

Powell's City of Books

25

WHERE TO SPEND A RAINY DAY

At the Oregon Zoo, you can get up close and personal with the wildlife.

Portland sees about 36 inches of rainfall per year. When things get wet, locals usually just go on doing what they were doing.

IF IT'S SPRINKLING:

- Explore **Mississippi Avenue.** Its shops, coffeehouses, and restaurants in close proximity make it easy to duck in and out.

- Take a hike in **Forest Park.** When it's damp, the park comes alive with the smells of the trees and, since many of the paths are paved, it's pretty easy to avoid getting muddy.

- Rainy days are also fun for taking in the **Portland Saturday Market.** Crowds tend to shy away when the weather gets wet, so it is easier to peruse the merchandise.

IF IT'S RAINING:

- Visit **Lan Su Chinese Garden.** Its many covered walkways make it easy to dodge the raindrops. Plus you can sip a cup of hot tea or eat a bowl of steaming dumplings at its teahouse.

- Rainy days are also perfect for a visit to the **Oregon Zoo.** There are fewer crowds and, for some reason, the rain just seems to bring the animals more out in the open.

- The **Portland Japanese Garden** is also a special experience when it's rainy. Raindrops reflect like jewels off the trees and create beautiful ripples in the koi pond.

IF IT'S ABSOLUTELY POURING:

- Take in a little history and explore **Pittock Mansion.** The French Renaissance-style home is 16,000 square feet; it will keep you out of the rain for a while.

- The **Oregon Museum of Science and Industry** is also a fun way to stay dry, with hands-on exhibits, touring showcases, a planetarium, and an enormous Omnimax theater.

- Grab some friends (or make some) at **Guardian Games,** a retail and table-gaming space where you can ride out the storm. Or head to **Ground Kontrol** and pass the time with classic arcade games.

plants, limestone rocks from Lake Tai in Suzhou, and many types of fir, gingko, and China pine. The garden offers twice-daily guided tours at no extra cost, and guests are encouraged to visit the teahouse to experience Chinese tea presentations along with traditional snacks and sweets.

MAP 2: NW 3rd Ave. and NW Everett St., 503/228-8131, www.lansugarden. org; mid-Mar.-Oct. daily 10am-7pm, Nov.-mid-Mar. daily 10am-4pm; $10 adults, $9.50 seniors, $7 students, free for children under 5

The Brewery Blocks

One of Portland's many nicknames is Beervana, thanks in part to Henry Weinhard, who established his iconic brewery here in the mid-1850s. For years, the Blitz-Weinhard Brewery served as the cornerstone of this former industrial area, and although it has been more than a decade since the sale of the brewery's property in 1999 ignited the development of Portland's glittering arts district, the Pearl, the beer giant's influence still shines through. The five blocks and 1.7 million square feet of gritty industrial space is now a mixed-use area sprinkled with luxury apartments, hip boutiques, a Starbucks, some galleries, and some of the city's favorite restaurants.

MAP 2: Between NW 10th Ave., NW 13th Ave., W. Burnside St., and NW Davis St., www.breweryblocks.com; merchant hours vary; free

The Armory

Built in 1891 to house the Oregon National Guard, the First Regiment Armory Annex (otherwise known as the Portland Armory) served as a home to soldiers during the Spanish-American War and World War I. It was opened to the public in the early 1900s, when the castle-like Romanesque Revival structure played host to operas, circuses, roller derbies, dances, boxing matches, and concerts. The building was one of only a few that could accommodate large crowds, as the truss system within the cavernous fortress allowed for unimpeded sight lines and free movement. Therefore, it served as the gathering spot where citizens heard speeches from the likes of Teddy Roosevelt, William Taft, and Woodrow Wilson.

In 2000, the Armory began a remarkable transformation when it was renovated (to the tune of $36.1 million) into an arts center that is now the permanent home of Portland Center Stage. Besides having two stages, a sprawling multilevel lobby, offices, work areas, and rehearsal spaces, the venue was the first on the National Register of Historic Places to receive platinum-level LEED certification for its sustainable design.

MAP 2: 128 NW 11th Ave., 503/445-3700, www.pcs.org; tours first and third Sat. of each month, noon-1pm; free

Chinatown Gate

With its multiple roofs, 78 dragons, 58 mythical characters, and two huge lions, the Chinatown Gate represents more than 135 years of Chinese history in Oregon and marks the official entrance to Chinatown. It's a popular place for photographs in an area that isn't always guidebook-presentable. The lions—Yin on the left side and Yang on the right—signify protection of the young and of the nation. The gate is both a beautiful landmark and a reminder of the era when Portland had the second-largest Chinese community in the United States. These days, Chinatown is compressed into just a few blocks, and with the exception of

Chinatown Gate

the gate, a few restaurants, shops, and grocery stores, much of the vibrancy the neighborhood saw in the 1890s is gone.

MAP 2: NW 4th Ave. and W. Burnside St.; daily 24 hours; free

Union Station

In the early days of P-Town, Union Station served as a hub for import, export, and transportation, thus supporting the movement of livestock, timber, produce, and most importantly, people. New arrivals came to Portland and marveled at the beautiful Romanesque and Queen Anne-style station with its elegant brick, stucco, and sandstone—and the iconic 150-foot clock tower that now urges passersby to "Go by Train."

Union Station still serves as the depot for all Amtrak and Greyhound service to and from Portland, and is worth a visit, especially for history buffs and train lovers. Look for the markers that will guide you through a walking tour beginning on Broadway and Hoyt. As you walk up the Broadway Bridge, check out the yards and the expansive views of the Portland skyline, then descend the steps to Naito Parkway and continue on across the east station esplanade through the yards. Climb the stairs to the Yards Plaza and cross the footbridge, where you'll get an up-close overhead look at the station platform.

MAP 2: 800 NW 6th Ave., 503/273-4865, www.amtrak.com; daily 5:30am-10pm; free

Jean Vollum Natural Capital Center

The Jean Vollum Natural Capital Center (also called the Ecotrust Building) was the first historical redevelopment in the United States to receive gold-level LEED certification from the U.S. Green Building Council. Originally constructed in 1895, this mixed-use building was redeveloped with a revolutionary focus on eco-friendly practices, materials, and design. Restoration of this beautiful space was done with environmentally friendly materials like recycled paint, wheatboard cabinets, and rubber flooring made from recycled tires. Inside, you will find Patagonia, a clothing company that adheres to a strong environmental ethic, and other like-minded businesses. It's a really pretty space and an innovative idea that has received a lot of attention. The public is welcome to wander through the atrium, mezzanine, and other public areas, and visitors can also inquire about event space and tours.

MAP 2: 721 NW 9th Ave., 503/227-6225, www.ecotrust.org/ncc; merchant hours vary; free

Northeast   Map 3

Beverly Cleary Children's Sculpture Garden

If you loved reading about the misadventures of the plucky but not always well-behaved Ramona Quimby, from the unforgettable children's series by Beverly Cleary, you'll want to visit

Ramona Quimby statue by Lee Hunt, Beverly Cleary Children's Sculpture Garden

Grant Park, where Ramona, Henry Huggins, and Henry's dog Ribsy are immortalized in bronze. Off the street in a patch of trees there is a fountain where the statues were placed to honor the author who made some of Northeast Portland famous. Cleary grew up in the neighborhood, and a number of her favorite childhood spots are remembered in the stories of Ramona and her sister, Beezus. Download a map from the Multnomah County website and take a self-guided walking tour of Ramona's neighborhood. You can see the homes where the author grew up or stroll down Klickitat Street (yes, it's real, and it's just four blocks from the park).

MAP 3: Grant Park, NE 33rd Ave. between Knott St. and NE Broadway, www.multcolib. org/parents/cleary; daily 5am-midnight; free

Chinese New Year at Lan Sun Chinese Garden

- **Chinese New Year at Lan Su Chinese Garden:** This urban garden comes alive each year with a two-week celebration involving lion dances, lanterns, cultural activities, and demonstrations.

- **Coastal Storm-Watching:** Whether you head to the Columbia River Gorge or the Oregon coast, you're not far from some pretty spectacular storm-watching. Come January and February, there's nothing like holing up behind a grand picture window by a warm fire while Mother Nature puts on a show.

- **Fertile Ground Festival:** This annual festival of new works, which is held in January,

Southeast Map 4

✪ Lone Fir Cemetery

Lone Fir Cemetery is a sometimes chilling but always moving representation of Portland's mottled past. Buried among the some 25,000 known and 10,000 unknown souls are many of the city's founders, including Asa Lovejoy, Socrates H. Tryon, J. C. Hawthorne, and Portland's first axe murderess, Charity Lamb. There's a lot of history here (not all of it flattering), and a stroll around this 30-acre arboretum will expose the tales of Chinese immigrants, pioneers, politicians, and soldiers. It was discovered in 2004 that several hundred patients from the Oregon Hospital for the Insane (which Hawthorne founded) are buried here in unmarked graves.

The grounds are well kept, and were it not for the gravestones, it would make a lovely park, speckled as it is with gingko trees, oaks, birches, firs, and dogwoods. If you visit in the summer months, you won't want to miss the Pioneer Rose Garden, where you'll find roses that were carried west with the pioneer women who made Portland their home. However, the memorials and grave markers are themselves is a fine example of why Portland is becoming a launch pad for creative and exciting new plays.

- **The Grotto:** More than half a million lights illuminate the National Sanctuary of Our Sorrowful Mother, a Catholic sanctuary that is more commonly called The Grotto. It's a breathtaking sight that you don't have to be Catholic (or celebrate Christmas) to enjoy.

- **Holiday Ale Festival:** Toast the dark, cold month of December at the only beer festival in the Northwest held outdoors, in Pioneer Courthouse Square. There are usually 30-40 beers on tap, all of which are special-edition winter ales.

- **New Year's Eve with the Portland Winterhawks:** At the turn of every year, Portland's hockey team hosts the Seattle Thunderbirds in what can easily be categorized as a civil war. The game starts at 8pm and is a good way to ring in the new year with the family.

- **The Nutcracker:** Every year, Portlanders know that the holiday season has begun when the Oregon Ballet Theatre begins dancing *The Nutcracker*. This is a holiday tradition that families flock to every year and the only West Coast production of George Balanchine's version of the famous ballet.

- **Portland Jazz Festival:** The city of Portland has a long and vibrant jazz history. This annual multi-venue festival features headlining talent such as Wayne Shorter, McCoy Tyner, Dianne Reeves, Regina Carter, Tom Grant, and Eddie Palmieri, along with a number of free showcase performances highlighting regional talent.

- **Ski Season:** Oregon has the longest ski season in North America thanks to all that precipitation. Putting up with a little rainfall in the city means an opportunity to carve some serious powder on the slopes of Mount Hood.

- **ZooLights Festival:** This annual holiday event is a delight. Each winter, the Oregon Zoo comes alive with thousands of lights, hundreds of musical groups, and the brightly lit Zoo Train. Stroll through after dark and see how active the animals get in the chilly night air.

worth the visit. Many date back to the mid-19th century and are surprisingly evocative of Portland's past.
MAP 4: SE Morrison St. and SE 20th Ave., 503/797-1709, www.friendsoflonefircemetery.org; daily sunrise-sunset; free

Lone Fir Cemetery

Vera Katz Eastbank Esplanade

One of Portland's numerous nicknames is Bridgetown, and if you head down to the waterfront, it's easy to see why. For years, the land on the east side of the Willamette River was an undeveloped industrial mess. In the late 1980s, developers and city planners began to envision a walkway that would extend north from the Hawthorne Bridge, past the Morrison and Burnside Bridges, to the Steel Bridge, where it would then link across the river to the already popular Tom McCall Waterfront Park on the west side. The finished esplanade contains markers that enumerate some of the area's vibrant history—all artistically lit to make them visible even at night.

While the area is a hotbed of activity—with Portlanders strolling, biking, skating, or simply exploring the underbellies of the city's many bridges—it is also a carefully planned habitat for fish and wildlife. Beavers and herons swim near boat docks as they try to nab salmon and steelhead, while pigeons and ducks nest on the rocks.

Take a quiet stroll down the walk and check out some of the public art installations, such as the ethereal Echo Gate and the bronze statue that commemorates the former mayor for whom the esplanade was named. Climb the steps and cross to the west side or head down to the lengthy floating walkway and feel the ebb and flow of the Willamette beneath your feet.

MAP 4: SE Water Ave. and SE Hawthorne Blvd., 503/823-2223, www.portlandoregon. gov/parks; daily 5am-midnight; free

Sellwood and Moreland   Map 5

✪ Oaks Bottom Wildlife Refuge

Oaks Bottom Wildlife Refuge is a 140-acre floodplain wetland on the east bank of the Willamette River that includes hiking and biking trails. The area is a favorite spot for bird-watchers, as more than 100 varieties of migratory birds manage to find their way to the refuge. You can hop on the trail at the SE Milwaukie Street entrance and head south along the edge of the pond, or opt for the paved Springwater Trail, which eventually connects to the south end of the Vera Katz Eastbank Esplanade.

In 1969, the city blocked development of this area into an industrial park because it was one of the few remaining marshlands around. Now the area is maintained by a volunteer organization that not only cares for the land but also works to restore the natural habitat of creatures such as wrens, raccoons, quails, kestrels, frogs, ducks, and the iconic blue heron.

MAP 5: SE Sellwood Blvd. and SE 7th Ave., 503/797-1709, www.portlandoregon.gov/ parks; daily 5am-midnight; free

Oaks Amusement Park

Going to Oaks Amusement Park is like stepping back in time to a Coney Island-style carnival complete with rides, bumper cars, games, and a giant slide. It's been around since the early 1900s and these days looks a little like something you would find in a *Scooby Doo* episode. The amusement park is only open on weekends during the spring and summer months, but the skating rink is open year-round and features special events outside of the park's regular hours for preschoolers (early morning) and adults (late at night). The park also hosts a fun Oktoberfest in September.

The Crystal Springs Rhododendron Garden is a lovely spot for a stroll.

MAP 5: 7805 SE Oaks Park Way, 503/233-5777, www.oakspark.com; amusement park Mar.-Sept. Sat.-Sun. noon-7pm, skating rink year round Tues. 3pm-5:30pm, Wed. 3pm-5:30pm and 7pm-9:30pm, Thurs. 3pm-5:30pm and 8pm-10:30pm, Fri.-Sat. 1pm-5:30pm and 7pm-10:30pm, Sun.1pm-5pm and 7pm-9:30pm; amusement park ride bracelets $17.25-39.25, skating rink admission $7-8

Crystal Springs Rhododendron Garden

It began as a "rhody" test garden in 1950, but now this 9.4-acre spot in the middle of Southeast Portland is a botanical oasis devoted to the flowering shrub that thrives better here than anywhere else. The cool, rainy Northwest climate is perfect for growing rhododendrons, but even when they are not in bloom, the garden is still a lush, romantic retreat. Packed with trails, waterfalls, ponds, shaded nooks, and benches, it's a beautiful spot to take a stroll, have a picnic, or capture some great photos of flora and fauna. Mind the geese and ducks, though. They more or less run the ponds and have been known to be a bit temperamental.

When the rhododendrons are in full bloom (usually late spring), Crystal Springs is an explosion of color. The garden houses a remarkable variety of blooms, some of which you can take home if you visit during the annual plant sale held during Mother's Day weekend in May.

Admission is free for all October-February, with a $5 charge for adults the rest of the year except Mondays. MAP 5: SE Woodstock Blvd. and SE 28th Ave., 503/771-8386, www.portlandoregon. gov/parks; Apr.-Sept. daily 6am-10pm, Oct.-Mar. daily 6am-6pm; $5 adults, free for children Mar 1.-Sept. 30 Tues.-Sun., free general admission Mar. 1-Sept. 30 Mon. and Oct.-Feb.

Mississippi Avenue

Ever-expanding and evolving, Mississippi Avenue was once considered "one of the best-kept secrets in Portland," but with an influx of new businesses and housing, it wasn't going to stay hush-hush for long. What was once a haven for drug deals and debauchery is now a harbor for both shoppers and foodies, thanks to a recent (and much-needed) shot in the arm from creative souls looking to establish themselves in the Rose City. Unable to settle into the expensive Pearl lofts or find space in the hotbed of the Alberta Arts District, artists and young entrepreneurs began to build their own neighborhood here, injecting it with their own ethos and style.

Mississippi Avenue is packed with some of the city's most creative restaurants, stylish bars, and quaint boutiques, but it's also a testament to Portland's commitment to sustainability. Near North Fremont Avenue stands the ornate Dada-esque facade of **The ReBuilding Center** (3625 N. Mississippi Ave., 503/331-1877), which hides a labyrinth of doors, windows, fixtures, and wood salvaged from homes all over the region and resold to locals who want to add unique touches to their home without creating a bigger carbon footprint.

MAP 6: N. Mississippi Ave., between N. Fremont St. and N. Skidmore St.; merchant hours vary; free

Peninsula Park & Rose Garden

Designed in the early 1900s as part of the City Beautiful movement, this park is equal parts elegant formal garden and community gathering space. Enter the sunken rose garden on Albina Avenue and stroll among the 6,500 rose plantings, which include more than 65 fragrant varieties. The heart of this garden, which is bedecked with lantern-style lights and stone pillars, is where you'll find a historic fountain; it's been the centerpiece of the park for nearly 100 years, and it is here that Portland's official city rose, Mme. Caroline Testout, was first cultivated and is maintained to this day.

Just past the formal garden, you'll find a grand octagonal gazebo, built in 1913 and preserved as a historic landmark, the last of its kind. Today, it is a popular spot for weddings and concerts. Beyond that are baseball fields, tennis courts, playgrounds, and a whimsical wading pool complete with a giant frog and flower sprinkler. At this end of the 16-acre park is also where you'll find Portland's first and oldest community center. The center, an Italian villa-style structure, has a 33-yard outdoor swimming pool that is a popular retreat for locals—and once served as the home for a number of Humboldt penguins awaiting transport to Washington Park Zoo.

MAP 6: 700 N. Rosa Parks Way, 503/823-2525, www.portlandoregon.gov/parks; daily 5am-midnight; free

Greater Portland

Map 7

SIGHTS

GREATER PORTLAND

❂ Washington Park

Washington Park is a sprawling public park home to a number of Portland's attractions, including the **Oregon Zoo, World Forestry Center, Hoyt Arboretum, Portland Children's Museum,** and **Portland Japanese Garden.** It's also home to the oldest continuously operated public test garden—the **International Rose Test Garden**—where more than 550 varieties of roses are cultivated and judged every year at the Portland Rose Festival. Also on the park grounds are an outdoor amphitheater, an archery range, tennis courts, and 40 acres of forest, trails, and playgrounds.

Take the MAX out to Washington Park and you will see the deepest transit station in North America, Portland's only underground stop. Despite being 260 feet below ground, the elevators can carry 35 people up to street level in about 20 seconds.

MAP 7: 400 SW Kingston Ave.; daily 5am-10pm; free

Pittock Mansion

❂ Pittock Mansion

One thousand feet above the city stands a monument to some of Portland's most fundamental qualities: natural beauty, progress, civic enthusiasm, and historical preservation. Pittock Mansion was built in 1914 by Henry and Georgiana Pittock, both active contributors to progressive mid-19th-century Portland. Henry (a newspaperman who developed what is now the *Oregonian*) made his way to Oregon at the age of 19, penniless but driven. He and Georgiana married in 1860 and began a life of hard work, committing countless hours to community service, all the while building an empire from their real estate, banking, railroad, ranching, and mining investments. The Pittocks had six children and 19 grandchildren, many of whom were raised on the 46-acre estate—which was purchased by the city of Portland (and thereby saved from demolition) for a mere $225,000.

The home was designed by Edward Foulks (who also designed the Tribune Tower in Oakland, California) in the French Renaissance style and boasts remarkably innovative features for its time, such as a central vacuum system, an intercom system, a walk-in freezer, and a Turkish smoking room. About 80,000 visitors tour the house each year (you can take a self-guided or docent-led tour) and then wander through the lush park-like gardens that blossom with rhododendrons and flowering cherries. There are also trails through **Pittock Acres Park** (daily 5am-9pm), which connect with the adjacent Forest Park and are popular with hikers and joggers for their verdant landscapes and spectacular views.

MAP 7: 3229 NW Pittock Dr., 503/823-3623, www.pittockmansion.org; Feb.-May and Sept.-Dec. daily 10am-4pm, June-Labor Day daily 10am-5pm; $11 adults, $10 seniors, $8 children ages 6-18, free for children under 6

✪ Portland Children's Museum

If you're traveling with kids, particularly very small children, this is a wonderful museum. Kids over eight might find it a bit boring; then again, even adults have been amused here. In Building Bridgetown, children can panel a wall, connect plumbing fixtures, take measurements, work the "button and latch" board, and build with blocks on the custom-designed building table. Water Works features a 12-foot-high waterfall, a hand-cranked "conveyor belt" that carries water in little recycled objects, a twirling collection of kitchen mops, and instruments that kids can play by spraying the water cannon. The museum provides waterproof smocks for this exhibit, which you will most definitely want.

MAP 7: 4015 SW Canyon Rd., 503/223-6500, www.portlandcm.org; daily 9am-5pm; $11 adults and children, $10 seniors, free for children under 1

Oregon Zoo

The Oregon Zoo has a lot of great animal exhibits, like the Red Ape Reserve, where you will find orangutans and gibbons, and the Africa Savanna, where you will see giraffes, hippos, and rhinos. The polar bears, penguins, sea lions, otters, and the African rainforest are always big winners, the latter with underwater viewing tanks that contain slender-snouted crocodiles. Over at the Asian elephant exhibit, you can learn about Packy the pachyderm and find out why he is Portland's sweetheart, or visit the zoo's exciting Predators of the Serengeti exhibit, which features lions, cheetahs, African wild dogs, African rock pythons, and caracals.

MAP 7: 4001 SW Canyon Rd., 503/226-1561, www.oregonzoo.org; late May-early Sept. daily 9:30am-6pm, early Sept.-late May daily 9am-4pm; $17.95 adults, $15.95 seniors, $12.95 children ages 3-11, free for children under 3

World Forestry Center

This 20,000-square-foot museum has interactive exhibits about the trees here in the Pacific Northwest and all over the world. So why go to a museum to learn about trees when you could just go to a forest? Well, the Forestry Center has a lot to say that those trees won't say themselves, like how to approach forest sustainability and how the intricate systems, structures, and cycles within the forests affect each other and us every day. Plus it's fun, since you can take a simulated ride down Class IV rapids, practice being a smokejumper, and try your hand at logging.

MAP 7: 4033 SW Canyon Rd., 503/228-1367, www.worldforestry.org; daily 10am-5pm; $7 adults, $6 seniors, $5 children ages 3-18, free for children under 3

Hoyt Arboretum

Part park, part museum of trees, the Hoyt Arboretum has miles of hills and trails showcasing tree life from all over the world. There are hours to be lost exploring all the 10,000 individual trees and shrubs, and sometimes, even with a map (provided outside the visitors center) it is quite easy to become disoriented. The walk is beautiful and full of lovely secluded places to think, explore, or have a woodland picnic. Mapped-out self-guided tours include one-, two-, and four-mile segments, portions of which have paved and ADA-accessible paths.

MAP 7: 4000 SW Fairview Blvd., 503/865-8733, www.hoytarboretum.org; visitors center Mon.-Fri. 9am-4pm, Sat. 11am-3pm; grounds daily 6am-10pm; free

Portland Japanese Garden

Portland Japanese Garden

If urban sprawl has you itching to find a much-needed moment of peace and tranquility, seek it among the winding stone steps, wooden bridges, waterfalls, and koi ponds of the beautifully landscaped Japanese Garden. High above the city, the garden is encircled by stately Douglas fir and western red cedar trees and the rolling green hills of Washington Park. Inside, the garden is divided into multiple spaces: the Entry Garden, the Sand and Stone Garden, the Natural Garden, the Flat Garden, the Tea Garden, and the Strolling Pond Garden with its exquisite Heavenly Falls and five-tiered pagoda lantern. It has taken years of cultivation to bring such serenity and authenticity to the gardens, but the

efforts have certainly paid off. In 1998, Kunihiko Saito, the Japanese ambassador to the United States, declared this "the most authentic Japanese garden, including those in Japan."

The Portland Japanese Garden offers several guided tours daily between April and October and once daily on weekends between November and March. Reservations aren't necessary for these tours, but you can also call ahead to set up a private group tour.

MAP 7: 611 SW Kingston Ave., 503/223-5055, www.japanesegarden.com; mid-Mar.-Sept. Mon. noon-7pm, Tues.-Sun. 10am-7pm, Oct.-mid-Mar. Mon. noon-4pm, Tues.-Sun. 10am-4pm; $14.95-16.95 adults, $12.95 14.50 seniors, $11.95 13.40 students, $10.45-11.50 children ages 6-17, free for children under 6

International Rose Test Garden

Portland's famous rose garden in Washington Park is the oldest continuously operated test garden in the United States. While the primary purpose of the garden is to test and protect new rose hybrids (a tradition that began in the midst of World War I when people from around the world sent roses to Portland to keep them safe from bombing), the 4.5 acres of blooms are a shining example of why Portland is known as the "City of Roses." You can picnic in the Shakespearean Garden, where you'll find blooms that are named for characters in the bard's plays scattered among the benches, archways, and graceful trees. As you near the garden's edge and enjoy a panoramic view of the city, amble along the Queen's Walk, where the Rose Festival Queens are remembered with a plaque that bears their names and signatures. Next, stroll past the sprawling outdoor amphitheater (a perfect spot for

International Rose Test Garden

a picnic), where you just might catch a summertime show or live music showcase.

MAP 7: 400 SW Kingston Ave., 503/823-3636, www.rosegardenstore.org; daily 7:30am-9pm; free

Portland Aerial Tram

The Portland Aerial Tram, a $57 million project, can accommodate up to 78 passengers on each of the Swiss-made silver cabins. As a visitor you likely won't have to take the tram for any practical purposes—it goes up to Oregon Health and Sciences University (OHSU), which footed much of the bill for construction of the tram; it serves as a valuable link between the main campus on the hill and the Center for Health & Healing at South Waterfront. But when the weather is clear, the view is spectacular, offering a vista that includes Mount Hood, Mount St. Helens, the Willamette River, and the city's downtown skyline. The tram takes about four minutes to travel the 3,300 feet up to OHSU at the top of Marquam Hill, a rise of 500 feet in elevation. Departures are about every six minutes. Note the ticket machine will not take dollar bills, but it will take quarters and credit or debit cards.

MAP 7: 3303 SW Bond Ave., www.portlandtram.org; Mon.-Fri. 5:30am-9:30pm, Sat. 9am-5pm, Sun. 1pm-5pm; $4.90

Portland Aerial Tram

Elk Rock Garden

The Garden of the Bishop's Close, known as Elk Rock, was created to show a collection of rare and native plants, magnificent trees, and remarkable views of the Willamette River and Mount Hood. It is a private garden and the home of the Episcopal bishop of Oregon. The family bequeathed the home to the church, leaving with it an endowment for the care and maintenance of the garden, and a requirement that it be left open to the public. It's a lovely, contemplative spot to visit, so long as you respect the rules. Dogs must be leashed; visitors may not bring picnics; and there is a prohibition against "frolicking"—all of which, actually, help to make this a peaceful place to visit. You won't find any signage on Highway 43 indicating the garden is there, which makes it all the more a treasure hunt, the reward of which is winding paths through magnolia trees, rhododendrons, giant sequoias, golden rain trees, gingkos, witch hazel, and burning bushes.

MAP 7: 11800 SW Military Ln., 503/636-5613, www.elkrockgarden.com; daily 8am-5pm; free

The Grotto

The National Sanctuary of Our Sorrowful Mother, or The Grotto, as it is more commonly called, is a 62-acre botanical garden and Catholic shrine that is a sight to see, for anyone, be they Christians, agnostics, or followers of the Flying Spaghetti Monster. Towering fir trees and imposing basalt cliffs bend to the careful artwork of peace and tranquility. A highlight of the visit is Our Lady's Grotto, a shrine to Mary that was carved out of the black cliffs in 1925 and features a marble replica of Michelangelo's famed work, the *Pietà*. Take a tour (call ahead to schedule) or stroll through on your own and explore the statuary hidden among the trees, streams, and passageways. Buy a token from the gift shop for $3.50 and ride the elevator to the upper level, which sits atop a 130-foot sheer rock cliff and offers unequaled views of the Columbia River and Mount St. Helens.

In the wintertime, The Grotto is home to one of Portland's most popular holiday events, the Festival of Lights. Volunteers spend months installing over half a million lights, animated displays, and fiber-optic representations of the holiday spirit. It is the only time of year when an admission fee is required, but tickets ($12 adults, $11 seniors, $6 children ages 3-12, free for children under 3) include concerts in the cathedral-like 500-seat chapel, petting zoos, and theatrical performances.

MAP 7: 8840 NE Skidmore St., 503/254-7371, www.thegrotto.org; Jan. daily 9am-5pm, Feb.-early Mar. daily 9am-5:30pm, early Mar.-day before Mother's Day daily 9am-6:30pm, Mother's Day-Labor Day daily 9am-8:30pm, day after Labor Day-Oct. daily 9am-6pm, Nov.-day before Thanksgiving daily 9am-5pm, day after Thanksgiving-Dec. daily 9am-3:30pm (closed Dec. 25); free, except evenings Thanksgiving Day-Dec.

Paul Bunyan Statue

Originally built to greet visitors to the Centennial Exposition for Portland's 100th anniversary on February 14, 1959, this big guy still looms tall over NoPo, as if watching over the adjacent Dancin' Bear, a famous local strip club. The legendary lumberjack of lore stands 31 feet tall and was recently added to the National Register of Historic Places.

P-TOWN FOR THE PINT-SIZED

Oregon Museum of Science and Industry

Portlanders are known for keeping their kids in tow instead of opting for nannies or baby-sitters. It's no surprise then that the city offers numerous places that appeal both to the young and the young-at-heart.

Young and old alike will find themselves wanting to touch, twirl, poke, and examine things around every corner of the **Oregon Museum of Science and Industry.** You can ride the motion simulator, check out a flick in the incredible IMAX theater, tour a real U.S. Navy submarine, or visit the latest traveling exhibition. You can also find fun for all ages

Composed mostly of steel, plaster, concrete, and paint, Paul is remarkably well constructed for his age (especially considering the fact that he was only intended to last six months). Thankfully, Paul has been lovingly cared for over the years by neighbors who saw him as a symbol of both the lumberjacks of Portland's past and the working class of today.

MAP 7: N. Interstate Ave. and N. Denver Ave.; daily 24 hours; free

Sightseeing Tours

WALKING TOURS

✪ Best of Portland Walking Tour

Did you know that Clark Gable once worked in the Meier & Frank tie department? Or that the local Elk Lodge boycotted the unveiling of the elk statue in the Plaza Blocks because they considered it an abomination? How about that Portland was named based on a coin toss? The guides that take you on this Portland 101 tour are equipped with all the inside tips, historical snippets, rumors, and realities you need to get to know the real Portland. Reservations are required, and the Best of Portland Tour, like many of the Portland Walking Tours, departs at exactly 10am daily.

at **Oaks Amusement Park.** Ride the Scream-n-Eagle, take a spin around the old-school skating rink, or have a picnic along the banks of the Willamette River.

Of course, the **Oregon Zoo** is a big draw for families, with its elephants, adorable penguins, majestic polar bears, fascinating fruit bats, and a plethora of animals from all corners of the world. In fact, on any given day, there are 2,200 specimens representing 260 species of birds, mammals, reptiles, amphibians, and invertebrates. You can check out the daily keeper talks or ride the Zoo Train, which takes you around the zoo and shows off some of the pretty forested areas of Washington Park. Wintertime visitors can also check out the **ZooLights Festival,** when the zoo is transformed into a colorful wintry wonderland and hours are extended past dark.

A great day trip with the kids is the 10-mile drive out to **Sauvie Island,** where there are U-pick farms as well as beaches and wildlife areas to explore in the warm months. In the fall there are mazes and pumpkin patches.

Portland Saturday Market has long been a favorite for kids, especially since it's the place where elephant ears were invented. Portland's Elephant Ears is one of many carts in the market's food court, but this one is a particular favorite among the small set. The smell of those ginormous fried dough treats is hard to resist, especially when you can douse them in marionberries, apple butter, cinnamon and sugar, or whatever you like. Kids are also pretty fond of touring the merchant booths, as there are a number of vendors with things to touch, test-drive, or try on.

There are great stops for the little reader in your life. **Powell's City of Books** has a truly jaw-dropping kids' room. In fact, it has been dubbed the "largest children's book section on the West Coast." There are tables and chairs for impromptu story time, and a staff person is on hand to help you or your child find exactly what you are looking for. Plus, it has a fun merchandise section with irresistible craft items, T-shirts, and cool educational toys. On the east side of the river, you'll find **Green Bean Books,** which has a fantastic collection of books for young readers and soon-to-be-bibliophiles. It also has an amusing collection of old vending machines that now distribute things like fake mustaches, finger puppets, and little fuzzy friends.

Downtown: meeting point Pioneer Courthouse Square, 503/774-4522, www.portlandwalkingtours.com; $23 adults, $19 seniors and children ages 11-17, $9 children ages 5-10, free for children under 5

Haunted Pub Crawl

The existence of ghosts may be debatable, but it sure is fun to hear about them. This tour combines two things that Portlanders love: beer and good stories. The one-mile, approximately two-hour tour winds through Old Town with stops for libations at two pubs along the way (beer is included in the price). Participants are treated to tales of Portland's sordid past with an emphasis on the gangsters and ne'er-do-wells that occupied the barstools and bedrooms of Old Town's historic buildings. The tour also includes a stop by the Merchant Hotel, a

spot featured on the Travel Channel's *Ghost Adventures.*

Downtown and Northwest: meeting point Kell's Irish Pub, 112 SW 2nd Ave., www.beerquestpdx.com; $45 plus booking fee

Secrets of Portlandia Tour

If you have about two hours to kill and enjoy corny jokes, check out the free Secrets of Portlandia tour, which runs seven days a week, rain or shine. The walking tour meets across the street from Pioneer Courthouse Square, and no reservation is required. Just show up and look for the guy in the bright green shirt. The tour is off-beat, silly, and occasionally inaccurate, but touches on many things like Voodoo Doughnut, *Portlandia* (the statue), the world's smallest park, food cart culture, and some suspected ghosts. Although the tour is free, it is customary to tip about $10-20 if you enjoyed it.

Downtown: meeting point across from Pioneer Courthouse Square on SW 6th Ave., www.secretsofportlandia.com; free

Underground Portland Tour

The Underground Portland tour, or "Worst of Portland Tour" as it is wont to be called, shines an un-flattering light on the prostitution, gambling, racism, and "crimping" of days gone by. Portland was ripe with the sort of people who made a busi-ness of the trade called "crimping." Drunken sailors might find them-selves pressed into service, kidnapped, or just plain tricked. One notorious crimper was Mary Boggs, who had a barge parked on the Willamette com-plete with saloon and bordello. Most of this tour takes place in Old Town and Chinatown, so you will also get a good peek at what life was like for the numerous Asian Americans who lived in Portland at a time when they were facing near-constant banishment and ridicule. And no tour about Portland's dirty underbelly would be complete without a few ghost stories, like those of the basement of Old Town Pizza, where ghosts are rumored to walk the halls. This tour is not recommended for children under 11.

Northwest: meeting point 226 NW Davis St., 503/774-4522, www.portlandwalkingtours.com; $23 adults, $19 seniors and children ages 11-17

MOTORIZED TOURS
Portland By Segway Tour

A fun way to do some sightseeing in downtown Portland is to hop aboard the Portland by Segway tour. The guides are equipped with some inter-esting facts about various landmarks and can answer question along the way. It is a one- to two-hour tour in-cluding a tutorial on how to ride the machine (it is easier than it looks once you trust it). This tour is more about taking in the sights than learning about the city, and a good alternative for people who have trouble biking or walking very far.

Downtown: meeting point 150 SW Harrison St., www.portlandbysegway.com; $55-65

Portland Gray Line Tours

If you'd like to see the city at your own pace but still benefit from the ex-pertise of a local guide, hop on board the Gray Line Tours Pink Trolley. The narrated 85-minute tour takes you to places like Washington Park, the Oregon Zoo, Portland Japanese Garden, Powell's City of Books, the Portland Saturday Market, and more. While your one- to two-day pass will have a designated start time, you're al-lowed to hop on and off the trolley as often as you like to spend more time at the various stops. Trolleys run every hour, so it's easy to grab the next one when you're finished looking around. A ticket booth is located in Pioneer Square, but you can also purchase a ticket from the driver at any desig-nated stop.

Various locations: 503/241-7373, www.graylineofportland.com; May-June and Sept. daily, first departure 10am, July-Aug. daily, first departure 9am; $34-44 adults, $17-22 children ages 6-12, free for children under 5

RESTAURANTS

Chefs have flocked to Portland over the last 10 years, much in the same way artists did 10 years before that, bringing with them a passion and energy that has moved the city's culinary status from the underground. Every quadrant is positively bursting with restaurants, food shops, food carts, and lounges, all devoted to the idea that fresh is best, local is key, and uniformity is passé.

Pick up a copy of the *New York Times, Bon Appétit,* or *Food & Wine* and you are likely to see Portland featured within their pages. Food and travel editors are in love with the city's energy and creativity. Celebrity chefs are made here, and their influence can be seen in cookbooks, on televisions, and in kitchens across the country. In Portland, it's not really about having a clever conceit or quirky angle; it's about finding better ways to use the ingredients you have, often by embracing old or forgotten ways of cooking and grilling.

Farm Spirit

Chefs and restaurateurs here create buzz by utilizing the bounties of the Pacific Northwest. In Portland, there is a joke that the "six degrees of separation" rule does not apply; here we have only three degrees, and the same can be said for our food. Greens come from neighborhood gardens, beef from local farms, and it's likely that the mushrooms were picked by the chef. The coffee is fair trade and roasted by "that guy down the block." The wines are biodynamic and made from grapes grown in a vineyard you can drive to in less than an hour.

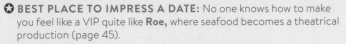

HIGHLIGHTS

✪ **BEST PLACE TO IMPRESS A DATE:** No one knows how to make you feel like a VIP quite like **Roe,** where seafood becomes a theatrical production (page 45).

✪ **BEST PLACE TO GET A LATE-NIGHT BITE:** Bargoers and travelers of all types flock to **Lúc Lác** for big bowls of pho and tasty cocktails, especially in the lively wee hours (page 48).

✪ **BEST PLACE TO BRAVE THE BRUNCH LINE:** Ambitious small plates and hearty favorites make **Tasty n Alder** worth the wait (page 52).

✪ **BEST PLACE TO FIND LOCALS GETTING DOUGHNUTS:** Voodoo may get the tourist glory, but the sophisticated flavors and perfectly balanced textures at **Blue Star Donuts** allure the locals (page 52).

✪ **BEST PLACE TO INDULGE A CHOCOLATE CRAVING:** If you've never tried drinking chocolate, get yourself to **Cacao;** this is not the hot chocolate of your youth (page 53).

✪ **BEST PLACE TO INDULGE YOUR INNER CARNIVORE:** Sip some wine while savoring wild boar sausage, succulent rotisserie chicken, or salami at **Olympia Provisions,** which handcrafts its meats and charcuterie (page 54).

✪ **BEST PLACE TO USE A TON OF NAPKINS:** An industrial-themed joint, **TILT** serves up big burgers and big slabs of pie (page 59).

✪ **BEST PLACE TO SCREAM FOR ICE CREAM:** Actually, try not to scream, but if you can make it through the line, **Salt & Straw** might just make you cry with joy (page 61).

✪ **BEST PLACE TO EAT AND GIVE BACK AT THE SAME TIME:** **Oregon Public House** donates 100 percent of its profits to charity (page 63).

✪ **BEST PLACE TO TAP INTO THE SPIRIT OF OREGON:** Eat an unforgettable, plant-based, multi-course prix fixe dinner at **Farm Spirit** (page 72).

✪ **BEST PLACE TO GET A PIECE OF PIE:** Forget ice cream, this pie doesn't need it. **Lauretta Jean's** unbeatable crust is the key, but fillings like salted honey, blueberry streusel, and banana chocolate cream don't hurt (page 80).

PRICE KEY

$	Entrées less than $10
$ $	Entrées $10-20
$ $ $	Entrées more than $20

PACIFIC NORTHWEST
Q Restaurant $$

When Portland's iconic Veritable Quandary restaurant closed after 45 years in 2016, some feared it marked the end of nostalgic Portland dining. Fortunately, VQ chef Annie Cuggino and much of the staff were not ready to throw in the pressed white napkin. Thus came Q, a restaurant with a familiar ambience and menu of upscale casual fare. Here you'll find dishes like salads with fresh Oregon berries, crispy duck fat potatoes, wild salmon, and a hearty osso buco. The menu changes daily, influenced by the season and supplied by local farmers. The restaurant also offers a prix fixe Monday night dinner series that often features fresh-caught fish and other local treats.

MAP 1: 828 SW 2nd Ave., 503/850-8915, www.q-portland.com; Mon.-Fri. 11:30am-3pm and 5pm-10pm, Sat.-Sun. 9:30am-3pm and 5pm-10pm

SEAFOOD AND STEAK
✪ Roe $$$

For a seafood lover, Roe is an experience that is sure to leave a lasting memory. Diners are offered a four-course "Theater Menu," which last about 1.5 hours, or the full seven-course menu, which typically goes 2.5-3 hours. The menu rotates constantly, showcasing the bounty of the region in unique and elevated ways. In one night, you could encounter a butterfish sashimi with shaved foie gras, cardamom-roasted lobster, and cold-smoked swordfish. There is also an optional caviar flight to really round out the experience. That said, you will

have to work for the experience a bit: Seatings are by reservation only and a $20-30 deposit per person is required to hold the booking. Finding the restaurant can be a bit of a challenge, too, as it is discretely signed and tucked into the mezzanine level of the otherwise fairly quiet Morgan Building.

MAP 1: Morgan Building, 515 SW Broadway, Ste. 100, 503/232-1566, http://roepdx.rest; Wed.-Sat. 5:30pm-10pm

El Gaucho $$$

El Gaucho is an anomaly among Portland restaurants. While most thrive on a balance of quality food with a laid-back setting, the tuxedo-clad servers at El Gaucho will come just short of cutting your 28-day dry-aged porterhouse for you. In fact, if you asked them to do it, they probably would. A meal will run you a pretty penny, but the steaks are some of the best. Skip the sides and focus on the collection of stellar appetizers, like the amazing (albeit ostentatious) seafood tower and the Caesar salad, prepared tableside. If you still have room, order the bananas Foster, also prepared tableside over an open flame.

MAP 1: 319 SW Broadway, 503/227-8794, www.elgaucho.com; Mon.-Thurs. 4:30pm-11pm, Fri.-Sat. 4:30pm-midnight, Sun. 4:30pm-10pm

Portland City Grill $$$

If you would like to get a greater perspective on the city of Portland, look no further than Portland City Grill. Resting 30 floors above the city in the "Big Pink" U.S. Bankcorp Tower, the restaurant provides not only spectacular views of town and the Cascades, but also a classy atmosphere perfect for special occasions. This place is all about making an impression, so if you can, make a reservation and secure a table by the window. The menu at City Grill is a mix of traditional steakhouse and high-end sushi joint. But whether you opt for a rib eye or some wild Northwest salmon, make sure you order some of the infamous Kung Pao calamari.

MAP 1: 111 SW 5th Ave., 503/450-0030, www.portlandcitygrill.com; Mon.-Thurs. 11am-midnight, Fri. 11am-1am, Sat. 4pm-1am, Sun. 9:30am-11pm

Southpark Seafood Grill & Wine Bar $$$

Riding the edge between the downtown core and the South Park Blocks, the exterior of Southpark Seafood Grill is deceptively unassuming. With little more of note than a statue of a bronze salmon bursting through the brick facade, the restaurant and wine bar seems like an innocuously quaint bistro. Inside, however, Southpark is a rock-solid example of Northwest cuisine, with an impeccable wine list and a staff knowledgeable enough to back it up. Of course, seafood is the forte, with fresh-caught crab, prawns, scallops, and fish starring on the menu. Daily specials are often fresh-from-the-sea, simple, and creative. Reservations are recommended, but if you don't have one or if you arrive early, you can visit the adjacent wine bar (open daily until midnight), sample some superb Northwest wines, and choose from a respectable selection of favorites from the full Southpark menu.

MAP 1: 901 SW Salmon St., 503/326-1300, www.southparkseafood.com; daily 11:30am-midnight

Jake's Famous Crawfish $$

Jake's is a Portland legend that has been a city landmark for more than 100 years. Inside, the deep burnished wood booths and rich decor lend a touch of masculine luxury and class to the place. The menu at Jake's is printed daily (and occasionally reprinted) to incorporate freshly caught fish and in-season specialties. While the seafood here is some of the best in the Northwest (and eventually launched an entire chain of restaurants for owners Bill McCormick and Doug Schmick), Portlanders love Jake's for its affordable and extensive happy hour—with nosh like the Jake's burger or shrimp ceviche for only $1.95. For that reason, it's a popular spot for locals to gather for post-work cocktails, Kobe beef sliders, and plate after plate of peel 'n' eat shrimp.

MAP 1: 401 SW 12th Ave., 503/226-1419, www.mccormickandschmicks.com; Mon.-Thurs. 11:30am-10pm, Fri.-Sat. 11:30am-11pm, Sun. 10am-10pm

CONTEMPORARY AMERICAN
Red Star Tavern & Roast House $$$

The best place to settle in at Red Star is one of the elevated booths in the bar. From there, you have a fantastic view of the restaurant and the enormous wall of booze that features one of the city's best collections of bourbon. The menu tends to focus on hearty dishes from the land and sea, with a heavy focus on Italian, French, and Mediterranean influences. Chef Dolan Lane—who has made his mark on several upscale Portland kitchens—continues with Red Star's longstanding tradition of using organic and local products whenever possible, so the menu changes often but always provides a healthy balance of vegetarian and carnivore-friendly dishes.

MAP 1: 503 SW Alder St., 503/222-0005, www.redstartavern.com; Mon.-Fri. 6:30am-11am, 11:30am-2pm, and 5pm-10pm, Sat. 8am-2pm and 5pm-10pm, Sun. 8am-3pm and 5pm-9pm

Imperial $$

If anyone could open a hotel restaurant and bar that does not suffer from being stodgy and overpriced, it is James Beard Award-winning Vitaly Paley (also owner of Paley's Place). Imperial is bold and unabashed with upscale decor that is gritty and masculine, like exposed brick, stone pillars, and bike chain chandeliers. The food is rich and portions large, often served on boards and in cast-iron pans. You can't go wrong with tails and trotters, or rib eye from the wood-fired grill,

but make sure you get some Parker House rolls and duck meatballs for the table.

MAP 1: 410 SW Broadway, 503/228-7222, www.imperialpdx.com; Mon.-Thurs. 6:30am-11pm, Fri. 6:30am-midnight, Sat. 8am-midnight, Sun. 8am-11pm

Jackrabbit $$

Jackrabbit is a carnivore's darling, helmed by *Top Chef Masters* winner Chris Cosentino. Pig is definitely the star here (although you can order a divine platter of rabbit) with such popular dishes as crispy pig ears, house charcuterie, and a pig's head served on a cutting board with tortillas, slaw, and salsa. Dinner choices are numerous and quite good, but if you go with a group, it's wise to order one of the sharcable entrées, like the rabbit or a decadent four-pound platter of 28-day-aged pin bone steak that comes with bone marrow dip. The

Red Star Tavern & Roast House

FOODIE TOURS

Portland offers numerous culinary delights, and if you'd like to take your food obsession a step further, you can embark on a tour or class while here.

The **Epicurean Excursion** (meeting point Pioneer Courthouse Square, 503/774-4522, www.portlandwalkingtours.com; $79) is a delightful tour through Portland's tastiest places. Guests can try any number of treats, like Oregon wine and imported mustards, gelato, sorbet, cheese, pizza, chocolate, and bread. As you sample and savor, you will also learn about how things are made, how sustainable practices work, and what Portland is doing differently that makes everything taste so good. Be sure you don't wear open-toed shoes for this walking tour, because you will be traipsing through some kitchens.

Portlanders really love their coffee. Many coffee shops in town roast their own beans, and now many coffee lovers are learning to do it themselves in their own kitchens. At **Mr. Green Beans** (3908 N. Mississippi Ave., 503/288-8698, www.diycoffeeroasting.com; $25), you can take a class and learn how to do just that with no special equipment, just a kitchen pan or popcorn maker. You will learn the principles of roasting as well as see demonstrations for every step of the process. After the class, you'll receive a DIY guide and a pound of green beans so you can test out your new skills at home.

---

space itself is open and rustic with wood from various sources and decor repurposed from bicycles and an old tannery. It gets a bit noisy in the main dining room, so if you prefer to have quieter conversation, opt for the more intimate back dining room or one of the booths.

MAP 1: 830 SW 6th Ave., 503/412-1800, www.gojackrabbitgo.com; Sun.-Thurs. 7am-11pm, Fri.-Sat. 7am-11:30pm

Picnic House $$

This cute American and French-style bistro is bright and open. When the owners of Picnic House pulled up the years of carpeting and paint to reveal the original dark wood and black-and-white tile, the rustic Prohibition-style Heathman Hotel setting immediately took shape. The menu is simple, with a few entrées and small plates featuring soups, salads, and sandwiches as well as charcuterie and desserts. You can even rent a fully loaded picnic basket of house-made treats and wine and eat it in the adjacent Park Blocks.

MAP 1: 723 SW Salmon St., 503/227-0705, www.picnichousepdx.com; Mon.-Sat. 11am-3pm and 5pm-10pm

Pine Street Market $$

This European-style food hall in Old Town is like a food court—if the shops in that food court were helmed by some of the city's top chefs. Inside, you'll find a number of individual restaurants, each with their own specialty. To name a few, there's Bless Your Heart Burgers from Drew Sprouse and John Gorham of Toro Bravo, an outpost of Olympia Provisions from top salumist Elias Cairo, Checkerboard Pizza from James Beard Award-winner Ken Forkish, and Wiz Bang Bar, a soft-serve ice cream bar from the people at Salt & Straw. A number of the spots also offer craft cocktails, beer, and wine, and there are happy hour specials.

MAP 1: 126 SW 2nd St., www. pinestreetpdx.com; daily, hours vary by restaurant

ASIAN
✪ Lúc Lác $$

This downtown hot spot is always packed with locals looking to find some homey Vietnamese specialties like aromatic pho, banh mi, and crispy rolls. Lúc Lác is *the* go-to spot for late-night dining, and its after-midnight menu extends until 4am on weekends. Besides the aforementioned favorites, try the papaya salad or the restaurant's namesake dish, which features beef tenderloin seared with garlic, peppercorn, Hennessy, and beurre de France. Order at the counter; you will be given a number and seated as soon as something is available. Depending on the size of your party, the wait can easily be 10-40 minutes, and you will not be allowed to order or sit until your whole party has arrived. This also means that they strictly enforce the "no late-joiners allowed" policy. It may seem harsh, but given how popular the place is, most people have come to accept the rules.

MAP 1: 835 SW 2nd Ave., 503/222-0047, www.luclackitchen.com; Sun.-Thurs. 11am-2:30pm and 4pm-midnight, Fri.-Sat. 11am-2:30pm and 4pm-4am

Saucebox $$

Since 1995, the folks at Saucebox have attempted to bring together fantastic food, perfectly crafted cocktails, exceptional music, and inspired decor to create an approachable, chic nightlife atmosphere. In short, they have spent a long time cultivating a "place to be seen" cocktail lounge. Saucebox's dinner menu features sushi and simple but cautiously creative pan-Asian dishes that put this place shoulder-to-shoulder with many of Portland's fine-dining destinations. Plates arrive with a beautiful presentation, but the use of fresh local and regional ingredients saves it from being too pretentious. You can order dim sum-style dishes like pot stickers, chicken dumplings, and salad rolls, or dig into a full-size entrée such as Korean ribs or grilled duck.

MAP 1: 214 SW Broadway, 503/241-3393, www.saucebox.com; Tues.-Thurs. 4:30pm-midnight, Fri.-Sat. 4:30pm-2:30am, Sun. 5pm-11pm

Chizu Bar $

Cheese lovers, rejoice. This little shop is devoted to all things creamy, stinky, buttery, and complex. The menu consists of an ever-changing variety of cheeses that are presented at perfect ripeness. Much like a sushi restaurant, you can choose your own experience by selecting as many types as you want to sample, or order *omakase*-style and name your price, then let the cheesemongers select for you. The results will be different every time. Perhaps you'll get an arrangement of goat and sheep cheeses alongside a drizzle of local honey, house chutney, and fresh fruit, or perhaps some Humboldt Fog goat cheese and Rogue Creamery blue cheese with some charcuterie, ginger pickles, and crostini. Whatever you choose, the experts here know exactly how to best bring out the flavors.

MAP 1: 1126 SW Alder St., 503/719-6889, www.chizubar.com; Wed.-Fri. 3pm-10pm, Sat. 1pm-10pm, Sun. 1pm-8pm

SUSHI
Masu Sushi $$$

Masu is to sushi what Bob Fosse is to choreography—sexy and surprising, but still introspective. The feel is all at once fluid and angular. During the daytime, Masu is open and bright, lit by the huge windows and white curtains that adorn this second-story space. At night, the space heats up with an amber glow that is perfect for intimate dining. It would appear that the specialty rolls are the real stars here—and they are worth their price, but since Masu is really more about the fish, not the sauce, the *nigiri* is not to be ignored. If that's not your thing, try the burger: This Kobe beef patty with kimchi mayo and caramelized onions is surprisingly delicious.

MAP 1: 406 SW 13th Ave., 503/221-6278, www.masusushi.com; Mon.-Thurs. 11:30am-11pm, Fri. 11:30am-midnight, Sat. 4pm-midnight, Sun. 4pm-10pm

FRENCH
Bistro Agnes $$$

James Beard Award-winning chefs Greg Denton and Gabrielle Quiñónez Denton are known for taking risks, and with this cozy bistro, named after Greg's grandmother, their risk paid off. In a city flooded with chefs rethinking cuisine, the Dentons have hit the mark by offering perfectly executed French cuisine made traditionally. Classic, comforting dishes like cassoulet, coq au vin, and beef bourguignon are the pillars of the menu, along with picture-perfect daily specials that include things like sweetbreads, tripe, and boudin blanc foie gras. If you order the burger, be prepared to get messy. It is superb, served "á la Française" with Wagyu-style beef, cheddar, and grilled onions sitting atop a pool of truffled bordelaise, like a burger-meets-French-dip delight.

MAP 1: 527 SW 12th Ave., 503/222-0979, www.bistroagnes.com; Sun.-Thurs. 11am-2pm and 5pm-10pm, Fri.-Sat. 11am-2pm and 5pm-11pm

Higgins $$$

Higgins is classic Portland-style dining meets French countryside, with its comfortable and classy dining room, attentive but not intrusive service, and robust, locally harvested menu. Higgins was doing vegetarian long before it caught on, and while it still does it right, the real specialty is meat.

House-cured charcuterie plates always satisfy. The seasonally prepared duck is a favorite among critics, and the Whole Pig Plate (a dish heaped with such things as roast loin, kielbasa, braised belly, and ribs) frequently shows up on lists of the top must-have dishes in Portland. Higgins is a popular pre-show spot, given its proximity to many of the downtown concert halls and theaters, so it's best to make a reservation.

MAP 1: 1239 SW Broadway, 503/222-9070, www.higginsportland.com; Mon.-Thurs. 11:30am-9:30pm, Fri. 11:30am-10:30pm, Sat. 5pm-10:30pm, Sun. 4pm-9:30pm

Little Bird $$

Sophisticated little sister to the award-winning east-side Portland favorite Le Pigeon, Little Bird opened in late 2011 to much acclaim. Little Bird features audacious French-inspired dishes but with a slightly simpler, more traditional palate. Reviews of the place border on salacious, with critics turning out lustful phrases about roasted marrow bones and charcuterie plates. There are many blush-worthy items on the menu, but don't overlook the Le Pigeon burger. It's pricey but well worth it. If you can manage to snag an upstairs table, do it. You will be treated to a slightly more intimate and quieter perch for people-watching.

MAP 1: 219 SW 6th Ave., 503/688-5952, www.littlebirdbistro.com; Mon.-Fri. 11:30am-midnight, Sat.-Sun. 5pm-midnight

ITALIAN
Il Solito $$$

The name of this restaurant means "the usual" and is intended to tap into that cozy, familiar feeling of getting that one beloved dish whenever you return to a place you adore. Chef Matthew Sigler—former executive chef of critic-favorite Renata—serves up New York-style Italian favorites, with handmade pastas taking the lead. You'll find traditional spaghetti and meatballs served with grilled garlic bread and a hearty rigatoni alla vodka, as well as a saffron carbonara with bacon, sea urchin, and English peas. Be sure to pay attention to the specials as well, because the kitchen occasionally turns out a particularly special ragù or ravioli that is worth skipping the menu for. The restaurant's interior is sleek and modern and looks like it was done by a graphic designer rather than a decorator, with sharp contrasts and bold imagery everywhere you look. The appearance is busy but not overwhelming, and it lends itself well both to the atmosphere and the plates being served.

MAP 1: 627 SW Washington St., 503/228-1515, www.ilsolitoportland.com; Mon.-Thurs. 7am-10:30am, 11am-2:30pm, and 5pm-10pm; Fri. 7am-10:30am, 11am-2:30pm, and 5pm-11pm, Sat. 8am-2:30pm and 5pm-11pm, Sun. 8am-2:30pm and 5pm-10pm

Mama Mia Trattoria $$

Mama Mia Trattoria is not the place to find traditional Italian, but if you are looking for comfort, this is the spot. Owner Lisa Schroeder is famous for her pillow-soft gnocchi and her Sunday gravy, a sauce she simmers all day and serves with penne, sausage, pork, and a meatball the size of your fist.

Despite its proximity to Portland's Cultural District, this place seems to have gotten lost on its way to New York. It's in an elite class for Portland, which otherwise lacks for true Italian American soul food. The food here seems like it was snatched from the kitchen of someone's *nonna*, yet

surprisingly, Mama Mia's has vegetarian options and will make many of the dishes vegan-friendly upon request. If you have room for dessert (or even if you don't), grab some out-of-this-world *zeppole* (fried dough balls sprinkled with powdered sugar) and a glass of moscato before you go.

MAP 1: 439 SW 2nd Ave., 503/295-6464, www.mamamiatrattoria.com; daily 11:30pm-9pm

DELIS AND DINERS
Kenny and Zuke's $$

Kenny and Zuke's was born out of a desire for more authentic Jewish deli food in Portland—more specifically, for good pastrami. Owner Ken Gordon went to work creating just that: a pastrami to serve as the backbone for a number of the dishes in this popular delicatessen. Waits can be long and prices can be steep, but the sandwiches are delicious and huge. You can get a traditional Reuben or pastrami sandwich or mix it up with coleslaw and chopped liver. If you really want to get crazy, try the pastrami burger. The best deal on the menu is the lunch special, a half sandwich served with a cup of soup (try the Hungarian mushroom) or a green salad. If you can't make lunch, happy hour (Mon.-Fri. 3pm-6pm) is also a less expensive option.

MAP 1: 1038 SW Harvey Milk St., 503/222-3354, www.kennyandzukes.com; Mon.-Thurs. 7am-8pm, Fri. 7am-9pm, Sat. 8am-9pm, Sun. 8am-8pm

The Roxy $$

A few things in life are constant. Around here, we take comfort in knowing the rain will always return and The Roxy diner will always offer sweet, fantastic French toast and bacon at 2am (unless it's Monday).

The food is good here, especially after a night sweating to 1980s pop. Check out the decidedly irreverent T-shirt collection and tip your server well (who else will bring you chili cheese fries at that hour?).

MAP 1: 1121 SW Harvey Milk St., 503/223-9160; Tues.-Sat. 24 hours; free

BREAKFAST AND BRUNCH
✪ Tasty n Alder $$

John Gorham is a bit of a legend in the Portland culinary scene—responsible for Tasty n Alder and its big brother Tasty n Sons (3803 N. Williams St., www.tastynsons.com, 503/621-1400) and their big daddy, Toro Bravo. You will find the occasional customer-favorite items on all the menus, like the bacon-wrapped dates or the chocolate potato doughnuts with crème anglaise. But, for the most part, each restaurant has its own, expertly crafted menu. There are few places in Portland where it is truly worth the potentially long brunch line, and this is one of them.

MAP 1: 580 SW 12th Ave., 503/621-9251, www.tastynalder.com; Sun.-Thurs. 9am-10pm, Fri.-Sat. 9am-11pm

Mother's Velvet Lounge and Café $$

With a name like Mother's, you can probably guess what sort of food owner Lisa Schroeder is famous for serving up. Comfort is key here, and while you stare at the ample plates full of such belly-rich dishes as the near-infamous crunchy French toast, you can almost hear your mother whisper, "Eat! You look skinny!" The sun-drenched dining room is a fine place to start your day, but make sure you come back and hunker down in the richly appointed Velvet Lounge, where Mom's Meatloaf & Gravy is served well into the night.

MAP 1: 212 SW Harvey Milk St., 503/464-1122, www.mothersbistro.com; Tues.-Thurs. 7am-2:30pm and 5:30pm-9pm, Fri. 7am-2:30pm and 5pm-10pm, Sat. 8am-2:30pm and 5pm-10pm, Sun. 8am-2:30pm

Blue Star Donuts

COFFEE AND DESSERTS
✪ Blue Star Donuts $

Blue Star opened its first location in December 2012. Now there are four locations around town, which still often close their doors by 3pm because the last doughnut is already gone. The difference is in the dough. Owner Micah Camden decided to go with a brioche-style dough, which is labor-intensive but results in a chewier, more pillow-like doughnut. The flavors are sophisticated as well with favorites such as Blueberry Bourbon Basil, Passion Fruit and Cocoa Nibs, and Cointreau Creme Brulee. Small children might be turned off by the more complex flavors, but they are likely to appreciate the Old Fashioned Buttermilk, which is just about the best thing you will ever put in your mouth.

MAP 1: 1155 SW Morrison St., 503/265-0410, www.bluestardonuts.com; daily 7am-8pm or until sold out

✪ Cacao $

There's nothing like a cup of hot chocolate to fight off the rain and cold, unless of course you have had a cup of drinking chocolate. What's the difference? Hot chocolate is made from cocoa powder containing only a small amount of cocoa butter, and drinking chocolate is made with whole chocolate, which naturally contains more than 50 percent cocoa butter. The flavor is rich and intense. It is all at once soothing and invigorating. If you are used to hitting a cup of coffee first thing in the morning, give Cacao a try. A small, thick cup of drinking chocolate might bring you quite surprising results.

MAP 1. 414 SW 13th Ave., 503/241-0656, www.cacaodrinkchocolate.com; daily 10am-6pm

Petunia's Pies & Pastries $

Whimsical and bright, this little shop got its start as a popular farmers market booth specializing in gluten-free and plant-based products. Vegans will delight at the variety of sweet and savory offerings, and non-vegans will likely be surprised to find that very few things here taste decidedly vegan. There are traditional items, like banana, carrot, and zucchini muffins, but also surprises like a coconut dulce de leche cake, chocolate brownie cream pies, and cheesecakes. A number of beverage options are also available, including coffee and espresso from nearby Coava Coffee as well as beer, wine, and cocktails. It also has some savory breakfast and lunch options.

MAP 1: 610 SW 12th St., 503/841-5961, www.petuniaspiesandpastries.com; Mon.-Wed. 9am-8pm, Thurs. 9am-9pm, Fri.-Sat. 9am-10pm, Sun. 9am-7pm

Stumptown Coffee Roasters $

Portlanders take their coffee pretty seriously (in a reusable or recyclable cup, thank you), and Stumptown is at the top of the list for most java hounds. Founded by Portlander Duane Sorenson but sold to Peet's in 2015, Stumptown still looms large in this town. Its beans are meticulously selected, sorted, roasted, and brewed so that you get the distinct flavor, sweetness, and complexity of the bean, not the scorched bean flavor that so many of us have become accustomed to. This particular hamlet of the Stumptown universe is near the ground floor of the all-too-hip Ace Hotel, and you are welcome to take your coffee and enjoy it in the comfy lobby of the hotel. Just don't forget to pick up a bag of beans to take home. You are going to want them later.

MAP 1: 1026 SW Harvey Milk St., 503/224-9060, www.stumptowncoffee.com; Mon.-Fri. 6am-7pm, Sat.-Sun. 7am-7pm

Voodoo Doughnut $

After the bartenders announce last call and the waitstaff swipe the empty glasses from all the tables of Portland's downtown bars, one late-night eatery is still going strong. Voodoo Doughnut in the Old Town neighborhood has been a haven

Voodoo Doughnut

for creatures of the night since its opening. Owners Tres Shannon and Kenneth Pogson reject conformity by offering such doughnuts as the Dirt Doughnut, covered in vanilla glaze and crushed Oreos, and the Maple Blazer Blunt, a cinnamon doughnut rolled to look like an oversized joint with a red sprinkled tip. Still, the real draw here is the peculiar atmosphere.

The offerings are quirky, queer, and not a bit serious. You can even get legally hitched under the giant Cruller Chandelier of Life. Voodoo is a cash-only establishment, and it has another brick-and-mortar location as well as a food truck across the river on the east side.

MAP 1: 22 SW 3rd Ave., 503/241-4704, www.voodoodoughnut.com; daily 24 hours

Northwest and the Pearl District

Map 2

PACIFIC NORTHWEST
Paley's Place $$$

Chef-owners Vitaly and Kimberly Paley are renowned in kitchens across the nation, having worked in some of the most illustrious restaurants on the map. Thankfully, the couple settled in Portland in the early 1990s for the blessed bounty of ingredients. Years after opening their intimate 50-seat restaurant, the Paleys are still receiving national acclaim for their French-influenced dishes that draw from Pacific Northwest ingredients, such as seasonal risottos and hearty cassoulets. After dinner, switch things up a bit and ask for a cheese course instead of dessert. Pair it with a glass of local wine for a perfectly rounded meal.

MAP 2: 1204 NW 21st Ave., 503/243-2403, www.paleysplace.net; Mon.-Thurs. 5:30pm-10pm, Fri.-Sat. 5pm-11pm, Sun. 5pm-10pm

CONTEMPORARY AMERICAN
Irving Street Kitchen $$$

Irving Street Kitchen is upscale without being snobby—so great for dates and business dinners. It's a touch high-concept, but the Southern-influenced New American cuisine feels both sophisticated and satisfying, with dishes like chorizo and squid ink risotto, smoked salt-baked salmon, and chicken-fried oysters. The menu also includes reliably delicious beef and chicken dishes as well as a pretty good dessert array. If you run out of room, order one of the butterscotch puddings with caramel sauce to go. Served in a reusable glass jar, it's a nice treat once your stomach is less full.

MAP 2: 701 NW 13th St., 503/343-9440, www.irvingstreetkitchen.com; Mon.-Thurs. 4:30pm-10pm, Fri. 4:30pm-11pm, Sat. 10am-2:30pm and 4:30pm-11pm, Sun. 10am-2:30pm and 4:30pm-10pm

✪ Olympia Provisions $$

Opened in 2009, Olympia Provisions is Oregon's first USDA-approved *salumeria* (cured-meat shop), and it operates out of two locations in Portland: the original Southeast Portland location (107 SE Washington St., 503/954-3663) and this one, tucked in a warehouse space under the Morrison

PACIFIC NORTHWEST CUISINE

One of the reasons Portland's food scene is so hot is because of the bounty of ingredients found so close to home. Pacific Northwest cuisine is farm-to-table at its finest, and made more personal by the fact that chefs may know their rancher by first name or even grow some of the restaurants' produce in their own backyard. The Oregon coast is just a skip away and offers some of the best seafood and shellfish in the world. Salmon spawn in our backyard, and the fertile valleys of the region give us wild mushrooms, nettles, asparagus, hazelnuts, blackberries, and other gorgeous fruits, not to mention spectacular wines. Here are some of the best places to experience Pacific Northwest cuisine:

Paley's Place

- **Paley's Place:** For over 20 years, this restaurant has been a favorite among locals thanks to the work of James Beard award-winning chef Vitaly Paley and his wife Kimberly, as well as the bounty of Pacific Northwest ingredients they incorporate into their French-Inspired fare (page 54).

- **Farm Spirit:** At this prix-fixe, plant-based restaurant, nearly everything you'll touch, including the plates, was sourced within 105 miles of the restaurant (page 72).

- **Jacqueline:** Portland's proximity to the Pacific Ocean means some of the freshest "tide-to-table" oysters and seafood, which Jacqueline showcases beautifully and without any excessive frills (page 73).

Bridge. At the back of this 30-seat house is a 4,000-square-foot all-purpose meat-curing facility, where award-winning salumist Elias Cairo crafts some of the finest charcuterie meats around. The menu is simple: a smattering of rustic European-inspired fares and Pacific Northwest favorites. And if cured meats really are king here, the queen is perhaps the signature roasted chicken, cooked to perfection on a vintage rotisserie and then crisped in a pan. You can order the famous Sunday Chicken Dinner (complete with salad and seasonal sides) to dine on there or take with you for a high-class picnic. But no visit to Olympia Provisions is complete without sampling the charcuterie. At the least, stop at the counter and purchase some to take with you.

MAP 2: 1632 NW Thurman St., 503/894-8136, www.olympiaprovisions. com; Mon. 11am-3pm, Tues.-Fri. 11am-10pm, Sat. 10am-10pm, Sun. 10am-9pm

ASIAN
Kim Jong Smokehouse $$
This hot spot is the brainchild of three chefs who have collaborated to make Korean street food using Southern-style barbecue techniques. Among them is Han Ly Hwang, who runs the food cart Kim Jong Grillin', a long-time local favorite. Hwang's bibimbap bowls are what made him famous around here, and they are a featured

Olympia Provisions

portion of the menu, along with steamed pork buns, house-made kimchi, and smoked spareribs. The bibimbap bowls are served with scorched rice, yam noodles, sesame sprouts, daikon and napa kimchi, seasonal pickles, a fried egg, and your choice of sauce. Try it as is with the kimchi mayo or Gochujang sauce, or opt for the cold smoked salmon or the brined and smoked oyster mushrooms to add depth and smoky complexity.

MAP 2: 413 NW 21st Ave., 503/239-0100; Sun.-Thurs. 11am-9pm, Fri.-Sat. 11am-10pm

Red Onion $$

Portlanders love Thai food, and Red Onion is a cut above. Former owner of two other local restaurants, Chef Dang Boonyakamol has made a name for himself by creating authentic northern Thai dishes—both traditional and unexpected. If you are a fan of heat, you will appreciate that they can actually bring it here without sacrificing the flavor. If you must, stick with the standards such as *pad kee mao* or chicken

curry, but if you are feeling adventurous, try one of the more distinctive specialties, like a crisp-skinned catfish or rolls filled with Chinese sausage, shrimp, egg, and cucumber and topped with Dungeness crab.

MAP 2: 1123 NW 23rd Ave., 503/208-2634, www.redonionportland.com; Mon.-Fri. 11am-3pm and 5pm-9:30pm, Sat. noon-9:30pm, Sun. noon-9pm

SUSHI
Bamboo Sushi $$

There are a number of really great sushi restaurants in Portland, but Bamboo Sushi made waves when it opened in 2008, not just because the sushi was top-notch, but also because this was the first certified sustainable sushi restaurant in the world. The NW 23rd location is the second and newest outpost to the immensely popular **Southeast Portland location** (310 SE 28th Ave., 503/232-5255), but it doesn't mean the lines will be shorter, so make reservations whenever possible. There are fun specialty rolls, like the Green

Machine with tempura asparagus, avocado, green onion, and cilantro sweet chili aioli, or the Highway 35 (a critic favorite), which has red crab, spicy sesame aioli, avocado, cucumber, and asparagus topped with sake-poached pears and eel sauce. Sample the sashimi and *nigiri* rolls, but don't overlook the Kobe burger. It is, arguably, one of the best in the city.

MAP 2: 836 NW 23rd Ave., 971/229-1925, www.bamboosushi.com; daily 4:30pm-10pm

FRENCH
St. Jack $$$

St. Jack is setting the bar high for French cuisine in Portland. Rather than getting cute or fussy, it focuses entirely on food from the bouchons of the French region of Lyon, such as sausages, foie gras, bone marrow, mussels, and duck. If it is hearty, meaty, or buttery, it is probably on the menu. The Mussels Provençal are rich, fragrant, and garlicky and pair beautifully with a French muscadet. Of course, there are also offer many variations on steak frites, including the bavette (sirloin), teres major (shoulder), and rib eye cuts. Situated at the neighborhood edge of the Alphabet District, St. Jack offers an unassuming but elegant atmosphere that is perfect for dates or special occasions.

MAP 2: 1610 NW 23rd Ave., 503/360-1281, www.stjackpdx.com; Sun.-Thurs. 4pm-11pm, Fri.-Sat. 4pm-midnight

Le Happy $

In one of the lesser-traveled areas of Northwest Portland is a tiny little café that specializes in the French equivalent of comfort food: the crêpe. Trust me now, these are nothing like your average pancake-chain crêpes. Besides being tasty and filling, the darn things are pretty versatile, too. You can order them savory or sweet in styles that range from elegant (such as the Saumon Fumé, with smoked salmon and white wine) to downright trashy (the Savoir Faire, with bacon and cheddar and an optional can of Pabst Blue Ribbon on the side). On the sweeter side of the menu, some local favorites are the simple clover honey and lemon crêpe and the delectable Spectac, made with Grand Marnier, Nutella, and banana flambé.

MAP 2: 1011 NW 16th Ave., 503/226-1258, www.lehappy.com; Mon.-Fri. 5pm-midnight, Sat. 10am-midnight, Sun. 10am-2:30pm

LATIN
Andina $$$

One of Portland's best restaurants, this Pearl District Peruvian tapas place has one of the most inspired and extensive small-plates menus in town. You can order traditional entrées—like pork tenderloin or Pisco-brined Cornish hen—but a better bet is to order two or three *pequeño* (small) plates each and share. The empanadas, filled with slow-cooked beef, raisins, and olives, are a must—as is the yucca root stuffed with cheese. Both floors of Andina get packed nearly every night, so expect a wait or book ahead online. Once seated, order a Sacsayhuamán cocktail (just say, "sexy woman") and soak in the atmosphere.

MAP 2: 1314 NW Glisan St., 503/228-9535, www.andinarestaurant.com; Sun.-Thurs. 11:30am-2:30pm and 5pm-9:30pm, Fri.-Sat. 11:30am-2:30pm and 5pm-10:30pm

Ataula $$

Ataula (ah-TOWL-ah) is a popular destination for food aficionados and critics from across the nation. This is *the* spot in Portland for traditional

Spanish tapas, house-made sangrias, and fragrant, hearty paellas. Chef Jose Chesa presents a menu that is thoughtfully curated and dishes both expertly prepared and beautifully plated. Start with the salt cod *croquetas*, a chorizo-stuffed goat cheese and membrillo lollipop, and mini *rossejat* (a traditional Catalan noodle dish). Finish your meal with a glass of the seasonal sangria and the spectacular Arros Negre, a traditional paella made with squid ink and grilled Spanish octopus.

MAP 2: 1818 NW 23rd Pl., 503/894-8904, www.ataulapdx.com.com; Tues.-Sun. 4:30pm-10pm

Isabel Pearl $$

Isabel Cruz, the California-based chef and owner of this Pearl District fusion café, draws influence from Puerto Rican, Cuban, Mexican, Japanese, and Thai cooking. While lettuce wraps and edamame alongside carnitas may seem strange, Cruz manages to make it work. Her food is akin to spa food—elegant, colorful, and oftentimes quite good for you. Order Cruz's signature Crispy Dragon Potatoes as a breakfast entrée with eggs and bacon or as an appetizer. For dinner, the Big Bowls are always reliable. The menu also includes a decent happy hour, but the breakfast and lunch offerings are still more extensive.

MAP 2: 330 NW 10th Ave., 503/222-4333, www.isabelscantina.com; Mon.-Fri. 8am-3pm and 4pm-9pm, Sat.-Sun. 8am-3pm and 5pm-9pm

VEGETARIAN
Laughing Planet $

Laughing Planet is a great option if you have meat eaters and vegetarians in tow. The generously sized burritos and bowls will satisfy herbivores and carnivores alike. At this quick-service café (and its multiple other Portland locations), you will find traditional offerings like a simple grilled chicken burrito with beans, organic brown rice, and Tillamook cheese, but also more exotic options, like the Che Guevara, with beans, plantains, sweet potatoes, rice, pico, and spicy barbecue sauce. The bowls make for a filling meal as well, with nods to Thai, Moroccan, Indian, and Latin American cuisine. If you don't finish your bowl, you can take it home and throw it into a tortilla later for an all-new twist on your meal.

MAP 2: 909 NW 21st Ave., 503/445-1319, www.laughingplanetcafe.com; Mon.-Sat. 11am-9pm, Sun. 11am-8pm

Mi Mero Mole $

For as much as the average Portlander would walk a mile in the rain for a good taco, it is pretty hard to find good, authentic Mexican food. It is even harder if you are a vegetarian. Enter Mi Mero Mole, where taco lovers can now get delicious tacos and authentic *guisados* (comfort food) just like you might score from street vendors in Mexico City. There are some great meaty dishes here, but the vegan and vegetarian dishes are hearty and satisfying and involve ingredients like cactus, squash, mushrooms, or seeds and nuts. You can also get an early morning fix with chilaquiles, customizable tacos, burritos, and bowls, and a steaming cup of cinnamon- and clove-infused coffee.

MAP 2: 32 NW 5th Ave., 971/266-8575, www.mmmtacospdx.com; Mon.-Thurs. 7:30am-9pm, Fri. 7:30am-10pm, Sat. noon-10pm, Sun. noon-9pm

Prasad $

In the Yoga Pearl healing arts center, Prasad stands out as one of Portland's favorite vegetarian cafés. Owner Karen Pride offers up remarkably varied dishes made from locally grown, organically farmed vegetables delivered each day by bicycle. It's a fine fit with the adjacent yoga studio, and although you are asked to keep it quiet out of respect for those meditating, the raw foods, salads, pastas, and smoothies on offer are touted to have you leaving feeling better than you did when you came in. Order the Chili Bowl—rice or quinoa, roasted garlic chilies, scallions, and avocado topped with green chili and garlic tahini sauce—and follow it up with a smoothie, a green tea *matcha* latte, or an invigorating shot of wheatgrass.

MAP 2. 925 NW Davis St., 503/224-3993, www.prasadcuisine.com; Mon.-Fri. 7:30am-8pm, Sat.-Sun. 9am-8pm

BURGERS
✪ TILT $$

If you want a good ol' burger, TILT is definitely on the top 10 list for a lot of Portlanders. Its motto is "handcrafted food and drink for the American workforce," and what that means is unapologetically big burgers, huge piles of fries, and pies that look straight out of a 1950s diner. Keep it simple with a classic cheeseburger or go crazy and try one of the signature burgers, like the Woody Royale with an onion ring, jalapeño slaw, brisket, bacon, and cheddar. The space is open and cavernous, having once been the home of a General Electric distribution plant, so the eatery can accommodate a lot of people, though the line to order still occasionally gets long. You'll find a number of little touches in keeping with the blue collar-industrial theme, like a bin of clean shop towels instead of napkins and flat metal trays instead of plates. You'll also find a lot

of concrete walls, exposed duct piping, and huge communal tables built out of concrete, wood, and steel.

MAP 2: 1355 NW Everett St., 503/894-9528, www.tiltitup.com; Sun.-Thurs. 7am-11pm, Fri.-Sat. 7am-midnight

Little Big Burger $

If you are paying attention, you will find LBB locations scattered all over the city. So popular are these little not-quite-sliders, but not-quite-burgers, that it is easy to support so many places. Micah Camden is the culinary giant who brings us LBB (as well as Blue Star Donuts, Boxer Ramen, and Son of a Biscuit), and it is the simplicity of his concept that makes it work so well. The options are quite limited and haven't changed since the first location opened in 2010 (except for the addition of pepper jack cheese). All burgers start with a quarter-pound beef patty topped with lettuce, red onion, and pickle on a brioche bun, and you can add cheese (cheddar, swiss, chèvre, blue, or pepper jack cheese) or bacon if you like. They also offer fries tossed in truffle oil and sea salt, fountain sodas, root beer floats, and beer. And that's it. Hungry eaters may want to order two or three of the little guys, but for light eaters or kids, the LBB is a perfect size.

MAP 2: 122 NW 10th St., 503/274-9008; daily 11am-10pm

BREAKFAST AND BRUNCH
The Daily Café $$

The Daily Café is just about as unassuming as its name, offering breakfast staples like omelets, hashes, French toast, and eggs Benedict as well as several rotating specials. They also offer a number of lighter-fare options like toasted Bowery Bagels, eggy

HOW TO HACK THE LINE

It's a long-running joke that Portlanders' favorite pastime is waiting in line, and a quick look around will make that seem very plausible. Lines for ice cream stretch around the block. Brunch lines groan out onto the sidewalks. Fortunately, there are a few tricks to help you avoid losing valuable time standing around.

Salt & Straw is nationally recognized for its amazing small-batch artisanal ice cream. Even on drizzly, wet days, you'll see a line of people waiting to sample a little Honey Lavender or Stumptown Coffee and Burnside Bourbon. Is it worth it? Yeah, it is—especially since you can sample as many flavors as you like before choosing. However, if you have an inkling of what you would like, simply walk in and grab a pint from the prepacked freezer. There's no need to wait in the line to pay.

Many pubs and markets also offer growler filling stations. You simply bring a glass jug (or buy one from the venue), and they will fill it and send you on your way. **Deschutes Brewery and Public House** in the Pearl District is happy to pour you a jug of its Inversion IPA, or whatever else you fancy. And **Fire on the Mountain,** despite being known for its wings, has its own brewery and offers both 32-ounce and 64-ounce growlers of its ale.

Feel peckish before the blues band you're about to see? If you are waiting for a show at the **Aladdin Theater,** pop into The Lamp lounge-restaurant next door and order some dinner. You'll receive a wristband to bypass the line when the doors open.

Sometimes, the key to getting what you want is to stake out the other locations of a Portland hot spot. Tourist favorite **Voodoo Doughnut** has a second and much larger location on the east side of the river (1501 NE Davis St., 503/235-2666).

Finally, with some places, you just have to know when to go. With touristy spots, you will have a better chance when the weather turns for the worse. Dinner in Portland is a bit of an affair, and people take their time getting to it. Skip the happy hour and head straight to dinner. At **Toro Bravo,** for instance, the dinner crowd gets thick around 7pm, so it's best to show up at 5pm. Don't eschew an opportunity to sit at the bar. You will get seated faster, and your service will be much more focused.

---

sandwiches, savory quinoa bowls, granola, and avocado toast. The atmosphere is pretty laid-back here; simply order at the counter and take a seat, but be prepared for a server to shout your name when your order is ready. It will be delivered to you, but you'll have to let them know where you land. **MAP 2:** 902 NW 13th Ave., 503/242-1916, www.dailycafeinthepearl.com; Mon.-Fri. 7am-4pm, Sat. 8am-4pm, Sun. 8am-3pm

Byways Café $

It has been over a decade since Byways Café got a little bit famous thanks to a visit from the Food Network, but locals still flock here to sample the omelets, scrambles, and corned beef hash. Byways is also known for its blue corn pancakes, made with ground blue corn and served with honey pecan butter. Don't get me wrong, the corn cakes are good, but nothing compares to

the amaretto-infused challah French toast. The weekend wait can be long here, as at many Portland breakfast joints. To make it more bearable, arrive early, bring something to read, and pick up something caffeinated on the way. Byways doesn't offer free sidewalk coffee, but servers will take your drink order if you ask. **MAP 2:** 1212 NW Glisan St., 503/221-0011, www.bywayscafe.com; Mon.-Fri. 7am-3pm, Sat.-Sun. 7:30am-2pm

St. Honoré Boulangerie $

If your idea of a good breakfast is a smooth latte and a buttery pastry, St. Honoré is a great place to start your day. Named for the patron saint of bakers, St. Honoré takes its influences from the bakery ovens of Normandy. The traditional clay brick oven was imported brick by kaolin clay brick to Portland—where the earthen sides retain moisture and provide for more even baking (in other words, perfectly flaky croissants and custard-rich *canalets*). If you don't have much of a sweet tooth, ask for a slice of freshly made quiche or the astounding *croque monsieur* sandwich (grilled brioche with Black Forest ham, Emmentaler cheese, béchamel sauce, and Dijon mustard) and grab a seat at one of the sidewalk tables.

MAP 2: 2335 NW Thurman St., 503/445-4342, www.sainthonorebakery. com; daily 6:30am-8pm

COFFEE AND DESSERTS

Moonstruck Chocolate Café $$

Moonstruck has a handful of café locations around the Portland area — and a mobile café truck as well. It also has some of the best coffee drinks around. A Mexican mocha is less of a morning pick-me-up and more of a decadent treat, especially since you get a free coin of dark chocolate to nibble on with your drink. The cafés have all manner of hot drinks throughout the year, and when summer comes around, they break out some pretty unbelievable ice cream shakes. While the coffee, hot chocolate, and truffles—did I mention the truffles?!—are enough to send any chocoholic into cardiac arrest, various cakes will satisfy that sweet tooth, too. There is also another location downtown (608 SW Alder St., 503/241-0955).

MAP 2: 526 NW 23rd Ave., 503/542-3400, www.moonstruckchocolate.com; Mon.-Sat. 8am-10pm, Sun. 9am-9pm

✪ Salt & Straw $

In a city like Portland, where you'll find an abundance of food carts and restaurants dedicated to very specific food passions, it makes sense that there would be an ice cream shop that

Salt & Straw

specializes in small-batch innovative concoctions. Owners Tyler and Kim Malek have collaborated with a number of Portland chefs to create a roster of flavors ranging from sea salt with a caramel ribbon and honey lavender to pear with blue cheese and arbequina olive oil. And while their ice cream continues to receive national acclaim, their Northwest Portland location includes a bakery where they serve up other goodies, like Stumptown Coffee, hand pies, doughnuts, and freshly baked scones, muffins, and cookies.
MAP 2: 836 NW 23rd Ave., 971/271-8168, www.saltandstraw.com; daily 10am-11pm

Coffeehouse Northwest $

Don't let the generic name fool you; Coffeehouse Northwest has been a longtime favorite in the Nob Hill area. They take the coffee-making process so seriously they would frankly rather you stay for a while and sip your cappuccino out of a real cup, not a paper to-go cup. The menu is simple and pared down to just a few basics—coffee, cappuccino, latte, espresso, and mocha—but each beverage is made with the utmost care. There are a couple of larger tables for gathering, but mostly, the place is lined with small tables and outlets for plugging in laptops. The exposed brick walls always have art adorning them, but with Edison lamps and woodwork all over, the place is a work of art on its own.
MAP 2: 1951 W. Burnside St., 503/248-2133; Mon.-Fri. 6:30am-6pm, Sat.-Sun. 8am-5pm

Cupcake Jones $

It doesn't take a thinking man to figure out why cupcakes have become so popular. They're sweet, portable, and provide infinite possibilities for creative flavor combinations. Cupcake Jones knows a thing or two about the business. The company is adamant about using locally sourced ingredients and giving everything they can back to the community. At the tiny Pearl District bakery (second location at 1405 NE Alberta St.), it's not uncommon to see a line of people out the door, waiting to get their hands on one of the daily specials. There are almost a dozen standard flavors available every day (among them Lemoncello, red velvet, carrot, and Boston cream) and a handful of seasonal offerings each day as well. Cupcakes can be ordered in miniature bite-size treats or jumbo-size filled cakes that are roughly the size of a softball. They have vegan and gluten-free options in some flavors, and even special cupcakes for dogs.
MAP 2: 307 NW 10th Ave., 503/222-4404, www.cupcakejones.net; Mon.-Sat. 10am-8pm, Sun. noon-6pm

Nola Doughnuts

Nola Doughnuts $

In a city full of doughnuts, it's hard to stand out, but Nola's doing a pretty good job. Its trademarked La'ssant dough is crafted using French pastry techniques over a meticulous three-day process to fold in European butter throughout, giving it complex layers and a rich flavor. The self-taught expert here is Rob Herkes, a Louisiana native. Also on offer is the Instagram-popular S'mores doughnut and made-to-order beignets with raspberry sauce. You can round out your experience with one of the chicory café au laits, espresso drinks, milk shakes, or sundaes.

MAP 2: 110 NW 10th Ave., 503/895-6350, www.noladoughnuts.com; daily 7am-9pm

Northeast Map 3

CONTEMPORARY AMERICAN

Laurelhurst Market $$$

Laurelhurst Market is equal parts American brasserie, butcher counter, lunchtime sandwich shop, and neighborhood diner. While a lot of places go overboard showing off the talents of a chef, Laurelhurst seems to revel in the simple touches, like a rib eye finished with blue cheese butter and garnished with fried Walla Walla sweet onions, or the expertly prepared mussels topped with steak frites, Dijon mustard, and crème fraîche. If you want to sample the wares but don't feel like shelling out the cash for dinner, stop by the sandwich counter and try one of the six daily special sandwiches, all constructed with Laurelhurst's own house-made deli meats.

MAP 3: 3155 E. Burnside St., 503/206-3097, www.laurelhurstmarket.com; dinner daily 5pm-10pm, butcher shop and sandwich counter daily 10am-10pm

Ned Ludd $$$

The rustic elegance of this Northeast Portland spot is immediately warm and inviting. With stacks of apple and pear wood tucked into corners, dishes piled high on every flat surface, and an open kitchen spilling over with market-fresh produce, this feels just like home—assuming you live in a beautiful cabin and know how to cook. Owner and chef Jason French has done something quite special with the house-made charcuterie and pickle plates, but it's that enormous brick hearth in the middle of the kitchen that makes this place so different.

Named after the same guy that tech-hating Luddites are, Ned Ludd eschews fancy technology in favor of a good old-fashioned wood-fired oven. That means meats, a whole roasted trout, and oven-baked cookies are all infused with the essence of fruitwood.

MAP 3: 3925 NE Martin Luther King Jr. Blvd., 503/228-6900, www.nedluddpdx. com; daily 5pm-10pm

GASTROPUB

✪ Oregon Public House $$

Oregon Public House is unlike anything in the world in that 100 percent of its net profits are given to charity. Its motto is "have a pint, save the world," and guests are asked at the end of their meal which of the partnered nonprofit charities they would like their bill to go toward. The charitable goals could be enough to encourage most locals to support this pub, but as it turns out, the food is quite good—including comfort food standards like nachos and burgers—and the selection of rotating local beers notable. OPH also offers an extensive gluten-free menu.

MAP 3: 700 NE Dekum St., 503/828-0884, www.oregonpublichouse.com; Sun.-Thurs. 11:30am-10pm, Fri.-Sat. 11:30am-11pm

FOOD CARTS
Fine Goose $

People seeking authentic French cuisine might be reluctant to order duck confit from a food cart—but they would be missing out in the case of Fine Goose. The cart is owned and run by Jean Broquere and Sebastien Guarderas, two chefs and best friends from the south of France, where sun-drenched soils provide a bounty of vegetables and fruits, and traditional recipes are humble, hearty, and reflective of the land. The Fine Goose menu is a collection of the chefs' favorite dishes from their childhoods, and from their many combined years in professional kitchens. The result is French food that feels fancy without all the fuss. The duck confit—slow-braised for hours in its own fat—is tender and juicy. And Chef Jean's ratatouille (a family recipe) is a perfect example of expertise put to good work with Pacific Northwest ingredients.
MAP 3: 1505 NE Alberta St., www. finegoose.us; Sun.-Tues. 8:30am-5pm, Wed.-Sat. 8:30am-9pm

The Grilled Cheese Grill $

Could anything be more inspired than a restaurant solely devoted to that childhood favorite, the grilled cheese sandwich? This place has Portland written all over it. Owner and grilled cheese enthusiast Matt Breslow turned an old Airstream trailer into a kitchen and set up picnic tables where hungry patrons can devour the cheesy delights. Somehow, even the most reticent adults get giddy as schoolchildren when they see the colorful school bus that's been redesigned into a cozy seating area. You can go for something basic, like a classic cheddar-on-white-bread sandwich (with or without crusts), or get a little crazy with bacon, apples, blue cheese, and swiss. If you're feeling particularly kinky, try the Cheesus Burger, a patty melt nestled between two grilled cheese sandwiches and garnished with lettuce, tomato, and grilled onion.
MAP 3: 1027 NE Alberta St., 503/206-8959, www.grilledcheesegrill.com; Sun.-Thurs. 11:30am-8pm, Fri.-Sat. 11:30am-2am

Gumba $

It's argued by some that some of the best-looking, most delicious pasta in Portland comes from this little cart. Gumba (pronounced GOOM-bah) makes its own pasta from scratch, and the difference is obvious from your first bite. You can't go wrong with whatever the spaghetti special of the moment is, tossed with a variety of ingredients such as shallots, lemon, sumac, or chilis, egg yolk, and house-made burrata. If you are a meat eater, don't miss the freshly made and perfectly tender pappardelle dish, topped with a hearty helping of braised short rib. Hours are a bit limited, in part because of Gumba's commitment to keeping the pasta fresh, but also because its inventory will occasionally sell out.

The Grilled Cheese Grill's Cheesus Burger

MAP 3: NE 23rd and NE Alberta St., www.gumba-pdx.com; Wed.-Thurs. 5pm-8pm, Fri.-Sat. 12:30pm-8pm and 9:30pm-12:30am, Sun. 12:30pm-8pm

PDX Dönerländ $

Doner kebab, the traditional Turkish dish of spit-roasted lamb, beef, or chicken, was brought to Germany after World War II, where it was given a new spin and new life to the extent that it's now considered quite characteristic of Berlin, where the sandwiches are hugely popular. PDX Dönerländ specializes in this Berlin-style doner kebab, which involves wrapping those delicious spit-roasted meats in homemade flatbread and serving them up with lettuce, tomato, onion, pepperoncini, and a delightful yogurt-dill sauce. All of the meats are cooked well and remain pretty juicy throughout the spit-roasting process, but the lamb seems to be treated with extra love and affection.

MAP 3: 625 NE Killingsworth St., www.pdx-donerland.com; Wed.-Sat. noon-9pm, Sun. noon-8pm

ASIAN
Hat Yai $$

Hat Yai is named for a Thai city along the country's southern border near Malaysia. So, naturally, it specializes in food from that region, specifically the southern Thai-style fried chicken you'd find from street vendors in Hat Yai itself. With a crispy outer coating that is thinner and lighter than Western-style fried chicken, the chicken is also less greasy, deeply aromatic, and spectacular dipped in curry. Order one of the combos (number five is the most popular), which comes with a rich curry and roti, a pan-fried bread. Word to the wise, however: If the menu designates something as "spicy," it will be delivered as such—this is not a place that mutes its spiciness for Western palates.

MAP 3: 1605 NE Killingsworth St., 503/764-9701, www.hatyaipdx.com; Sun.-Thurs. 11:30am-9pm, Fri.-Sat. 11:30am-10pm

Izakaya Kichinto $$

An *izakaya*, a relaxed Japanese pub, is a place to gather after work and partake in drinks and sharable plates. Izakaya Kichinto is great representation of this style of venue, with sushi hand rolls, pork gyoza, fried chicken, and homemade ramen noodles. You won't find courses or entrées here, and plates come out in Japanese fashion—as they're ready—so ordering a variety of dishes offers the most satisfying experience. Don't be afraid to put in orders at various points as is customary, but save that bowl of ramen for last. The shoyu ramen, especially, has a broth that's full-bodied without being greasy, and perfectly chewy noodles, a warm end to your meal.

MAP 3: 102 NE Russell St., 971/255-0169; Mon. and Wed.-Thurs. 4pm-10pm, Fri. 11:30am-2:30pm and 4pm-11pm, Sat. 11:30am-11pm, Sun. 11:30am-10pm

Pok Pok Noi $$

Andy Ricker, chef and owner of Pok Pok and its handful of locations, is a star in the food scene, and not just in Portland. Ricker has gained notoriety (and a James Beard award) for using his experience as a chef and world traveler to build a menu of flavorful dishes that ardently adhere to traditional north and northeast Thai ingredients as well as traditional preparation techniques. His wings are popular, marinated in fish sauce, garlic, and sugar, fried, and then tossed in a caramelized sauce with spices

and garlic. This northeast location is pretty cozy, but a little less crowded than some of the other locations.
MAP 3: 1469 NE Prescott St., 503/287-4149, www.pokpoknoi.com; daily 11:30am-10pm

Frank's Noodle House $

Housed in a cute yellow Victorian home, this eatery has a prim, no-frills charm about it, from the unadorned tables to the bright tennis balls affixed to each chair leg to protect the hardwood floors. It doesn't matter if ambience is lacking, because, as its name suggests, the reason to visit Frank's is the noodles, which are hand-pulled every day by Frank himself and his wife. The resulting noodles are thick, chewy, and perfectly cooked, whether served in a steaming bowl of soup or tossed with cabbage, peppers, onions, chili flakes, and your choice of chicken, beef, pork, shrimp, or squid.
MAP 3: 822 NE Broadway, 503/288-1007, www.franksnoodlehousepdx.com; Mon.-Sat. 11am-3pm and 5pm-9pm

SUSHI
Zilla Saké House $$

Zilla Saké House is pleasant, dark, and cozy, with high-backed booths and rain-colored walls adorned with funky decor. The staff is knowledgeable and helpful without a hint of pretentiousness. For that reason, and thanks to the sheer volume of options, it is a great place to become a burgeoning sake drinker and sushi eater. If you like to nibble slowly, order the edamame, seasoned with ginger in addition to the traditional sea salt and pepper. The spicy *ika* (dried squid jerky) is a surprisingly delightful choice, especially with wasabi mayo on the side. The sashimi, particularly the *hamachi*, is all quite good and served with real wasabi that is grated right in front of you.
MAP 3: 1806 NE Alberta St., 503/288-8372, www.zillasakehouse.com; Mon.-Sat. 4pm-10pm, Sun. 4pm-9pm

FRENCH
Beast $$$

Chef-owner Naomi Pomeroy is a legend in the Portland food scene, named one of the Best New Chefs of 2009 by *Food & Wine* and featured in *Bon Appétit* within months of opening. Pomeroy has drawn eyes thanks to her unabashed approach to "French grandma-style" cooking. She was even a competitor on *Top Chef Masters* in 2011 and has been a recurring judge on the series *Knife Fight*. The prix fixe dinner is $125 per person for six courses, and it changes each week. Each meal usually begins with a delicate soup followed by a charcuterie plate stocked with such nibbles as foie gras bonbons, chicken liver mousse, and pickled seasonal vegetables. For the main course, you might find stuffed rabbit, braised duck, or pork cheeks (if you're lucky). As long as you are splurging, opt for wine pairings in addition to the meal ($50 for six small glasses).
MAP 3: 5425 NE 30th Ave., 503/841-6968, www.beastpdx.com; Wed.-Sat. dinner seatings at 6pm and 8:45pm, Sun. brunch seatings at 10am, 11:30am, and 1pm, dinner seating at 7pm

Verdigris $$

Verdigris is a small, elegant eatery that feels contemporary, but still classically French. The menu changes with the seasons and with the availability of local greens, meats, and produce, but the beef short rib bourguignon remains an anchor, and for good reason. It is a beautiful bowl of rich, hearty gravy, roasted root vegetables, and melt-in-your-mouth tender meat. If you can't make up your mind, you can opt for the remarkably affordable chef's choice menu, which will run you about $35 for three courses. Verdigris is also quite popular for brunch, where they serve French-style omelets and a life-changing 60-minute sous vide egg with ham or hash.

MAP 3: 1315 NE Fremont St., 503/477-8106, www.verdigrisrestaurant. com; Tues.-Sun. 5pm-10pm

Petite Provence $

Whether you stop by Petite Provence for breakfast or lunch, make sure you take away one of the buttery pastries in a bag for later. If you can get past the cream puffs, caramel tarts, and opera cakes, take a gander at the full menu, stocked with French egg dishes, grilled sandwiches, and country-style salads. The Colette omelet is a neighborhood favorite, with its combination of basil and eggs topped with artichoke hearts, tomatoes, and mozzarella and then placed under the broiler until it's bubbly. For lunch, salads are a good bet. The goat cheese salad is simple enough, with medallions of cheese tossed with greens, onions, red peppers, roasted walnuts, and a light vinaigrette dressing. It's satisfying and refreshing, but still leaves room for a bowl of French onion soup and an almond croissant.

MAP 3: 1824 NE Alberta St., 503/284-6564, www.provence-portland.com; Sun.-Thurs. 7am-9pm, Fri.-Sat. 7am-10pm

GERMAN
Stammtisch $$

Stammtisch (which means "regular table") is German comfort food at its best. You can get small plates of nibbles such as a warm Bavarian pretzel, currywurst, or potato pancakes with applesauce. Medium-size plates include beautifully executed classics such a beer- and bacon-braised rabbit, thick dumplings with duck confit, and trios of sausages. Try to come with friends because a couple of the large plates are not to be missed. Of course, there's Wiener schnitzel, crispy, juicy, and as big as the platter it comes on. But it's the Schweinshaxen that's worth making dinner buddies over. It is a comically large pork shoulder that is brined for five days and slow-roasted and then served on a bed of spaetzle and red cabbage.

MAP 3: 401 NE 28th Ave., 503/206-7983, www.stammtischpdx.com; Mon.-Thurs. 3pm 1:30am, Fri. 11:30am-1:30am, Sat.-Sun. 11am-1:30am

Swiss Hibiscus $$

Though the Hawaiian-inspired decor may tell a different story, this little hole-in-the-wall family establishment is all about Switzerland. The owner and chef of the café can thank her Swiss father and Hawaiian-born mother for that. The menu speaks to her heritage, with Swiss comfort foods served with a side of aloha spirit. You'll find Wiener schnitzel, gravlax, goulash, and bratwurst heaped with caramelized onions. House salads are served with the restaurant's famous Swiss dressing (available for purchase), or get a sampler plate of all the salads with a superb bowl of Swiss onion soup. To wet your whistle, they have bottled beers and a small selection of wine in addition to canned sodas and water.

MAP 3: 4950 NE 14th Ave., 503/477-9224, www.swisshibiscus.com; Tues. and Thurs. Sat. 3pm-9pm, Wed. 11:30am-2:30pm and 5pm-9pm

ITALIAN
D.O.C. $$$

If you think you've seen an open kitchen, you have never seen one like D.O.C.'s (Denominazione di Origine Controllata, the Italian food and wine control). Walk through the front door of this tiny establishment, just past the windows with red-checkered curtains and mason jars stacked in the sills, and you will find yourself smack-dab in the middle of the kitchen. It can be a bit disconcerting at first, but soon you find yourself mesmerized by the tidiness and efficiency with which things are run. The restaurant opened in June 2008 and still receives accolades for providing polished and chic, yet intimate, dining. Chef Steven Malloy prepares a weekly menu that incorporates local produce and pasture-raised meat, and his cuisine nears perfection with dishes like tagliatelle, beef cheeks, and risotto. Order in courses or opt for the chef's tasting menu ($75), which gives you six courses, including dessert.

MAP 3: 5519 NE 30th Ave., 503/946-8592, www.docpdx.com; Tues.-Sat. 6pm-10pm, Sun. 4pm-9pm

Ciao Vito $$

Ciao Vito is a diamond in the rough in the otherwise artsy, granola-crunching Alberta Arts District. The menu includes simple, elegant, well-prepared dishes like pork *sugo* with crispy fried polenta, Bolognese *ragu* with fettuccini, and arguably the best beet salad in Portland. Start with the calamari and antipasti plate, served with bread from Ken's Artisan Bakery and spicy olive oil. When your entrée comes, don't be afraid to nibble at it and save room for dessert. Many of the heartier dishes here reheat well as leftovers, and Ciao Vito's vanilla panna cotta topped with raspberries is not to be missed.

MAP 3: 2203 NE Alberta St., 503/282-5522, www.ciaovito.net; Wed.-Fri. noon-10pm, Sat.-Sun. 4:30pm-10pm

MEXICAN
Autentica $$

As you can probably guess, Autentica is Spanish for authentic, and at this Concordia neighborhood restaurant, they mean it. The dishes hail from the Guerrero region of Mexico, which is as diverse in horticulture as the Pacific Northwest. There are the beaches (think Acapulco) that bring an abundance of seafood, but there are also plains and mountains and tropical regions that offer other more exotic flavors. Don't expect to get bowls of chips and salsa. Instead, you will find fresh ceviche, creamy soups, moist and flavorful pork tacos, and sensational tamales. On Thursday night, don't miss the pozole, a tasty, traditional Mexican stew steeped in tradition.

MAP 3: 5507 NE 30th Ave., 503/287-7555, www.autenticaportland.com; Tues.-Fri. 5pm-10pm, Sat.-Sun. 10am-2pm and 5pm-10pm

La Bonita $

This little taquería may not look like much from the outside, but the food is quick, inexpensive, and delicious— and the walls display the work of local artists. La Bonita is family-owned and claims to be "as authentic as Mexican gets." It comes darn close with the *al pastor* tacos and unbelievably good carne asada. The burritos are enormous and run about $9 each. If you stop in a little early or want to plan ahead for tomorrow, grab a breakfast burrito, filled with eggs, chorizo, and hash browns.

MAP 3: 2839 NE Alberta St., 503/281-3662, daily 10am-10pm

SOUTHERN AND CREOLE

Screen Door $$

One of the most secretly celebrated restaurants in Portland, Screen Door never takes itself too seriously. This is where you're likely to find off-shift chefs and bartenders, and it's no co-incidence. The menu spits in the face of the hoity-toity low-carb or raw food mentality, but still manages to use some of the best local ingredients in its soul-quenching dishes. This is food the way it was meant to be eaten. Crispy fried oysters dripping with *gribiche* sauce (an egg sauce) or fried green tomatoes with remoulade, followed by some of the best fried chicken in the city, will have you singing the praises of this quaint little Burnside joint. Will you wait for a table? Yes, probably. Will you clutch your belly in gluttonous joy as you roll yourself out the door? It's quite likely. Will it be worth every sticky, drippy, carb-laden bite? Absolutely.

This is another one of Portland's popular brunch spots. If you manage to get a table, don't walk away without sampling Screen Door's infamous praline bacon and equally notorious Bloody Mary.

MAP 3: 2337 E. Burnside St., 503/542-0880, www.screendoorrestaurant. com; Mon.-Fri. 8am-2pm and 5:30pm-10pm, Sat. 9am-2:30pm and 5:30pm-10pm, Sun. 9am-2:30pm and 5:30pm-9pm

TAPAS

Aviary $$$

Smack dab in the heart of Portland's Alberta Arts District, Aviary is a pretty and minimalistic site. But if they spared a little flourish in the decor, they certainly spent it on the menu. Everything is delivered in such an artful way you almost hate to eat it. Chef and owner Sarah Pliner has a fine résumé of experience in both New York City and Portland, and it shows in her use of classic French techniques with a nod to Asian cuisine. Stand-out dishes include the duck liver toasts, crispy pig ears, and charred octopus, but the menu changes with available meat and produce.

MAP 3: 1733 NE Alberta St., 503/287-2400, www.aviarypdx.com; Mon.-Thurs. 5pm-10pm, Fri.-Sat. 5pm-11pm

Urdaneta $$$

This Alberta neighborhood tapas place features dishes from northern Spain and the Basque region. The restaurant is named after the owner's mother (her surname), and many of the menu items reflect that familial connection as well. The menu is constantly changing, but you may find things like halibut cheek croquettes, hand-carved aged jamon, or a lovely crispy-skin black cod. The ambience is warm and cozy but buzzing with energy, especially in the extremely open kitchen at the center of the room. Since Urdaneta allows reservations for parties of 1-6 people, it is a good idea to plan ahead or be prepared for quite a wait.

MAP 3: 3033 NE Alberta St., 503/288-1990, www.urdanetapdx.com; Sun. and Tues.-Thurs. 5pm-10pm, Fri.-Sat. 5pm-11pm

Navarre $$

The food at Navarre is like improv; you never quite know what you're going to get, but the off-the-cuff brilliance is impressive. Chef James Melendez builds his menu daily around the ingredients he gets from a nearby CSA. If parsnips are in season, they might just get tossed into a warm crab salad. Fresh greens may be tucked under foie gras. Cauliflower is transformed into gratin. Green tomatoes are breaded and fried. Whatever you choose, make sure you order some bread (from Ken's Artisan Bakery down the street) to soak up all the bits of sauce and dressing from the other plates. Since it's technically a wine bar, Navarre has more than 50 different wines by the glass, so it's easy to pair a vintage with the eclectic array of plates on the table. Ask your server for recommendations if you get overwhelmed.

MAP 3: 10 NE 28th Ave., 503/232-3555, www.navarreportland.com; Mon.-Thurs. 4:30pm-10:30pm, Fri. 4:30pm-11:30pm, Sat. 9:30am-11:30pm, Sun. 9:30am-10:30pm

Toro Bravo $$

Toro Bravo set Portland on its ear when it opened in 2007. Dinner here is an event, a whirlwind of noise and activity, a mishmash of fast-moving plates and eager conversation. The general excitement is palpable because everyone is waiting for their next little morsel to arrive. The tapas are expertly crafted, right down to the last loving detail. Must-try dishes include the bacon-wrapped dates in warm honey, oxtail croquettes, and delectable olive oil cake with caramel. The wait for a table can be agonizingly long, so be prepared. Don't come when you are ravenous. Reservations aren't offered for parties with fewer than seven people on weekdays and not at all on Friday and Saturday. Come early, put your name on the list, and head upstairs to the Secret Society Lounge, where you can imbibe cocktails and snack while you wait.

MAP 3: 120 NE Russell St., 503/281-4464, www.torobravopdx.com; Sun.-Thurs. 5pm-10pm, Fri.-Sat. 5pm-11pm

SANDWICHES
Basilisk $

In Harry Potter fandom, the Basilisk is a beastly serpent that was hatched from a chicken egg beneath a toad. At this little shop (located in the grown-up food court that is the Zipper building), the specialty of the house is a beast of a chicken sandwich. It towers high with crispy slabs of buttermilk-dredged chicken, slaw, and pickles all stacked in a Pearl Bakery bun. The sandwich is so tall, in fact, that it is held together with a steak knife instead of toothpicks, making it seem far more daunting to eat than it actually is. Also available are a number of notable vegetarian and vegan options, like the fried tofu sandwich and the must-try Dan Dan fries, which are covered with Szechuan peanut sauce, chili oil, baby dill pickles, peanuts, green onions, cilantro, and lime.

MAP 3: 820 NE 27th Ave., 503/234-7151, www.basiliskpdx.com; daily 11am-10pm

BREAKFAST AND BRUNCH
Helser's on Alberta $$

If you go to Helser's for any reason, go for the German pancake (also known as a Dutch baby, but that seems a little macabre). The eggy puffed pancake is baked until golden brown and approximately the size of a bowler hat. One is enough to feed a couple of people, especially if you order Scotch eggs on the side (hard-boiled eggs wrapped in bratwurst, then breaded and fried). If that's not your cup of tea, try the brioche French toast or the smoked salmon hash topped with poached eggs and hollandaise. Order a mimosa made with fresh orange juice and you are well on your way to a food coma.

MAP 3: 1538 NE Alberta St., 503/477-9058, www.helsersonalberta.com; daily 7am-3pm

Pine State Biscuits $

When Portlanders talk about brunch lines, there are a couple of places that frequently top the list of "worth the wait." Pine State is one of those places. After getting their feet wet with a popular farmers market booth, the three owners (all Southerners who missed the food from home) opened their first shop in 2008. Since then, business has been very, very good. Pine State appeared on the Food Network and has been featured in *Food & Wine, Bon Appétit,* the *New York Times,* and *Town & Country.* Nowadays, there are three locations throughout Portland, and people continue to be stacked at the door waiting to get their hands on those fluffy, flaky biscuits, mouthwatering gravy, and tender buttermilk chicken (otherwise known as the ever-popular Reggie sandwich).

MAP 3: 2204 NE Alberta St., 503/477-6605, www.pinestatebiscuits.com; daily 7am-3pm

COFFEE AND DESSERTS

Pix Patisserie $$

Pix is a dessert place in the strictest sense of the word, and it's all about indulgence. Beautiful cakes and tarts looking like they belong on a wall in a gallery instead of on a cake plate sit in ordered, anticipatory silence. Colorful macarons in flavors such as raspberry, rose, and passion fruit beckon to be touched and tasted. A signature dish here is the Amelie, an orange-vanilla crème brûlée atop a glazed chocolate mousse with caramelized hazelnuts, praline crisp, and Cointreau génoise. Check out the website for upcoming events like Flamenco Fridays with live entertainment and tapas, or the weekend tea service with over a dozen sweet and savory bites alongside Townshend's Tea.

MAP 3: 2225 E. Burnside St., www. pixpatisserie.com; Mon.-Fri. 4pm-midnight, Sat.-Sun. 2pm-midnight

Pie Spot $

Pie Spot specializes in adorable individual pies with flavors such as brandied apple, marionberry, banana cream with salted caramel, and brown butter pecan. Like many other Portland foodie favorites, Pie Spot got its start as a food cart before popularity eventually inspired the opening of a brick-and-mortar store. Pies (regular and gluten-free) are sold individually or by the baker's dozen and are perfect for picnics or grab-and-go treats. If you are looking to make a whole meal out of pie (and who isn't), you can also buy mini chicken or mushroom pot pies and quiches.

MAP 3: 521 NE 24th Ave., 503/913-5103, www.pie-spot.com; Mon.-Thurs. 7am-9pm, Fri. 7am-11pm, Sat. 8am-11pm, Sun. 8am-9pm

PACIFIC NORTHWEST

✪ Farm Spirit $$$

At Farm Spirit, they are all about local. Like, super local. It calls its cuisine "Cascadian" because everything from the ingredients to the plates they're served on is sourced from no farther away than the edges of Oregon and southern Washington. You're seated at a communal counter (which is made from Oregon ash) as the chefs prepare each dish in front of you. Everything on the menu is plant-based, but don't let that deter you if you usually prefer meat. Each dish that Chef Aaron Adams and his team turn out is stunning, surprising, and seductive. They are creative and complex, but they don't try to be meat. Instead, the flavors of Nebrodini mushrooms play off smoky collard greens, and sous vide carrots reach a depth of flavor that most people haven't experienced before.

MAP 4: 1414 SE Morrison St., 503/736-9228, www.farmspiritpdx.com; Wed.-Fri. 6pm and 8:30pm, Sat. 4pm, 6pm, and 8:30pm

Castagna Restaurant $$$

Portland diners are pretty laid-back. It's not uncommon to see jeans and T-shirts alongside business casual and semi-formal in the dining rooms of most area restaurants. This is not to say, however, that Portland does not do fancy dining. Castagna may be out of the price range of a lot of people, but the experience is worth saving for. The chef's tasting menu runs

Farm Spirit

about $165 per person (with wine pairings for an additional $85), but for that, Chef Justin Woodward delivers a full orchestra of flavors and a 90-minute experience that is elegant, surprising, and unlike anything else in town. Offerings might incorporate Dungeness crab, geoduck clams, and albacore tuna.

MAP 4: 1752 SE Hawthorne Blvd., 503/231-7373, www.castagnarestaurant. com; Wed.-Thurs. 5:30pm-9pm, Fri.-Sat. 5:30pm-10pm

Clarklewis $$$

Deep in the gritty industrial area of Portland's inner Southeast is an old loading dock that has been transformed into one of the city's swankiest restaurants. With small, elegant tables set into a cement and steel backdrop, the place is romantic without an overdose of femininity. In the cooler months, when they can't open the great garage-style doors to let in light, the dinner hour can get downright dark. It's often so dark, in fact, that your server will bring you a tiny flashlight to read your menu by.

Its Pacific Northwest menu is Italian-inspired, and offerings change daily based on what's in season. Your best bet is to chuck the menu and go for the Chef's Choice, a prix-fixe four-course meal ($60 per person). For an additional $45, wine pairings will accompany each course. Be sure to tell them if you have any allergies, and then sit back and eat like an expert epicurean.

MAP 4: 1001 SE Water Ave., 503/235-2294, www.clarklewispdx.com; Mon.-Thurs. 11:30am-2pm and 4:30pm-9pm, Fri. 11:30am-2pm and 4:30pm-10pm, Sat. 4:30pm-10pm

Willow $$$

Tucked upstairs above a coffee shop, the lobby here is really more like a modern living room. The setting is intimate—very intimate. With only 11 guests per seating, it's easy for chefs Doug Weiler and John Pickett to greet each guest personally and talk with them about what the meal will be like. Seats are at the counter overlooking the kitchen, and guests are encouraged to watch, ask questions, and learn little stories about the food being cooked. Willow is pretty vegetable-forward because the chefs try to showcase the bounties of the Pacific Northwest, but it is not strictly vegan or vegetarian (although they can make those accommodations). An occasional beef tartare, braised cheek, or trout might show up, depending on the season. Combined with the personal attention and compassion for food, this makes for a unique experience.

MAP 4: 2005 SE 11th St., 814/933-4458, 631/478-8414, www.willowpdx.com; Wed.-Sat. seatings at 6pm and 8:30pm

Jacqueline $$

Portland is fortunate to have access to some pretty spectacular seafood, and Jacqueline is taking full advantage. One of the best things this place has to offer is its selection of "tide to table" oysters from all along the Oregon and Washington coast. You will also find Dungeness crab, fresh halibut, cedar-planked Oregon trout, and the like, all passionately prepared. Don't worry about it being too stuffy, though: The atmosphere and the menu are both pleasant and quirky, and loving in detail. In an homage to Wes Andersen, a painting of Bill Murray (in his *The Life Aquatic with Steve Zissou* role) hangs on the wall, and the restaurant takes its name from the title character's ex-wife.

MAP 4: 2039 SE Clinton St., 503/327-8637, www.jacquelinepdx.com; Mon.-Sat. 5pm-10pm

OK Omens $$

If Castagna is out of your price range, pop next door and check out its sister restaurant, OK Omens, where Chef Justin Woodward lets his more laidback, playful side show. Here you'll find beignets filled with Tillamook cheddar, buttermilk fried chicken with Szechuan peppercorn, and a burger accented with smoked beef fat remoulade. OK Omens also offers some fun desserts, like a cake of the day and Blizzard-style seasonal milk shakes. The wine selection is thoughtful and affordable with cute categories like "what we drink when we are not helping you drink" and "juice for skiing (Alpine wines)."

MAP 4: 1758 SE Hawthorne Blvd., 503/231-9939, www.okomens.com; daily 5pm-midnight

Pyro Pizza

FOOD CARTS

Pyro Pizza $$

Pizza from a trailer? Oh, yeah. This is really good, Italian-style, wood-fired pizza made in a hand-built brick oven from locally sourced ingredients like Rogue Creamery cheese and Nicky USA meats. If that seems like a lot of hyphenated words, it's because so much personal attention has gone into the creation of these pizzas. It's a popular late-night stop for folks on their way home from the bar, because those little pizzas are total comfort food. Each pie feeds approximately 1.5 people, and you can get some classic flavors like Margherita, arugula and mushroom, or fennel sausage with red onion and basil.

MAP 4: 1207 SE Hawthorne Blvd., 503/701-5149, www.pyropizzacart.com; Sun.-Thurs. 11:30am-midnight, Fri.-Sat. 11:30am-1am

Fried Egg I'm In Love

Fried Egg I'm in Love $

Fried Egg is a music-themed cart that is silly in name but serious in delivering a tasty breakfast. The menu consists of a series of sandwiches, all served on lightly toasted sourdough bread, with all but a couple built around eggs. The signature dish is the Yolko Ono—a fried egg with "magic egg dust," a hand-pressed seasoned sausage patty, and a layer of pesto and parmesan cheese. Non-meat eaters have a lot of options here too, as any sandwich can be made vegetarian (or gluten-free). At this location (there is also one in Pioneer Square, downtown), you can also order mimosas, beer, and wine.

MAP 4: 3207 SE Hawthorne Blvd., 503/610-3447, www.friedegglove.com; Wed.-Fri. 8am-3pm, Sat.-Sun. 8:30am-6pm

Potato Champion $

In the midst of Cartopia, one of Portland's favorite pods of late-night carts, you will find Potato Champion, a colorful cart that serves up fries in small or large paper cones. These are not the greasy, soggy mess from some state fair; the fries at Potato Champion are hot, salty, and crispy on the outside, while still being soft and warm on the inside. They're good on their own, but just for kicks, PC offers an array of dips like rosemary ketchup, sweet hot mustard, tarragon anchovy mayonnaise, and remoulade. If you're feeling really indulgent, try the *poutine*, a Canadian treat that involves smothering fries with cheese grits and gravy.

MAP 4: 1207 SE Hawthorne Blvd., 503/683-3797, www.potatochampion. tumblr.com; Sun.-Thurs. 11am-1am, Fri.-Sat. 11am-3am

Viking Soul Food $

It's the only Norwegian cart in the city, with a menu that focuses on *lefse* (pronounced lef-suh) in true Scandinavian style. The thin potato flatbread is

Le Pigeon

warmed up on the griddle and topped with any number of ingredients, from sweet (like lingonberries and cream cheese) to savory (Norse meatballs, *gjetost* cheese sauce, and pickled cabbage). One of the best might be the house-smoked salmon rolled with dill crème fraîche, lightly pickled shallots, and watercress. Make sure you get at least one of those. While the taste may be fit for a Viking, the portions are not. Order more than one if you plan to make a meal out of it.

MAP 4: 4255 SE Belmont St., 971/506-5579, www.vikingsoulfood. com; Sun.-Thurs. noon-8pm, Fri.-Sat. noon-8:30pm

SUSHI

Yoko's Japanese Restaurant $$

Word to the wise: The wait at Yoko's is always long. Arrive mere moments after the doors open and it's still likely be an hour. To make things easier, leave your cell phone number on the sign-up sheet and head next door to C Bar, where the bartenders are happy to serve you a cocktail and offer a sympathetic sigh.

Once inside the tiny sushi shack, peruse the extensive sake menu and order some rolls to share family-style. Yoko's is known for creative, artful creations, and that is where it really excels. If you just stick to the things you know, you might be disappointed. Try the rainbow roll or the popular Batman Roll, made with eel and cream cheese. Whatever you do, don't skip the Taka's tuna, a local favorite.

MAP 4: 2878 SE Gladstone St., 503/736-9228; daily 5pm-9pm

FRENCH

Le Pigeon $$$

Portland has its fair share of vegan and vegetarian joints, but Le Pigeon ain't

FOOD CART FEASTS

Some of the best food in Portland doesn't come from fancy kitchens; it comes from food carts. There's even a website devoted to the phenomenon, **Food Carts Portland** (www.foodcartsportland. com), which provides details on locations, menus, prices, and hours. Across the city, countless Twitter pages and Facebook updates discuss the mobile culinary culture with an excitement otherwise reserved for major music festivals and show openings.

Cartlandia food cart pod sign

Food carts in P-Town have fixed locations and are usually clustered together, like miniature food courts. Each cart tends to keep its own hours, although within pods there's typically some consistency. Here are some of the most notable food cart pods in Portland:

DOWNTOWN

- **SW 5th Avenue and Oak Street** is set along the MAX line and popular with downtown business traffic at lunch time. It's a great place to find Indian food, like vegetable-filled samosas and paneer, Korean-style tacos, hearty Mexican food, and Middle Eastern fare. Most of the carts here are open primarily during extended lunch hours, but a few also offer breakfast.

- **Alder Street Food Cart Pod** is arguably one of the city's largest, located between SW Alder and SW Washington Streets and from 9th to 10th Avenues; within that block and the surrounding streets there are over 60 carts to choose from during the weekday lunch hour, when the whole block is positively jamming. Whether you're looking for a snack or a hearty meal, a wide variety of cuisine is to be found here, from pumpkin and green curries to belly-warming soups to Hawaiian plate lunches and savory Chinese crepes.

SOUTHEAST

- **Cartopia** (SE Hawthorne Blvd. and SE 12th Ave) was the city's first sceney food cart pod. It opened in 2008 and offered something Portland was truly

one of them. This place is all about indulgence, particularly the carnivorous kind. Chef Gabriel Rucker has achieved celebrity status for his use of classic French techniques with a modern twist. How about a pork belly salad or seared foie gras? The menu changes according to the chef's whim (and

what's available at the local markets), but if you get a chance to try the beef cheeks, do not pass it up. The meat absolutely melts in your mouth. This is a great spot if you're feeling adventurous, because it's not uncommon to find pig's tail, sweetbreads, and, yes, even pigeon on the menu.

lacking in back then—late-night food options. Nowadays, the Cartopia pod is a popular place for post-show and post-bar crowds as many of the carts stay open until 3am, offering comfort food and occasionally entertainment. It also has a huge heated and covered patio in the middle of the carts where you can munch on cones full of fries from **Potato Champion** or slices from **Pyro Pizza** while witnessing a big slice of local culture.

- **The Bite on Belmont** (SE Belmont St. and SE 42nd Ave.) offers a little culinary trip around the world, with Brazilian, Hawaiian, Mexican, Japanese, and Scandinavian food carts (try **Viking Soul Food** for the latter). Covered tables protect you from the elements, and there's even a cart offering local beer, wine, and mimosas here. The pod doesn't stay open terribly late, so this is a good stop for a mid-afternoon meal, happy hour, or dinner.

NORTH PORTLAND

- **Prost! Marketplace** (N. Mississippi Ave. and N. Skidmore St.) is tucked into the side patio of Prost!, a German beer and food hot spot on Mississippi Avenue, where you'll find a collection of carts that can be accessed whether you're visiting the bar or not. The pod attracts some top names in the industry, and food options include everything from breakfast sandwiches and cold brew cocktails to Texas-style barbeque, Korean tacos, and pastrami sandwiches. You can hunker down at the ample outdoor seating or take your food inside the pub to eat it (as long as you order a drink).

GREATER PORTLAND

- **Portland Mercado** (7238 SE Foster Rd., www.portlandmercado.org) is a sprawling Latin American public market and community hub with 19 businesses, including a coffee shop, butcher shop, and grocery store, in addition to a pod of food carts. Since its opening in 2015, the Mercado has continued to solidify itself as a cornerstone for cultural development and a delicious place to eat, with particularly delightful options including mole, Cubano sandwiches, and el pastor tacos.

- **Cartlandia** (8145 SE 82nd Ave., 503/358-7873, www.cartlandia.com) in deep Southeast Portland is a hub for more than 30 food carts—one of the largest in Portland—and is hugely popular because of its abundant parking and seating, as well as proximity to a bar that welcomes cart food. Its wide variety of offerings include Pacific Northwest cuisine, cheesesteaks, burgers, barbecue, pancakes, fried chicken, ramen, and bagels, as well as Thai, Indian, Mexican, and Italian food. A covered, family-friendly beer garden is at the center of the action, and the Blue Room Bar just across the parking lot lets you order cocktails and cold beer to go with your food cart finds. Also here is an outpost of **Voodoo Doughnuts,** selling out of a bright pink truck until the doughnuts are gone.

MAP 4: 738 E. Burnside St., 503/546-8796, www.lepigeon.com; daily 5pm-10pm

Bar Avignon $$

At this neighborhood favorite, comfort and ambience are the foundations of success. Bar Avignon is technically a wine bar, and its well-curated list contains more than 80 reasonably priced bottles from all around the globe. I say technically, because its food menu elevates Bar Avignon from the bevy of other wine bars in the region that meagerly offer only olives and cheeses along with their wines. Here you will find small plates like mussels, fresh vegetables, or risotto, and full entrées like pork coppa or hanger steak. Of course, it also has olives and a sophisticated selection of cheese and charcuterie. The intimate atmosphere and small-plate options both lend themselves to dining alone or with someone special.

MAP 4: 2138 SE Division St., 503/517-0808, www.baravignon.com; daily 5pm-close

SOUTHERN AND CREOLE
Le Bistro Montage $$

Visiting Le Bistro Montage is almost a rite of passage for Portlanders. The service can be abrupt, abrasive, or almost absent, but the various "Macs" are cheap, filling, and worth any abuse you might suffer. It's tempting to try the oddities on the menu, like frog legs and alligator linguini, but you're better off sticking with the Montage classics. The original macaroni and cheese recipe, Old Mac, was featured on the Food Network, and is a simple garlic, parmesan, and heavy cream delight. Another staple is the jambalaya, hearty and spicy with Cajun gravy and your choice of chicken, catfish, rock shrimp, crawfish, scallops, oysters, andouille sausage, or, yes, even alligator. The kitchen keeps late hours, making it destination for late-night dining; crowds come in buzzed with enthusiasm around 1am.

There are no boring doggie bags here. Instead, leftovers are wrapped in foil and sculpted into a veritable cornucopia of shapes, like snails, flowers, swords, and cats.

MAP 4: 301 SE Morrison St., 503/234-1324, www.montageportland.com; Sun.-Thurs. 5pm-2am, Fri.-Sat. 5pm-4am

PIZZA
Apizza Scholls $$

When was the last time you waited an hour for a table to get a pizza? While it might seem crazy, Portlanders do it almost every night at Apizza Scholls. It's not uncommon for folks to be lined up outside the place when the doors are unlocked. That's because Apizza has achieved that terrific balance required to make really good pizza. The crust is tantamount to pizza's success, and this one is crispy on the outside, soft on the inside, and still maintains a flavor of its own that does not compete with the toppings.

MAP 4: 4741 SE Hawthorne Blvd., 503/233-1286, www.apizzascholls. com; Mon.-Fri. 5pm-9:30pm, Sat.-Sun. 11:30am-2:30pm and 5pm-9:30pm

Ken's Artisan Pizza $$

Ken's Artisan Pizza formed out of necessity when the bakery of the same name was flooded by requests for its hand-tossed, wood-fired pizzas—much like what you would find in Italy. The wait is long here. Reservations aren't accepted, and staff won't seat a group larger than 10. To-go pizzas are occasionally done at the discretion of the staff (according to how busy they are) and are limited in number. Pizzas come in one size, which is perfect for one or two people, and there are appetizers (try the lamb and pita) and salads to round out the meal.

MAP 4: 304 SE 28th Ave., 503/517-9951, www.kensartisan.com/pizza.html; Mon.-Thurs. 5pm-9:30pm, Fri. 5pm-10pm, Sat. 4pm-10pm, Sun. 4pm-9pm

SANDWICHES
Lardo $$

At Lardo, meat is definitely on the menu. Rick Gencarelli's food-cart-turned-brick-and-mortar kingdom is built upon towering sandwiches piled with meat and house-made sauces. There's a Korean pork shoulder sandwich, dripping with Sriracha mayo and pickled vegetables, or the Double Burger, which is big enough to share. If that doesn't provide enough meat for you, you can also get an order of fried pig ears, or the Dirty Fries, which are topped with pork scraps, marinated peppers, parmesan, and fried herbs. Chef Gencarelli frequently includes a special "Chefwich" on the menu, which is a collaboration with another local chef. These specials are often quite exciting, and a portion of the proceeds are donated to a charity of the collaborating chef's choice. Seating is a hot commodity indoors here, but fortunately, they have a spacious outdoor patio that provides street-side people-watching opportunities.

MAP 4: 1212 SE Hawthorne Blvd., 503/234-7786, http://lardosandwiches.com; Sun.-Thurs. 11am-10pm, Fri.-Sat. 11am-11pm

BREAKFAST AND BRUNCH

Broder $$

Broder, so popular it now has several other locations, manages to not be just like all the other breakfast spots in town by being the only place in Portland to serve up authentic Swedish favorites. No, really, and it goes way beyond meatballs. Here you will find fluffy *aebleskiver* with lemon curd or lingonberry jam, apple fritters with baked eggs and sausage, and *lefse* filled with the daily special ingredients. If you have heroic battles to endure over the course of your day, perhaps you should try the Swedish Breakfast Bord—brown bread and rye crisp, cured meat, smoked trout, hard cheese, seasonal citrus yogurt with fruit and granola, and daily salad. Pair

that with a little nip of aquavit and you should be able to accomplish anything. MAP 4: 2508 SE Clinton St., 503/736-3333, www.broderpdx.com; daily 8am-3pm

Slappy Cakes $$

It was Tessie Tura from the musical *Gypsy* who said, "You gotta get a gimmick," and Slappy Cakes was listening. This breakfast spot is bustling on weekends thanks to pancake griddles cleverly built into the dining tables. Instead of ordering a boring old stack of round pancakes, you order a bottle of batter (there are four types) and a side of add-ins like chocolate chips, berries, or bacon. It's a lot of fun to create your own shapes, and the process is surprisingly idiot-proof. If you don't feel like cooking, the staff at Slappy Cakes is happy to do it for you. Plus, there are a number of other great items on the menu, like pork belly Benedict and chicken-fried bacon. Yes, you read that right: chicken-fried bacon. MAP 4: 4246 SE Belmont St., 503/477-4805, www.slappycakes.com; Mon.-Fri. 8am-2pm, Sat.-Sun. 8am-3pm

Waffle Window

Waffle Window $

The Waffle Window is pretty much just what it sounds like. Alongside the Bread and Ink Cafe, there is a little

Lauretta Jean's

blue window that serves liege-style waffles, adapted from a classic Belgian recipe. The waffles are well made, with a little crispness around the edges and a soft, fluffy inside. You can order them sweet and plain with just a little crushed pearl sugar on top, dipped in hard chocolate, or topped with a variety of items like cheesecake, strawberries, or peanut butter. The window also has a number of delightful savory options like The Three Bs, which consists of bacon, basil, and brie. Once you order your waffle, you can take it to go, sit at the covered picnic tables next to the window, or head inside the Bread and Ink Cafe where there's an area for Waffle Window customers.

MAP 4: 3610 SE Hawthorne Blvd., 971/255-0501, www.wafflewindow.com; Sun.-Thurs. 8am-6pm, Fri.-Sat. 8am-8pm

COFFEE AND DESSERTS
✪ Lauretta Jean's $

So, you are out on Division Street, craving something sweet and, of course, the line at Salt & Straw is halfway down the block. Never fear, just head up the street to Lauretta Jean's. This little bakery is, first and foremost, a pie shop, and they have, hands down, some of the best pies in town. It all comes down to the amazing crust, which has just the right balance of tenderness and flakiness. You can pick up a slice or a whole pie, or just sit and eat your wedge of salted honey pie while enjoying a cocktail from the 1950s-inspired menu.

MAP 4: 3402 SE Division St., 503/235-3119, www.laurettajeans.com; Sun.-Thurs. 8am-10pm, Fri.-Sat. 8am-11pm

PACIFIC NORTHWEST
Relish Gastropub $$

This Sellwood spot is a cozy, modern space where seasonal components play along with classic American cuisine. It's all so cozy and comfortable you just might forget that you are sitting in a former funeral parlor. Topping the list of must-eats is the Relish signature burger with sweet onion jam, arugula, and white cheddar, or perhaps the fresh Pacific Northwest salmon prepared with seasonal butter and vegetables. These fresh, local, and seasonal classics are matched by a list of some of Oregon's best wines and beers and a list of craft cocktails that employ house-made ingredients like ginger beer and sour mix.

MAP 5: 6637 SE Milwaukie St., 503/208-3442, www.relishgastropub.com; Tues.-Thurs. 3pm-8pm, Fri. 3pm-10pm, Sat. 10am-10pm, Sun. 10am-8pm

CONTEMPORARY AMERICAN
Papa Haydn $$

This chic but slightly more understated sister to the Papa Haydn in Northwest Portland (701 NW 23rd Ave., 503/228-7317) is a fine place for desserts, but the elegant, airy atmosphere also makes it a nice stop for a meal or Sunday brunch. If you go for dinner, start with the gorgonzola and fontina fondue, order some entrées to share, like a rich, seasonal risotto or braised pork cheeks. And then see if you have room for fresh berry cobbler or peanut butter mousse cake. Go early for quick seating; at both Papa Haydn outposts, the dining room fills up later in the evening when people come for dessert.

MAP 5: 5829 SE Milwaukie Ave., 503/232-9440, www.papahaydn.com; Mon.-Thurs. 11:30am-10pm, Fri.-Sat. 11:30am-midnight, Sun. 10am-9pm

FOOD CARTS
Hurry Back Ice Cream $

Hurry Back Ice Cream makes small-batch, Philadelphia-style ice cream right in its cart. Philly-style uses no eggs, so no custard is required, and while you might think this would lead to a less scrumptious treat, you would be wrong at this cart. Its core flavors, like Ghirardelli chocolate, orange blossom, or grasshopper (to name a few) are surprisingly rich and dense. It also has a seemingly endless list of limited offerings that occasionally pop up and beg to be tried, like cardamom chocolate chip. This is a beloved spot for vegans since the cart has a number of regular flavors and rotating specials made with coconut milk, cream of coconut, and cane sugar—many of which are as complex and delicious as their dairy counterparts.

MAP 5: SE 13th St. and SE Lexington St., 503/737-9727, www.hurrybackicecream.com; Tues.-Thurs. 3pm-8pm, Fri. 3pm-10pm, Sat. 10am-10pm, Sun. 10am-8pm

ASIAN
Jade Teahouse & Patisserie $$

Do not be deceived into thinking that Jade Teahouse is a bustling fast-food place, despite the counter service. This calm, peaceful restaurant invites lingering, and with countless excellent teas, free Wi-Fi, and some of the best Vietnamese food in town, it's easy to do so. The salad rolls are fresh and spicy, with a great balance of texture and flavors, and the french fries with truffle oil alone are worth the trip.

MAP 5: 7912 SE 13th Ave., 503/477-8985, www.jadeteahouse.com; Mon.-Sat. 11am-9pm

Wei Wei $$

In a neighborhood full of antiques shops and quaint little houses, Wei Wei looks a little unassuming tucked into a strip mall, but the food makes up for the lack of ambience. If you are an aficionado of Taiwanese soup, then you will definitely want to order the beef noodle soup. It is heavenly and aromatic, made with braised beef and handmade noodles. Another dish that should not be missed is the steamed *baos,* handmade dumplings that are made to order (so they may take a bit of time). You can choose from grilled chicken, pork belly, or braised beef (or all three), and each will come served with fermented bean sauce, cilantro, and crushed peanuts.

MAP 5: 7835 SE 13th Ave., Ste. 102, 503/946-1732, www.weiweirestaurantpdx. com; Tues.-Sat. 11am-10pm, Sun. 11am-9pm

ITALIAN
A Cena Ristorante $$$

A Cena (pronounced a-CHAY-na) focuses on seasonal, locally grown produce for a contemporary yet modern take on simple Italian cuisine. The extensive wine list features regional Italian wines and several local selections, and the two rustic dining rooms offer an intimate experience that lends itself well to the meaning of the name—"come to supper." But it is the handmade breads, pastas, and cheeses and freshly cured meats that have made this casual Italian restaurant a popular place to grab lunch or brunch with friends or family. If it's on the menu, don't miss the lobster

agnolotti. If it's not, ask for recommendations. The seasonal specials are usually quite good, and the servers are happy to give suggestions as to what will best suit your palate.

MAP 5: 7742 SE 13th Ave., 503/206-3291, www.acenapdx.com; Mon. 5pm-9pm, Tues.-Thurs. and Sun. 11:30am-2:30pm and 5pm-9pm, Fri.-Sat. 11:30am-2:30pm and 5pm-10pm

Gino's $$

Gino's is a great place to find traditional Italian soul food: good old-fashioned cioppino; hearty ravioli tossed with seasonal sauces; chicken marsala; and a simmered-on-the-stove-all-day tomato, pork rib, and beef sauce tossed over penne. If you're on a budget, skip the expensive steaks, which are good but not exceptional. Instead, opt for the hearty pastas and a family-size Caesar salad. If you're dining on the bar side, there is also a very small, inexpensive bar menu that occasionally includes some specialty dishes.

MAP 5: 8051 SE 13th Ave., 503/233-4613, www.ginossellwood.com; Sun.-Thurs. 4pm-10pm, Fri.-Sat. 4pm-11pm

BREAKFAST AND BRUNCH
Bertie Lou's $

Bertie Lou's is the Estelle Getty of the breakfast world in PDX. She's tiny, colorful, and a bit rough around the edges, but oh boy, does she pack a punch. Bertie's offers a truly extensive collection of standard breakfast offerings like biscuits and gravy, Benedicts, scrambles, and omelets with witty descriptions like "bigger than a saddlebag and cheesier than a Christian rock band" and "the things I do for money." Make sure you bring some cash, because the eatery will not take cards or checks.

MAP 5: 8051 SE 17th Ave., 503/239-1177; Mon.-Fri. 7am-2pm, Sat.-Sun. 8am-2:30pm

Fat Albert's $

You won't really want to linger at Fat Albert's. For one thing, there is a sign that discourages you from "camping." For another thing, there's probably going to be a horde of hungry people eyeing your table and drooling over every plate of home-style potatoes that goes by. It's not the sort of place that will fuss over you, so don't expect anyone to spread jelly on your toast or cut up your chicken-fried steak for you. This place is all about no-nonsense, good food. The portions are generous and the food is great, which is really all that matters. Bring cash.

MAP 5: 6668 SE Milwaukie Ave., 503/872-9822; Mon.-Fri. 7am-2pm, Sat.-Sun. 7am-3pm

North Portland

Map 6

PACIFIC NORTHWEST
EaT: An Oyster Bar $$

Owners Ethan Powell and Tobias Hogan (the E and T of the restaurant's name) get shipments each week from different oyster farms, making their bivalves just about the freshest in town. A chalkboard on the wall announces the most recent arrivals from Oregon, Washington, and the East Coast. If you're new to eating oysters, ask your knowledgeable server for guidance. The freshness of the raw oysters, served on the half shell, really speaks for itself, but EaT also makes a mean oysters Rockefeller. Baked and topped with a puree of watercress, garlic, and spinach and then finished with a touch of absinthe, they are remarkably rich and earthy.

MAP 6: 3808 N. Williams Ave., Ste. 122, 503/281-1222, www.eatoysterbar.com; daily 11:30am-10pm

Quaintrelle $$

A quaintrelle is a woman who emphasizes a life of passion, who seeks out joy and finds it in the world around her. That pursuit of life's charms is expressed here in this farm-to-table bistro with soft candlelight and an air of femininity. Chef de Cuisine Ryley Eckersley presents a seasonally curated menu of sophisticated dishes using the best local ingredients he can find. These plates aren't fussy, but they are quite pretty and seem to express a passion for letting ingredients speak for themselves whenever possible. In Eckersley's hands, squash, radishes, and beets are given as much appreciation as a flat iron steak, which makes for some really amazing sides and salads.

MAP 6: 3936 N. Mississippi Ave., 503/200-5787, www.quaintrelle.co; Sun. and Wed.-Thurs. 5pm-9pm, Fri.-Sat. 5pm-10pm

FOOD CARTS
Eurodish $

If you get one thing at this cart, make it the pierogis. They are soft and tender with a lovely mash of potatoes, meat, spinach, or cabbage and mushroom and served in a traditional way with caramelized onions and sour cream. If you are feeling a little more adventurous (or are just incredibly hungry), opt for the Polish Plate and you can sample the pierogis, bigos (a hunter's stew), stuffed cabbage, and a grilled kielbasa all on one platter. The kielbasa is juicy and packed with smoky flavor, the stuffed cabbage is hearty and comforting, and the bigos with its various meats and sauerkraut nicely unifies the plate. It is also a pretty great deal for all the food that you'll get; the portions here are as generous as the welcoming service.

MAP 6: 1331 N. Killingsworth St., 971/344-3704; Mon.-Fri. 11am-8pm, Sat.-Sun. 11am-7pm

Wolf & Bear's $

Over the years, Wolf and Bear's has developed a dedicated community of fans. Its falafel is arguably one of the best in town, even garnering support from celebrities like Jerry Seinfeld and Fred Armisen, who visited the cart while filming *Comedians in Cars Getting Coffee.* The Sabich is one of its most popular items, with hard-boiled egg, cucumbers, eggplant, homemade hummus, onion, and mango pickles wrapped in a pita. Three locations can be found around town, but this cozy nook on Mississippi has some seating right off the street, which provides ample opportunities for people-watching while you nibble on olives and warm pita.

MAP 6: 3925 N. Mississippi Ave., 503/453-5044, www.eatwolfandbears.com; daily 11am-9pm

MEXICAN
¿Por Que No? $

If you're looking for cheap and sublime tacos, this is the place. Try the delicious and juicy carnitas with braised local pork in handmade tortillas, or wild shrimp, sautéed and served with a dollop of *crema.* The ceviche (line-caught snapper and wild shrimp marinated in seasoned lime) is superb, and it's served with

house-made tortilla chips. If you're thirsty (and you should be after that), try a pomegranate margarita, which tastes like summer. Or order a glass of *horchata,* which is creamy, sweet, and delicious, especially when spiked with rum. There is a **second location** (4635 SE Hawthorne Blvd., 503/954-3138), and both almost always have a line, so bring a friend to chat with.

MAP 6: 3524 N. Mississippi Ave., 503/467-4149, www.porquenotacos.com; Mon.-Sat. 11am-10pm, Sun. 11am-9:30pm

¿Por Que No?

The Spicy Spoon $

Looming above the taco hot spot ¿Por Que No? is a modest and cozy shop, barely bigger than a food cart, where traditional American barbecue blends with Mexican dishes. Many delightful options are on the menu, but the pulled pork taco is where it's at, especially when topped with seasonal fruit like pineapple or mango. The fish tacos are also excellent, so fresh and flavorful they don't need to be fried. The Spicy Spoon remains a well-kept secret despite having reviews in national publications like *Travel* । *Leisure,* which named Spicy Spoon one of the best places for tacos in the United States. The word is getting out, however, especially to those tired of waiting in line next door.

MAP 6: 3540 N. Mississippi Ave., 503/477-7715; Mon. 5pm-8pm, Tues.-Sat. 10am-8pm, Sun. 11am-5pm

BARBECUE AND BUFFALO WINGS
Fire on the Mountain $

If you are hankering for wings, most Portlanders will send you to Fire on the Mountain for some of the freshest wings around, with over 10 different homemade sauces to slather them in. You have the option of standard wings (made with all-natural, free-range chicken, of course), boneless wings, or vegan nuggets; or burgers, sandwiches, or salads if wings are not your thing. The smallest order is six wings (served with celery and dressing), and you may want to save room for dessert. If you have never had a deep-fried Twinkie or Oreo, this is the place to try one. There are **two other locations** (1708 E. Burnside, 503/230-9464 and 3443 NE 57th Ave., 503/894-8973).

MAP 6: 4225 N. Interstate Ave., 503/280-9464, www.portlandwings.com; daily 11am-11pm

The People's Pig $

This book could include a whole chapter on popular restaurants that started as popular food carts, and The People's Pig would be one of those spots. Pit Master Cliff Allen ran a cart for five years and eschews all arguments that his meats are not traditional or regionally specific. He has a right to be proud of his work because his standout dish, an amazing pork shoulder with a beautiful crust of charred fat, is among the best smoked meats in the city. Also notable are the beef brisket, smoked fried chicken sandwich with jalapeño jelly, and dry-rubbed St. Louis-style ribs.

MAP 6: 3217 N. Williams St., 503/282-2800, www.peoplespig.com; Sun.-Thurs. 11am-9pm, Fri.-Sat. 11am-10pm

BREAKFAST AND BRUNCH
Gravy $$

A great spot for a good old American greasy spoon breakfast, Gravy is a testament to the joys of gluttony. Biscuits and gravy get a lot of attention here and deservedly so. The biscuit is the size of a plate and smothered with a decidedly un-Atkins-approved portion of gravy. A single order is enough to share between two people. The weekday lunch menu leans to the Southern side: You can get a salad, but why would you when there are fried egg sandwiches, tuna melts, and gravy-soaked fries?

Word to the wise: The wait can be long on weekends, as for any Portland breakfast joint. Come prepared with a cup of coffee from one of the many nearby coffeehouses.

MAP 6: 3957 N. Mississippi Ave., 503/287-8800; daily 7:30am-3pm

Radar $$

Hints of Scandinavian influences, from Swedish pancakes to latkes and smoked bluefish, grace the Radar menu, alongside a small handful of American breakfast staples. Offering such rare treats as a marrow bone served with toast and a soft scrambled egg or smoked pork shoulder grit cakes, the menu offers welcome departures from the typical breakfast, and Radar's husband-and-wife team employ responsibly sourced local ingredients. Look for the Radar Standard on the menu, which will give you the opportunity to choose three items from a long list of house favorites to create your own perfect combo.

MAP 6: 3951 N. Mississippi Ave., 503/841-6948, http://radarpdx.com; Mon.-Thurs. 5pm-9:30pm, Fri. 5pm-10pm, Sat. 10am-2pm and 5pm-10pm, Sun. 10am-2pm and 5pm-9pm

COFFEE AND DESSERTS

Either/Or $$

Either/Or is many things. It's a coffee shop, a bar, a place to grab some comfort food served up in a bowl while you listen to some music on the twin turntables. You can find a selection of coffee drinks, specialty cocktails, and mocktails here, but the highlight of the menu is its selection of coffee and tea flights. The espresso flight, which changes weekly, is served with a double shot of two different rotating single-origin espressos, sparkling water, and small-bite pairing. You can also get a flight with a double shot and your choice of a cappuccino, macchiato, or cortado.

MAP 6: 4003 N. Williams St., 503/284-8928, www.eitherorpdx.com; Sun.-Thurs. 7am-midnight, Fri.-Sat. 7am-1am

Fresh Pot $

Fresh Pot is a cute little café housed in the historic Rexell Drug Building, and it is a truly charming place with all the atmosphere one might expect from an old-time coffee shop. In fact, it was the set of the 2007 film *Feast of Love,* which captured the coffee shop's inherently welcoming vibe. Fresh Pot serves local favorite Stumptown Coffee, as well as pastries from Bittersweet, Pearl, and Black Sheep Bakeries; and it has free Wi-Fi, so you are welcome to plug in, sip some coffee, and feel transported to a place that's just a little more relaxed.

MAP 6: 4001 N. Mississippi Ave., 503/284-8928, www.thefreshpot.com; Mon.-Fri. 6:30am-6pm, Sat.-Sun. 7am-6pm

Jory Coffee $

In a land where coffee reigns supreme, Jory Coffee is setting itself apart by offering, almost exclusively, pour-over coffees. A proper pour over requires expertise, and Jory has it. Its precise process allows the baristas to adjust the pouring style and consistency, giving each cup the proper bloom. If you are accustomed to relying on espresso drinks or drip-brewed coffee, give your coffee a taste before adding any cream or sweeteners. With less water being pushed through the grinds and carefully controlled water temperatures, the resulting cup often needs less adjustment than one might expect.

MAP 6: 3845 N. Mississippi Ave., 480/369-4712, www.jorycoffee.com; daily 8am-6pm

PACIFIC NORTHWEST

The Country Cat Dinnerhouse and Bar $$

The Country Cat has been a long-time anchor of Southeast Portland's Montavilla neighborhood. The popular spot has been serving farm-to-table Pacific Northwest-inspired brunches and dinners with ingredients that often come from the farmers market just down the street. Critics and regulars rave about the cast-iron skillet fried chicken, which can be ordered brunch-style with a toasted pecan-bacon spoonbread and optional maple syrup, or dinner style with bacon braised collard greens and mashed potatoes with smoky bacon and sausage gravy. Reservations for parties larger than four are definitely recommended, especially for brunch.

MAP 7: 7937 SE Stark St., 503/408-1414, www.thecountrycat.net; Sun.-Thurs. 9am-2pm and 5pm-9pm, Fri.-Sat. 9am-2pm and 5pm-10pm

The Observatory $$

The Observatory may seem unassuming, but that's because it gets so many things right. The venue lighting is a perfect balance between practical and serene. The menu is both elegant and approachable. The drink menu is populated with champagne cocktails, negronis, manhattans, and old-fashioneds. The beer and wine list gives nods to famous locals and familiar imports. For starters, try the oregano fry bread (served with basil crème fraîche and tomato puree) or the apple and beet salad. Move on to the catch of the day special, the pulled pork sandwich, or the lamb burger with feta, balsamic tomatoes, *tzatziki* sauce, and marinated onions.

MAP 7: 8115 SE Stark St., 503/445-6284, www.theobservatorypdx.com, Mon. 11am-11pm, Tues.-Fri. 11am-midnight, Sat. 9am-midnight, Sun. 9am-11pm

Seasons & Regions Seafood Grill $$

This homey little seafood restaurant in Portland's Multnomah Village is known for serving fresh clams, salmon, crab, and various other fresh finds from the sea, but the menu is surprisingly well-rounded. In fact, there's a full menu with appetizers, entrées, salads, and desserts for vegetarian diners and for those with gluten allergies (just ask). If you get there before they run out, try the salmon cakes. The specials change regularly, but you will always see some Pacific Northwest favorites like chinook salmon or red snapper. Everything tends to reflect what is fresh and in season. In fact, Seasons & Regions has its own 13-acre farm just outside of Estacada, where they grow heirloom fruits, vegetables, herbs, and flowers. Parking is tight, but there is overflow parking across the street.

MAP 7: 6660 SW Capitol Hwy., 503/244-6400, www.seasonsandregions. com; Mon.-Fri. 11:15am-9:30pm, Sat. 9am-9:30pm, Sun. 9am-9pm

ASIAN

HK Cafe $$

Just as they love their brunches, Portlanders also love their dim sum. Old Town and Chinatown used to be the place to go, but now most of the Asian markets and restaurants have moved out to 82nd Avenue in a neighborhood affectionately known as the Jade District. HK Cafe is located in a strip of businesses along the outer edge of Eastport Plaza, a shopping center that is otherwise not known for excellent dining experiences. It looks small from the outside, but inside is a sprawling and bustling dining room where silver carts wheel around steaming plates of pork *shu mai* (dumplings), chicken feet, and *hum bao* (a steamed pork-filled bun). Despite the enormous dining room and ample seating, weekend wait times can still get up to 30-45 minutes, so the earlier you arrive, the better. Dim sum service is until 3pm.

MAP 7: 4410 SE 82nd Ave., 503/771-8866; daily 9:30am-midnight

Nudi Noodle Place $$

Nudi is a place full to the rafters with whimsy. The outside looks like a mashup between a Swiss chalet and a Hobbit house, and the interior looks a bit like it was decorated by a magpie. Bits of moss hang from the walls and the chandelier. Lights sparkle through holes in the ceiling like stars in the sky. The menu is also whimsical, with an Asian-fusion take on some classic Thai dishes and a bevy of soup bowls. Try the Lak Sa, a house specialty with rice noodles, sliced pork, prawns, poached egg, bean sprouts, and peanut sauce or a spicy brisket ramen with spinach and enoki mushrooms. Cocktails here are equally fun, like the Gin and Sonic made with Bombay Sapphire, sweet lychee liqueur, tonic water, lime, and a handful of lychee fruit pearls.

MAP 7: 4310 SE Woodstock Blvd., 503/477-7425, www.nudipdx.com; Mon.-Fri. 11am-3pm and 5pm-10pm, Sat. noon-10pm, Sun. noon-9pm

BAVARIAN
Otto & Anita's European Restaurant $$

At this quaint underground Bavarian restaurant, everyone is talking about dill pickle soup. Invented by Otto himself, it is both terrifyingly green and remarkably delicious. The decor is casual and kitschy, and the rest of the menu is rounded out with a variety of schnitzels and sausages. The *zigeunerschnitzel* (two pieces of pork loin in a red wine paprika sauce with vegetables and spaetzle) is phenomenal, and so is the *maultaschen,* a Swabian dish of noodles filled with spiced pork and served in a beefy onion broth. Save room for dessert (or take some to go), because this is Anita's specialty. Black Forest cake, coconut cream cake, and a rum-soaked chocolate cake are just a few that top the list.

MAP 7: 3025 SW Canby St., 503/425-1411, www.ottoandanitas.com; Tues.-Fri. 11am-2pm and 5pm-9pm, Sat. 5pm-9pm

SOUTHERN AND CREOLE
Delta Café $$

In the heart of the Woodstock neighborhood, Delta Café is a favorite haunt for nearby Reed College students on a carbohydrate binge and families who know kids love nothing more than

Nudi Noodle Place

ooey-gooey mac and cheese. If you can get past the appetizer menu—with its hush puppies, cornbread, sweet potato fries, and catfish bites—settle into a plate of fried chicken or a bowl of crawfish étouffée. Or simply order a sampler platter. Delta also has a fantastic cocktail menu that utilizes a variety of house-infused vodka, tequila, rum, and whiskey.

MAP 7: 4607 SE Woodstock Blvd., 503/771-3101, www.deltacafepdx.com; daily 9am-midnight

Po'Shines Café de la Soul $

Po'Shines is worth a visit. Not just because it serves up some of the best Southern soul food in town, and not just because the hush puppies that accompany most baskets and platters are deep-fried gems. You may not even notice it as you scarf down ribs, smoky brisket, and fried okra, but this restaurant is a nonprofit organization helping train people in the community for work in restaurants. In fact, most employees, from the server to the chef, volunteer their time to the cause of strengthening the community.

MAP 7: 8131 N. Denver St., 503/978-9000, www.poshines.com; Mon. 8am-3pm, Tues.-Thurs. 8am-8pm, Fri. 8am-9pm, Sat. 9am-9pm

CARIBBEAN
Salvador Molly's $$

Salvador Molly's is just plain fun. They call it "pirate cookin'" because they have stolen cuisine concepts from all over the Seven Seas. You'll find Caribbean jerk chicken, Baja fish tacos, Hawaiian kalua pork, and Creole jambalaya—and that's just a smattering of the eclectic entrées. Some starters you won't want to miss,

like the unforgettable Cheesy Poofs, which are fried mashed potato fritters with a touch of cheese and chipotle chiles. But if you really want an adventure, order the Great Balls of Fire. If you can manage to eat all five habanero cheese fritters with the sauce, you'll get your picture on the Wall of Flame.

MAP 7: 1523 SW Sunset Blvd., 503/293-1790, www.salvadormollys.com; Mon.-Tues. 11:30am-9pm, Wed.-Thurs. 11:30am-10pm, Fri.-Sat. 11:30am-11pm

BREAKFAST AND BRUNCH
Marco's Café & Espresso Bar $$

This quaint Multnomah Village café is a neighborhood favorite, which is why you don't hear much about it in the city. With friendly service and reliably good breakfasts, this charmer is a well-guarded secret. The extensive menu has a heavy emphasis on scrambles, omelets, and Benedicts; everything is organic and fresh. If you're not a fan of egg-heavy breakfasts, opt for a hearty veggie breakfast burrito filled with brown rice, black bean chili, corn, tomato, avocado, and pepper jack cheese, or try the superb tofu scramble with mixed veggies in a tandoori or Korean barbecue marinade.

MAP 7: 7910 SW 35th Ave., 503/245-0199, www.marcoscafe.com; Mon.-Fri. 7am-9pm, Sat.-Sun. 8am-9pm

Toast $$

Toast is a cozy and casual neighborhood restaurant that makes a point of using local and seasonal products. It bakes fresh breads and pastries and grinds meats for its sausages and burgers in-house. Brunch diners are treated with complimentary fresh scones upon arrival, a nice gesture considering the wait for a table can be kind of long. Try the Dismal Times, a tasty dish of ground hanger steak, white cheddar, seasonal greens, and fried eggs with a potato *rosti* on the side. If you are unfamiliar with potato *rosti,* you are in for a treat. The Swiss dish is similar to hash browns but cooked in a circular mold for a crispy outside and a soft, creamy inside.

MAP 7: 5222 SE 52nd Ave., 503/774-1020, www.toastpdx.com; daily 8am-2pm

Fat City Café $

Fat City Café has numerous awards for its quirky style and delicious food; for many locals, it's the perfect place to enjoy classic diner favorites in generous proportions. Cinnamon rolls the size of a baby's head are the big star at this neighborhood café; the recipe hasn't changed since 1974. Breakfast is the specialty here, served all day, but there's also a terrific lunch menu full of burgers, sandwiches, and other such things.

MAP 7: 7820 SW Capitol Hwy., 503/245-5457; daily 6:30am-3pm

NIGHTLIFE

Portland's nightlife scene is not about seeing and being seen but about experiencing the joys that life has to offer, whether it's a glass of hoppy IPA or a beautifully executed old-fashioned.

When people in Portland go out, they like to talk, share, imbibe, and indulge. You won't find many dance clubs pumping out top 40 hits, and if you do, it's not the locals crowding the floor. Splashy theme or concept bars have a tendency to fall flat in these parts, as locals tend to gravitate toward more eclectic spots with interesting back stories, great libations, and comfortable gathering spaces.

Craft brewers draw upon the region's resources—its hops and delicious water—creating innovative beers that receive international acclaim and continue to put Portland on the map as a haven for beer lovers.

Doug Fir Lounge

The city's cocktail culture is treated with almost the same reverence as its food scene, and is likewise featured on television and in magazines and blogs across the country. Industry stars utilize the bounty of the Pacific Northwest's fruits and distillations.

The Pacific Northwest has also long been considered a key player in the independent music scene. But long before bands like the Decemberists, Pink Martini, Modest Mouse, the Dandy Warhols, or the Shins called Portland home, it was a favorite stop for many jazz, blues, and bluegrass players.

HIGHLIGHTS

Shift Drinks

⊕ **BEST PLACE TO DRINK LIKE A PROFESSIONAL: Shift Drinks** is a spacious, modern bar where the drinks are so well-executed that ardent fans include local bartenders as well as cocktail mavens (page 93).

⊕ **BEST PLACE TO DANCE ON AIR:** For 90 years, music lovers have flocked to the **Crystal Ballroom** to dance on the legendary "floating" dance floor (page 95).

⊕ **BEST PLACE TO BEAT YOUR HIGH SCORE:** Part bar, part well-appointed arcade, **Ground Kontrol** will make the kid in you squeal with delight (page 99).

⊕ **BEST PLACE TO MEET MARVELOUS DAMES:** After 40 years, **Darcelle XV** is more than just a drag show—it's a Portland rite of passage (page 99).

⊕ **BEST PLACE TO PUT YOURSELF UNDER LOCK AND KEY:** If you're looking for a laid-back place with a lot of swagger, cute cocktails, retro decor, and sweet tunes, **Keys Lounge** is about as groovy as it gets (page 102).

⊕ **BEST PLACE TO DREAM ABOUT YOUR NEXT OUTDOOR ADVENTURES: Base Camp Brewing** is reminiscent of a ski chalet, serves a signature S'more Stout, and has an outdoor patio with fire pits (page 105).

⊕ **BEST PLACE TO GRAB A PINT: Horse Brass Pub** has arguably one of the best selections of drafts from around the globe (page 105).

⊕ **BEST PLACE TO KISS OVER A COCKTAIL:** The cocktails are pretty and the lighting is low at **Slow Bar** (page 106).

BREWPUBS AND TAPHOUSES

Bailey's Taproom

Bailey's Taproom is like a library for beers. The selection is extensive and constantly changing. It even sends out tweets and posts of what's new. While it doesn't serve food, Bailey's allows you to bring in anything you like—or you can order from the Mexican joint next door and have the food delivered to your table. Keep an eye on the digital menu that displays real-time keg levels on each of the taps.

MAP 1: 213 SW Broadway, 503/295-1004, www.baileystaproom.com; daily noon-midnight

COCKTAIL LOUNGES

✪ Shift Drinks

Shift Drinks bills itself a "professional drinking establishment," and it isn't just talking itself up. With its vaulted ceilings and sleek, seductive vibe, it is *the* go-to spot for bartenders and craft cocktail makers across the city, which says a lot. The cocktail menu is unique and delicious, with well-balanced flavors and fun concoctions that will satisfy a variety of palates. The wine list has been curated as carefully as a playlist to a lover. The name Shift Drinks comes from the restaurant tradition of rewarding employees with an alcoholic drink at the end of their shift, and in keeping with that tradition, the venue appeals to the varied after-work crowd by offering rotating happy hour deals all day, every day. You will find a number of snacks and sandwiches for less than $5 as well as super cheap deals on drinks including beers ($3), rare wines ($7), and cocktails ($5-7).

MAP 1: 1200 SW Morrison St., 503/922-3933, www.shiftdrinkspdx.com; Mon.-Fri. 4pm-2:30am, Sat.-Sun. 5pm-2:30am

Multnomah Whiskey Library

At Multnomah Whiskey Library, cocktails never tip over into the silly or sweet category. This is a serious bar with one of the most impressive collections of Scotch and whiskey in the states. The atmosphere is that of an exclusive club with oak paneling, chandeliers, library ladders, and walls of gleaming bottles. The wait is long (unless you fork over the considerable amount of cash it takes to become a member), but it is worth it. The old-fashioned, made with Henry McKenna single barrel bourbon, is so well crafted, it will ruin you for all other wannabes.

MAP 1: 1124 SW Alder St., 503/954-1381, www.multnomahwhiskeylibrary.com; Mon.-Thurs. 4pm-midnight, Fri.-Sat. 4pm-1am

Pepe Le Moko

This little crown jewel—named for a 1937 French film about a gangster hiding out in the Casbah—is a smarter, more sophisticated sibling to the popular Clyde Common restaurant around the corner, and all about reclaiming what has been lost: the art of the cocktail. From the 10th Avenue entrance, it looks the size of a one-chair barbershop. But this 36-seat subterranean bar is not to be missed. At first glance, the cocktail menu looks like a collection of bad ideas. The Blue Hawaii, the Amaretto Sour, the Long Island Ice Tea all sound like drinks for

THE HAPPIEST HOURS

Happy hour culture is a special thing in Portland. The Oregon Liquor Control Commission (OLCC) requires that all establishments that serve alcohol offer at least five different and substantial food items on their menu, so many of the city's bars have embraced this and offer great food as well as happy hour deals on not just drinks but eats. Deep discounts on specialty cocktails, beer and wine, or wells can put drinks under $5. Many places offer their most popular dishes for about half the cost during happy hour as well. And at some bars, happiness comes twice a day (post-work and late night). Here are some of the best places to experience happy hour in Portland:

- **Shift Drinks:** Shift Drinks lives by the creed that happy hour was meant to offer working people cheap food and drinks after they clock out—but since everyone works different hours, the bar has developed a truly unique happy hour menu that lasts all day, every day. On that ever-changing menu, you'll find some rare wines for $7, beer for just $3, cider and sake for $5, and a bevy of cocktails with a featured spirit (like mezcal) for around $5-7 (page 93).

- **Bartini:** Sample your way through the 100-plus martini menu at Bartini during its happy hour (Mon. 4pm-close, Tues.-Sat. 4pm-6:30pm and 9:30pm-close, Sun. 4pm-close), when the drinks are half-price (page 97).

- **Swift Lounge:** Swift's happy hour (Mon.-Fri. 4pm-8pm, Sun. 9am-2am) boasts $5 16-ounce mason jar cocktails, $4 wines, and $1 off drafts, as well as a food menu ranging $3-5 that includes things like red beans and rice, chicken satay, and several pairs of sliders (page 101).

- **EastBurn:** EastBurn has two happy hours daily. "Recess" (daily 3pm-5pm), as it's called, offers $2 off appetizers and handheld food (e.g., burgers and sandwiches), and the menu for the late-night happy hour (Sun.-Thurs. 10pm-midnight) includes some serious snackables, like soft pretzels, goat cheese kale dip, and chicken fingers (page 108).

- **Oaks Bottom Public House:** This Lompoc Brewing pub has two happy hours every day (daily 3pm-6pm and 9pm-close), each offering a long list of $6 full-sized plates, $4 pints, and $1 off cocktails (page 114).

a college sports bar, not a lush, intimate lounge. But in the hands of cocktail genius Jeffery Morgenthaler, these old concoctions are reclaimed. This is not a place for fussy garnishes and state-of-the-art smokes and ices; this tiny cocktail lounge does not reinvent the daiquiri but instead brings it back to its heyday.

MAP 1: 407 SW 10th Ave., 503/546-8537, www.pepelemokopdx.com; daily 4pm-2am

BARS AND PUBS
Jack London Bar

In the basement of the Rialto Poolroom, Jack London Bar is nothing like its upstairs neighbor. A little dark with a slight speakeasy resemblance, it hosts jazz nights, open mics, art shows, and burlesque shows. This bar is for music nuts, history buffs, and bookish cool cats. It was named not for the legendary author, but after the hotel atop the space, at the time called the Jack London Hotel.

MAP 1: 529 SW 4th Ave., 503/228-7605, www.rialtopoolroom.com; hours vary, usually closed Wed. and Sun.

Kells Irish Pub

If you're out roving for a pint, Kells Irish should be where you point your feet. With a fantastic collection of beers on tap and a fine collection of whiskey, Kells can be a lot of fun, with live Irish music many nights. It's also a fine place to chat or watch soccer. Hand your server a dollar and a couple of quarters and ask to see "the dollar trick." You'll lose the money, but it's for a good cause.

MAP 1: 112 SW 2nd Ave., 503/227-4057, www.kellsirish.com; Mon.-Wed. 11:30am-midnight, Thurs. 11:30am-1am, Fri. 11:30am-2:30am, Sat. 8am-2:30am, Sun. 8am-midnight (happy hour Mon.-Thurs. 3pm-6:30pm and 10pm to close, Fri. 3pm-6:30pm, Sun. 7pm-close)

Shanghai Tunnel

Learn a little about Portland's history and you'll understand why Shanghai says it's to "bars what Bruce Campbell is to horror films." The dark, seedy journey into the bowels of Old Town is part of the novelty, but it's also a pretty good bar. Skip straight to the narrow staircase to the basement, where the cocktails are stellar and pool is $0.50 a pop. Shanghai isn't classy, but that's okay because it never means to be.

MAP 1: 211 SW Ankeny St., 503/220-4001, www.shanghaitunnel.com; daily 5pm-2:30am (happy hour daily 5pm-close)

GAY AND LESBIAN

Scandals

Scandals launched on the scene about 30 years ago now as the first gay bar in the area. Nowadays it's a favorite haunt for pretty boys and sassy girls who like cheap, strong drinks, and a more laid-back, hospitable crowd than many of the popular meat markets nearby. Scandals is a great spot to sit and linger before heading off to dance or see a show, and it's also a perfect place to decompress afterward.

MAP 1: 1125 SW Harvey Milk St., 503/227-5887, www.scandalspdx.com; daily noon-2:30am (happy hour daily 4pm-8pm); free most nights

LIVE MUSIC

TOP EXPERIENCE

❂ Crystal Ballroom

The McMenamin brothers have made a name for themselves in the Pacific Northwest for breathing life into some pretty remarkable historic venues. The Crystal Ballroom is no exception, having seen a lot of action in its 90 years: dance revivals, police raids, fabled rock concerts, and even near demolition. It is rumored that Little Richard once fired Jimi Hendrix mid-concert on the Crystal's stage. But what people can't seem to stop talking about is the floor. One of only a few like it in the country, it moves on ball bearings, giving a whole new meaning to "dance on air."

MAP 1: 1332 W. Burnside St., 503/225-0047, www.mcmenamins.com/venues; box office daily 11:30am-6pm, later for shows (happy hour daily 3pm-6pm and 10pm-close); price varies

Dante's

Spend an evening at Dante's and you can practically hear "In-a-Gadda-Da-Vida" seeping through the walls. Dante's has a long and sordid history, having been a brothel, flophouse, punk club, and gambling hall. These days, it's the home of two must-see weekly events: Sinferno Cabaret, a weekly mash-up of fire dancing, burlesque, and debauchery; and Karaoke from Hell, where wannabe rock stars can sing with a live band.

MAP 1: 1 SW 3rd Ave., 503/226-6630, www.danteslive.com; daily 11am-2:30am (happy hour Mon.-Fri. 4pm-6pm); price varies

Kelly's Olympian

If Portland has a biker bar, this is it. Kelly's looks like a kitschy downtown diner by day, chock-full of motorcycle memorabilia and fully restored bikes, but when night falls, it becomes a hot venue for local punk, indie, and underground rock shows. You won't see many hipsters here, rather a lot of post-work bartenders and servers, actors, and retail denizens. Besides the great music, Kelly's has all the good dive bar elements: stiff drinks, hot bartenders, and fried late-night nosh. **MAP 1:** 426 SW Washington St., 503/228-3669, www.kellysolympian. com; daily 10am-2am (happy hour daily 4pm-7pm); free-$7

Northwest and the Pearl District

Map 2

BREWPUBS AND TAPHOUSES

Bridgeport Brewing Company

A longtime award-winner and staple in the local microbrew scene, Bridgeport has a terrific ale called Blue Heron, released in 1987 as a special tribute to the Audubon Society. The pale ale is round and soft on the palate, but finishes crisply. Of course, Bridgeport is probably better known for its IPA, a consistent Gold Medal winner in the World Beer Championship. Fans of the show *Leverage* may recognize Bridgeport as the setting for the fifth season of the show, which used some interior and exterior shots of the pub as its home base. **MAP 2:** 1313 NW Marshall St., 503/241-3612, www.bridgeportbrew. com; Sun.-Wed. 11:30am-10pm, Thurs.-Sat. 11:30am-11pm (happy hour Mon.-Fri. 4pm-6pm)

Deschutes Brewery and Public House

For more than 20 years, Deschutes Brewery has been hand-crafting ales that are popular all over the world, like Mirror Pond Pale Ale and Black Butte Porter. The Portland pub (sister to the flagship in Bend, Oregon) has become a favorite spot for folks to grab a pint before they hit the theater or galleries. Order a sampler tray and try six brews for just slightly more than the price of a single pint. The Portland pub also features a 100 percent gluten-free Hazy IPA, which is derived from rice syrup, Belgian candy syrup, and honey with mango and peach puree. **MAP 2:** 210 NW 11th Ave., 503/296-4906, www.deschutesbrewery.com; Sun.-Tues. 11am-10pm, Wed.-Thurs. 11am-11pm, Fri.-Sat. 11am-midnight (happy hour daily 4pm-6pm)

Rogue Ales

There's a pirate in every bunch, and Rogue Ales, based in Newport on the Oregon Coast, is Portland's resident scallywag. Rogue has a truly impressive lineup of beers, but it does dark best. In particular, the Shakespeare Stout is rich, chocolatey, and earthy. Another popular one is the Dead Guy Ale, which is done in the German maibock style. The pub is a reasonably

Bridgeport Brewing Company

large space, with a bar area that includes shared benches and some cozy tables. The dining area is a popular spot for large groups and families with children.
MAP 2: 1339 NW Flanders St., 503/222-5910, www.rogue.com; Mon.-Thurs. 11am-midnight, Fri.-Sat. 11am-1am, Sun. 11am-11pm (happy hour Mon.-Thurs. 4pm-6pm and 10pm-close)

10 Barrel

When Bend, Oregon-based darling 10 Barrel announced it was selling to Anheuser-Busch, beer lovers were crushed. But the company promised that nothing would change with the beer the fiercely loyal fans had come to expect. The sale did allow them to upgrade and expand the brewpub in the Pearl District. Check out the brew board for what's on tap, like the specially made Pearl IPA, with a strong hoppy punch but smooth finish. The brewpub is also quite popular with non-beer drinkers for its cucumber and raspberry sours, which offer a

crisp and refreshing alternative to the rest of the ales on its tap list.
MAP 2: 1411 NW Flanders St., 503/224-1700, www.10barrel.com; Sun.-Thurs. 11am-11pm, Fri.-Sat. 11am-midnight

COCKTAIL LOUNGES
Bartini

The name of the game here is creative, colorful cocktails with giggle-worthy names like Snickertini, a concoction of vanilla-infused vodka, crème de cacao, and Frangelico shaken with cream and topped with caramel. This is a particularly popular spot with the ladies because there is a veritable fruit basket of cocktails to sample, like the hot-sweet spicy mango martini and the blueberry smash, with rum, blueberries, and mint.
MAP 2: 2108 NW Glisan St., 503/224-7919, www.urbanfondue.com; Mon.-Thurs. 4pm-midnight, Fri.-Sat. 4pm-1am, Sun. 4pm-11pm (happy hour Sun.-Mon. 4pm-close, Tues.-Sat. 4pm-6:30pm and 9:30pm-close)

DESIGNATED DRIVERS: PORTLAND BEER TOURS

If you'd like to tour Portland's many breweries without doing the driving or walking, or just want to leave the itinerary up to someone else, you have some options.

If you're looking to learn why some people refer to Portland as "Brewvana," hop aboard the short bus by **Brewvana** (2580 NW Upshur St., 503/729-6804, www.brewvana. com; $69-109) and you'll gain an education. Each of these little beer-themed buses takes passengers on daily all-inclusive tours of various breweries. You can take a Coffee, Beer, and Doughnuts tour, where you'll sample all the delights the title indicates, or a Pacific Northwest tour, which will take you to four breweries determined to prove that the West Coast is the best coast. For each tour, you'll also receive a souvenir pilsner glass, pretzel necklace, and tasting guide.

You can also imbibe some of Portland's finest and visit places like Lucky Labrador and Widmer Brothers Brewery via the **Portland Brew Bus** (503/647-0021, www.brewbus.com; $45). On this fun, educational tour, you'll learn about the history of craft brewing, different styles of beer (ales, lagers, porters, stouts), and why Portland is the home of craft brewing. The bus takes you around Portland to three or four breweries, where you can sample different beers and ask questions of the resident brewers.

Alternatively, if you'd like to embark upon some collective biking activity with your beer, you can always hop aboard the **Pedalounge** (page 156), where a captain steers a human-powered trolley on a voyage to as many as four breweries, pubs, and dive bars.

Pope House Bourbon Lounge

This little Southern-themed lounge and restaurant in an old Victorian serves up an extensive array of whiskey and bourbon, everything from the bottom-shelf Old Crow to the hidden-somewhere-safe 23-year Pappy Van Winkle. Order some hush puppies and ask your bartenders for recommendations. They know their stuff. And if you really, really love bourbon, join the Pope House Bourbon Derby: Sample 50 or more types of bourbon and be immortalized on a horseshoe on the wall.

MAP 2: 2075 NW Glisan St., 503/222-1056; daily 4pm-midnight (happy hour Mon. 4pm-close, Tues.-Sun. 4pm-7pm)

Teardrop Cocktail Lounge

This is the spot for classic cocktails with a DIY Portland twist. The owners make their own bitters, tinctures, specialty liqueurs, and tonic. Teardrop's menu changes regularly to reflect the season and what ingredients are locally available. Utilizing a wide range of both local and international top-shelf spirits, Teardrop has a truly awe-inspiring menu that most second-rate bartenders could only hope to pronounce, let alone prepare. If you need proof that these guys know what they are doing, just look around at the clientele; chances are, most of them are bartenders themselves.

MAP 2: 1015 NW Everett St., 503/445-8109, www.teardroplounge.com; Mon.-Thurs. 4pm-12:30am, Fri.-Sat. 4pm-2am (happy hour Mon.-Fri. 4pm-7pm)

WINE BARS
M Bar

Arguably one of the smallest bars in Portland (think big closet, but with wine, beer, and sake), M Bar packs a lot of charm into its tiny space. The selection is simple, and the happy hour prices (which last until 8pm) are laughably low. There are no fussy menus here; a chalkboard mounted above the bar declares the choices for the day.

MAP 2: 417 NW 21st Ave., 503/228-6614; daily 6pm-2:30am (happy hour daily 6pm-8pm)

ARCADE BARS
✪ Ground Kontrol

What could be more appealing than an arcade full of classic games, from Galaga to Street Fighter, that also serves cocktails and hosts regular Dance Dance Revolution and Rock Band tournaments? Thought so. Ground Kontrol is a time warp into the days of Atari, Pumas, and Apple IIe . . . but with beer. It's basically a hands-on museum to the bleep, bleep, whirr digital past, but also a really fun way to spend a date or an evening out with friends when you tire of playing pool for the umpteenth time.

MAP 2: 511 NW Couch St., 503/796-9364, www.groundkontrol.com; daily noon-2:30am (happy hour daily 5pm-7pm); free

GAY AND LESBIAN
✪ Darcelle XV

"That's no lady, that's Darcelle!" She's an icon in Portland, and has been for more than 40 years. The girls at Darcelle's perform weekly shows that are full of bawdiness, humor, and sparkle. Make reservations before you go and catch the late Saturday show if you can. It's followed by a stripped-down and sexy performance by The Men of Darcelle at no additional charge.

MAP 2: 208 NW 3rd. Ave., 503/222-5338, www.darcellexv.com; Wed.-Thurs. 6pm-11pm, Fri.-Sat. 6pm-2:30am; $20 most shows

Hobo's

Had Old Blue Eyes and the rest of the Rat Pack been gay, this is where they would have hung out. Dark and comfortable, each table feels a little bit private, and with the addition of flickering candlelight and the soft piano, it's downright romantic. The Hobo's staff is friendly and attentive, and it's

an elegant choice for anyone seeking clandestine conversation over cocktails and delectable entrées.

MAP 2: 120 NW 3rd Ave., 503/224-3285, www.hobospdx.com; Sun.-Fri. 4pm-2:30am, Sat. 3pm-2:30am (happy hour Mon.-Fri. 4pm-7pm)

LIVE MUSIC
Wilf's Restaurant and Bar

If you picture a piano bar (the elegant kind, not the cheesy kind), you'll get an idea of an evening at Wilf's. High-backed red chairs and the dark, deep-colored surroundings make for a swank affair. In fact, Wilf's somehow manages to feel an awful lot like an affair: secretive, romantic, and unpredictable. The talent is reliably great, and it is not uncommon to feel as though you have stumbled into *A Star Is Born*.

MAP 2: 800 NW 6th Ave., 503/223-0070, www.wilfsrestaurant.com; Tues.-Fri. 11:30am-10:30pm, Sat. 5pm-midnight (happy hour Tues.-Fri. 5:30pm-7pm); price varies

COMEDY
Brody Theater

This downtown theater hosts open mic comedy twice a week, usually on Monday and Wednesday, and improv shows, tournaments, and stand-up other nights of the week. There is a full bar inside the theater that also serves bagels, wraps, and paninis. Open mic nights are free with the purchase of one item (which doesn't have to be booze).

MAP 2: 16 NW Broadway, 503/224-2227, www.brodytheater.com; Mon. and Wed. 9:30pm; free with drink purchase

ComedySportz

If you are familiar with shows like *Whose Line Is It Anyway?* then you'll get ComedySportz. The troupe of sketch comedians has been performing fast-paced, hilarious (but clean) comedy in Portland since early 1993 and is still going strong. Two teams of comedians take turns making up scenes, playing games, and singing songs. There's a lot of audience participation, and at the end the audience decides which team did better. On select Sundays, the group performs a ComedySportz 4 Kids show, focusing on games and suggestions from the 12-and-under crowd; they even give a bunch of the audience members a chance to be in the spotlight.

MAP 2: 1963 NW Kearney St., 503/236-8888, www.portlandcomedy.com; Fri.-Sat. 8pm; $15-55

KARAOKE
Voicebox

If you love belting out some karaoke, but hate listening to strangers, you will love Voicebox. Guests get private rooms, each slightly different but comfortably fitting 6-30 people. The song selection is decent and controlled with a remote, so no cheesy KJ banter either. Table service comes to the rooms, and there is a selection of sake, sake cocktails, beer, and wine as well as an assortment of appetizers, sandwiches, and silly things like a plate of gummy worms.

MAP 2: 2112 NW Hoyt St., 503/303-8220, www.voiceboxpdx.com; Mon.-Thurs. 4pm-midnight, Fri. 4pm-2am, Sat. 2pm-2am, Sun. 2pm-midnight (happy hour Thurs.-Tues. 4pm-7pm and Wed. 4pm-midnight); $7 and up

Northeast   Map 3

BREWPUBS AND TAPHOUSES
Alameda Brewhouse

This tiny brewhouse got its start in 1996 in the Beaumont Village area of northeast Portland. It was just five barrels (155 gallons) back then, but has since grown to be a recognized name on Portland taps. Alameda Brewhouse has won a number of awards, particularly for its Black Bear XX Stout. The Klickitat Pale Ale—which shares a name with the real street made famous by Beverly Cleary's Ramona Quimby books—is another great beer with bold hops and a caramel finish.

MAP 3: 4765 NE Fremont St., 503/460-9025, www.alamedabrewhouse. com; Mon.-Sat. 11am-11pm, Sun. 11am-10pm (happy hour Mon.-Fri. 3pm-6pm)

Burnside Brewing Company

It has taken a few years for Burnside Brewing Company to hit its stride, but it surely has now. Popular for its dependable Burnside IPA and Sweet Heat (made with heaps of apricots and imported Jamaican Scotch Bonnet peppers), the brewery also makes some seasonal ales that keep people excited with anticipation all year, such as the winter ale Permafrost. It often has a number of guest taps as well, with a rotating collection of ciders.

MAP 3: 701 E. Burnside St., 503/946-8151, www.burnsidebrewco.com; Mon.-Tues. 11am-10pm, Wed.-Thurs. 11am-11pm, Fri.-Sat. 11am-midnight (happy hour daily 3pm-6pm and 9pm-close)

Laurelwood Brewing Co.

Laurelwood Brewing Co., a locally owned, certified-organic brewery and collection of pubs, is popular with many locals thanks to the stellar Tree Hugger Porter, Free Range Red, and especially the Workhorse IPA, which bears a larger-than-life hop flavor and a 6.7 percent alcohol-by-volume kick. It's quite popular with families and often packed with small children who can hang out in a dedicated playroom while their parents sip on beers and munch on plates of fries.

MAP 3: 5115 NE Sandy Blvd., 503/282-0622, www.laurelwoodbrewpub. com; daily 11am-10pm (happy hour daily 3pm-6pm)

COCKTAIL LOUNGES
Angel Face

This bar is about as precious as it gets, a quiet little sister next door to the bustling Navarre restaurant, which is owned by the same people. The limited food menu has things like almonds with lavender, oysters, and cheese boards. There is no cocktail menu, but rather a stellar selection of top-shelf spirits, and the bartenders are experts at designing a cocktail to complement your small plates. The fun part is the surprise. You tell them you like, for instance, vodka, but don't care for sweet things, and let them do the rest. It is a concept that could come off as snooty and impersonal, but instead feels special, hospitable, and consciously crafted. Notice the meticulously hand-painted wallpaper at this place.

MAP 3: 14 NE 28th St., 503/239-3804, www.angelfaceportland.com; Sun.-Thurs. 5pm-midnight, Fri.-Sat. 5pm-1am

Secret Society Lounge

With its rich decor, low lighting, and classic cocktail menu, the Secret Society Lounge makes you feel hipper than you are. Try the corpse reviver (Aviation gin, Lillet, lemon juice, and absinthe), a lounge favorite. The Moscow mule and the chrysanthemum cocktail are also lovely. If you're a woman, check out the bathroom, as the "ladies lounge" is almost cooler than the bar.

MAP 3: 116 NE Russell St., 503/493-3600, www.secretsociety.net; Sun.-Thurs. 5pm-midnight, Fri.-Sat. 5pm-1am (happy hour Sun.-Thurs. 5pm-7pm and 10pm-close)

Swift Lounge

Swift feels like a backyard party thrown by that guy from high school who never really stopped throwing parties. The list of "dranks" includes a number of 16-32-ounce mason jar cocktails with names like Bitchy Parrot and Guilty Sparrow. It's charmingly unpretentious and a little bit eccentric. The happy hour at Swift is hugely popular thanks to great deals on both food and drink, so the place gets quite busy in the post-work hours and late at night.

MAP 3: 1932 NE Broadway St., 503/288-3333; Mon.-Fri. 4pm-2am, Sat.-Sun. 9am-2am

WINE BARS
Noble Rot

If your wallet is a little light but you still want to sip some great wines, Noble Rot is your new best friend. The bottle markup here is only $7 above retail. The selection of flights changes almost nightly—as does the extensive tapas-style menu, which includes items accented by greens grown on the rooftop garden. The 3,000-square-foot garden (which you can tour if you ask) is just one example of The Rot's eco-friendly focus.

POTLAND: CANNABIS IN THE CITY

After Oregon voters approved Measure 91 in 2014, cannabis became legal for nonmedical purposes. It took a bit to work out all the kinks, but in 2015, dispensaries began selling marijuana to recreational users over the age of 21. What followed was a boom of dispensaries; there are currently more pot dispensaries than there are Starbucks in Portland.

RULES AND REGULATIONS

It can be a little confusing to navigate the laws regarding recreational purchase and use, so here are a few tips:

- Bring your ID with you to dispensaries. You'll need to show it to gain entrance and likely again to make a purchase. Dispensaries are required to keep an internal record of that purchase, but that record cannot be used for background checks, nor is it reported anywhere outside of the store.

- Bring cash with you. You'll most often need to make your dispensary purchases in cash. However, most keep an ATM on-site, inside their secured entrances.

- It's prohibited to smoke on-site or in public spaces, which includes bars, restaurants, music clubs, sporting venues, public streets, and parks (although you are still likely to see this occasionally).

- One ounce of cannabis is the legal amount you're allowed to carry on your person in public.

- It's illegal to cross state lines carrying cannabis.

DISPENSARIES

- **Oregon's Finest** (1327 NW Kearny St., 503/239-1150, www.oregons-finest.com; daily 8am-10pm) is a local grower-owned and -operated dispensary that has two locations in Portland (the second is across from the Convention Center). It specializes in small-batch craft cannabis. This is the boutique shopping of weed.

MAP 3: 1111 E. Burnside St., 503/233-1999, www.noblerotpdx.com; Mon.-Thurs. 5pm-10pm, Fri.-Sat. 5pm-11pm, Sun. 5pm-9pm (happy hour Mon.-Fri. 5pm-6pm)

MAP 3: 455 NE 24th Ave., 541/531-7653, www.pairingsportland.com; Mon.-Tues. noon-8pm, Wed.-Sat. noon-10pm, Sun. noon-7pm

Pairings

Wondering what kind of wine pairs with the news of the day? Or perhaps with your outfit? Or what kind of wine goes with Harry Potter? (It's an Oratorie St. Martin "Les Douyes" Cairanne '12, by the way.) Jeff Weissler can tell you. His fun with pairings is what makes the experience at this wine bar so lighthearted and enjoyable. There is no food, but you are encouraged to bring food in with you from one of the nearby food spots like Basilisk or Pie Spot.

BARS AND PUBS
✪ Keys Lounge

This hidden gem on Killingsworth used to be a key store and locksmith. The original building has been overhauled yet maintains much of its charm, exuding a retro, somehow familiar feel, even for first-time visitors. The decor hints at the bar's origin story, from the giant letters spelling out K-E-Y-S atop the roof to the old keys set in resin on the bartop. The cozy space is dimly lit, with a fireplace in one corner, ample seating, and rugs

- **Electric Lettuce** (203 NE Weidler St., 971/983-8357, www.electriclettuce; Mon.-Sat. 10am-9:45pm, Sun. 10am-6:45pm) is hard to miss with its colorful psychedelic exterior. It sells cannabis in all forms, from flower to topical salve, and its website is helpful as it describes its strains using words like "groovy," "mellow," "easy," and "aware."

- **Treehouse Collective** (2419 NE Sandy Blvd., 503/894-8774, www.pdxtreehouse.com; Mon.-Sat. 10am-10pm, Sun. 11am-8pm) has a number of really good live resins (cannabis concentrates), and staff is knowledgeable about storage and use, which is especially helpful for people trying them out for the first time.

- **Farma** (916 SE Hawthorne Blvd., 503/206-4357, www.farmapdx.com; Mon.-Sat. 10am-9.45pm, Sun. 11am-7pm) is designed like a high-end pharmacy and is a great shop for beginners. Staff is super knowledgeable and can walk you through the various strains and products.

- **Shango** (8056 SE Harold St., 503/788-7005, www.goshango.com; daily 10am-10pm) operated as a medical marijuana shop before recreational licensing was in place. It has several cultivation facilities and has partnered with celebrities like Tommy Chong and Kyle Turley to create specific strains, and also makes some of its own edibles, including the very popular CBD and THC gumdrops.

TOURS

- **High Five Tours Multnomah Falls Adventure Tour** (503/303-2275, www.high5tours.com; Fri. 11am, $89) meets at **Jayne** (2145 NE Martin Luther King Jr. Blvd., www.jaynepdx.com), where you can purchase weed products before hopping on the Yellow Pot Bus. This tour visits the Vista House at Columbia River Gorge, Multnomah Falls, Ruby Jewel ice cream shop, and finally, Homegrown Apothecary, where you'll learn all about organic cannabis and receive discounts on products. Snacks and water are included.

- **The Potlandia Experience** (503/409-3975, www.potlandiaexperience.com; Thurs.-Sat. 11am, $75) is an introduction to Portland like you've never seen. The bus stops at dispensaries and microbreweries along the way as it takes passengers to iconic city stops like Voodoo Doughnut. The tour meets at the first venue of the tour, which changes occasionally, but is sent out with confirmation of the tour.

all around. A DJ station plays everything from groovy 1960s French pop and surf guitar to cool lounge, soul, and jazz. The cocktail list emphasizes classic cocktails (try the Damn Vivien), and the food menu boasts fun twists on bar snacks, like gin-soaked olives, pimento croquettes, and Cheat-Charones (vegan soy skin "pork rinds").

MAP 3: 533 NE Killingsworth St., 503/719-7409, www.keyspdx.com; daily 3pm-2am (happy hour daily 3pm-7pm and 11pm-2am)

Billy Ray's Neighborhood Bar

Billy Ray's is as unassuming as it gets. It's the sort of bar you drive by for months and never think twice about, which may be part of its charm, or like that accidentally hot, soft-spoken friend you've had for years who suddenly grows on you. Nothing outside claims it as "Billy Ray's" or announces

craft cocktail at Keys Lounge

that *Playboy* named it one of the top dive bars in America or *Portlandia* filmed an episode there; it is just too cool to make a fuss.

MAP 3: 2216 NE Martin Luther King Jr. Blvd., 503/287-7254; daily noon-2am (happy hour daily 4pm-7pm)

Hale Pele

Hale Pele is a tropical tiki bar that celebrates rum, fruity flavors, and the spectacle of times past. You can find traditional tropical drinks on the menu like the mai tai or the zombie punch, all made with fresh juices, premium spirits, and locally made syrups. Order a Flaming Volcano (which can be ordered for 2-6 people); it arrives with a tower of flame and cinnamon sparks. Small plates on the menu also stick to the Hawaii theme, with offerings like pulled pork sandwiches on Hawaiian bread and a pineapple upside-down cake.

MAP 3: 2733 NE Broadway, 503/662-8454, www.halepele.com; daily noon-2am (happy hour daily 4pm-7pm)

LIVE MUSIC
Wonder Ballroom

Easily one of the top venues for big acts, the Wonder has recently become an active part of the live music scene. The 1914 ballroom, beautifully restored in 2005, now hosts big-name bands, fashion shows, and raucous charity events. There's a fairly spacious dance floor, and the balcony (if open) is a fine place to escape with a drink while you rest your feet. Make sure to check out Bunk Bar downstairs, which has delicious food for around $10-11 and a happy hour daily 3pm-6pm.

MAP 3: 128 NE Russell St., 503/284-8686, www.wonderballroom.com; show nights 5pm-midnight; price varies

COMEDY
Curious Comedy

Curious Comedy is a nonprofit that hosts a number of shows each week. On Thursday nights, Open Court is a sort of improv open mic. The next evening, the popular Curious Comedy Showdown takes the stage for a competitive improv game where only one comic will be victorious. It also hosts several popular late-night events, like Friday Night Fights where improv teams face off against each other. The focus of this comedy stage is to push boundaries and foster community, so it's a great place to discover fresh comics and to find some easygoing improv.

MAP 3: 5225 NE Martin Luther King Jr Blvd., 503/477-9477, www.curiouscomedy. org; showtime varies; price varies

KARAOKE
Spare Room

The book lover in me hopes this bar is named after Lucy's home beyond the wardrobe in the *The Chronicles of Narnia*, but even if it isn't, it has a magical sort of quality about it. Karaoke happens Monday-Wednesday, and if you are lucky, you can catch Karaoke From Hell, providing a live band backup instead of canned tunes (don't worry, they still give you the lyrics). Adding to the charm, you can order a "Mystery Shot" for only $2.50. A dice roll decides what you get. Spoiler: It's not always pretty.

MAP 3: 4830 NE 42nd Ave., 503/287-5800, www.thespareroompdx.com; daily 7am-2:30am (happy hour daily 3pm-6pm); free karaoke, show prices vary

BREWPUBS AND TAPHOUSES

✪ Base Camp Brewing

Base Camp Brewing is a favorite among backpackers and adventurous sorts—not only because it happens to package beer in backpack-friendly aluminum bottles, but also because the beer inside them is exceptional. Try the S'more Stout. It's served with a toasted marshmallow. The inside of the brewpub very much resembles a ski chalet with high, beamed ceilings, but the outdoor area is the place to be no matter the weather, with its huge tented seating area, large tables at which to gather, and food trucks from which to grab a burrito or something else tasty to go with your brew.

MAP 4: 930 SE Oak St., 503/477-7479, www.basecampbrewingco.com; Sun.-Thurs. noon-10pm, Fri.-Sat. 11am-midnight (happy hour Mon. noon-10pm, Tues.-Fri. 3pm-6pm)

✪ Horse Brass Pub

Named one of the best bars in America by *Esquire*, this is a public house in the true sense of the term. The sprawling interior is welcoming and warm with wood paneling and decor that belie its Pacific Northwest location. Inside it's easy to believe you've hopped the pond. There are more than 50 beers on tap (and some of the best from around the world, at that), but the menu really hollers for a good nip of Scotch to wash down the delicious fish-and-chips or Scotch eggs. With brewpubs popping

Hopworks Urban Brewery

SOUTHEAST

up all over, Horse Brass is still the best spot to toss a few darts or sip an IPA. **MAP 4:** 4534 SE Belmont St., 503/232-2022, www.horsebrass.com; daily 11am-2:30am

Hopworks Urban Brewery

Portland's first eco-brewpub, Hopworks Urban Brewery (HUB) makes organic brews from locally grown ingredients on-site in its sustainability-focused facility. This is where the beer snobs of Portland debate the use of adjuncts (like raspberry, peach, or chocolate) in the brewing process. Try the boozy Hopworks float made with vanilla ice cream and the signature Organic Survival "Seven Grain" Stout. **MAP 4:** 2944 SE Powell Blvd., 503/232-4677, www.hopworksbeer.com; Sun.-Thurs. 11am-11pm, Fri.-Sat. 11am-midnight (happy hour Mon.-Fri. 3pm-6pm and 9pm-close, Sat.-Sun. 9pm-close)

Lucky Labrador Brew Pub

There are few things Portlanders love more than their beer and their dogs—and at Lucky Lab, you can sip a pint with your pup at your side. Absolutely unpretentious and packed with some of the most laid-back native Portlanders, it's a great place to linger on the patio, munch on hand-tossed barley flour pizza, and enjoy a glass of Stumptown Porter. **MAP 4:** 915 SE Hawthorne Blvd., 503/236-3555, www.luckylab.com; Mon.-Wed. 11am-11pm, Thurs.-Sat. 11am-midnight, Sun. noon-10pm

COCKTAIL LOUNGES

✪ Slow Bar

This bar is sexy—like it was built for secret meetings and intimate affairs. Dim, slightly reddish lighting, high-backed curved booths, and cozy corners only add to the ambience. Just sip on your Dark and Stormy in secluded comfort and hide from the world. When you get hungry, order a Slowburger, a consistent winner of the "who has the best burger in Portland" argument and that has even spawned a mini-restaurant. **MAP 4:** 533 SE Grand Ave., 503/230-7767, www.slowbar.net; daily 11:30am-2:30am (happy hour Sun.-Thurs. 3pm-6pm and midnight-2:30am, Fri. 3pm-6pm)

Night Light Lounge

At the edge of the Clinton Street neighborhood favored by the DIY youth culture sits an outpost for Portland's artistic scene. Writers, musicians, artists, and the like flock to the Night Light, crowd into the dark booths or huddle on the couches, and sip on PBRs while engaging in the (only partially) accidental task of seeing and being seen. The Night Light makes great cocktails, and the food menu is both elegant and affordable. It's all very upscale, but in a laid-back atmosphere with prices that do not offend. **MAP 4:** 2100 SE Clinton St., 503/731-6500, www.nightlightlounge.net; Mon.-Fri. 2pm-2:30am, Sat.-Sun. 10am-2:30am (happy hour Sun.-Thurs. 3pm-7pm and 11pm-1am, Fri.-Sat. 3pm-7pm)

Furry friends are welcome at the Lucky Labrador

BOTTLE SHOPS IN BEERVANA

The grocery store beer aisle can be a challenging place in a city full of so many options. Will you prefer something hoppy or fruity? Do you even like sour ales? Fortunately, Portland is equipped with a number of bottle shops where you can talk to the experts, sample some brews, and narrow down your choices to a few great options. They're also often great, low-key spots at which to drink beer among other craft brew lovers.

- **The Beermongers** (1125 SE Division St., 503/234-6012, www.thebeermongers.com; Mon.-Thurs. 11am-11pm, Fri.-Sat. 11am-midnight, Sun. 11am-11pm) has more than 600 bottles from which to choose, as well as some taps so you can just order a pint and hang out in the spacious shop, which has a few tables and a small bar.

- **Imperial Bottle Shop** (3090 SE Division St., 971/302-6899, www.imperialbottleshop.com; Mon.-Thurs. noon-10pm, Fri.-Sat. noon-midnight, Sun. noon-10pm) has a diverse selection of drafts and bottles that can be consumed on the premises or taken home. Almost 20 taps are here, with everything from stout to cider with which to fill your growler. No worries if the bottle you choose is not cold; a cooler here will chill it in mere seconds.

- **Belmont Station** (4500 SE Stark St., 503/232-8538, www.belmont-station.com; bottle shop Mon.-Fri. 10am-10pm, Sun. 11am-9pm; Beircafé Mon.-Fri. noon-11pm, Sat. 11am-11pm, Sun. 11am-10pm) has long been a destination for beer lovers, with almost 1,400 beers to choose from at the bottle shop (which you can consume on the premises or take to go) as well as a number of taps for tasting and growler filling on the café side.

- **Saraveza** (1004 N. Killingsworth St., 503/206-4252, www.saraveza.com; daily 11am-midnight) features vintage 1940s beer coolers; owner Sarah Pederson found them at an old marketplace and transformed them into the focal point of her north Portland bottle shop. Those coolers contain a curated collection of local favorites, rare finds, one-offs, and vintage beers. She also offers in-house pours of 5-16 ounces and mason jars or growlers to go.

- **John's Marketplace** (3535 SW Multnomah Blvd., 503/244-2617, www.johnsmarketplace.com; Sun.-Thurs. 9am-9pm, Fri.-Sat. 9am-10pm) is one of the largest beer markets in the city and also offers $5 draft pours and $10 flights, as well as sizable burgers for less than $5.

Rum Club

Where do the practiced Portland bartenders go to get a drink when they are not working? The Rum Club has one of the most extensive collections of rum in the city and also makes many of its syrups, tonics, and bitters in-house. Everything in here, from the cocktail menu to the decor, is a nod to Ernest Hemingway (whether intentional or not)—a perfect balance of rugged and romantic. Try the daiquiri. No, really. It will forever ruin you for all other daiquiris.

MAP 4: 720 SE Sandy Blvd., 503/265-8807, www.rumclubpdx.com; daily 4pm-2am (happy hour daily 4pm-6pm)

Sapphire Hotel

There's something about the soft, red ambience of The Sapphire that makes everyone feel a bit more romantic and beautiful. The space was once the lobby of a rather questionable hotel. These days, the hotel is gone, but the lobby continues to be a gathering place. The cocktail menu is full of tongue-in-cheek references to the bar's sordid past, like Going Up?, made with serrano pepper-infused tequila muddled with cilantro, lime juice, and sweet and sour.

MAP 4: 5008 SE Hawthorne Blvd.,
503/232-6333, www.thesapphirehotel.com;
Mon.-Sat. 4pm-2am, Sun. 4pm-midnight
(happy hour Sun.-Thurs. 4pm-6pm and
10pm-close, Fri.-Sat. 4pm-6pm)

Victory Bar

If you're not that familiar with Belgian beer, the options here can be a bit intimidating. Still, *Imbibe* magazine rated Victory as one of the best places in the United States to have a beer. That is reason enough to go, but the dark, cozy, ambient environment helps—as does the impressive cocktail list, with such classics as the corpse reviver, old-fashioned, and French 77. The bar is not shy about saying that it's a "bartender's bar," and it has a following of industry leaders to prove it.

MAP 4: 3652 SE Division St.,
503/236-8975, www.thevictorybar.com;
Mon.-Sat. 5pm-1am, Sun. 5pm-midnight
(happy hour Mon. 6pm-close, Tues.-Fri.
6pm-7pm)

BARS AND PUBS
Creepy's

Creepy's is, in fact, a delightfully creepy bar, but not in a horror-film kind of way—more in a carnival fashion, but as described by Ray Bradbury. It's a pretty fun place for a bar covered in clowns, but be sure to keep your eye on that painting behind the bar, because it is definitely watching you. The menu includes a seriously killer spicy fried chicken sandwich and a rotating collection of other fried things like zucchini, pickles, and hushpuppies. The game room in the back has both pinball and pool, as well as a photo booth in case you need to document your creepy stay.

MAP 4: 627 SE Morrison St., 503/889-0185,
http://creepys.business.site; daily
3pm-2:30am

Creepy's

Dots Cafe

The Clinton Street district (all six blocks of it) has so much charm. Much of this comes from the high concentration of youthful artists frequenting the bars along this stretch. Dots serves cocktails, wine, and beer, but its cozy, kitschy diner atmosphere—except it has velvet wallpaper, you're more likely to hear Radiohead than Chubby Checker blasting through the sound system, and you can't help but wonder if someone forgot to turn on the lights—and food menu make it a prime destination for those who want some post-drinking eats before committing themselves to bed. While the food here is great—featuring favorites like chili cheese fries, burgers, and tuna melts, as well as vegetarian options like falafel wraps and vegan burritos—and the drinks (especially the lime rickey) are delightful, the real star is the late-night people-watching.

MAP 4: 2521 SE Clinton St., 503/235-0203;
daily 2pm-2:30am (happy hour Mon.-Fri.
2pm-7pm and 11pm-1am)

EastBurn

When it comes to hangout spots for Portlanders, EastBurn is at the top of the list. Is it the skee-ball? The year-round closed-in patio with mosaic fire tables, outdoor heaters, and chair swings? The fact that its happy

BEST LATE-NIGHT EATS

Doug Fir

After a night of drinking, dancing, or rocking out in the city, you can sate your food cravings at these late-night spots:

- **Lúc Lác:** With steaming bowls of pho and bahn mi sandwiches, this is a great spot for comfort food with a chill downtown lounge vibe. It stays open until 4am on weekends (page 48).

- **The Roxy:** Generations of young Portlanders cut their "going out" teeth by hanging out at this 24-hour diner, digging into huge breakfast plates and tasty burgers (page 51).

- **Cartopia:** When no one in your group can make a decision about what to eat, the Cartopia food cart pod is the solution, offering pizza, fries, sweets, sandwiches, and more all in one easy, outdoor (covered and heated) spot, with some carts open until 3am on weekends (page 76).

- **Le Bistro Montage:** Montage was for decades one of only a couple of places in Portland to get food after the bars closed (open until 4am on weekends), and the restaurant's still going strong with to-die-for mac and cheese and Southern comfort food (page 78).

- **Dots Cafe:** If late-night food for you means burgers, nachos, and smothered fries, this bar is the place for you, especially if you have both vegans and meat eaters in your group (page 108).

- **Reel 'M Inn:** It may not look like much, but this dive bar has some of the best fried chicken and potatoes in town. It takes awhile to make, but it is well worth the wait (page 110).

- **Doug Fir:** This live music venue is also a boisterous gathering place for refueling; the menu practically shouts its offerings at you: Fir Burger! Oysters! Corn "Dougs" (page 111)!

hour is called "recess"? It's probably all that, plus the great selection of locally produced beer and wine as well as a menu with favorites such as the Grover's Mackin' Cheese. EastBurn's laid-back, sports-bar style makes it a great place to watch a game or catch a drink and some great conversation.

MAP 4: 1800 E. Burnside St., 503/236-2876, www.theeastburn.com; Mon.-Fri. 11am-2am, Sat.-Sun. 10am-2am (happy hour Sun.-Thurs. 3pm-5pm and 10pm-midnight, Fri.-Sat. 3pm-5pm)

Elvis Room

Where would Elvis go if he were alive and visiting Portland? Ever since the 24 Hour Church of Elvis—an Elvis-themed storefront that offered weird wedding services and tchotchkes—closed back in the 1990s, we haven't had a clear answer. Thankfully, the folks responsible for revamping classic, kitschy bars like The Alibi have brought us the Elvis Room. This opulent two-floor bar features Elvis-themed decor, signature champagne cocktails, and a build-your-own burger menu worthy of the King of Rock and Roll. The upstairs feels like on-stage Elvis: bright, over-the-top, and a bit brazen. Downstairs, however, is like Elvis in his darker years: brooding, contemplative, and hidden away with a peanut butter burger in his hand.

MAP 4: 203 SE Grand Ave., 503/235-5690; daily 4pm-2:30am

Reel 'M Inn

This Clinton-area dive bar has cheap stiff drinks, brassy bartenders, and a constant stream of regulars along with free pool, an online jukebox, and poker machines. So what sets this dive apart? It has the best fried chicken in town, that's what. It goes through about 800 pounds of chicken each week. It's simple, cheap, and served with enormous jojo potatoes and a six-pack of dipping sauces.

MAP 4: 2430 SE Division St., 503/231-3880; Mon.-Sat. 10am-2:30am, Sun. 10am-1am

ARCADE BARS
Quarterworld

Quarterworld is a huge retro arcade that sits right in the middle of the "Barmuda Triangle" of southeast Hawthorne, where a collection of bars converge. It has more than 30 different pinball machines and more than 60 classic and new arcade games to play. Games take quarters, dollar bills, and credit cards via a mobile app, so it's easy to drop some serious dough trying to beat that high score. Fortunately, there is a full bar and cheap things to eat like corn dog bites, pizza, and deep-fried Twinkies.

MAP 4: 4811 SE Hawthorne Blvd., 503/548-2923, www.quarterworldarcade. com; Tues.-Fri. 3pm-1am, Sat.-Sun. noon-1am (happy hour Tues.-Sun. 3pm-6pm); free

GAY AND LESBIAN
Crush Bar

A favorite queer-friendly bar, Crush also happens to be a favorite hangout for performers, bartenders, and servers. There are burlesque shows several times a month, movie nights, and DJ dance parties. It even hosts a monthly Dr. Sketchy's event where models pose in various themed costumes (and occasionally states of undress) for life drawing. The vibe here is welcoming to all. It even implemented one of the city's first all-gender bathrooms; only the stalls are private.

MAP 4: 1400 SE Morrison St., 503/235-8150, www.crushbar.com; Mon.-Fri. noon-2am, Sat. 11am-2am, Sun. 11am-midnight (happy hour Mon. 3pm-midnight, Tues.-Sun. 3pm-7pm); free most nights, show prices vary

LIVE MUSIC
Aladdin Theater

Since its days as a vaudeville house, the Aladdin has hosted some of the greatest performers of our time, particularly for blues, jazz, bluegrass, soul, and pop. The 600-plus-seat house lends intimacy to the experience, whether it's a quiet sit-down show, a screaming punk show, or the occasional music festival. Arrive early and grab some food and a pint at The Lamp (get it?) next door if you have your tickets already. When it comes time for entry, you can get a wristband to jump the line, which often snakes around the block.

MAP 4: 3017 SE Milwaukie Ave., 503/234-9694, www.aladdin-theater.com; box office Mon.-Sat. 11am-6pm; price varies

Doug Fir

Doug Fir is a popular music venue, housed in the basement of the Jupiter Hotel. It often programs indie acts in its intimate, primarily standing-room space, and has great acoustics. A plucked-from-the-1950s bar-diner above the space makes a great late-night hangout spot even if you're not there for a show, attracting a fascinating collection of nocturnals with its menu that spans from gut-busting breakfasts to the cheeky Fir Burger. Guests often spill onto the patio, where there are outdoor firepits and smoking lounges. The party at Doug Fir has been known to rage on late.

MAP 4: 830 E. Burnside St., 503/231-9663, www.dougfirlounge. com; bar-diner daily 7am-2:30am (happy hour Sun.-Thurs. 3pm-6pm and 10pm-midnight, Fri.-Sat. 3pm-6pm), showtime varies, price varies

Revolution Hall

Revolution Hall is a state-of-the-art performing arts center based in the historic former Washington High School, which closed in 1981. The school's old auditorium is now an 850-seat venue that hosts big musical acts and indie bands. It's also the Portland home of sex columnist Dan Savage's HUMP! Film Fest, which showcases amateur porn (think sex-positive shorts) made by regular people and celebrating the sexual spectrum, from gay and lesbian to hetero, mono to poly, vanilla to kink, funny to sexy. Revolution Hall also has two on-site bars, including a gorgeous rooftop bar with views over the city skyline and beyond.

MAP 4: 1300 SE Stark St., 503/288-3895, www.revolutionhallpdx.com; price varies

DANCE CLUBS
The Goodfoot

The Goodfoot is like the Odd Couple subletting a bar together. Upstairs, there's the tidy and bright Felix with his art and carefully arranged pool tables; in the basement is Oscar, with his windowless, squat space filled with duct-taped benches and odd-tiled floors. Surprisingly, both atmospheres are ideal for their purpose. The music downstairs is some of the best and least predictable in town, particularly the Soul Stew spins on Friday nights with DJ Aquaman.

MAP 4: 2845 SE Stark St., 503/239-9292, www.thegoodfoot.com; daily 4pm-2:30am (happy hour daily 5pm-8pm); free upstairs, $1-15 downstairs

Holocene

Holocene has a stark industrial feel, and while it seems spacious at the outset, the open spaces fill up quickly some nights. The club plays

SEX-POSITIVE STRIP CLUBS

In other cities, strip clubs are treated as something to be whispered about. But Portland is unabashed and unapologetic, is in fact proud of its strip clubs, whose proliferace is a sign of the city's progressive, sex-positive culture. Portland has more strip clubs per capita than anywhere else in the world (including Las Vegas)—or at least it did until the tiny town of Springfield, Oregon, opened its seventh club—knocking Portland off the top seat. Thanks to a liberal free-speech clause in the state constitution and several rulings by the state supreme court, Oregon strip clubs and other sex-oriented businesses are practically untouchable.

Several factors play into the city's unique strip club scene. Many of the most popular clubs embrace the Portland ideal of self-expression and individuality. Dancers are not likely to look like models out of gentlemen's magazines, instead often sporting natural breasts, tattoos, and piercings, and maybe wearing tube socks instead of fishnets. You'll also see dancers in a vast array of sizes, styles, ages, shapes, and gender-embodiments. And this inclusivity extends to the audience as well. On any given night at some clubs, the clientele is likely to be split pretty evenly between men and women, scattered through all age brackets from 21-70, and comprising singles, couples, and groups of friends. There's also often no cover charge to get into strip clubs in the city. And in addition to featuring nude entertainment with wildly athletic individuals, top spots often feature extensive tap lists as well as delicious and affordable food. Portland allows nude performers within a full bar environment, unlike some locales that only allow topless performances where alcohol is served.

Follow a few rules of thumb if you decide to check out a strip club while in town, and you'll be fine: 1) Note that tipping the dancers at least $1 per dance is customary, and if you're sitting at the rack (the seats at the edge of the stage behind the railing), it's required. 2) Absolutely no touching is allowed. Dancers may touch you if you're at the rack, but be respectful and keep your hands to yourself. 3) Cell phone use is not allowed in performance areas. If you are seen using a phone or, god forbid, taking photos, you will be kicked out immediately.

Here are some of the best strip clubs in town:

some great music here, with some of the city's most fashionable DJs spinning every week. One popular event is Double Down, a hot and sweaty queer-friendly dance party the last Saturday of each month. Holocene gets big props for the sunken projection-lit dance floor, which looks like a living room in the midst of a gritty industrialized loft.

MAP 4: 1001 SE Morrison St., 503/239-7639, www.holocene.org; Wed.-Thurs. and Sat. 8:30pm-2:30am, Fri. 5pm-2:30am, open select Sun.-Tues. for shows; price varies

Lovecraft Bar

This horror-themed goth bar named for the granddaddy of the genre, H. P. Lovecraft, is creepy, but in the cutest way possible. Black lights

illuminate animal skulls and random bones on walls and shelves. Painted tentacles adorn the walls. Near the bathrooms is a shrine of old movie posters and dead horror legends. The Gate of the Necronomicon is painted on the ceiling. This is the place to catch some great industrial, goth, and metal nights, as well as belly dancing, burlesque, art classes, and movie nights.

MAP 4: 421 NE Grand Ave., 971/270-7760, www.thelovecraftbar. com; Sun.-Thurs. 8pm-2:15am, Fri.-Sat. 4pm-2:15am; free-$6

COMEDY
Helium Comedy

Helium Comedy hosts a number of big headliners and fun comedy events. It also has one of the most popular

- **Mary's Club** (129 SW Broadway, 503/227-3023, www.marysclub.com; Mon.-Sat. 11am-2:30am, Sun. 11:30am-2:30am) is Portland's oldest strip club, open since 1954. It's laid-back and a little lazy. Dancers choose their own songs from the jukebox before beginning their number. Courtney Love famously stripped here in the 1980s.

- **Sassy's** (927 SE Morrison St., 503/231-1606, www.sassysbar.com; daily 10:30am-2:30am) is arguably one of the most popular clubs in town, with an impressive tap list featuring 24 microbrews. It also has a happy hour (daily 3pm-8pm) to rival most regular bars, with $2.50 beers and $5 food items, but with the added benefit of some of the—yes, I'll say it—sassiest dancers in town.

- **Devil's Point** (5305 SE Foster Rd., 503/774-4513, www.devilspointbar.com; daily 11:30am-2:30am), a tiny rock and roll strip club, features staff and dancers who look like they stepped out of a Suicide Girls photoshoot. This is the home of the popular weekly **Stripparaoke** (Sun. 9pm), where you pick your song and sing as the dancer strips around you. It gets crowded, so arrive early.

- **The Acropolis** (8235 SE McLoughlin Blvd., 503/231-9611, www.acropolispdx.com; Mon.-Sat. 7am-2:30am, Sun. 11am-2am) is an icon in Portland for two reasons: First, it hires a lot of very talented dancers, and, second, it serves really cheap ($4-10) and truly delicious steaks—the owner has a cattle ranch. Seriously. Brunch is also really good, and 65 beers and two wines are on tap.

- **Casa Diablo** (www.casadiablo.com) has two locations, the original (2839 NW St. Helens Rd., 503/222-6610; daily 2pm-2:30am) and the sequel (8445 SE McLoughlin Blvd., 503/222-6610; daily 2pm-2:30am), which is located right next to The Acropolis. They are 100 percent vegan strip clubs, from the dancers to the food on the menu. Their motto is "Vixens not veal," and they mean it. Dancers are also prohibited from wearing any fur, feathers, leather, or wool when they perform.

open mic comedy nights in town on Tuesday, when a number of comedians are allowed 3-7 minutes on the mic. Admission for the open mic is free with a two-item purchase, and you can order food or beverages. Stick with the well drinks if you decide to get a cocktail. The specialty cocktails get pretty pricey. **MAP 4:** 1510 SE 9th Ave., 503/477-9477, www.heliumcomedy.com; Tues.-Thurs. 5pm-11pm, Fri.-Sat. 5pm-2am; free-$27

BREWPUBS AND TAPHOUSES

Oaks Bottom Public House

This addition to the Lompoc family was named for the Oaks Bottom Wildlife Refuge, just west of the pub. It's everything a neighborhood pub is supposed to be: cozy, welcoming, and blessed with good beer. The expected Lompoc brews are available, but you can also find some very unique guest beers on tap. Regular patrons sing the praises of the limited but pleasing menu, which includes "totchos," an unholy mash-up of tater tots and nachos.

MAP 5: 1621 SE Bybee Blvd., 503/232-1728, www.newoldlompoc. com; Mon.-Sat. 11am-midnight, Sun. 11am-10pm (happy hour daily 3pm-6pm and 9pm-close)

WINE BARS

Corkscrew

It's a little like drinking inside a wine barrel, what with all the reclaimed wood and vaulted ceilings, but Corkscrew is cozy. The wines rotate regularly, and there are small-plate options to accompany your vintage, like artisan cheese, charcuterie, and bread with olive oil. The bottles are organized by flavor profiles, and bartenders are happy to suggest pairings or flights. Patrons frequently wander in while waiting for a table at nearby Saburo's, and are often treated to live music or open mic entertainment.

MAP 5: 1665 SE Bybee Blvd., 503/239-9463; Sun.-Thurs. 4pm-10pm, Fri.-Sat. 4pm-midnight (happy hour Mon.-Thurs. 4pm-6pm)

LIVE MUSIC

Muddy Rudder

This neighborhood pub in a converted home has cozy, rustic decor and a laid-back homey feel. It has a full bar, beer, and live music gravitating toward bluegrass, blues, acoustic, and Irish. The pizzas are homemade with local organic flour and produce. It's not large, and finding a place to see when music is playing can be difficult, but if you just want to listen, you can hear just fine. A dog-friendly patio is out back.

MAP 5: 8105 SE 7th Ave., 503/233-4410; Mon.-Wed. 4pm-10:30pm, Thurs. 4pm-11:30pm, Fri.-Sat. noon-11:30pm, Sun. noon-10:30pm (happy hour daily 4pm-6pm)

BREWPUBS AND TAPHOUSES

5th Quadrant

The 5th Quadrant is part of the Lompoc family of brewpubs, favored by locals who appreciate fine, locally made beer. Sip on a glass of LSD (Lompoc Strong Draught) or sink into a hoppy C-Note Imperial Pale. If you don't know what you'd like, the servers here are more than happy to direct you. The brewpub has a heated, dog-friendly patio, which is helpful when it's happy hour and things get a little crowded. In addition to happy hour, there's Tightwad Tuesdays, when pints go for $3.

MAP 6: 3901 N. Williams Ave., 503/228-3996, www.newoldlompoc. com; Mon.-Fri. 11am-midnight, Sat. 10am-midnight, Sun. 10am-11pm (happy hour daily 3pm-6pm and 10pm-close)

Prost!

This German-themed pub anchors the north end of Mississippi Avenue, serving European ales in traditional glassware. Belgian ales get a tulip, scotch ales get the thistle, wheat beers get the skinny-on-the-bottom, wide-on-top Weizen glass. And then there is The Boot, a two-liter beer served in a shaped glass and meant to be shared and passed without letting it touch the table. Prost has a sizable beer garden with outdoor heaters and access to a pod of food carts. It also has a full kitchen with traditional German wares.

MAP 6: 4237 N. Mississippi Ave., 503/954-2674, www.prostportland, com; Mon.-Fri. 11:30am-2:30am, Sat.-Sun. 11am-2:30am

Widmer Brothers Brewery

Widmer Brothers Brewery is probably the most widely recognizable Pacific Northwest brewer, thanks to its wildly successful Hefeweizen. Operating since 1984 and now partly owned by Anheuser-Busch, its other notable beers include the Drop Top Amber Ale and Broken Halo IPA. In 2017, Widmer dramatically revamped its brewpub, doing away with its full-service menu entirely so the focus would be on the taproom. So, although you will no longer find steaming bowls of goulash, you will find far greater care being given to the presentation of the brewery's beers.

MAP 6: 929 N. Russell St., 503/281-2437, www.widmer.com; Mon.-Fri. 3pm-10pm, Sat.-Sun. noon-10pm (happy hour Mon.-Tues. and Thurs.-Fri. 2pm-5pm, Wed. 3pm-10pm)

COCKTAIL LOUNGES

Box Social

Box Social is a self-proclaimed "cocktail parlor," and while that may seem a bit self-serving, it's pretty accurate. Everything here is made to order with precision and care. Ice is hand crushed, fresh citrus is squeezed, and "smoked" cocktails require matches. The atmosphere is dark and romantic, and the service is attentive, but not fussy. Try the Beatnik, made with bourbon, Amaro CioCiaro (a bitter orange digestif), tawny port, and burnt lemon peel.

MAP 6: 3971 N. Williams St., 503/288-1111, www.bxsocial.com; Sun.-Wed. 4pm-1am, Thurs.-Sat. 4pm-2am (happy hour Sun.-Thurs. 4pm-6pm and 11pm-close, Fri.-Sat. 4pm-6pm)

DON'T JUST DRINK, DO SOMETHING

Drinking can be fun. Especially with all the great beer, wine, and craft cocktails to be found in this fair city. But Portlanders don't tend to sit still for very long, so it makes sense that there would be a number of events catering to the idea of drinking and doing something a little bit different.

Kennedy School

If you fancy yourself a history buff, check out **History Pub Mondays** (www. mcmenamins.com) at the McMenamins' Kennedy School. You can enjoy a pint of McMenamins ale or sip a glass of wine while listening to exciting presentations about local and regional history from the Oregon Historical Society and the Holy Names Heritage Society.

Got a nose for science instead? You can check out **Science Pub** (www.omsi. edu), a twice monthly lecture (with booze!) about such subjects as engineering, earth science, volcanology, forensics, and nano-technology. The lectures are held at places like the historic Hollywood Theatre or Mission Theater, both of which offer local beers, ciders, wine, and pizza. There is also **Science on Tap** (www.viaproductions.org) at the Clinton Street Theater, which offers a laid-back but informative lecture once a month.

You can also explore the Oregon Museum of Science and Industry without the crowds of small children at the popular **OMSI After Dark** (www.omsi.edu). You can taste the difference between grain and potato alcohol, try on some "beer goggles" that simulate different levels of impairment, or test your stability in the earthquake simulation house.

Artistic types can engage their muse at **Dr. Sketchy's Anti-Art School** (www. drsketchy.com), which meets on the last Sunday of every month at Crush Bar. Themes come in all shapes and sizes with a focus on dynamic characters like pirates, burlesque stars, comic book heroes, and H.P. Lovecraft creations. Costumed models pose for small and long stretches of time, and artists can sketch, share their work with other artists, or simply draw in silence.

At **Bottle and Bottega** (1406 SW Broadway St., 971/205-5070, www. bottleandbottega.com), you can learn how to paint while imbibing some wine or beer. The studio offers reasonably priced classes every day that include materials, instruction, and a take-home canvas of your very own work. It features Tap It Tuesdays (with specials on beer), Wine Down Wednesdays (with wine specials), Thirsty Thursdays, and the Mimosa Mornings class, which offers daytime weekend lessons complete with bubbly. Or try your hand at some arts and crafts at **DIY Bar** (3522 N. Vancouver St., www.diybar.co), where the "craft-tenders" not only serve you booze but walk you through a DIY project that includes all the materials you might need. Learn how to make a wallet, leather beer koozie, or succulent pot, and then take home the fruits of your labor.

Finally, if you are looking for a team-building activity, there are a number of bars that offer weekly pub trivia, a very popular activity for locals. The Wednesday night **Quizis-sippi** (www.mississippipizza.com/geeks) at Mississippi Pizza is frequently voted most popular, as is **Geeks Who Drink** (www.geekswhodrink.com), a rotating group that holds trivia events at multiple places around the city on various nights.

No Bones Beach Club

No Bones is one of those bars that is so good, you might never notice it's vegan. It's the second vegan tiki bar in the world and garnering a lot of attention from vegans and carnivores alike. The bar has nachos, pineapple radish wontons, avocado tacos, and amazing jackfruit flautas. What's more, the cocktail menu offers interesting twists on some classic tiki drinks, like the coconut mojito and beet hibiscus margarita. Try the shark shot if you're feeling adventurous; it's a shot served in the mouth of a plastic shark atop a bed of "bloody" crushed ice. The environment at No Bones is dark and a bit loud, but the tiki vibe is nice and not too over the top, making it a good casual place to meet with friends.

MAP 6: 3928 N. Mississippi Ave., www. nobonespdx.com; Tues.-Thurs. 4pm-10pm, Fri.-Sat. 11am-11pm, Sun. 11am-10pm (happy hour daily 4pm-6pm)

The Old Gold

The Old Gold is a whiskey and bourbon bar—just the sort of watering hole North Portland needed. This bustling bar lives somewhere between cozy neighborhood dive and cocktail lounge. On the wall hangs a handmade wooden sign that's a nod to the famous White Stag sign over downtown and reads "Drink in Oregon." Check the board for the rotating booze selections as well as the ever-changing local taps. If you are feeling really fancy, you can push the "Champagne Button" and your server will appear with champagne. No, really.

MAP 6: 2105 N. Killingsworth St., 503/894-8937, www.theoldgoldpdx.com; Mon.-Tues. 4pm-midnight, Wed.-Thurs. 4pm-1am, Fri.-Sat. 4pm-2am, Sun. noon-midnight (happy hour Mon.-Fri. 4pm-7pm)

LIVE MUSIC
Mississippi Pizza

Mississippi Pizza and the siren-themed Atlantis Lounge in the back is a popular spot any night of the week. Tuesday is for the popular Baby Ketten Karaoke, and Wednesday crowds pack in for the Quizissippi pub trivia. The rest of the week features live music of all walks, from a Romanian and Balkan band to Zydeco or a comedy folk band. On the weekends, there's often live music for little ones and occasionally even a pub trivia geared just toward the 12-and-under set.

MAP 6: 3552 N. Mississippi Ave., 503/288-3231, www.mississippipizza. com; Mon., Wed.-Thurs., and Sun. 11am-midnight, Tues. and Sat. 11am-1am (happy hour Sun.-Wed. 3pm-5pm and 10pm-close, Thurs.-Sat. 3pm-5pm), free most nights

Mississippi Studios

This former Baptist church turned music venue is in the heart of the artistic Mississippi Avenue neighborhood. The intimate venue is known for having great acoustics and offering up nearly 500 local, regional, national, and international acts each year. All shows are general admission (cash only), and if the on-site bar is too crowded, your ticket allows you access to Bar Bar, the attached bar with two large outdoor patios and a garden in the back. Seating is limited to the balcony and is first-come, first-served, but still quite close to the stage. In summer months, watch for the "Summer Sessions" series— free concerts by local artists on the outdoor patio.

MAP 6: 3939 N. Mississippi Ave., 503/288-3895, www.mississippistudios. com; daily 11am-2am (happy hour daily 4pm-6pm); free-$20

KARAOKE
The Alibi

Comfortable as an old sweater—complete with holes—and as friendly and helpful as a Smurf, The Alibi tops many a local's list for after-work drinks, happy hour, and karaoke. It's a bit kitschy, but maybe that's why we like it. After a full day, what we need is a drink—and $2.50 chicken strips—served up with a "Hey, how are ya?" There is the added charm of feeling like you're drinking in the Tiki Room at Disneyland.

MAP 6: 4024 N. Interstate Ave., 503/287-5335; daily 11:30am-2:30am (happy hour Mon.-Sat. 2pm-7pm, Sun. 11:30am-2:30am); free

ARTS AND CULTURE

Portland is a creative city. It thrives because it seeks to welcome all ideas and desires. Where else can you find such a celebration of self-expression?

Oregon Ballet Theatre

Maybe that's why so many artists, writers, and performers flock here. In this town, there is an assumed license to reinvent, redefine, or completely obliterate the boundaries of normalcy. One of the most compelling things about Portland's arts scene is the expectation that whatever you are is exactly what you should be, so long as it brings you inspiration and pleasure. Portlanders want to do it all, and if "it" doesn't exist yet, "it" is created. It's terribly comforting and exhilarating all at the same time.

Portland also has the best of both worlds. You can spend an afternoon in the art museum looking at Van Gogh and Monet or hit the galleries on Last Thursday and meet an artist who makes encaustic art. Attend a gay pride festival, plunder with pirates, and ride your bike naked through the streets. See classic symphony or ballet shows, or catch performances by local and international emerging artists.

You might think the weather would be prohibitive. Sure, it rains a lot, but the locals take it in stride. It's the price one pays to live in such a lush state. But look around and you'll see that maybe those months spent bundled up and indoors are worth it in other ways—they give us all the more time to work on that painting, develop that performance, or write that novel.

HIGHLIGHTS

a production of *Astoria: Part Two*, produced by Portland Center Stage for the Fertile Ground Festival

✪ **BEST PLACE TO FIND ART WITH A STORY:** At **Sequential Art Gallery + Studio** you can explore the amazing life of comic book art (page 124).

✪ **BEST THEATER PERFORMANCE:** Portland's biggest theater company, **Portland Center Stage** balances its season between daring new works and classic plays (page 125).

✪ **MOST UNIQUE THEATER:** Housed in an old church, **Portland Playhouse** puts on surprising and thoughtful plays (page 128).

✪ **BEST PLACE TO FALL IN LOVE WITH SCIENCE:** Where else but the **Oregon Museum of Science and Industry** can you experience an earthquake, visit the Milky Way, climb aboard a submarine, and trip out in the Omnimax theater (page 130)?

✪ **BEST PLACE TO SEE A FIRST-RUN MOVIE IN STYLE:** The Colonial Revival architecture of the **Bagdad Theater & Pub** makes it a grand space in which to catch a film (page 131).

✪ **BEST WAY TO EXPERIENCE A BLEND OF NEW AND OLD:** **Portland Cello Project** performs the music of artists not normally associated with the cello—like Kanye West or Britney Spears—adding a vibrant old-world twist (page 133).

✪ **BEST CELEBRATION OF BIKE CULTURE:** Portland's DIY spirit and love of bicycling come together for free, themed, volunteer-led rides around the city during **Pedalpalooza** (page 137).

✪ **BEST FEST TO SIP ON PACIFIC NORTHWEST BREWS:** If you love craft beer, don't miss the **Oregon Brewers Festival,** where you can sample craft beers as well as ciders from over 80 brewers (page 139).

MUSEUMS

Oregon Historical Society

The Oregon Historical Society (OHS), founded in 1898, is Oregon's premier history museum. Its permanent exhibit, called "Experience Oregon," has an immersive build that allows visitors to walk through a covered wagon and explore the themes of water, land, and home through compelling artifacts and state-of-the-art technology. It also includes a 360-degree theater and several interactive games that allow you to test your survival skills on the Oregon Trail, ride a bucking bronco like the African American cowboy George Fletcher, or try to save rock and roll at the Vortex Music Festival. OHS also presents major traveling exhibitions on a variety of themes, from the history of Claymation to Northwest traditions.

MAP 1: 1200 SW Park Ave., 503/222-1741, www.ohs.org; Mon.-Sat. 10am-5pm, Sun. noon-5pm; $11 adults, $9 seniors and students (with ID), $5 children ages 6-18, free for children under 6

Oregon Maritime Center and Museum

To get a real understanding of the significance Portland played in maritime travel and commerce in years past, you'll want to visit this intriguing museum. Housed on the steam-powered *Portland* moored at Tom McCall Waterfront Park, the floating museum's exhibits feature navigation instruments, model ships, photographs, memorabilia, and artifacts from vessels of the region's maritime past. Other attractions include "Mom's Boat," a fishing boat from the late 1920s, and the barge *Russell*. Lectures and educational programs are often offered, and there is a gift shop on-site.

MAP 1: 115 SW Pine St. in Tom McCall Waterfront Park, 503/224-7724, www. oregonmaritimemuseum.org; Wed. and Fri.-Sat. 11am-4pm, Sun. 12:30pm-4:30pm; $7 adults, $5 seniors, $4 students, $3 children ages 6-12, free for children under 6

Portland Art Museum

The Portland Art Museum (PAM) was founded in 1892, which happens to make it the oldest art museum on the West Coast and seventh oldest in the United States. At 240,000 square feet, it is also one of the 25 largest art museums in the United States. Galleries begin with European Impressionism and transition to more current pieces, in addition to whichever major traveling exhibit is here. The permanent collection display is constantly changing and showcases more than 42,000 works of art, with a center for Northwest art, Native American art, Asian art, African art, and contemporary art, sculpture, and photography. PAM is also home to the Northwest Film Center.

Native American crafts at the Portland Art Museum

PORTLAND PUBLIC ART

Portland is filled with works of art, from its galleries to its shops to its streets. There are more than 1,000 pieces of public art on display for everyone to see. You can even download an app (Public Art PDX) that will tell you all about each piece and where to find it.

Allow Me: This guy has been in more selfies than the average teenage girl. Also known as *Umbrella Man*, this bronze sculpture features a man with an umbrella with one hand raised as if hailing a cab. Because of his visibility in Pioneer Courthouse Square, he is often used as a meeting spot.

Animals in Pools: This series of fountains and bronze sculptures that line the blocks of Yamill and Morrison Streets between 5th and 6th Avenues are another popular photography spot, particularly with children. They feature bears, salmon, seals, beavers, deer, ducks, and otters. In 2014, the otters acquired their very own sweaters, knitted for them by "yarn bombers."

Animals in Pools

Kvinneakt: Better known as the "Expose Yourself to Art" lady, this life-size sculpture of a wind-swept nude was once featured in a poster with soon-to-be mayor Bud Clark, who held his raincoat open away from the camera, flashing the bronze lady in return.

Nepethes: These giant glass sculptures are some of the newest art pieces in Portland, and they have been receiving mixed reviews since they were erected in 2013 along Northwest Davis Street in Old Town. The bulbous pieces represent tropical carnivorous plants of the same name. At night, the statues are fully illuminated thanks to photovoltaic cells.

The People's Bike Library: Otherwise known as the *Zoobomb pile*, this sculpture is a lot more than just art. It is also a bike rack, a bike lending library, and a visible testimony to the offbeat history of Portland. The piece was created in 2009 in honor of the Zoobombers, a group that meets weekly to ride down the west hills on child-size bicycles at unbelievable speeds.

Portlandia: Arguably the city's most famous and not famous piece of art. She could have been our Statue of Liberty, but her image is fiercely protected by the artist who created her. So you will never see her on a keychain.

Skidmore Fountain: On the other end of the spectrum from Nepethes is Skidmore Fountain, Portland's oldest piece of public art. It was designed after the fountains in Versailles that its namesake Stephen Skidmore saw over the course of his travels. He wished to have a gathering place that men, horses, and dogs could all drink from.

MAP 1: 1219 SW Park Ave., 503/226-2811, www.pam.org; Tues.-Wed. and Sat. 10am-5pm, Thurs.-Fri. 10am-8pm, Sun. noon-5pm; $20 adults, $17 seniors and students (with ID), free for children under 18

GALLERIES

Augen Gallery

The building housing Augen Gallery was erected in 1894 and stands in the Yamhill Historic District three blocks from the center of the business district and two blocks from the Willamette River. The gallery now occupies 10,000 square feet on two floors and showcases contemporary prints and works on paper by well-known and emerging artists. There's a second gallery in the Desoto Building arts complex, which houses four galleries and the Museum of Contemporary Craft. Both are worth a visit, especially if you can make it out for expanded First Thursday hours (until 8:30pm).

MAP 1: 817 SW 2nd Ave., 503/224-8182, www.augengallery.com; by appointment only; free

ORCHESTRAL MUSIC

Oregon Symphony

The Oregon Symphony has a long history in Portland, stretching back to 1896 when it was known as the Portland Symphony Society. These days, the orchestra entertains some 225,000 people per season with classical concerts, pops concerts, shows geared specifically for children, and special guest performances. Arrive one hour early for any of the classical series concerts and hear 30-minute conversations between the music director, conductor, and symphony musicians as they chat live on the radio about the music, the composers, and the history of the piece that will be performed

MAP 1: Arlene Schnitzer Concert Hall, 1037 SW Broadway, 503/228-1353, www. orsymphony.org; price varies

THEATER AND DANCE

Artists Repertory Theatre

Formed in 1982, Artists Repertory Theatre (ART) is Portland's oldest continuously run theater company. In the early days, ART (which is always pronounced spelled out "A-R-T") performed in a 110-seat venue in a YWCA. The company has come a long way and now has its own two-stage venue (which has been renovated to allow easier access between the two

Arlene Schnitzer Concert Hall at Portland'5 Centers for the Arts

stages). ART has survived as long as it has in part because since its inception it has committed to performing new, innovative works and taking dramatically different approaches to classics.

MAP 1: 1515 SW Morrison St., 503/241-1278, www.artistsrep.org; box office Tues.-Sun. noon-6pm; price varies

Oregon Ballet Theatre

Oregon's premier classical dance company, Oregon Ballet Theatre (OBT) was the product of a 1989 merger of Ballet Oregon and Pacific Ballet Theater. Under artistic director James Canfield, a former dancer with the Joffrey Ballet, the company repertoire grew to comprise over 80 ballets, from evening-length works to contemporary pieces. Every holiday season, the company performs the West Coast production of George Balanchine's *The Nutcracker*, which includes OBT's full company and nearly 100 students from the OBT School.

MAP 1: Keller Auditorium, 222 SW Clay St., 503/227-0977, www.obt.org; $29-146

Portland'5 Centers for the Arts

The Portland'5 Centers for the Arts (formerly Portland Center for the Performing Arts) is actually three separate buildings: the Keller Auditorium, the Arlene Schnitzer Concert Hall, and Antoinette Hatfield Hall, which houses the Newmark and Dolores Winningstad Theatres and Brunish Hall. Five resident companies and several presenting arts companies call the center home, among them Portland Opera, Oregon Ballet Theatre, Oregon Symphony Orchestra, Oregon Children's Theatre, White Bird Dance Company, and Broadway in Portland.

MAP 1: 1111 SW Broadway, 503/248-4335, www.p5pa.com, box office Mon.-Sat. 10am-5pm; price varies

Northwest and the Pearl District

Map 2

MUSEUMS

Freakybuttrue Peculiarium

It doesn't get much weirder than the Freakybuttrue Peculiarium. If you are looking for a break from the fancy galleries or just want to capture a little of the real Portland weirdness, this is the place for you. At the front is a small, weird gift shop that looks like the direct descendent of the 24-hour Church of Elvis—a wacky and weird relic of Portland's history where you could pay homage to the King of Rock and Roll, pick up a trinket, even get married. Past the gift shop is the museum, which you can explore for a small fee. You will find an assortment of oddities, gruesome dioramas, and sci-fi art and exhibits devoted to urban legends like Krampus, a demon-like counterpart to Santa. It's a quick walk through, but for lovers of everything unique and freaky, it certainly won't disappoint.

MAP 2: 2234 NW Thurman St., 503/227-3164, www.peculiarium.com; daily 10am-8pm; $5

Oregon Jewish Museum

The Oregon Jewish Museum is the only Jewish museum in the Pacific Northwest, and therefore serves as a museum for historical materials from the entire region, not just Oregon. At any time in the museum there is a wide array of Jewish art, cultural pieces, and historical artifacts. It also has a surprisingly extensive collection of organizational records, family papers, photographs, and ephemeral materials dating from 1850 to the present—the largest documented and visual history of Oregon's Jews—which is available to researchers, students, and scholars.

MAP 2: 310 NW Davis St., 503/226-3600, www.ojm.org; Tues.-Thurs. 10:30am-4pm, Fri. 10:30am-3pm, Sat.-Sun. noon-4pm; $8 adults, $5 seniors and students, free for children under 12

GALLERIES

✪ Sequential Art Gallery + Studio

Sequential Art is a gallery that loves a good story. As the name implies, it focuses on works carrying a sequential narrative. It often showcases paintings, photography, mixed media, fabric, and other forms of art in a single panel or whole collections that are part of a larger story. Here you will find the work of comic book legend Matthew Clark, known for his work on *The Amazing Spiderman, Punisher,* and *Ghost Rider.* The gallery also features rising stars and works to foster the idea that comic books and comic art deserve a place in the company of other fine art. While you are there, be sure to say hello and give some scritches to Mochi Manju, the gallery cat.

MAP 2: 328 NW Broadway, 503/916-9293, www.sequentialartgallery.com; Thurs. 3pm-7pm, Sat. 11am-5pm, or by appointment; free

Blue Sky Gallery

Blue Sky Gallery, also known as the Oregon Center for the Photographic Arts, is a nonprofit space focused on educating the public about photography. You may not already know the work of the local, national, and international artists on display at Blue Sky, but you will soon. Blue Sky has been credited with the best record for discovering new photographers of any artists' space in the country. As a nonprofit, Blue Sky is largely supported by grants and its membership program, which costs as little as $40 and comes with a gaggle of incentives and gifts. MAP 2: 122 NW 8th Ave., 503/225-0210, www.blueskygallery.org; Tues.-Sun. noon-5pm; free

Bullseye Gallery

Bullseye Glass Company has been a maker of colored glass for art and architecture since 1974 and was the first company in the world to formulate and manufacture glass that is factory-tested for fusing compatibility. Chances are, if you know an artist who works with glass, some of his or her materials come from Bullseye. The company has also supported individual artists and art-school programs by developing new materials technologies that have helped change the field of kiln-formed glass artistry. Its Bullseye Gallery works with a group of international artists in the field of kiln-formed glass and showcases some of the most dynamic creators through exhibitions and projects. MAP 2: 300 NW 13th Ave., 503/227-0222, www.bullseyegallery.com; Tues.-Sat. 10am-5pm, or by appointment; free

Elizabeth Leach Gallery

Established in 1981 and considered the second-oldest gallery in Portland, the Elizabeth Leach Gallery offers a comprehensive selection of contemporary fine art. It is definitely a high-caliber place, with excellent work on display that will particularly delight serious collectors. The gallery occupies a 4,000-square-foot space in the Pearl District, and it features a video and light installation *Light on the Horizon* by Portland light artist Hap Tivey, who has long been active on the local arts community boards. MAP 2: 417 NW 9th Ave., 503/224-0521, www.elizabethleach.com; Tues.-Sat. 10:30am-5:30pm, or by appointment; free

Waterstone Gallery

Waterstone Gallery was founded in 1992 by four established artists who believed that an artist-run gallery would provide uniquely intimate interaction with their clientele. Today, Waterstone still offers clients the opportunity to have direct contact with the artists who own and operate the space—though it has grown to include 14 nationally and internationally known artists. You will always find creative, contemporary, original art that is carefully crafted and beautifully presented. MAP 2: 124 NW 9th Ave., 503/226-6196, www.waterstonegallery.com; Tues.-Sat. 11am-5:30pm, Sun. 11am-4pm; free

THEATER AND DANCE
✪ Portland Center Stage

The sparkling (and super-sustainable) renovation of its home, the Gerding Theater at the Armory, would be reason enough to make Portland's second-oldest theater company worth a visit. The circa-1895 Armory became the first historic renovation and the first theater to achieve LEED platinum certification for green practices. The result? An airy, visually stunning lobby (complete with Wi-Fi and a cafe) and two state-of-the-art performance spaces. On the 599-seat Main Stage, you'll find hit musicals like *Ain't Misbehavin'* and *Sweeney Todd* mixed with national bestsellers like *A Streetcar Named Desire* and *Othello*, plus world premieres and readings at the theater's annual playwrights festival, JAW. The downstairs studio space, the 200-seat Ellyn Bye Studio, leans toward smart, cutting-edge performances scaled for the stage's more intimate advantage.

MAP 2: 128 NW 11th Ave., 503/445-3700, www.pcs.org; box office daily noon-5:30pm, noon-7:30pm on performance days; $25-92

HISTORIC MOVIE HOUSES

Mission Theater

Probably the most varied past of the McMenamin brothers' kingdom belongs to Mission Theater. Built in 1912, the site once housed the Portland Swedish Mission Covenant congregation, very focused on mission work that took them all over the world. By 1954, however, the community had outgrown the space in a neighborhood becoming much more commercial. When the gentle Swedes moved out, dockworkers moved in, and the venue became a hiring hall for longshoremen. The McMenamins opened the Mission Theater and Pub in 1987, the first of what would become a long list of pub-based theaters. The success of the cheap movie concept was staggering, and the Mission still stands as a community-based gathering place, hosting concerts and TV showings in addition to second-run movies.

MAP 2: 1624 NW Glisan St., 503/223-4527, www.mcmenamins.com; Mon.-Fri. 5pm-close, Sat.-Sun. 2pm-close; $2-4 for screenings

Alison Bechdel's *Fun Home*, produced by Portland Center Stage

ART WALKS

First Thursday in the Pearl (www.firstthursdayportland.com) is one of the most popular and well-attended art walks. Most of the galleries launch new exhibits on this day, hosting receptions with free wine and goodies, where you can meet the artist in person and listen to live music. Generally, the hours are 6pm-9pm, but some parties can last well into the night. Stroll through the streets and stop at whichever gallery, shop, or restaurant calls to you.

Last Thursday on Alberta (www.artonalberta.org) is the splashy, wild child in the bunch. Year-round, the crowds on Last Thursday are thick with people searching for affordable art, a little nip of wine, or just a good time. Officials close down about 15 blocks of NE Alberta Street between 10th and 30th Avenues, which alleviates some of the crowding. It's a good thing, because the real focus is the street vendors who set up their art on sidewalks, tables, trees, patches of dirt, or chain-link fences. Be sure to hit the streets for some unparalleled people-watching. It is not uncommon to see an impromptu parade, a live band on someone's porch, or a stilt walker strolling by.

Central Eastside Arts District First Friday Art Walk (www.firstfridaypdx.org) is less of a walk than an opportunity to check out the launch of some new exhibits, as it is scattered as far north as NE Broadway and as far south as Sellwood. A good area to hit is East Burnside Street, where you will find a few galleries and a number of restaurants to relax in. There's a lot to see, but with it being spread out across much of the city's inner core, it can be a bit of a scavenger hunt. The website provides a map of galleries, shops, restaurants, and bars that are participating.

Third Thursday in Kenton (www.facebook.com/kentonthirdthursday) is the first art walk for the north side of town. The Kenton neighborhood (home to the giant Paul Bunyan statue) has seen a significant influx of new restaurants and shops along North Denver Avenue, but it still maintains a homey, small-town feel. The monthly art walk is a great chance to explore boutiques, cafés, and galleries that are new on the scene.

Northeast   Map 3

GALLERIES

Antler Gallery

Antler Gallery is so named because owners Susannah Kelly and Neil Perry believe that an antler is the perfect marriage of form and function, both adornment and tool. The natural world is a strong theme at Antler, and the pieces on display are a mixture of contemporary art and innovative craft. There are a few well-curated items for sale, and the owners are very knowledgeable about art and delightful to talk to.

MAP 3: 2728 NE Alberta St., 503/285-6757, www.antlerpdx.com; Thurs.-Mon. noon-6pm; free

Guardino Gallery

Guardino Gallery has been doing monthly rotating art shows since 1997, which is a long time for a gallery to last. The building housing Guardino also hosts four other businesses, so there is a lot to see under one roof. The gallery occupies two of the six storefronts and has a reputation for presenting great contemporary works by Northwest artists and select special guests. There is also a retail shop with a great selection of contemporary crafts and fine gifts.

MAP 3: 2939 NE Alberta St., 503/281-9048, www.guardinogallery.com; Tues. 11am-5pm, Wed.-Sat. 11am-6pm, Sun 11am-4pm; free

THEATER AND DANCE
✪ Portland Playhouse

When Portland Playhouse came on the scene in 2008, it wasn't exactly a splashy entrance. The original company made use of an old church in the NE King neighborhood, an area quite lacking in exposure to the arts. For the first few performances, attendance was abysmal. But soon the company began to produce the kind of work that spoke to the neighborhood and inspired conversation. After they almost lost the church in 2012 due to city rules about the use of church space, it was the community that stepped in and demanded they be allowed to stay. The request was granted, and the company has since continued to grow and become one of the most talked-about theater companies in the city for its polished, professional, and evocative performances.

MAP 3: 602 NE Prescott St., 503/281-4215, www.portlandplayhouse.org; Tues.-Fri. 10:30am-4pm (by phone only); $25-59

HISTORIC MOVIE HOUSES
Hollywood Theatre

A stroll through the Hollywood District wouldn't be complete without a look at the majestic Hollywood Theatre. Built as a 1,500-seat vaudeville house in 1926, the Hollywood has one of the most ornate theater fronts in the Pacific Northwest, with a stunning marquee and Byzantine rococo tower. The theater is currently split into three venues, each capable of screening films. There is a 468-seat main auditorium, which was the original orchestra level, a 180-seat venue (one-half of the original balcony), and a 190-seat venue (the other half of the original balcony). The theater was purchased in 1997 by the nonprofit Film Action Oregon (FAO), which has been on an aggressive campaign to renovate and save this old Portland landmark. The Hollywood has also returned to its vaudeville roots to welcome live theatrical performances, concerts, and lectures.

MAP 3: 4122 NE Sandy Blvd., 503/281-4215, www.hollywoodtheatre.org; daily 1pm-9pm; $7-9 for screenings

Kennedy School

When this elementary school was built in 1915, it was as rural as it got. Most nearby residents lived without electricity, running water, or telephones. After 1975 the building served as a community center, but

Hollywood Theatre

THE McMENAMINS KINGDOM

In addition to owning nearly 60 brewpubs, microbreweries, music venues, historic hotels, and theater pubs, Mike and Brian McMenamin are rather like historians. A number of their pubs and hotels are salvaged historical buildings that have colorful pasts as, for example, an elementary school, a bathhouse, a vaudeville house, and a church. The "McBrothers" have a reputation for breathing new life into buildings that would have otherwise met with a wrecking ball, while still holding on to the venues' original charms. Given the nature of their business, the brothers take history pretty seriously, and their kingdom (as they call it) employs a full-time historian to dig up and preserve stories. There are numerous ways to experience the whimsical world of the McMenamins in Portland and vicinity, including overnight stays at the **Crystal Hotel, Kennedy School,** or **White Eagle Motel,** seeing a movie at the **Mission Theater** or **Bagdad Theater & Pub,** catching live music at the **Crystal Ballroom,** and putting the golf course at **Edgefield.**

was then threatened with demolition. With the help of the community and the Portland Development Commission, it was successfully spared, and the McMenamin brothers began putting their signature style on the space in 1997. The school's auditorium now lets you grab a slice and watch older and second-run movies from the comfort of some pretty cushy couches. Hey, you might still get an education, but at least you can have a beer while you do it.

MAP 3: 5736 NE 33rd Ave., 503/249-3983, www.mcmenamins.com; Mon.-Fri. 5pm-close, Sat.-Sun. 11am-close; $2-4 adults for screenings

The Laurelhurst

The owners of the beautiful art deco Laurelhurst Theater, Prescott Allen and Woody Wheeler, had been regulars of the Bagdad Theater on Hawthorne when Allen discovered a run-down old theater that needed new life. The space was built as a single-screen venue in 1923 and was equipped with an orchestra pit and grand organ. In the 1950s, Laurelhurst was adorned with a small retail space and a soda fountain—which is now an additional screening room. The venue now offers four screens that show modern and independent first- and second-run movies, as well as classic films. Concessions, most of which are provided by local businesses, include pizza, microbrews, and wine. Despite its classic Hollywood look, this surprisingly environmental gem now runs on wind power.

MAP 3: 2735 E. Burnside St., 503/232-5511, www.laurelhursttheater.com; Mon.-Fri. 4pm-close, Sat.-Sun. 1pm-close; about $6-9 for screenings

Southeast

Map 4

MUSEUMS

✪ Oregon Museum of Science and Industry

Oregon Museum of Science and Industry (OMSI) is one of the top science centers in the world, offering a variety of exhibits and activities guaranteed to entertain and engage both children and adults. Take a tour of the USS *Blueback*, the U.S. Navy's last non-nuclear, fast-attack submarine, which appeared in the movie *The Hunt for Red October* (claustrophobics, beware). Watch a film on the five-story domed IMAX projection screen or a laser light show in the Kendall Planetarium, or explore your way through some of the most exciting exhibits touring the world today. Admission to the Omnimax theater, planetarium, submarine, and the museum's multisensory motion simulator are not included in admission. Also hosted by the museum is **OMSI After Dark** ($15), typically held once a month on Wednesday, when it stays open late for adults over 21, with food and alcoholic beverages available.

MAP 4: 1945 SE Water Ave., 503/797-4000, www.omsi.edu; Tues.-Sun. 9:30am-7pm; $14.50 adults, $11.25 seniors, $9.75 children ages 3-13, free for children under 3, parking $5

GALLERIES

Nucleus Portland

Nucleus is a rather new idea for a gallery space, operating both as a showcase for art and a collaborative space to drink and create. In its stark white space, it highlights illustrated, graphic, and contemporary art by both local and international artists. In addition to regular monthly gallery showings, it also hosts regular events, workshops, and classes that allow artists to connect with the community. A popular happening is the weekly drink-and-draw event, where guests can bring their sketchbooks to work on while sipping local brews.

MAP 4: 1445 SE Hawthorne Blvd., 503/231-2702, www.nucleusportland.com; Wed. 5pm-10pm, Thurs.-Sun. noon-6pm; free

THEATER AND DANCE

Do Jump!

Do Jump! calls its performers "actorbats." It is a fitting term because their shows are a unique blend of theater, dance, aerial work, acrobatics, dynamic visuals, and live music that defies categorization. The company was established in 1977 as a group of volunteers under the direction of Robin Lane. Today, Do Jump! has progressed into a troupe of salaried players, with Lane still at the helm. Many also serve as teachers for Do Jump!'s Movement Theater School, which offers classes in trapeze, acrobatics, and aerial yoga.

MAP 4: The Echo Theatre, 1515 SE 37th Ave., 503/231-1232, www.dojump.org; price varies

Milagro Theatre

Milagro Theatre produces a broad array of works focused on celebrating Latino culture and language, sometimes bridging it with American theater traditions. The company is consistently—and delightfully—different, whether presenting a vibrant Día de los Muertos (Day of the Dead) combination of dance, music, and theater or a dark, compelling historical piece. Milagro manages to keep things fresh while holding on to its Latino heritage. The company occasionally performs in Spanish (usually with projected supertitles), but even if you don't understand the language, the performances are full of heart and compelling to watch. Purchase tickets online, by phone, or in person at the box office (425 SE 6th Ave.) or at Milagro Theatre one hour prior to a performance.

MAP 4: Milagro Theatre, 525 SE Stark St., 503/236-7253, www.milagro.org; box office Mon.-Fri. 9am-5pm; $20-35

Third Rail Repertory Theatre

Third Rail Repertory Theatre burst on the scene in 2003 with a core group of actors already known for solid, dynamic performances. As the company began putting together progressively risky and exciting works, everyone kept expecting—but dreading—the moment when it would stumble. In fact, the company managed to remain a darling among the temperamental and often obstinate local theater critics. It performs at the Imago Theater in Southeast Portland, and you can purchase tickets online or by phone.

MAP 4: 17 SE 8th Ave., 503/235-1101, www.thirdrailrep.org; box office Mon.-Fri. 10am-4pm; $25-45

HISTORIC MOVIE HOUSES
✪ Bagdad Theater & Pub

One of Portland's most notable historic theaters—immortalized in the 2004 film *What the Bleep Do We Know!?*—the Bagdad Theater & Pub is a McMenamin brothers restoration success story. Built in 1926 with the help of Universal Pictures, it was intended to be a vaudeville house, but by the early 1930s, vaudeville

Oregon Museum of Science and Industry

was dead. The site then became a cinema-only venue, and Mike and Brian McMenamin purchased it in 1991 and began serving beer and pizza alongside film screenings. It shows first-run movies. The brothers also converted the unused backstage space into a bar that stretches seven stories high. The space, now appropriately known as the BackStage Bar, was large enough to house a full fly system for the theater's vaudevillian past, but now it houses an enormous

Bagdad Theater & Pub

mural that depicts the building's theatrical beginnings.

MAP 4: 3702 SE Hawthorne Blvd., 503/249-7474, ext. 1, www.mcmenamins. com/theaters; Mon.-Thurs. 11am-midnight, Fri.-Sat. 11am-1am, Sun. noon-midnight; $7-10 for screenings

Clinton Street Theater

Clinton Street Theater was built in the early Craftsman style in 1914, and it is said to be the oldest continuously operating movie house west of the Mississippi. The theater plays host to underground and independent movies and festivals, such as Filmed by Bike, with screenings devoted to bike-themed independent shorts, and the Portland Underground Film Festival (PUFF). The theater is best known, however, for playing the *Rocky Horror Picture Show* every Saturday night since 1978. Fans of the cult classic line up for the midnight showing in full costume armed with rice, toast, newspapers, and other appropriate props to wield or throw as they scream, sing, and dance along with the movie.

MAP 4: 2522 SE Clinton St., 503/238-8899, www.clintonsttheater.com; doors open 30 minutes before each show; price varies

Sellwood and Moreland   Map 5

MUSEUMS

Ping Pong Puppet Museum

If you have fond memories of watching *The Muppet Show* or *Mr. Rogers*, chances are you will be absolutely charmed by the Puppet Museum. Operated by puppet builders and enthusiasts Steve Overton and Marty Richmond, this space is full of all your favorite characters and clever

new ones. The guys have a storied history in the puppetry industry, having built puppets for Walt Disney, Tears of Joy Theater, and Will Vinton. You will often find them in the midst of constructing a new puppet, and they are happy to show you the inner workings. They also give demonstrations of the different forms of puppetry—string, sock, rod, hand, and electronic.

MAP 5: 906 SE Umatilla St., 503/865-8733, www.puppetmuseum.com; Thurs.-Sun. 2pm-8pm; free

GALLERIES
12x16 Gallery

This Sellwood gallery is an artist collective producing the art on display either collaboratively or as individuals. There are about a dozen members of the collective at 12x16, and while each has a distinct style and form, there is a through line that pulls them together. So you often find similar themes and styles that play off each other and add to the richness. The gallery changes once a month and occasionally features guest artists from around the Pacific Northwest.

MAP 5: 8235 SE 13th Ave., #5, 503/432-3513, www.12x16gallery.com; Thurs.-Sun. noon-5pm; free

HISTORIC MOVIE HOUSES
Moreland

This theater hasn't changed since it first opened its doors in 1926. Back then, it was still called Moreland Theater and showed vaudeville acts along with silent films. Pretty soon, the vaudeville acts went away and the silent films became talkies, but the theater remains largely unchanged. This is both great and terrible. Seats are sometimes uncomfortable, and there is nary a cup holder in sight. What it lacks in comfort it makes up for in charm. The tickets are cheap, and the theater shows first-run films. Oh, and one more thing that hasn't changed: they don't accept any of that newfangled plastic money, so you better bring cash.

MAP 5: 6712 SE Milwaukie Ave., 503/236-5257, www.morelandtheater.com; doors open 15 minutes before first show; $7.50 for screenings

Various Venues

ORCHESTRAL MUSIC
✪ Portland Cello Project

This "indie cello orchestra" is as hip as it gets, oftentimes collaborating with the likes of the Dandy Warhols, the Builders and the Butchers, Loch Lomond, and 3 Leg Torso or playing from a repertoire that includes everything from Bach and Beethoven to Britney Spears and Led Zeppelin. When the 8-16 cellists get together, they are just as likely to play any of those songs as they are to invent something completely new. With their quirky attitudes and undeniable ability to attack any song with the passion and fervor of a moth around a porch light, it's no surprise that they have a rock star following in Portland.

Various venues: www.portlandcelloproject.com; price varies

Portland Baroque Orchestra

Presenting mostly 17th- and 18th-century music, the Portland Baroque Orchestra performs baroque and classical music on centuries-old instruments or truly authentic replicas to match when the music was composed. Using the lute, harpsichord, lirone, and other options, they can play the music in a way that modern orchestras

PORTLAND ON FILM

Oregon is blessed with a beautiful landscape, which filmmakers have long sought because of its versatility. If some of the scenery you encounter looks familiar, don't be surprised. Here's just a sampling of the films that were made in Portland:

- *Body of Evidence:* The movie, which featured Madonna and Willem Dafoe, was largely considered a clunker, but many scenes in this erotic thriller were filmed in Portland, including a number at the Governor Hotel.

- *Come See the Paradise:* This historical drama set before and during World War II is about the treatment and internment of 100,000 Asian Americans. The movie starred Dennis Quaid and was filmed in Astoria, Portland, and the Willamette Valley.

- *Coraline:* Neil Gaiman's creepy-cool story of a plucky young girl who wishes for better parents was painstakingly animated in the Portland stop-animation studio Laika.

- *Drugstore Cowboy:* This film, which was Gus Van Sant's second, starred Matt Dylan and Kelly Lynch. It was filmed in and around areas such as the Nob Hill Pharmacy on NW Glisan and the Irving Apartments near NW 21st and Irving. While the film was set in the 1970s, a number of buildings appear on screen that were not built until the 1980s.

- *Feast of Love:* This film starring Morgan Freeman, Greg Kinnear, Radha Mitchell, and Selma Blair was set at Portland State University but filmed at Western Seminary and Reed College.

- *The Hunted:* Directors of this film starring Benicio del Toro and Tommy Lee Jones picked Portland because they needed a lot of rain for filming. Sadly for them, Portland was visited by an unusually dry spell that lasted several weeks.

- *Into the Wild:* This adaptation of the Jon Krakauer book starred Emile Hirsch, Marcia Gay Harden, and William Hurt. The graduation scene was filmed at Reed College.

can't—and the way it was originally intended. The approach brings a whole new complexity to Beethoven, Handel, Vivaldi, and Bach, and the results are particularly noticeable when you hear something like Handel's *Messiah*.
Various venues: 503/222-6000, www. pbo.org; price varies

Third Angle New Music Ensemble

Third Angle turns the traditional concept of chamber music on its ear with modern and inventive expressions of works by 20th- and 21st-century composers. They have presented over 90 programs of contemporary music, commissioned more than 20 new works, and released five recordings to much critical acclaim. The ensemble produces 3-5 programs each year, interspersed between recording

projects and educational outreach projects. The company has garnered a well-deserved reputation for musical excellence and interesting, positively electric performances.
Various venues: 503/331-0301, www. thirdangle.org; price varies, free for children under 3

THEATER AND DANCE
Pendulum Aerial Dance Theatre

Boundaries are tested and then distinctly ignored by Pendulum Aerial Dance Theatre. Using various aerial apparatuses, from a trapeze to darn near anything they can suspend themselves from, the multitalented and captivating company puts on quite a show. In some moments, the movements are so smooth and controlled, it is as if they are underwater. At the

- **Men of Honor:** The Cuba Gooding Jr. film about the first African American U.S. Navy diver filmed some restaurant exterior shots in Portland.

- **Mr. Holland's Opus:** The Richard Dreyfuss film about a composer who agrees to teach music in order to support his family was filmed in and around Grant High School in Northeast Portland.

- **My Own Private Idaho:** Gus Van Sant's sad film about two young men on a journey of personal discovery was set in Van Sant's hometown and favorite locale, Portland.

- **Paranoid Park:** The Gus Van Sant film about a teenage skateboarder who accidentally kills a security guard was set in and filmed in Portland—in particular, the Burnside Skatepark, the Willamette River, and the Steel Bridge.

- **Short Circuit:** Number 5 came alive in Oregon. The 1986 comedy starring Ally Sheedy and Steve Guttenberg was filmed in Astoria, Portland, the Cascade Locks, and other portions of the Columbia River Gorge.

- **Untraceable:** This thriller starring Diane Lane as an FBI agent on the hunt for a serial killer was filmed in a number of Portland locales, including Oaks Amusement Park and the Broadway Bridge.

- **What the Bleep Do We Know!?:** This documentary-style film about quantum physics and human consciousness was filmed at the Bagdad Theater & Pub on Hawthorne, in the Pearl District, and in the MAX tunnel, which serves as the Washington Park Zoo stop.

- **Wild:** Portland author Cheryl Strayed's harrowing tale of her own journey along the Pacific Crest Trail. Portland shooting locations included Hotel deLuxe, The Driftwood Room, Mississippi Studios, and Casba Mediterranean Café in Northeast Portland.

core of their physically demanding performances is sheer physical prowess and strength, and a whole new concept of dance that is one part circus, one part burlesque, and a whole lot of imagination.

Various venues: www. pendulumdancetheatre.org; price varies

White Bird

White Bird brings established and emerging companies and choreographers to Portland that audiences here wouldn't otherwise see. It has commissioned several new works, developed numerous partnerships, thought up some otherwise unimaginable collaborations, and retained a strong relationship with the local performing arts community. Since 1997, partners Walter Jaffe and Paul King have presented more than 118 companies from all over the world and given Portland a remarkable helping of modern dance. As the audience has grown more sophisticated, so has White Bird, bringing in increasingly more complex and compelling companies and challenging returning companies to perform more innovative works.

Various venues: 503/245-1600, www. whitebird.org; price varies

Festivals and Events

SPRING
Spring Beer and Wine Fest

More than 80 different beers and 25 wineries can be found at the Spring Beer and Wine Fest, which turns the Oregon Convention Center into a mecca for brew connoisseurs and vino aficionados alike every March. A wide assortment of breweries—like Full Sail, Bridgeport, and Deschutes—serve up frosty mugs of their most popular hoppy concoctions, while wineries the likes of Cooper Ridge or Naked Winery will gladly pop a cork of their latest vintage for your imbibing pleasure. You will also find several local distilleries like Dry Fly and Big Bottom Whiskey offering samples of their spirits. Of course, there's food to sample as well, from barbecue to seafood—not to mention artisan cheeses, specialty chocolates, and chef's demonstrations. You must purchase souvenir beer or wine glasses and tokens to fill your glass with the beverage of your choice.

Northeast: Oregon Convention Center, 777 NE Martin Luther King Jr. Blvd.; Mar.; www.springbeerfest.com; $10

Red Dress Party

What started out as a party in the basement of a North Portland home has blossomed into one of the most anticipated fundraising events to grace our city. Over the years, the annual Red Dress Party has raised more than $87,000 for charities that work with youth, adults, and seniors living with HIV and AIDS. The event seeks to entertain party-goers with hosted food, beverages, red cocktails, fire spinners, and music. There's just one rule: Everyone—yes, *everyone*—must wear a red dress to get in.

Various locations: www.reddresspdx. com; Apr. or May; $75-150

Cinco de Mayo Festival

The largest Cinco de Mayo Festival in North America celebrates the colors, cuisine, arts, music, and folklore of Mexico—more specifically, Guadalajara, Portland's sister city. The four-day fiesta usually kicks off bright and early with a ribbon-cutting ceremony followed by a naturalization ceremony. After that, it's time to enjoy all manner of music, food, and entertainment and a magnificent fireworks display come nightfall. There's an interactive children's area, and Guadalajara artisans and jewelers demonstrate their crafts on-site and sell their wares.

Downtown: Tom McCall Waterfront Park, www.cincodemayo.org; early May; $10 adults, $7 seniors and children, free for children under 6

SUMMER
Portland Rose Festival

The big daddy event for Portland is the Rose Festival, held every year from the end of May through the first two weeks of June to celebrate the riches of the Pacific Northwest heritage and environment. It's all about bringing the city together, but also about extending a hand to communities across the world. The spectacular Grand Floral Parade, which is the centerpiece of the festival, is the second-largest floral parade in the nation and the biggest spectator event in the state of Oregon. But the festival has events

THE ROSE SOCIETY

Portland's annual **Rose Festival** is quite the event. It's all thanks to the Rose Society, which was founded in 1888 by Georgiana Pittock, the flower-loving wife of *Oregonian* publisher Henry Pittock. But it started long before that, when in 1837, the first rose plant was brought to Oregon and presented to Anna Maria Pittman, the bride of missionary Jason Lee and the first European woman to be married, give birth, die, and be buried in Oregon. After much of the mission was destroyed by a fire years later, pioneer and legislator John Minto salvaged the rose and transported it to his home. The plant flourished in Portland's climate, and, thanks to Minto's willingness to share clippings, the city soon fell in love with the thorny beauty.

In an effort to teach and encourage amateur gardeners to plant and cultivate roses, a group of Portlanders decided to form a society, which would one day become the oldest of its kind in the United States. While the city's first rose show occurred in 1889—a tradition that is still practiced during the festival to this day—the first official Rose Festival didn't happen until 1907.

In the early days of its existence, a king, Rex Oregonus, was chosen to rule over the festival. His identity (masked by a gigantic beard) was kept secret until being revealed at an annual celebratory ball. In 1914, the king was replaced by a queen, a socialite chosen from Portland's elite. The tradition continued until 1930, when the city decided to let each of the area high schools choose a representative from their senior class to serve as a Rose Festival princess. One year later, the title came with a college scholarship. Nowadays, the princesses (sometimes called "ambassadors") are not chosen for their beauty and social status; instead, they must have a minimum grade-point average of 2.75 and demonstrate exemplary citizenship. As ambassadors for their schools and the city, they are evaluated for their character, communication skills, and presence.

that are worth checking out besides that. Kids are released from school early to march through the Hollywood District in the Junior Parade. After the sun goes down, the Starlight Parade, which winds through the streets of downtown, is always fun, and the party is always raging at Tom McCall Waterfront Park, with music, vaudeville acts, exhibits, acres of food, and Funtastic rides.

Portland Rose Festival's Grand Floral Parade

Downtown: Tom McCall Waterfront Park, www.rosefestival.org; May-June; $7, free for children under 7

✪ Pedalpalooza

Each June, the Pedalpalooza bike festival features an unbelievable lineup of events. The festival is very DIY in nature, as the rides are all led by volunteers and, in fact, anyone is welcome to organize a ride and contribute to the fun. Nearly all rides are free, and there is a little something for everyone, from family-friendly tricyclerider (like Kidical Mass) to daredevil (like Unicycle Polo). There are even bike crawls that will take you on tours of pubs, vegan restaurants, or spokenword joints. Or, if you really want to see a spectacle, check out Cirque du Cycling—part circus, part parade—which lights up Mississippi Avenue. Cirque du Cycling events in the past have included parades, races, and biker performers. Also taking place as part of Pedalpalooza is Portland's

THE WORLD'S LARGEST WORLD NAKED BIKE RIDE

Portland's version of the **World Naked Bike Ride** (WNBR, www.pdxwnbr.com; free)—which, as its name suggests, takes place internationally—is the largest of its kind, typically drawing around 10,000 participants. The ride takes place every June and coincides with **Pedalpalooza.** Intended as a peaceful protest to bring attention to our country's dependence on oil, the ride has also become a way to highlight the lack of safety for vulnerable people as well as encourage body positivity. Nudity as protest is protected by Oregon law, so the ride is legal, and in fact the city's cops help cork the streets for bicyclists during the event. The celebratory mass ride often includes body glitter, playful bike decorations, and speakers playing music, and is a major happening in the life of the city. It might seem intimidating, but anyone can join; simply bring your own bike or other human-powered vehicle (e.g., rollerskates, skateboards) to the route's starting point, which changes every year. Despite the ride's name, there's no requirement to ride naked; you can ride comfortably "as bare as you dare." Portland's WNBR typically snakes through multiple neighborhoods, to the cheers and high fives of spectators, before ending with jubilant after-parties.

massive **World Naked Bike Ride**, a two-wheeled party through the city. **Various locations:** www.shift2bikes.org; June; free

Portland Pride Festival

If you really want to see a party, head down to the waterfront in June and check out the Portland Pride Festival. The event is intended to encourage and celebrate the positive diversity of the lesbian, gay, bisexual, trans, and queer communities and allow an opportunity to gather together and celebrate with music, entertainment, food, demonstrations, and exhibits in Tom McCall Waterfront Park. The whole shebang lasts only one weekend and builds up to a fantastic and colorful parade through the streets of downtown on the last day of the event. If you miss that, however, there are other fun events around the city during the festival and in the weeks before and after it. The Pride Glow Run, for instance, is a night race where participants are encouraged to adorn themselves with all manner of glow sticks and lights or, at the very least, wear something bright and outrageous. With mixers and parties and parades galore, the whole

celebration is more fun than a barrel of sequins and a bottle of spray glue. **Downtown:** Tom McCall Waterfront Park, www.pridenw.org; June; $8

Safeway Waterfront Blues Festival

The Safeway Waterfront Blues Festival is one of the largest blues festivals in the nation (second only to Chicago), attracting more than 120,000 blues lovers from all over the world. Fans show up to catch just a few of the 150 performances that happen on the festival's four stages over the July 4th holiday. Proceeds from the festival benefit the Oregon Food Bank, a nonprofit organization

Portlanders occasionally use umbrellas—but usually just as an accessory.

that provides food to low-income people in Oregon and southwest Washington. With such fantastic performances from such legends as Marcia Ball, Keb' Mo, and Isaac Hayes, the festival is able to raise around $500,000 and more than 80,000 pounds of food (by collecting donations of money and nonperishable foods at the gate). If the crowds are a bit much for you, consider taking one of the Blues Cruises on the *Portland Spirit,* which sails down the Willamette to Oregon City. On board, you'll be treated to live music and a no-host hors d'oeuvres buffet and full bar.

Downtown: Tom McCall Waterfront Park, www.waterfrontbluesfest.com; early July; $15

✪ Oregon Brewers Festival

If there is anything we truly love in Portland, it's beer. It's no wonder, then, that we would host an entire festival in its honor for four days every summer. The annual Oregon Brewers Festival is regarded by many as one of the finest craft beer festivals you can find. In years past, more than 60,000 people have attended the event—and the numbers climb each year for beer lovers of all walks seeking a sampling of local favorites, new brews, and micros from all over, but with a heavy regional bent. Food is provided by local restaurants, and there's always live entertainment. Admission is usually free—unless, of course, you want to drink. A souvenir mug (required for tasting) will cost you $7, and you can buy as many $1 tokens as you'd like (but it will take about four to fill a mug).

Downtown: Tom McCall Waterfront Park, www.oregonbrewfest.com; July; free

Pickathon

Every summer on the first weekend in August, Pickathon features nationally acclaimed folk and indie bands on multiple stages at a sprawling farm just outside Portland. It typically spans four days and has been going strong for over 20 years, featuring the likes of Built to Spill, Dinosaur Jr., and the Blind Boys of Alabama. There are six stages total, and the main stage has a view of Mount Hood. Two intimate stages are in barns. Another particularly picturesque stage is just a short hike into the woods under a canopy of trees, with hammocks and hay. Some of the artists also make a weekend out of it, giving multiple performances and catching other artists between shows. Pickathon has a particularly Portlandy ethos of sustainability, requiring attendees to bring their own dishware and utensils or to buy reusable versions to use over the weekend (they also make nice souvenirs), and the festival also runs a shuttle from the closest mass transit hub. Tent camping on the farm is included with the weekend pass.

Greater Portland: Pendarvis Farm, Happy Valley; www.pickathon.com; early Aug.; day and weekend pass prices vary

The Bite of Oregon

Food lovers drop their triple cream brie and put away their reduction sauce to come out for The Bite of Oregon, a festival that celebrates the bounty of fantastic restaurants, breweries, and wineries in the Pacific Northwest. Lots of great entertainment, celebrity chefs, and the annual Iron Chef Oregon competition make it worth the price of admission, but the real draw here is the plethora of food, wine, and beer. Plus, the event

Bridge Pedal

benefits the Special Olympics, so you're eating that deep-fried asparagus for a reason, right?

Downtown: Tom McCall Waterfront Park, www.biteoforegon.com; Aug.; $10, free for children under 12

Bridge Pedal

Even in bike-friendly Portland, it can be a pretty harrowing experience to navigate some city streets. Oh, the narrow bike paths, car doors swinging open, and missed signals! And that's just on the streets—never mind making your way across some of the many bridges. For one day in August, cyclists of all walks and all ages get a rare chance to ride freely over many of the bridges that span the Willamette River—including such forbidden territory as the Fremont and Marquam Bridges (which are basically freeways). Bridge Petal is a popular event, and the city works hard to keep traffic moving in a reasonable fashion by shutting down only portions of

the bridges to vehicles and only for short durations. A portion of the proceeds from the event goes to the Bicycle Transportation Alliance and the Providence Hospital Heart and Vascular Institute.

Various locations: www.providence. org/bridgepedal; Aug.; $25-40, free for children under 12

Portland Adult Soapbox Derby

Every summer, some of Portland's most adventurous folks head to the top of Mount Tabor and then hurl themselves down the hill in homemade contraptions built for speed and whimsy. Participants build elaborate gravity-powered vehicles and race each other to the bottom while crowds that frequently number in the thousands cheer them on. There are two loosey-goosey categories (Art and Science), and teams receive awards for engineering, speed, creativity, and other criteria. The city issues a special permit for the event, so feel free to bring beer and wine (no hard alcohol). The race almost always proves to be a raucous good time.

Art in the Pearl

Rounding out a Portland summer filled with as much inspiration and entertainment as can be packed into the warm months, Art in the Pearl is a lovely gathering of artists, entertainers, and art lovers in the northwest Park Blocks. Here, you can dance to world music, sample delicacies from around the globe, and check out the jury-selected work of 130 artists from across the United States and Canada. You can also work on building your art collection, as there are usually well over 100 artists showing and selling works ranging from jewelry to furniture at very reasonable prices.

Northwest and the Pearl District: Northwest Park Blocks, between W. Burnside and NW Glisan at NW 8th Ave., www.artinthepearl.com; Labor Day weekend; free

Swift Watch

At the end of summer, people gather at dusk on picnic blankets and chairs to watch Mother Nature get a little bit weird and a little bit wild. Each year, thousands upon thousands of Vaux's swifts take up roost in the chimney of Chapman Elementary School during their fall migration. Swifts are loyal to their roosts and the population that holes up in the Chapman chimney has been returning to this location since the 1980s. The birds are a truly spectacular sight to see, with swarms the size of large clouds circling and darting through the sky as they come to settle in for the night. The swifts can be viewed over the period of about a month, before they continue on their way to Central and South America. Audubon Society of Portland volunteers are often on hand each night to answer questions.

Northwest and the Pearl District: 2701 NW Vaughn St., http://audubonportland.org; late Aug.-Sept one hour before sunset; free

FALL

MusicFest Northwest

What started as North by Northwest—a smaller, grungier version of Austin's annual South by Southwest Festival—has blossomed into a pretty exciting event. Now called MusicFest Northwest (MFNW), this is Portland's multiday extravaganza of rock music, and it brings in some pretty stellar acts from all over the nation. As interest builds around Portland as a music town, more and more big acts are adding their names to the roster. The festival also manages to give a platform to the lesser known, hardworking local musicians that keep Portland's music community feeling so alive.

Various locations: www.musicfestnw. com, Sept., price varies

MusicFest Northwest

PICA's T:BA Festival

Stimulate your senses all over the city at the Time-Based Art Festival (T:BA), an exploration of every form of contemporary art—including dance, music, new media, and visual. Unique to Portland, Pica's T:BA Festival provides a forum for contemporary as well as emerging artists from Portland and around the world. With well over 100 workshops, installations, lectures, and performances, this 10-day festival is packed with opportunities to experience art as you never have before. Since the festival happens all over the city, you can buy a pass that will allow you access to more than you can possibly see—or you can buy tickets to individual performances and events, available on the day of the show at the venues themselves.

Various locations: www.pica.org/tba; Sept.; price varies

Portland Lesbian & Gay Film Festival

The Portland Lesbian & Gay Film Festival has been around unofficially since the early 1990s, but officially began in 1997 when the first annual festival was launched. By the third year, things really started to take shape with sold-out screenings, world premieres, Oscar-winning features, and emotionally moving forums. Each year the festival showcases feature, documentary, and short films from all over the world that are made by, about, or of interest to the LGBT community. Films are selected based on the quality of storytelling, uniqueness, and overall appeal. The festival now works through a partnership with Film Action Oregon.

Northwest and the Pearl District: Cinema 21, 616 NW 21st Ave., www.plgff.org; late Sept.-early Oct.; $10-100

FASHIONxt

Portland has garnered quite a name for maintaining a high standard of eco-friendliness and creative design, and that attitude is creating a buzz in the fashion industry these days, too. In October, the annual FASHIONxt (pronounced "Fashion Next") rolls out the runway, and designers from across the world unveil their upcoming spring and summer collections. For several years, FASHIONxt (formerly Portland Fashion Week) has been illuminating the Northwest style scene with a focus on lifestyle, technology, and innovation, and now, the world is paying attention—and not just to chuckle about a Northwest show that features only fleece and hiking boots. It's no wonder. It may have been laughable 10 years ago, but each year, more talented Portland designers emerge onto the scene. Portland-area designers have claimed the top prize on Lifetime's *Project Runway* four times, and the winners and all-stars frequently showcase their work at this event. Attendees can choose from a variety of tickets ranging from a one-night soiree to a whole-week affair and from VIP seating to general admission.

Various locations: http://fashionxt.net; Oct.; $30-185

H. P. Lovecraft Film Festival

Twentieth-century American author Howard Phillips (H. P.) Lovecraft has a name synonymous with blood-curdling screams, night terrors, and noisome monsters like "the green, sticky spawn of the stars." His stories dominated the literary scene with a new genre labeled "weird fiction," which encompassed horror, myth, and science fiction. In 1995, producer, author, and avid fan Andrew Migliore founded the H. P. Lovecraft Film

Festival so that professional and amateur filmmakers could transport to the screen what Lovecraft had so brilliantly put on the page. There's no better way to kick off the month of October than by attending the H. P. Lovecraft Film Festival, where goosebumps are a guarantee and horror is a form of art. The festival takes place at the historic Hollywood Theatre, lending a creep factor that is likely to make you believe that Cthulhu himself could crawl out of the balcony.

Northeast: Hollywood Theatre, 4122 NE Sandy Blvd., 503/281-4215, www.hplfilmfestival.com; Oct.; $18-58

Reel Music

Reel Music, the Northwest Film Center's annual celebration of music on film, is a cinematic love letter to music's most intriguing artists (both legendary and unknown). Not limited to any particular genre, the festival highlights jazz, rock, reggae, bluegrass, bossa nova, and indie rock. Featuring everything from vintage performance clips to new documentary and dramatic films, to cutting-edge music videos and animation, it's an interesting way to explore the ways sounds and images play off each other to affect the human experience.

Downtown: Whitsell Auditorium, 1219 SW Park Ave., www.nwfilm.org; Oct.; $12 adults, $10 seniors and students

Northwest Filmmakers' Festival

With so many eyes and cameras on the Northwest these days, it is not surprising that we need our own film festival just to behold a portion of it. Since the 1970s, the Northwest Filmmakers' Festival has presented feature-length, short, and documentary films showcasing Northwest talent. Typically,

there are about 50 films shown over the course of a week in November, all of them made by artists from Alaska, Oregon, Washington, British Columbia, Montana, or Idaho. The festival is a showcase of what's on the minds of Northwest filmmakers, and an opportunity to seek inspiration and connections. The Northwest Film Center, which hosts the festival and is part of the Portland Art Museum, was established as a resource for media arts in the region. It offers a variety of film and video exhibitions in addition to education and information programs throughout the year and during the festival.

Downtown: Whitsell Auditorium, 1219 SW Park Ave., www.nwfilm.org; Nov.; price varies

The Swashbuckler's Ball

The Swashbuckler's Ball is an annual fundraising event that has come to be known as the "pirate prom." Pirates are a big thing in Portland, and while there are a number of events throughout the year that cause people to throw on a tricorn hat, this event is the biggest and most extravagant. Piratical bands come from all over the country to play for this event, which raises money for a different charitable organization each year. There are often two levels of entertainment to choose from, such as live bands and dancing in the main ballroom and burlesque shows and more intimate concerts in the cabaret lounge below.

Southeast: Melody Ballroom, 615 SE Alder St., www.swashbucklersball.com; Nov.; $40

WINTER

Providence Festival of Trees

The Providence Festival of Trees is your opportunity to stroll through nearly 50 decorated trees, as well as

ZooLights Festival

wreaths and holiday vignettes created by the city's top designers, businesses, and volunteers. Held the last weekend of November, the festival lights up the season in style and raises funds to support critically needed health-care services at Providence Hospital. The public show features children's activities, including the adorable Teddy Bear Hospital and Santa's Workshop, live entertainment, model trains, gingerbread houses, and a holiday bookshop. Tickets can be purchased at the door, and there are often coupons on the festival website that will save you money at the gate.

Northeast: Oregon Convention Center, 777 NE Martin Luther King Jr. Blvd., www.providence.org/festivaloftrees; late Nov.; $10 adults, $9 seniors, $8 children, free for children under 3

Festival of Lights at The Grotto

For more than 20 years now, The Grotto, a 62-acre Catholic shrine and botanical garden, has hosted the Festival of Lights at The Grotto, which is open nightly from around Thanksgiving through December 30 (except for Christmas Day). The spectacle features 150 musical performances, more than 500,000 lights, petting zoos, puppet shows, carolers, family entertainment, and more. Local choirs perform at the Chapel of Mary, a remarkable cathedral constructed of rock quarried from a cliff; it's an awe-inspiring display of polished marble, magnificent statues, and beautiful murals, and the acoustics are said to rival some of Europe's finest cathedrals. During the festival, The Grotto is open nightly 5pm-9:30pm.

Greater Portland: 8840 NE Skidmore St., 503/254-7371, www.thegrotto.org; Nov.-Dec.; $12 adults, $11 seniors, $6 children ages 3-12, free parking

ZooLights Festival

Every evening (except Christmas Eve and Christmas Day) from November 28 until December 28, the Oregon Zoo transforms into a holiday fairyland for its annual ZooLights Festival.

It's a spectacular event for the entire family. Decorated with nearly a million lights, this winter wonderland is a more whimsical display than your traditional holiday light show, with swinging monkeys instead of snowmen, slithering snakes instead of nodding reindeer. Sip some cocoa from the Zoo Café or ride the special Christmas train, brightly decorated and aglow with lights, as it winds through the zoo.

Greater Portland: Oregon Zoo, 4001 SW Canyon Rd., 503/226-1561, www. oregonzoo.org; Nov.-Dec.; $17.95 adults, $15.95 seniors, $12.95 children

Christmas Ship Parade

The Christmas Ship Parade started back in 1954 when one guy with a sailboat decked the bow with lights and sailed the Willamette. Each year since then, the fleet has grown, and now it averages 55-60 boats between the Columbia and Willamette River fleets. The parade happens nightly for two weeks beginning in early December. The displays are elaborate and brightly lit, and can be seen from bank to bank on each river, which is a real treat for those dining, staying, or strolling riverside. Book well in advance if you want to witness this event from the warmth of a restaurant or hotel room. The skippers pay for their own fuel, decorations, and other expenses, so they welcome donations to keep the tradition going. The website provides a means for donations, plus gives an overview of hotels, restaurants, and viewing spots that offer a good vantage point.

Various locations: www.christmasships. org; early to mid.-Dec.; free

Holiday Ale Festival

The annual Holiday Ale Festival features some of the season's best craft beers (with names like Auld Nutcracker, Lumpa Coal, Ebenezer, and Sled Crasher). A large, clear tent keeps patrons dry but allows views of the city. Beer lovers sample robust brews, listen to seasonal music, and warm themselves by the gas heaters that surround the city's enormous holiday tree. Admission includes a souvenir mug and 12 beer tickets. Don't miss the annual **Brewers Brunch** (tickets can be purchased on the website), where breakfast and local and imported beers not otherwise available at the festival are served.

Downtown: Pioneer Courthouse Square, www.holidayale.com; Dec.; $35

Santacon

If you are visiting Portland in December, and you happen to see a large gathering of people dressed like Santa, don't be alarmed. You are simply witness to one of the city's most mysterious and talked-about events: Portland's version of Santacon. Revelers dress up as Santa and engage in a daylong pub crawl that takes them to several bars, a few parks, and the occasional stop for (relatively) innocent mischief. The event is so popular, it has spawned a number of copycat events. As such, the details of when and where the Santas meet is kept

Holiday Ale Festival

very much a secret until right before the event. Joining the crawl isn't hard if you do your research and make sure you are following the right event. While you are there, be sure to behave yourself in a manner befitting a true Portland Santa (don't be a jerk, bring cash, and above all, be nice to the city and your fellow Santas).

Various locations: www. portlandsantacon.com; Dec.; free

Fertile Ground Festival

All right, so January in Portland isn't exactly a "showcase" month. Tourism is down, the skies are gray, and the weather is, at best, unpredictable. It's tempting to sulk about the house, but frankly, a whole month indoors is just not natural for most Portlanders. Thank goodness this city is full of creative folks who are not willing to give up on January. Thanks to them, the city suddenly has a reason to get out of its collective pajamas and experience something truly original. In 2008, Portland launched its first citywide performing arts festival devoted entirely to new works. More than two years in the making, the Fertile Ground Festival is an ambitious 10-day event that unites more than a dozen performing arts groups to present a series of world premiere productions. Portland has always been a "fertile ground" for playwrights and premiere performances, so it's no surprise that so many companies are consistently able to develop their seasons around the idea of producing something new and groundbreaking during this event.

Various locations: www. fertilegroundpdx.org; Jan.; price varies

Portland Seafood & Wine Festival

While you are busy savoring all the bounties that the Northwest has to offer, you'll want to save some room for the Portland Seafood & Wine Festival. Taste some of the state's most savory seafood and most veritable vino, all while enjoying local live music. Show up early and be one of the first 300 people through the door and you'll receive a commemorative wineglass to sip from all year long. Food prices range $2-15, and wine samplings start at $0.50.

Northeast: Oregon Convention Center, 777 NE Martin Luther King Jr. Blvd., www. pdxseafoodandwinefestival.com; early Feb.; $15 adults, $12 seniors and children, free for children under 5

Annual Portland Golf Show

Kicking off the annual Pacific Northwest golf season, the Portland Golf Show gives enthusiasts a chance to get their swing into shape. You can try out the latest technology in clubs in the Green Demo Room, take the 50-foot putting challenge, get some free lessons from some of the area's top instructors, and shop the 5,000-square-foot clearance center, where you can replace all those balls you lost in a lake for a fraction of what you paid the first time. There's even a kiddie area where pint-size golfers will receive a custom-made club and a mini lesson for free.

Northeast: Oregon Convention Center, 777 NE Martin Luther King Jr. Blvd., www. portlandgolfshow.com; Feb.; $13 adults, $12 seniors, free for children under 12

Portland International Film Festival

Portland International Film Festival annually draws an audience of over

35,000 over two weeks in February, making it the biggest film event in Oregon. It premieres over 100 international shorts and feature films to film-loving audiences and hosts visiting artists and talkback sessions throughout. This is often a great place to catch foreign films that are creating an Oscar buzz, or check out Short Cuts, a program of experimental films presented by Cinema Project and the Northwest Film Center. In addition to films, there are also a number of parties and special events surrounding the festival, a full schedule of which can be found on the website.

Downtown: Whitsell Auditorium, 1219 SW Park Ave., www.nwfilm.org; Feb.; price varies

Portland Jazz Festival

The Portland Jazz Festival showcases local talent as well as widely known performers like Branford Marsalis, Esperanza Spalding, Bill Frisell, and Charlie Hunter. Spread out over various venues around the downtown area, the festival offers a unique look at both the future and history of jazz. It's not uncommon to see up-and-coming musicians take the stage with the legends who inspired them in the first place. Ticket prices for the headliners can run about $30-60, but there is something even for jazz fans on a budget. The festival always offers a number of free and low-priced music performances, jam sessions, films, lectures, and exhibits.

Downtown: www.pdxjazz.com; Feb.; price varies

RECREATION

Around here, we don't wait for the sun to start shining to enjoy the outdoors.

Portland is a city that bikes.

We're blessed in Portland to have access to more than 290 municipal parks that are perfect for walking, jogging, or simply enjoying a little rest and relaxation. You'd also be hard pressed to find a city more suited to cycling or hiking than Portland. Locals are all about living the two-wheeled or two-legged lifestyle, and the sheer number of bike lanes, trails, and pedestrian bridges in town is a testament to this.

There are many ways to experience the city. Go DIY and rent a bike or hitch yourself up to one of the many biking tours offered in town. You can hike up a trail and see the city from above or traipse into the marshlands and meet some of the local wildlife. Scream your lungs out in the stands of the Portland Timbers Army or sniff a bloom in a rose garden. Whatever your preferred adventure, Portland has a little something for everyone.

HIGHLIGHTS

Forest Park

○ **BEST WAY TO DRINK AND BIKE:** If you're looking for a party and an active way to visit some of Southeast Portland's popular brew-pubs, jump aboard **Pedalounge,** a human-powered bicycle built for 12 (page 156).

○ **BEST DIY BIKE ADVENTURE:** Bike some of the 20-plus miles comprising the easily accessible **Springwater Corridor.** Pop off as you like for fun of your choosing, whether that means exploring a wildlife refuge or a giant food cart pod (page 156).

○ **BEST PLACE TO SEE PORTLAND AT PLAY:** When the sun comes out, **Colonel Summers Park** is alive with picnickers, hula hoopers, jugglers, frisbee enthusiasts, and more (page 157).

○ **BEST PARK TO HUG A HUNDRED TREES:** Deep in the hills of Northwest Portland, **Forest Park** is one of the country's largest urban parks, with more than 5,000 acres of trees, trails, and topography to explore (page 159).

○ **BEST SPOT TO SEE A REAL SMACKDOWN:** The roller derby queens of **Rose City Rollers** are tough and seriously entertaining (page 162).

BIKE RENTALS AND TOURS
Pedal Bike Tours

Pedal Bike Tours is a bike rental place and tour guide company rolled into one. Tours range from simple rides around the city to a nine-mile jaunt through the Columbia River Gorge. Tours are themed and include the bike rental, helmet, and all the other equipment you might need. Take a trip through historic downtown and Old Town, go on an ecotour, or cruise the five-mile Oregon Brewery Tour past several of the area's most popular breweries and take a tour of one. Pedal Bike will custom-design a tour for you if you have something special you want to do. Want a tour of coffee shops and roasteries? Just ask.

MAP 1: 133 SW 2nd Ave., 503/243-2453, www.pedalbiketours.com; daily 10am-6pm; tours $59-99 per person, bike rental $10-20 per hour

Waterfront Bicycle

If you're looking to rent a cruiser for a little downtown exploration, Waterfront Bicycle has top-notch equipment and service. Hybrid bikes, cruisers, and road bikes all come with a helmet, bike bag, map, and lock. Road bike rentals also come with blow-out bags and a pump for fixing any flats. For kids in tow, they have trailers, trailer bikes, and kid-size rides, or for two, rent a tandem cruiser, which always looks adorable, by the way.

MAP 1: 10 SW Ash St., 503/227-1719, www.waterfrontbikes.com; Mon. and Wed.-Sat. 10am-6pm, Sun. 10am-5pm; bike rental $30-65 for 24 hours

BIKE TRAILS
Waterfront Bike Loop

This 12-mile loop on both sides of the Willamette is a great way to see the city without dodging cars. Westside access is found in Tom McCall Waterfront Park, along the seawall and bollards. On the east side, it's best to enter along the Vera Katz Eastbank Esplanade. If you would like to do a shorter route and stick with spectacular downtown views, loop between Hawthorne Bridge and Steel Bridge. If you want the full route going as far south as Sellwood Bridge, download a map from the "Getting Around" section of www.downtownportland.org by clicking on "PDOT Bike Maps." It will show you the exact route, telling you about places where you should be cautious of traffic, children, and narrow passages.

MAP 1: western access Tom McCall Waterfront Park; eastern access: Vera Katz Eastbank Esplanade; daily 5am-midnight; free

SPECTATOR SPORTS
Portland Timbers

The Timbers are more than just a soccer team, they are practically a way of life. The acronym RCTID (Rose City 'Til I Die) you'll spot on bumper stickers, scarves, and bathroom walls all over the city is not just a mantra in support of Portland, it is a catchphrase for unwavering support of the Portland Timbers. Enthusiastic supporters known as "The Timbers Army" describe themselves as "part carnival, part mosh pit, part revival meeting, part Christmas morning, filled with people from every part of

Portland Timbers game

the community and every walk of life." Taking in a soccer game can be a lot of fun, even if you aren't seated in the sea of green and white with the Army. The Timbers are tough competitors and, who knows, you might find yourself moved to join in when the crowd starts singing "You Are My Sunshine" at the 80th minute. It's a tribute to the former mascot Timber Jim.

MAP 1: Providence Park, 1844 SW Morrison St., www.timbers.com

MINI GOLF
Glowing Greens

Glowing Greens is a mini golf course like no other. This underground course in the midst of downtown is like a radioactive mash-up of Pirates of the Caribbean meets Alice in Wonderland. Only in Portland would you find an indoor black light 3-D miniature golf course (yes, 3-D). Animated creatures, psychedelic sea scenes, and stimulating sound effects pretty much turn your average Putt-Putt on its butt-butt. Opt for the 3-D glasses, but don't be afraid to take them off. They're trippy and fun, but not exactly helpful when making a shot.

MAP 1: 509 SW Taylor St., 503/222-5554, www.glowinggreens.com; Sun.-Thurs. noon-9pm, Fri.-Sat. noon-11pm; $11 adults, $9 seniors and children

BIKE CITY, USA

Portland has long been a city for cyclists and is frequently bestowed honors for being one of the most bike-friendly cities in the United States (and sometimes the world) by the likes of *Forbes*, *Bicycling* magazine, and the Travel Channel. Here are a few things to know about kicking up the kickstand in Portland.

- **Bike Lanes:** You'll find bicycle lanes painted on most Portland streets (sometimes with whimsical twists). Particularly hazardous lanes are sometimes painted blue to alert cyclists and motorists of added danger. When bike lanes aren't present, cyclists are expected to ride with the flow of traffic at a reasonable pace and as close to the edge of the roadway as safely possible.

- **Bike Maps:** Many bike maps are available online from various sites, including Portland's Department of Transportation, where you can download a pdf map or access an interactive map that tells you the best route to take on your adventure.

- **Bike Share:** It's hard to miss the bright orange bicycles all over town. **Biketown** (various locations, www.biketownpdx.com; daily 24 hours; $5 sign-up fee, $0.08 per minute), the Nike-sponsored bike share program, brings pay-as-you-go bicycles to everyone, tourist and local alike. Its bikes are specifically designed for urban riding, with adjustable seats, integrated lighting, and an eight-gear shift built into the handlebars. To use the bikes, you'll need to sign up for a membership online, on their mobile app, or at one of the bike kiosks; there are long-term as well as pay-as-you-go options. When finished with your ride, simply return the bike to any Biketown station or lock it to any public bike rack (for an additional fee).

- **Bridges:** Cycling is allowed on most Portland bridges, and sidewalks are widened to allow cyclists to share the space with pedestrians. On one day every summer, the city closes the bridges to all except bicyclists (and pedestrians) during **Bridge Pedal.**

- **Green Bike Boxes:** The City of Portland added these "Advanced Stop Line Boxes" to some difficult intersections to prevent the accidents that occur when a motorist is turning left and a cyclist is continuing forward. As a

Northwest and the Pearl District
Map 2

BIKE RENTALS AND TOURS

Cycle Portland

Cycle Portland was one of the first companies in the city to offer tours by bike. Founder Evan Ross was surprised that it wasn't something more bike shops and enthusiasts offered. The tours Ross and his team put together are engaging and educational; you can tell that they really love their city. While the Essential Portland tour, which takes you through the streets of downtown and the Pearl District, cyclist, if you come to a green box intersection, simply ride to the front of the box and wait for the light to change. If you are a motorist, stop behind the box and allow cyclists to move to the front.

- **Helmets:** Helmets are mandatory for everyone under the age of 16 unless wearing a helmet "would violate a religious belief or practice of the person." While adults over 16 are not required to wear helmets, it is a pretty good idea to do so anyway.

- **Limited Visibility:** Gray, rainy conditions mean less visibility, which is especially dangerous for cyclists. A front white light visible from at least 500 feet is required in these conditions and at night, as is a red rear reflector. But it's a good idea to also attach a flashing light to yourself or your backpack to increase visibility.

- **May:** The month of May is Portland Bike Month, and Portland is alive with celebrations all over the city as well as workshops and classes geared toward bike safety and advice.

- **Parking:** It is often easier to find bike parking than automobile parking. Many businesses have free bike parking on the sidewalk or in small sections of the street. You will need to bring your own lock. Bike lockers are also available for long-term rental throughout Portland through the Portland Department of Transportation.

- **Pedalpalooza:** Pedalpalooza is a monthlong happening in June, with volunteers guiding bike rides all over the city for free, many with zany themes. Portland's famous iteration of the **World Naked Bike Ride** also takes place in conjunction.

- **Sharing the Road:** Most Portland drivers are accustomed to sharing the road with cyclists, but you should follow the basic rules of safety. Ride with the flow of the traffic, not against it. Wear visible colors and lights, especially on rainy days or in the dark. Obey all traffic signals and maintain control of your bicycle.

- **Transit:** The buses, the streetcar, the aerial tram, and the MAX are all equipped with bike holders, and it does not cost extra to transport your bike.

is very enlightening, it is more fun to go off book and let the guides run deep into their Portland nerdery with a custom tour. Ross has been known to put together a Simpsons tour around the long-running popular show and its Portland-based creator Matt Groening, as well as a tour that features many of the locations from the IFC show *Portlandia*.

MAP 2: 117 NW 2nd Ave., 844/739-2453, www.portlandbicycletours.com, tours $39-59 adults, bike rental starting at $5 per hour or $20-35 per day

PARKS AND GARDENS
Jamison Square

When developers were planning the Pearl District in the early 1990s, they wanted to create open gathering spaces within the urban sprawl. Located on the full city block between NW Johnson and NW Kearney, Jamison's real gem is the interactive fountain and tidal pool. It's a popular spot for families in the heat of the summer. Children splash in the low pools and chase the ever-changing flow of water while their parents take advantage of the free Wi-Fi or chat with others. The park is on the streetcar line and adjacent to a number of coffee shops, pizza joints, and other restaurants, so it's a great spot to grab a bite and do some people-watching—providing you like children, of course, since this park is a haven for shrieking, but happy, tykes.

The park also features several sculptures, streetcar access on both sides, and a wooden boardwalk that connects it to Tanner Springs Park two blocks away.

MAP 2: 810 NW 11th Ave., 503/823-7529, www.portlandoregon.gov/parks; daily 5am-midnight; free

Northeast   Map 3

BIKE RENTALS AND TOURS
Everybody's Bikes

Everybody's Bikes highlights the culture and lifestyle of the Northeast and North Portland neighborhoods. The Beer and Parks tour takes you by a number of great eastside breweries and four area parks. The other tour introduces urban farms and treats you to baked goods, gourmet doughnuts, and sandwiches. Rental is affordable and available by the day or week. Everybody's Bikes has a number of well-maintained vintage bikes in addition to touring bikes and rugged steel-framed road bikes. They will find a bike that suits you and make the necessary adjustments to make it a perfect fit.

MAP 3: 305 NE Wygant St., 503/358-0152, www.portlandbicycletours.com; tours $45 adults, bike rental starting at $25 per day

PARKS AND GARDENS
Grant Park

Lovers of Beverly Cleary's Ramona books will want to grab a picnic and head to this Northeast Portland park. In addition to having tall, shady trees and vast expanses of green grass, it shelters sculptures of Ramona, Henry Huggins, and Henry's dog Ribsy.

The neighborhood was once home to Cleary, and many of the streets will look familiar to fans, especially Klickitat Street, the site of Ramona's home. There is a splash pad (which is similar to a fountain, but with little or no standing water), a playground, and an accessible restroom, so it is a great place to spend a sunny afternoon.

MAP 3: NE 33rd St., 503/823-7529, www.portlandoregon.gov/parks; daily 5am-midnight; free

SPECTATOR SPORTS
Portland Trail Blazers

Love them or hate them, the Portland Trail Blazers have been an active part of professional basketball since 1970 and always a Portland team. Portlanders tend to be loyal in their support but fickle in their devotion. Blazer fever kicks in with a vengeance whenever the team is successful, but when it is failing, the same base is rather nonplussed. That was all different in 1976, when Bill Walton led the team to a 49-33 season and the 1977 championship. Blazer mania peaked again in the early 1990s, shortly after billionaire Paul Allen purchased the team. With team legend and sentimental favorite Clyde "The Glide" Drexler as charismatic forward and a starting lineup including Buck Williams, Jerome Kersey, and Kevin Duckworth, the team was back in its fans' good graces.

What followed a decade later is what most Portlanders refer to as the "Jail Blazers" era. Every day it seemed that another player was facing arrest. Players such as Rod Strickland, Isaiah Rider, Ruben Patterson, and Qyntel Woods seemed to get more press for their off court behavior than their game skills. Hot-headed Rasheed Wallace was repeatedly ejected from games. Despite the continued wins, fans were giving up on the Blazers in droves. These days, the fans are slowly starting to regain trust in their team. With a number of strong (and well-behaved) players like Damian Lillard, Meyers Leonard, and CJ McCollum, the now very young team is starting to remind Portlanders of the days when the "Rip City Rhapsody" (a team spirit

song written for and recorded by the 1990s-era Blazers) was on everybody's brain.

MAP 3: Rose Garden Arena, 1 N. Center Court St., 503/797-9600, www.nba.com/blazers

Portland Winterhawks

The Portland Winterhawks are a major junior ice hockey team in the Western Hockey League based in western Canada and the Pacific Northwest. It is one of three leagues that make up the Canadian Hockey League, the highest level of nonprofessional hockey in the world. Most home games are at the Memorial Coliseum, though typically a few each season go to Rose Garden Arena. A great number of Winterhawks have graduated to play in the National Hockey League, including Mike Vernon, Gary Yaremchuk, Clint Malarchuk, Ray Ferraro, Adam

Portland Trail Blazers game

Deadmarsh, Steve Knowalchuk, Glen Wesley, Nolan Pratt, Byron Dafoe, Brendon Morrow, Jozef Balej, and Richie Regeh. The Winterhawks have won the Memorial Cup twice—in 1983 and again in 1998. They are known for doing fundraising events, like the Teddy Bear Toss, wherein fans toss brand-new bears onto the ice, which will then be donated to children's charities by the team. Portland broke the record in 2006 for most bears donated on one night, and then broke it again in 2007 when they collected 20,372 animals in one night. The 2015 record went to the Calgary Hitmen with 28,815 bears.

MAP 3: Memorial Coliseum, 300 N. Winning Way, 503/238-6366, www. winterhawks.com

Southeast

Map 4

BIKE RENTALS AND TOURS
✪ Pedalounge

This isn't so much a bike tour as a human-powered trolley trip. Twelve passengers—or "Loungers"—sit along a rail facing each other and pedal (there are also two spots for non-pedaling passengers), while a captain steers the way on a 2.5-hour voyage to as many as four breweries, pubs, and dive bars. Loungers can drink at the stops and also choose from a number of designated stops. But the journey is really the best part as the party rolls through the streets of Southeast Portland, ringing bells, singing songs, and waving to passersby.

MAP 4: 1125 SE Division St., 503/285-4844, www.pedalounge.com; $22-25

Clever Cycles

Clever Cycles is very clever indeed. In a city positively teeming with bike enthusiasts, they tapped into a market many bike shops had missed. Here it's not about the rising cost of oil or the newest fad in fitness bikes; the bikes are geared (pun intended) toward practical transportation. The company has about 20 bikes to rent out, and during the peak summer months, those are often sold out. The majority are Brompton folding bikes, which are sturdy and comfortable for people of all heights. The beauty of the folding bike is that it is easily carried on mass transit and in vehicles, making it much simpler to decide when you are done with your ride.

MAP 4: 900 SE Hawthorne Blvd., 503/334-1560, www.clevercycles.com; Mon.-Fri. 11am-6pm, Sat.-Sun. 11am-5pm; bike rental starting at $30 per day

BIKE TRAILS
✪ Springwater Corridor

The multiuse Springwater Corridor starts just south of the Vera Katz Eastbank Esplanade in Southeast Portland. It heads about 21 miles east to the amusingly named town of Boring, taking you past numerous places where you can hop off the route and explore, like **Oaks Bottom Wildlife Refuge** (around mile 2.5), **Sellwood** (around mile 3.5), and the excellent food cart pod **Cartlandia** (around mile 8.5). You can find a map on the Portland Parks & Recreation website. The corridor follows a former railroad route that ceased service in 1989. Most of it is paved and bordered by fields and trees, and though it does span some busy streets, most are equipped with crossing lights. It can get crowded on the weekends with bicyclists, runners, and walkers at the western starting point, but the farther out you head, the less populous and more abundant in flora and fauna.

MAP 4: SE Ivon St. and SE 4th Ave., www.portlandoregon.gov/parks; daily 24 hours; free

Springwater Corridor

Vera Katz Eastbank Esplanade

A leisurely ride along the waterfront is a great way to get a good look at the city, and from the Eastbank Esplanade, you have a choice of heading north and following the route across the Steel Bridge into downtown or south to the Springwater Corridor. There are several urban markers depicting the eastside city grid, and interactive panels provide information on the river and the city's history. The esplanade is named for former Portland mayor Vera Katz, and a statue of the lady herself smiling and saving a spot for you on a bench is near the Hawthorne Bridge.

MAP 4: SE Water Ave., 503/823-7529, www.portlandoregon.gov/parks; free

PARKS AND GARDENS
✪ Colonel Summers Park

This park may not seem like much if you don't catch it at the right time. Other than picnic tables, a basketball court, and an adorable community garden, it's mostly open lawn space. But on sunny weekends and Monday evenings—dubbed "Monday Funday," during which epic dodgeball games take place and others gather to kick off the week—the area buzzes with energy as jugglers, hula hoopers, hacky sackers, and fire dancers converge to hang out, practice, and collaborate. With its relaxed and welcoming vibe, it has become an unofficial meeting spot for area bohemians.

MAP 4: SE 17th Ave. and SE Taylor St., 503/823-7529, www.portlandoregon.gov/parks; daily 5am-10pm; free

Ladd Circle Park & Rose Gardens

Though his name may be cursed by drivers trying to navigate through the mystery that is Ladd's Addition, William Sargent Ladd was actually quite clever. He came west during the California Gold Rush and settled in Portland in 1851. The productive businessman and one-time mayor of Portland owned a 126-acre farm on Portland's east side, which he decided to subdivide in a manner similar to Pierre L'Enfant's plan for Washington, D.C. Ladd's design is based on a diagonal street system surrounding a central park and four rose gardens located on the points of a compass. It was a radical departure from the common grid pattern of the expanding city and one that still confuses drivers, who get stuck in a seemingly endless maze.

The central park was designed in 1909 by park superintendent Emanuel Mische, who planted camellias, perennials, and a lawn area, as well as numerous rosebushes with the intention of creating a stained-glass effect. The garden is still quite lovely, with over 3,000 roses of 60 varieties.

MAP 4: SE 16th Ave. and SE Harrison St., www.portlandoregon.gov/parks; daily 5am-midnight; free

Laurelhurst Park

Laurelhurst Park has a little bit of something for everyone. Within its 31 acres, there is a basketball court, soccer field, tennis court, volleyball court, playground, off-leash dog zone, horseshoe pit, picnic tables, a stage, and restrooms. There are also multiple paths winding through and around the park for strolling and observing some flora and fauna. The pond in the center of the park is well populated with ducks; you are not supposed to feed them, but they are fun to watch anyway.

MAP 4: 3756 SE Oak St., 503/823-7529, www.portlandoregon.gov/parks; daily 5am-10:30pm; free

Laurelhurst Park

WATERSPORTS
Willamette Jetboat Excursions

If you are not the floating and paddling sort, maybe you would rather see the Portland waterfront whiz past you while you enjoy sights, history, and scenic beauty from the seat of a jet boat. This tour shows off giant ships, bridges, elegant riverfront homes, historic Oregon City, and the majestic Willamette Falls. Each boat holds about 50, and there are both one- and two-hour excursions available. Reservations are highly recommended, particularly in the height of summer. Oh, and by the way, do wear sunblock and expect to get a little wet.

MAP 4: 1945 SE Water Ave., 503/231-1532, www.willamettejet.com; $39 adults, $25 children ages 4-11, free for children under 4

HIKING

✪ Forest Park

If you really want to get away from it all, look no farther than Forest Park, the 5,200-acre urban forest—one of the country's largest—that sits just outside of downtown Portland in the Tualatin Hills. Inside Forest Park's peaceful vastness, it's hard to imagine there's a city just outside its perimeter. Extending along the east ridge above the Willamette River, Forest Park is bounded by West Burnside Street on the south, and abuts the Alphabet District in Northwest Portland, making it a popular retreat for those who seek peace and solitude close by. It features 70 miles of trails for hikers, as well as bikers and horseback riders, and is abundant in flora and fauna; the massive canopy of trees offers a safe and prosperous habitat for 112 species of birds and 62 species of mammals. Whether you're looking for a quick jaunt without leaving the city or want to lose yourself in tall trees, moss, flowers, birds, and quiet, this is your park.

If you're feeling ambitious, take a 12-mile jog from the Leif Erickson Drive entrance, which is conveniently metered at each quarter mile with a white pole sign. There are some spectacular views along the way, especially at Mile 3, where you get a great view of the city. Another picturesque trail is the Lower Macleay Trail, which you

Forest Park

GREATER PORTLAND

RECREATION

Sauvie Island (http://sauvieisland.org), pronounced either SO-vee or SAW-vee, is just 10 miles northwest of downtown Portland, past Forest Park, and makes a great day trip. During the summer months, it offers a number of **U-pick berry, flower, and stone fruit farms** as well as **nature trails** and **fishing spots.** The tiny island is also home to a number of wide, sandy **beaches** for sunbathing along the Columbia River, including Collins Beach, a popular clothing-optional beach. Sauvie is particularly busy in the fall when Portlanders come out in droves to the **pumpkin patches** of **Kruger's Farm** (17100 NW Sauvie Island Rd., 503/621-3489, www.krugersfarm.com; mid-Apr.-Nov. daily 9am-7pm) to pick out a pumpkin, ride on a hay truck, or tackle the haunted corn maze.

To get here, just take Highway 30 west toward St. Helens and turn right to cross over the Sauvie Island Bridge. Due to the single-bridge access, the time it takes to make the trip can vary a lot, especially during peak times (sunny summer days and Oct.), but about a half-hour is standard. To park in any of the wildlife areas, which include all the beaches, you'll need a **parking permit** ($10), which can be purchased from a few spots on the island, including the **Oregon Department of Fish and Wildlife** (18330 NW Sauvie Island Rd., 503/621-3488) and **Cracker Barrel Grocery** (15005 NW Sauvie Island Rd.).

GREATER PORTLAND

can find at Macleay Park (near NW Thurman and NW 29th). It's a pleasant, short hike through shady trees and small streams. Stick to the trail and you'll end up at the Audubon Sanctuary, which has its own circuit of beautiful trails. At the southeastern end of the park, the popular Wildwood Trail—which winds some 30 miles through Forest Park—passes Pittock Mansion and offers breathtaking panoramic views of Mounts Hood, St. Helens, Rainier, Adams, and Jefferson.

MAP 7: NW 29th Ave. and Upshur St. to Newberry Rd., www.forestparkconservancy. org; daily 5am-10pm; free

Audubon Sanctuary

This 150-acre nature sanctuary, nestled against Forest Park, is only five minutes from downtown, but it feels miles away. Chock-full of native flora and fauna, it has over four miles of forested hiking trails. At various times during the year, you can find over 40 species of birds and 60 species of mammals making their home in this sanctuary. Pick up a trail guide at the Audubon House, which will provide you with a look at all three trails. The Pittock Bird Sanctuary trailhead is

most accessible from the parking lot, but try finding the Founders trailhead first (across the street). It offers more exercise and lovely forest scenery as well as a view of Oregon's native plants unfettered by the invasive effects of English ivy and other nonnative plants.

MAP 7: 5151 NW Cornell Rd., www. audubonportland.org; daily dawn-dusk; free

Tryon Creek State Natural Area

Tryon Creek State Natural Area is a 645-acre park that lies between Boones Ferry Road and Terwilliger Boulevard in Southwest Portland. The park includes hiking trails and horse trails, and a paved bicycle path runs along the east edge of the park toward Lake Oswego. The park once belonged to pioneer settler Socrates Hotchkiss Tryon Sr., who left the land to his family when he died. Years later, the land was sold, and a few decades were spent logging the cedar and fir trees until the infamous Columbus Day Storm blew down most of the remaining trees. In 1969, Multnomah County bought 45 acres in the hopes of establishing a municipal park. Citizens banded together to help and eventually formed the nonprofit Friends of Tryon Creek, which to this day helps raise funds, purchase land, and maintain the beauty and health of the reserve.

These days, the land is beginning to thrive as Douglas firs, western red cedars, and bigleaf maples tower over trilliums and sword ferns. As you stroll, it's not uncommon to see owls, woodpeckers, blue herons, and deer, as well as steelhead trout, Coho salmon, salamanders, banana slugs, and beavers.

MAP 7: 11321 SW Terwilliger Blvd., www.tryonfriends.org; daily dawn-dusk; free

PARKS AND GARDENS
Harper's Playground at Arbor Lodge Park

It took several years of work, but this playground finally came to life thanks to the efforts of one family, countless donations, and the steadfast support of the Portland Timbers Army. After watching their disabled daughter struggle to play at other local parks, the Goldberg family dreamed up a park that would be all-inclusive by reimagining play structures in ways that would allow children of all types to play. Harper's Playground is a place that people drive from all over the state to visit, and it is a truly joyous place to experience.

MAP 7: N. Delaware and N. Bryant St., 503/823-2525, www.portlandoregon.gov/parks; daily 5am-midnight; free

Leach Botanical Gardens

If you head deep into Southeast Portland, you'll discover hidden treasure at the Leach Botanical Gardens. Named for Lilla Leach—who is famous for botanical research, her exploration of the Siskiyou and Klamath Mountains, and discovering five plant species new to science—and her husband, this combination of forest and garden offers a woody feel. The original Leach residence is still on the property and serves as one of several entries to the garden's nine acres of walkable land. This botanical garden—or living museum—sits next to Johnson Creek and offers 2,300 planted species, a rock garden, physics garden, fern collection, wildflowers, and even a composting demonstration center.

MAP 7: 6704 SE 122nd Ave., 503/823-9503, www.leachgarden.org; Tues.-Sat. 9am-4pm, Sun. 1pm-4pm; free

Mount Tabor

Mount Tabor Park is named for the eponymous dormant volcanic cinder cone that it surrounds. It wasn't until 1912, many years after the neighborhood and the park had been established at its base, that it was discovered that the mountain was actually a volcano (extinct for 3,000 years), one of only two urban volcanoes in North America. It's a popular spot for many reasons, including its great views over the city. In the summer, you will find many a Portlander picnicking or sunning themselves on the grassy hillsides. The beautiful 195-acre park was designed by the Olmsted brothers and includes basketball courts, picnic areas, play areas, off-leash dog areas, horseshoe pits, a stage, tennis courts, and volleyball courts. Numerous paved and unpaved trails also make Mount Tabor a great spot for walking as well as biking, for cyclists and dirt bikers alike. Find a trail map on the Portland Parks & Recreation website. Mount Tabor is also the home of the annual Adult Soapbox Derby, a riotous event in which grown men and women race each other down the hill in their home-built nonmotorized cars at breakneck speeds.

MAP 7: SE 60th Ave. and Salmon St., www.portlandoregon.gov/parks; daily 5am-midnight; free

SPECTATOR SPORTS
✪ Rose City Rollers

The Rose City Rollers, a collection of roller derby divas, have been tearing up tracks in Portland since 2004. Sure, they have tongue-in-cheek names like Madame Bumpsalot, Layla Smackdown, and Rocket Mean (their cofounder and executive director), and their costumes often involve fishnet stockings under their knee pads, but once the skates go on, they take their sport pretty seriously. At the derby, teams battle it out for points, with five girls from each team on the track at any given time. While one player fights her way through the crowd, earning one point for every member of the opposite team that she passes, her teammates try to ensure that she can stay on her feet, all the while endeavoring to stop the opposition from passing. Basically, it's a whole lot of elbows, shoulders, and knees flying about at (literally) breakneck speed. Rose City Rollers events often draw as many as 2,500 spectators, and oftentimes sell out the seats of the Expo Center.

MAP 7: Portland Expo Center, 2060 N. Marine Dr., www.rosecityrollers.com

WATERSPORTS
Milo McIver State Park

There are a number of rivers and streams that are fun spots to float, swim, or soak when the weather gets warm. Estacada's Milo McIver State Park on the lower Clackamas River is a great spot for inner tubing or raft floating. Flotation devices can be purchased at most outdoor stores, Fred Meyer stores, or tire shops. There are some mild rapids along the Clackamas, so wearing a life vest is always a good idea—as is avoiding any alcohol until after you're out of the water.

MAP 7: 24101 S. Entrance Rd., Estacada, 503/630-7150, www.oregonstateparks.org/park_142.php; daily 7am-10pm; $5 per day

Smith and Bybee Wetlands Natural Area

The Smith and Bybee Wetlands Natural Area, consisting of around 2,000 acres of protected wetlands, is the largest of its kind within an American city. Surrounded by industrial areas in North Portland, this fragile ecosystem was developed for waterborne activities such as paddling. There's also a short trail with wildlife-viewing platforms from which you can spot beavers, river otters, and one of the largest western painted turtle populations in the state.

MAP 7: 5300 N. Marine Dr., 503/797-1850; daily 5am-sunset; free

GOLF
Gendoveer Golf Club

Glendoveer has 36 holes, and when it's in tip-top shape, it's considered by many to be the best public course in the city. Many regular users prefer the East Course because it's hillier and more heavily treed, which presents interesting challenges depending on how the wind picks up over the hills. The West Course is easier for most because it lacks the tight, tree-lined passages and does not have any water hazards. The weekends can get crowded and require more patience while you wait for your opportunity to hit, so book on a weekday or during off-hours if you can. This course also has a jogging trail (open to the public) that circles the greens. With all the huge, old trees and rolling greens, it makes for a really beautiful walk or run, whether or not you golf.

MAP 7: 14015 NE Glisan St., 503/253-7507, www.golfglendoveer.com; daily 6:30am-9pm; $11-39 per 18 holes

Heron Lakes Golf Club

Heron Lakes has two 18-hole, par 72 courses: Greenback and the Great Blue. There's water everywhere, so bringing a handful of extra balls is not a bad idea. The Great Blue is a traditional links-style track where you will find the par 4, 466-yard 8th hole, which has a 90-degree dogleg left and a dangerous slough. Greenback is a better course for beginners but comes with plenty of challenges for more seasoned players as well (like numerous trees that must be avoided). Tee times can be booked online through the website or over the phone.

MAP 7: 3500 N. Victory Blvd., 503/289-1818, www.heronlakesgolf.com; daily 6am-9pm; $13-36 per 18 holes

The Pub Courses at Edgefield

There are many reasons to head out to Edgefield. Meandering through the stately property and the Pub Courses are at the top of the list. There are two separate pitch-n-putt courses, including a 20-hole course (West) and a 12-hole course (East). The holes range about 40-80 yards throughout, and there is one mat tees for all hitters. The newest portion, which opened in the spring of 2008, was modeled after Burningbush, the fantasy fairways from Michael Murphy's *Golf in the Kingdom,* and includes 15 holes. It's a good place to practice your short game or simply entertain yourself while gathering with friends and drinking some of the famous McMenamins beer.

MAP 7: 2126 SW Halsey St., Troutdale, 503/492-5442, www.mcmenamins.com; hours vary seasonally; $12-20

SHOPS

Portlanders don't tend to get too fancy when it comes to fashion, but they do

Cargo

tend to have a lot of personality. While suits and jeans commingle in most of the city's restaurants and arts venues, a night out on the town just might call for a vintage statement necklace or a fedora. Fortunately, Portland is a hotbed of jewelry and clothing makers, haberdashers, and handbag artists who are all about giving you the icing for your cake. P-Town has become known for its creative boutiques and concept stores, as well as a distinctive style and personal touch.

A mantra for many Portlanders is "Shop Local." While you'll find a handful of malls, department stores, and chains scattered about the city, most citizens prefer to purchase everything, from the shoes on their feet to the paint on their walls, from people who live near their own backyards.

Hence the fervent indie shop scene, often featuring locally made products. The city's fashion sense has been built on the back of its DIY roots, and, for many designers and makers, the core motivation comes from a sense that if someone else can make it, it can be done better and greener right here in Portland.

HIGHLIGHTS

Tender Loving Empire

⊗ **BEST PLACE TO BUY A UNIQUE GIFT:** Every weekend, artists bring their wares out to the **Portland Saturday Market,** the largest continuously operating market in the United States (page 167).

⊗ **BEST PLACE TO FIND YOUR PERFECT PORTLAND SOUVENIR:** Whether it's a plushy cloud or bottle of Portland rain, **Tender Loving Empire** has an adorably weird gift to commemorate your trip (page 168).

⊗ **BEST PLACE TO FIND YOUR INNER CHILD:** Even the most straitlaced adult has a hard time not squealing for joy at **Finnegan's Toys & Gifts** (page 171).

⊗ **BEST PLACE TO BEGIN YOUR I DOS:** At **Gem Set Love** you're likely to find an engagement ring that is one-of-a-kind and has a history that bears repeating (page 173).

⊗ **BEST PLACE TO PICK UP SOMETHING FOR YOUR FOODIE FRIEND: Providore Fine Foods** is a one-stop-shop for specialty Pacific Northwest sauces and marinades, beers and wines, and locally produced cookbooks and gifts (page 180).

⊗ **BEST PLACE TO ENGAGE IN HERO WORSHIP:** An inclusive, judgment-free comic book shop, **Books with Pictures** is a great place to discover new titles and revisit classics (page 185).

⊗ **BEST PLACE TO DIG FOR RARE VINYL:** Independent record retailer **Music Millennium** has a remarkable selection of used and new CDs, vinyl, and DVDs, as well as memorabilia (page 186).

⊗ **BEST PLACE TO FILL A SOCK DRAWER:** Socks for Christmas were never much fun until **Sock Dreams** came along; the beloved company makes black socks seem like an insult to your feet. (page 189).

SHOPPING DISTRICTS

Downtown

Shopping in downtown Portland is remarkably accessible, thanks to its dense concentration and affordable parking options. It is best to head near SW Yamhill between SW 3rd and SW 4th Avenues, where there are a number of parking options adjacent to the Pioneer Place Mall and other local shops.

MAP 1: bounded by W. Burnside to the north, I-405 to the west and south, and the Willamette River to the east

The Pearl District

High-end boutiques, sophisticated salons, and fashionable cafés mix to make these streets infinitely charismatic, particularly during the monthly First Thursday art walk. This is where you will find a number of Portland's hottest boutiques, like Sloan and Hanna Andersson. It's also the home of the iconic Powell's City of Books. Don't worry if you get overwhelmed; you can rest as often as you like in one of the many cafés or martini lounges.

MAP 2: bounded by the Willamette River to the north, W. Burnside to The Pearl

NW 23rd and NW 21st Avenues

Block-for-block, this district is Portland's prime shopping area. The Alphabet District is packed from A to Z (actually, from B to T is more accurate) with unique boutiques and a few high-end chain stores. Begin at West Burnside Avenue. You'll pass by some chain stores on your way to NW Glisan, where the street really kicks into gear. Try to hit one side and then double back to catch the other side before you head a few blocks over to NW 21st Avenue.

MAP 2: NW 23rd Ave. and NW 21st Ave. between W. Burnside and NW Thurman St.

Alberta Arts District

Sprinkled with galleries and artsy boutiques, Alberta Street is a perfect neighborhood to find something unique and inspiring. It takes a bit of walking to hit all the great shops along this 20-block spread, but the street is always alive and vibrant with activity. Once a month, when Alberta hosts the Last Thursday art walk, galleries and stores invite guests to partake in special discounts, treats, and meet-and-greet opportunities with designers, artists, and special guests. If you are not a fan of crowds, avoid Last Thursday altogether and come in the afternoon when things are decidedly less chaotic.

MAP 3: Alberta St. between NE 12th Ave. and NE 33rd Ave.

Hawthorne Boulevard and Belmont Street

On SE Hawthorne Boulevard and SE Belmont Street, the vibe is laid-back and independent. This is the area where Portland's counterculture has put down its bohemian roots, opening up funky coffeehouses, indie music stores, and hip and inexpensive clothing stores. Weird isn't weird on these parallel streets (separated by five blocks); it's the standard. While Belmont appeals with its sweet charm and quiet devil-may-care attitude, Hawthorne is a bit more like San Francisco's Haight-Ashbury with its mash-up of hippies and hipsters.

MAP 4: SE Hawthorne Blvd. between SE 11th Ave. and 55th Ave., SE Belmont St. between SE 31st Ave. and 60th Ave.

Sellwood

Sellwood keeps a firm grip on the past. Some two dozen antiques and vintage stores populate the neighborhood's **13th Avenue,** known as **Antique**

BEST SOUVENIRS

COFFEE
Find locally roasted coffees at **MadeHere PDX** and **Stumptown Coffee Roasters.**

LOCAL ARTS AND CRAFTS
Pick up locally made souvenirs and gifts at places like the **Portland Saturday Market, Tender Loving Empire,** and **Land Gallery.**

BEER GROWLERS
Pretty much every brewery sells a branded refillable beer growler, but **Deschutes Brewery and Public House** and **Base Camp Brewing** have particularly nice ones.

WILLAMETTE VALLEY WINE
A number of tasting rooms are scattered throughout the city, but you can also purchase a bottle to take home at **Providore Fine Foods.**

MadeHere PDX

Row. It's been a destination for collectors for nearly 40 years. Mixed in with all of the street's coffee shops, cafés, restaurants, and boutiques, this is a great stretch to spend a few hours exploring knickknacks, rummaging through records, or discovering some cool costume jewelry or collectible art.

MAP 5: 7875-8027 SE 13th Ave.

Mississippi Avenue
Mississippi Avenue is a six-block-long walkable stretch of North Portland and home to a number of quirky, local boutiques, as well as restaurants and bars. One of Portland's youngest hot neighborhoods, it has a youthful, hipster vibe.

MAP 6: N. Mississippi Ave. from N. Fremont Ave. to N. Skidmore St.

Downtown   Map 1

LOCAL GOODS
✪ Portland Saturday Market
Portland Saturday Market is the nation's largest open-air craft market. Each Saturday and Sunday (it's open both weekend days, despite its name), artists haul their paintings, sculptures, lawn art, clothing, and jewelry down to Old Town and assemble one of the best displays in town, with row after row of stalls to peruse. The east side of the market is where you'll find the best handmade merchandise. Every artist on this side of the market was chosen by a jury. If you are short on time, skip the other side, which is an international import market focused on jewelry, clothing, incense, tapestries, and other such things.

MAP 1: 48 SW Naito Pkwy., 503/241-4188,
www.portlandsaturdaymarket.
com; Mar.-Dec. Sat. 10am-5pm, Sun.
11am-4:30pm

✪ Tender Loving Empire

This record label turned mini-empire
(it has four locations, including one at
the Portland airport) has been offering small-batch artisan jewelry, small
press books, indie comics, quirky
gifts, and locally produced vinyl records for over a decade now. It col-
laborates with local artists to stock
its stores with unique items that can't
be found anywhere else, so it's a great
spot for Portland-themed gifts like
T-shirts, glassware, hats, prints, and
plush critters. You'll also find a listening station where you can sample some
of the music from the label and pick up
the albums you like on vinyl or on CD.
MAP 1: 412 SW 10th Ave., 503/243-5859,
www.tenderlovingempire.com; daily
10am-7pm

Tender Loving Empire

Boy's Fort

In this 2,500-square-foot shop, owners Richard Rolfe and Jake France
have assembled a fun collection of locally made products as well as vintage
finds unlikely to be seen anywhere
else. There is a distinct masculine vibe

Portland Saturday Market

here, with everything from beard oil
to box guitars and hand-forged bottle
openers for sale. The shop also carries
men's leather bags, wallets, and jewelry, as well as custom-built furniture
(like a truck bed turned sleeping bed)
and reclaimed light fixtures.
MAP 1: 1001 SW Morrison St.,
503/223-9510, www.boysfort.com;
Sun.-Mon. 11am-6pm, Tues.-Sat. 11am-7pm

Crafty Wonderland

Here you will find jewelry, T-shirts,
greeting cards, retro aprons, miniature shrines, kitschy barrettes, stuffed
robots, handmade candles, and more.
Everything has that inexplicable
Portland charm, so this is a great place
to find a gift to commemorate a visit
to the city. Crafty Wonderland is basically the Portland Etsy community
come to life. In fact, many of the artists featured here have their own Etsy
store, and it is fun to see it all in one
place. The store started as a pop-up retail version of the hugely popular annual bazaar of the same name.
MAP 1: 808 SW 10th Ave., 503/224-9097,
www.craftywonderland.com; Mon.-Sat.
10am-6pm, Sun. 11am-6pm

GIFTS AND HOME
Canoe

Canoe is a pretty little store full of
crafts, housewares, gifts, and other

such things from around the world. It focuses on finding unique, hand-crafted pieces that showcase artistry and design. The space is tidy, warm, and welcoming, and the staff is friendly, if aloof. It's a great place to shop for gifts or trinkets to spruce up your home. Everything here is modern and beautiful, and while you might not need any of it, you sure will want it.

MAP 1: 1233 SW 10th Ave., 503/889-8545, www.canoeonline.net; Mon.-Sat. 10am-6pm, Sun. 11am-5pm

CLOTHING AND ACCESSORIES

Adorn

Adorn is a trendy women's boutique that carries a wide selection of brands, including Prairie Underground, Hailey and Co, Velvet, Michael Stars, and Halston Heritage, as well as premium denim brands like Citizens of Humanity, Hudson, and 7 For All Mankind. You'll find a lot of light-weight, easygoing fabrics and some wardrobe staples to match the cool palette of the Pacific Northwest. Stylists here do a good job of tying local designers in with bigger name brands, and they're quite happy to introduce you to some local pieces or put together that perfectly breezy outfit for you.

MAP 1: 1016 SW Washington St., 503/206-6208, www.shopadorn. com; Sun.-Wed. 11am-6pm, Thurs.-Sat. 11am-7pm

Danner

In the early days of Portland, the city was filled with loggers, pioneers, and working men who stomped around in rugged boots. By the early 1930s, a lot of those boots were Danner boots. Long recognized as a maker of durable work boots, the brand has recently embraced a more lifestyle-focused

Boy's Fort

approach. Located in the swanky Union Way shopping arcade, this is Danner's first stand-alone retail shop. In it, you can find the sort of rugged boots Danner is known for, but also its Stumptown collection, a line that mixes the modern with the vintage in an homage to the Portland of the past.

MAP 1: 1022 W. Burnside St., 503/262-0331, www.danner.com; Mon.-Sat. 11am-7pm, Sun. 11am-6pm

Frances May

Frances May has long been a Portland favorite for fashion-forward women's and men's clothes. Owned by a grandmother-granddaughter team, it blends modern-day panache with sweet, old-fashioned whimsy. In addition to offering some amazing one-of-a-kind vintage pieces, the shop carries the latest from hot local designers like Bright Volume, Kate Towers, and Another Feather. Throughout the season, you can also find vintage-inspired jewelry from various designers and a timeless collection of shoes and belts by Rachel Comey. Frances May has also started selling its own line of upscale-casual clothing, born of a collaboration with designer Rachel Turk.

MAP 1: 1003 SW Washington St., 503/227-3402, www.francesmay.net; Mon.-Sat. 11am-7pm, Sun. noon-6pm

John Helmer Haberdashery

For about 80 years now, the Helmer family has been outfitting Portland with some pretty distinguished styles, focusing on menswear, accessories, and tailoring. Whether you're the sort to don a leather driving cap or an English derby, chances are the shop will have the hat for you. Also here is a very small selection of ladies' hats (particularly around the Kentucky Derby season). Shopping at John Helmer is like stepping back into a time when hats, scarves, and sock garters were de rigueur. The staff is still mostly Helmers (second and third generation), and just as knowledgeable and friendly as the originals.

MAP 1: 969 SW Broadway, 503/223-4976, www.johnhelmer.com; Mon.-Fri. 9:30am-6pm, Sat. 9:30am-5:30pm

Mario's

Mario's is to a department store like Kobe beef is to an overcooked sirloin. The service is intended to be attentive and hospitable instead of merely advantageous. The first floor of this downtown shrine to excess is devoted to menswear; ladies will find their haven upstairs, where sales associates offer a glass of wine or champagne to sip while you shop. If you're looking for labels, Mario's has all the drool-worthy ones, like Prada, Pucci, Vera Wang, Dolce & Gabbana, and Christian Louboutin. Yes, the prices are high, but the sales are spectacular.

MAP 1: 833 SW Broadway, 503/227-3477, www.marios.com; Mon.-Sat. 10am-6pm, Sun. noon-5pm

underU4men

This small boutique offers every kind of men's underwear, sleepwear, and swimwear you could hope to find, from basic to exotic. Underwear comes in a multitude of colors, shapes, material, and support levels, turning this store into a hipper, sportier version of Victoria's Secret—for men. Items here are comfortable, athletic, and sexy enough to make anyone blush, but don't expect such style to come cheap. You can expect to pay $20-100 for each pair of underwear and considerably more for sleepwear and swimwear. An apothecary and barbershop are also located on-site, making it a pretty useful stop for the gentleman who wants a little more out of life than boxers or briefs.

MAP 1: 800 SW Washington St., 503/274-2555, www.underu4men.com; Mon.-Thurs. and Sat. 10am-7pm, Fri. 10am-9pm, Sun. 11am-6pm

VINTAGE AND ANTIQUES
Rebels and Heroes

If you love vintage Levi's 501s, Pendleton flannels, and motorcycle memorabilia, this is the shop for you. Its selection is well curated, so although you won't find screaming deals here, it is a great place to find unique and iconic pieces that inspire nostalgia and old-school Americana vibes. The shop specializes in men's wear, with particular focus on sturdy denim, leather, fleece, and flannel—so if you find yourself struggling in the cool Pacific Northwest weather, this is a good place to find clothes that'll have you looking like a local in no time.

MAP 1: 429 SW 10th Ave., 541/639-1661; Sun.-Fri. 11am-7pm, Sat. 11am-9pm

GOURMET TREATS
Portland Farmers Market at Portland State University

The biggest of many farmers markets in Portland, this Saturday market fills up the Park Blocks with as many as 250 produce stands, art booths, and food vendors. You can't get fruits, vegetables, and flowers any fresher than this, short of growing them yourself. The market is a great place to grab a bite to eat, listen to some music, or stock up on special handmade treats like freshly smoked salmon from The Smokery or lavender-infused jelly from Sundance Lavender Farm. For a special evening indulgence, pick up some of Rogue Creamery's world-class blue cheese, a bottle of Shy Chenin Blanc from Twist, and a Pearl Bakery baguette.

MAP 1: Portland State University in the South Park Blocks between SW Harrison St. and SW Montgomery St.; Apr.-Oct. Sat. 8:30am-2pm, Nov.-Dec. Sat. 9am-2pm

CHILDREN'S STORES
✪ Finnegan's Toys & Gifts

Spacious but stuffed to the rafters with smiling penguins, wind-up birds, colorful trains, and every game under the sun, Finnegan's is a gem. Find classic and collectible toys like Raggedy Ann, Playmobil, Curious George, and Radio Flyer, as well as fun newfangled robots and crazy building sets from Melissa & Doug, HK Kites & Design, and Lego. There are some wooden toys and games to keep little hands busy, and when it's time to leave, there are small, inexpensive trinkets to distract them from that expensive toy they're likely to cling to. Finnegan's is a popular spot for families to stop in and play, thanks to its proximity to the Multnomah County Library and the MAX line.

MAP 1: 820 SW Washington St., 503/221-0306, www.finneganstoys.com; Mon.-Sat. 10am-6pm, Sun. 11am-5pm

SHOPPING CENTERS
Pioneer Place Mall

Inside downtown's side-by-side shopping towers, Pioneer Place, you will find a fairly walkable mall that houses such upscale retailers as Louis Vuitton and Coach, as well as more affordable favorites like Forever 21, Gap, and J. Crew. A food court is on the bottom floor, and sky bridges over the streets take you between the two buildings.

MAP 1: 700 SW 5th Ave., 503/228-5800, www.pioneerplace.com; Mon.-Sat. 10am-8pm, Sun. 11am-6pm

Union Way

Upscale boutiques like Danner and Self Edge, a men's denim retailer, are packed into this modern shopping arcade at Portland's West End, across from Powell's Books. You can also find special treats and eats here from shops like Wailua Shave Ice, a Kauai-based shave-ice spot.

MAP 1: 1022 W. Burnside St., 503/922-0056; hours vary by shop

Danner at Union Way

PET SUPPLIES
Urban Fauna

For the pet owner interested in unique items and accessories, Urban Fauna is the place to go. This store specializes in difficult-to-find, high-quality items from around the world. Urban Fauna offers obedience classes that can turn excessively energetic and unruly dogs into upright citizens, and there are also doggy day care and grooming services for pet owners on the go. It stocks chew-friendly toys, comfortable leashes, and cozy beds, as well as a good selection of high-quality food. Products in this store go way beyond man's best friend and cater to the needs of cats, birds, fish, and reptiles as well.

MAP 1: 939 SW 10th Ave., 503/223-4602, www.urbanfauna.com; Mon.-Fri. 7am-7pm

Northwest and the Pearl District   Map 2

LOCAL GOODS
Hello From Portland

If you are looking for some art, clothing, or trinkets to celebrate or remember the distinct personality of Portland, this little shop should be right up your alley. It has a ton of beer koozies, stickers, magnets, T-shirts, and accessories celebrating things like the Oregon rain, Sasquatch, and bridges. If you have a little one in your life, look for the Larry the Dog books, where you can follow the adventures of Larry as he explores all that makes Portland the city it is. The shop also has a selection of Stumptown Coffees, Jacobsen Salt Co. candies, and infused salts.

MAP 2: 514 NW Couch St., 971/279-2787, http://hellofromportland.net; Mon.-Sat. 10:30am-6pm, Sun. noon-6pm

MadeHere PDX

Founded by a former footwear product developer and a former Fender executive, MadeHere PDX is a shop that highlights the talents of Portland-based designers, artists, and makers. MadeHere is more art gallery than cute memorabilia shop, and a great place to discover some of the artists who make their mark on the world through welding, stitching, brewing, and building. You will find locally roasted coffees, drinking vinegars from Pok Pok, beard grooming essentials from Damn Good Soap, and BlaqPaks, as well as countless other items.

MAP 2: 40 NW 10th Ave., 503/224-0122, www.madehereonline.com; Sun.-Wed. and Fri. 11am-6pm, Thurs. 11am-7pm, Sat. 10am-7pm

MadeHere PDX

CLOTHING AND ACCESSORIES
✪ Gem Set Love

If you're in the market for a unique engagement ring or one-of-a-kind piece of jewelry, Gem Set Love is likely to have something you can't live without. The cozy boutique has an immense selection of vintage and antique jewelry, mostly purchased from estate sales. Many of the rings here hail from the 1880s to the 1940s, and each has a story. Find a wedding set that belonged to high school sweethearts married for 60 years, or try on a cocktail ring that adorned a flapper's finger. In addition, the shop sells a selection of new, locally made jewelry and accessories, like delicate droplet earrings from Brunet, bright-colored lockets, and mixed-media statement pieces.

MAP 2: 720 NW 23rd Ave., 503/226 0629, www.gemsetlove.com; Mon.-Sat. 11:30am-6pm, Sun. noon-5pm

Dr. Martens

The United States headquarters for this iconic United Kingdom boot brand with roots in the punk scene is located in Portland's Pearl District—and although you might think it out of place among the chichi boutiques of the neighborhood, the brand fits right in. At the base of its headquarters, crowned with a giant boot, you'll find its retail shop carrying many of the iconic Doc looks, some artistic collaborations and unique styles, as well as bags, backpacks, key chains, and maintenance supplies. This store is small, but packed with items that are hard (if not impossible) to find elsewhere.

MAP 2: 2 NW 10th Ave., 503/552-9000, www.drmartens.com/us; Mon.-Sat. 10am-8pm, Sun. 11am-7pm

Folly

Folly's stylish pieces, made in-house by owner Sarah Bibb, have a following, and offer great construction and wearability. Bibb employs a lot of soft, feminine silhouettes with flowing dresses, simple slips, and elegant wraps that are classic and comfortable.

MAP 2: 1005 NW 16th St., 503/954-1334, www.follypdx.com; Mon.-Fri. 10am-7pm, Sat. 11am-6pm

Foundation

If you've ever wondered where your money is going when you buy that new scarf or handbag, lay down your worries at Foundation. Yes, it is a stylish women's fashion boutique in the heart of the Alphabet shopping district, but this little shop donates all—yes, all—of its profits to a different charity each quarter. Its goal is to raise social awareness. Of course, it doesn't hurt that the shop's offerings—monochromatic basics, breezy dresses, classic outerwear, and an abundance of denim—are stylish and timeless.

MAP 2: 919 NW 23rd Ave., 503/345-2689, www.foundationpdx.com; Mon.-Fri. 11am-6pm, Sat. 11am-7pm

Halo Shoes

This little boutique specializes in unique, high-quality brands and small designers. It specifically seeks out designers with limited distribution and incredible attention to detail and workmanship. The staff is happy to give suggestions on new designers or point you toward something unusual or exceptional. The shop also carries some luxury brands like Chloe, Fiorentini + Baker, and Red Wing. It can also ship your purchases home for you.

MAP 2: 938 NW Everett St., 503/331-0366, www.haloshoes.com; Mon.-Sat. 11am-6pm, Sun. noon-5pm

Lizard Lounge

Lizard Lounge is a local hangout, especially during First Thursday, when it has live music, free beer or wine, and art showings. If you miss the monthly event, it's still a great place to grab some free Stumptown Coffee, play some Ping-Pong, or make use of the free Wi-Fi or iMac station while you browse through stylish, laid-back, and earth-conscious clothes. As it should be with any great lounge, the staff is friendly, stylish, and accommodating, and chances are, know something about every piece or designer in the shop. Lizard Lounge features both men's and women's fashion, stocking a bunch of Toad & Co apparel and its high-end, Portland-based, ecofriendly line, Nau. The clothing can be a little pricey, so check for sales or be prepared to pay a little more for something durable and guilt-free.

MAP 2: 1323 NW Irving St., 503/416-7476, www.lizardloungepdx.com; Sun.-Fri. 11am-7pm, Sat. 10am-7pm

Oh Baby!

This is where good girls go to be naughty and naughty girls go to be even naughtier. The award-winning lingerie boutique is filled to the bedposts with lingerie in sizes 32A to 42G for all shapes and tastes. At the center of the shop, you will find a queen-size bed strewn with pretty panties in satin and lace. The girls who work here are experts at fitting and can no doubt put you in a bra that will make you wonder how you ever got along without it. They specialize in bridal lingerie and corsets, which you are welcome to try on in the private fitting room outfitted with floor pillows and enough room for an audience of one. If you're a little out of your element amid all the ribbons and lace, the staff will help you pick out something fabulous that would make a perfect bridal shower or bachelorette gift, or just a self-indulgent treat.

MAP 2: 722 NW 23rd Ave., 503/274-4190, www.ohbabylingerieshops.com; Mon.-Sat. 11am-7pm, Sun. noon-5pm

Sloan Boutique

This locally owned and operated women's boutique has three locations around town, each well-appointed with apparel, shoes, and accessories for women of all ages and styles. The brands featured are mostly affordable to moderately pricey and range from well-known to distinctly obscure designers. There is a little something for every taste and body style, although the shop keeps little in stock over size 12-14. Sloan's staff is friendly and excited about fashion, and seem to really enjoy putting together a new look for someone; if you like having someone walk you through the shopping process, you will find something akin to a personal stylist experience here.

MAP 2: 735 NW 23rd Ave., 503/222-6666, www.sloanpdx.com; Mon.-Fri. 10:30am-7:30pm, Sat. 10am-8pm, Sun. 11am-6pm

3 Monkeys

If a burlesque dancer, a fashion designer, and a costume designer shared an apartment, it might look a little like 3 Monkeys. The shop is a colorful extravaganza of hats, handbags, masks, bow ties, costume jewelry, candles, flasks, and more tiaras than a beauty pageant. They also carry a number of quirky gift ideas and cool wall art. The store looks small from the outside, but be sure to explore both levels and maybe pick up a unicorn or chicken mask for your next costume party.

MAP 2: 803 NW 23rd Pl., 503/222-5160; daily 11am-7pm

3 Monkeys

Upper Playground

Upper Playground is an urban-chic clothes source (selling T-shirts, hoodies, and hats) and an art gallery. Street and graffiti art adorns the walls, and there's a full-blown gallery in the back. This outpost of the Bay Area brand has screen-printed shirts by metro artists Alex Pardee, David Choe, and Jeremy Fish. It has Portland-themed shirts, which make great gifts for people who want a little piece of Portland with more character than your average tourist-trap buy. If you don't mind a crowd, stop by on First Thursday. You can shop, sip beer or wine, check out the newest art in the gallery, and listen to a DJ spin some tunes.

MAP 2: 23 NW 5th Ave., 503/548-4835, www.upperplayground.com; Mon.-Sat. 11am-8pm, Sun. noon-6pm

OUTDOOR GEAR
REI

If you are unaccustomed to the Pacific Northwest weather, or if you plan to explore the Oregon wilderness while you're here, take a trip by this retailer founded in Seattle. The gear and apparel are high quality and designed and sold by people with an expertise and passion for outdoor recreation. Shopping here can be especially invigorating for women who may have felt overlooked or simply nonplussed about the bland athletic-wear options at other retailers.

MAP 2: 1405 NW Johnson St., 503/221-1938, www.rei.com; Mon.-Sat. 10am-9pm, Sun. 10am-7pm

GOURMET TREATS
Elephants Delicatessen

For Elephants, the word "delicatessen" doesn't even begin to cover it. It is part grocery, with an amazing array of cured meats, fine cheeses, olives, capers, anchovies, pickles, gourmet chocolates, and hand-crafted caramels, but it is also a popular lunchtime spot, catering company, and happy hour bar. It's a perfect place to stop and grab the makings for a simple gourmet picnic before you head out to Washington Park. Or check out the gift box section of the website and preorder a basket with a perfectly paired bottle of Northwest wine.

MAP 2: 115 NW 22nd Ave., 503/299-6304, www.elephantsdeli.com; Mon.-Sat. 7am-8:30pm, Sun. 8am-6:30pm

Pearl Specialty Market & Spirits

Oregon's liquor laws can be pretty persnickety. You can't purchase hard alcohol in grocery stores, and the liquor stores close early and are often closed on Sunday. What's more, if you want to make a truly artisan-style cocktail with fancy bitters or gourmet olives, you usually have to make several stops. Pearl Specialty Market & Spirits was given special permission by the Oregon Liquor Control Commission to be open seven days a week and maintain longer hours, as well as the right to sell things like chocolate, crackers, olives, cheese, caviar, cigars, and Willamette Valley wine. Pearl Specialty also has an unbelievable selection of—get this—luxury water, in pretty, reusable decanters and Swarovski crystal-encrusted bottles.

MAP 2: 900 NW Lovejoy St., #140, 503/477-8604, www.pearlspecialty.com; Mon.-Sat. 9am-10pm, Sun. noon-8pm

Smith Teamakers

Before his death in 2015, Steven Smith was sort of the big daddy of tea in the Pacific Northwest. Dubbed the "All-Star Alchemist of Top-Shelf Tea" by the *Wall Street Journal,* Smith definitely did his part to change how tea was made in this area and far beyond. After launching both Stash Teas and Tazo into success, the cofounder then moved on to create Steven Smith Teamakers, a lovingly refined company that is arguably some of his best work. In this former blacksmith's shop, you can smell, sample, and imbibe the small-batch, artisanal teas before choosing something to take home. In addition to the brand's core teas, you'll find a seemingly endless supply of rare loose-leaf teas in pretty bags and tins as well as lovely gift boxes. The teamakers on hand are always happy to tell you the stories behind the teas and their creator as they help you select your favorites.

MAP 2: 1626 NW Thurman St., 503/719-8752, www.smithtea.com; daily 10am-6pm

Smith Teamakers

BEAUTY AND WELLNESS
Aesop

Aesop is an Australian brand offering high-quality skin-care products that smell amazing and can save your skin from the trauma of the ever-changing Pacific Northwest weather. Earthy fragrances like cedar, rosemary, bergamot, and coriander permeate the air. The staff is happy to help you find a scent profile that you like and give you samples. They're also knowledgeable about skin types and can offer suggestions, as well a warm washcloth or towel so you can refresh yourself.

MAP 2: 827 NW 23rd Ave., 503/224-0032 www.aesop.com; daily 11am-7pm

Blush Beauty Bar

This adorable little boutique in the Alphabet District promotes the idea of shopping local and still carries a fairly extensive selection of top-of-the-line cosmetics and skin-care products (from brands like Nars, Bare Escentuals, Lorac, and Mario Badescu). The prices are not inflated, as you might suspect they would be in this neighborhood, and the staff is knowledgeable. Book a makeover and a team member will teach you all the tricks you need and walk you through the products. It costs $50-150 depending on whether you want a 55- or 90-minute lesson, and the cost can be redeemed in products. They also offer threading, waxing, and facials.

MAP 2: 513 NW 23rd Ave., 503/227-3390, www.blushbeautybar247.com; Mon.-Fri. 11am-7pm, Sat. 11am-6pm, Sun. noon-6pm

Lush

It's hard to miss Lush when you can smell it from a block away. This bath and body shop is loaded with hand-made bath bombs, body butters, creams, soaps, shampoos, and lotions. If you are new to the line, explore the bath bombs first. They're a fragrant and luxurious treat to use in a hotel bath or carry home as gifts. While Lush isn't a Portland-based company, the ideology certainly fits with the Portland dogma, since all the products are fresh, ecofriendly, and never tested on animals.

The sales team can be quite helpful (sometimes overly so) in aiding you in finding the products that will best suit your needs. Don't be afraid to tell them that you just want to explore and will ask if you have questions.

MAP 2: 708 NW 23rd Ave., 503/228-5874, www.lush.com; Mon.-Sat. 10am-8pm, Sun. 11am-7pm

New Renaissance Bookstore

Many Portlanders are committed to whole body health, so no matter which neighborhood you're in, you'll find a number of metaphysical shops and bookstores nestled in with all of the yoga studios and acai bowl shops. New Renaissance, however, is the largest of them all, spanning four Victorian attached houses along the bustling shopping area of 23rd Avenue. Inside, you'll find crystals, smudging equipment, singing bowls, malas, essential oils, chakra tea, and, of course, books. The store also offers a number of services such as tarot, palm, psychic, astrological, Enneagram, and energy readings on various days.

MAP 2: 1338 NW 23rd Ave., 503/224-4929, www.newrenbooks.com; Mon.-Thurs. and Sat. 10am-9pm, Fri. 10am-9:30pm, Sun. 10am-8pm

CHILDREN'S STORES

Hanna Andersson

When you want high-quality children's clothes that are extremely durable, this is the place. While many think this company—which specializes in cotton togs in a rainbow of colors—is a Swedish business, it was founded right here in Portland. Every button, stitch, zipper, and swath of fabric undergoes rigorous eco-testing to guard

New Renaissance Bookstore

against chemicals and harsh radicals. Hanna stocks soft and comfy sweaters, leggings, sweatpants, and dresses (with some matching mommy-and-me outfits) in styles and colors designed to last through generations of hand-me-downs.

MAP 2: 327 NW 10th Ave., 503/321-5275, www.hannaandersson.com; Mon.-Fri. 10am-6pm, Sat. 10am-5pm, Sun. 11am-5pm

PET SUPPLIES
Hip Hound

This store is a favorite stop for travelers (and locals) with fur babies. It carries toys, treats, leashes, harnesses, dog and cat food, human and dog clothing, and even CBD for dogs. Just inside the door, you'll find Java Hound, a coffee bar that features coffees, espresso drinks, and teas, as well as puppuccinos (goat milk with a meat topper) for your four-legged friends. In addition to being a pup boutique, Hip Hound also hosts a number of events like Yappy Hour every third Thursday with in-store treat demos, wine and beer, regular meet-and-greets, adoption events, and dog yoga sessions.

MAP 2: 610 NW 23rd Ave., 503/841-5410, www.hiphoundpdx.com; daily 9am-7pm

Northeast   Map 3

CLOTHING AND ACCESSORIES
Amenity Shoes

Amenity Shoes is a locally owned and operated resource for comfy shoes that don't look like they came from your grandma and grandpa's closet. The owners have a background in art and shoe manufacturing, clearly evident from the store's selection, which is cute, modern, and comfortable all at once. Women's shoes range from colorful, embroidered flats to classy patent-leather T-strap sandals. The stock of men's shoes is equally well balanced and modern, with brands like Sole, Kenneth Cole, and Fly London leading the pack.

MAP 3: 3430 NE 41st Ave., 503/282-4555, www.amenityshoes.com; Mon.-Sat. 10am-6pm, Sun. 11am-5pm

The Pencil Test

It's no secret that most women are wearing the wrong size bra. Our bodies fluctuate with the seasons, life changes, and age, so it is hard to keep up on proper fitting. It doesn't help that shopping for bras can be so daunting, confusing, and at times embarrassing. The Pencil Test (named for the informal test developed by Ann Landers to determine whether or not a woman could go braless in public) is a place that aims to fix that by providing measurement service to all their customers. They carry a number of larger cup sizes (read: closer to the middle of the alphabet) in styles that are not the beige, matronly ones buxom girls find in most places.

MAP 3: 2407 NE Alberta St., 971/266-8611; Tues.-Fri. 11am-6pm, Sat. 10am-6pm, Sun. 11am-5pm

Popina Swimwear

I know what you're thinking: a swimwear store in Portland? Yes, even if it rains nine months of the year in these parts—or maybe because of it—we occasionally need to chuck the raincoat and head off to sunny Mexico or Hawaii. Heck, we'll settle for a dip in a nearby hot springs or even a friend's Jacuzzi. And if Portlanders need a swimsuit, they go looking for something with panache. Enter Pamela Levenson, a swimwear designer specializing in women's retro-styled suits. Try on one of the many in her shop just off of Alberta Street; if it doesn't fit perfectly, they will alter it for you at a surprisingly small cost. There is also a **Popina Boutique in the Pearl District** (318 NW 11th Ave., 503/243-7946). Both locations are free of fluorescent lighting and will offer you a free Kona beer while you are shopping.

MAP 3: 4831 NE 42nd Ave., 503/282-5159, www.popinaswimwear.com; Mon.-Wed. 10am-6pm, Thurs.-Sat. 10am-7pm, Sun. noon-5pm

Redux

At Redux you'll find fascinating pieces—many repurposed from other items like typewriters, PBR cans, or bicycle chains—hanging from every wall and hook. Owner Tamara Goldsmith stocks jewelry designed by many local folks and has artwork on display by great local artists as well. Ladies, grab a pair of delicate earrings with dangling bits of raw crystal or a set of leather cuffs made from a recycled belt. You'll also find some kitschy home wares here, like animal-shaped coffee mugs, moon-faced clocks, macramé art, or planters built out of oddball things like a doll's head. Prices are remarkably affordable for such distinctive pieces

MAP 3: 811 E. Burnside St., Ste. 116, 503/231-7336, www.reduxpdx.com; Mon.-Sat. 11am-7pm, Sun. 11am-5pm

Well Suited

If you are in need of a suit but don't have the money to shell out for the usual designer store prices, Well Suited may be for you. The unassuming storefront hides a remarkable selection of high-end suits by designer labels like Prada, Hugo Boss, and Armani—as well as some beach-style shirts and basic business-casual wear. Since the store is a consignment shop, you can find a great suit for about 50-80 percent of what you might pay anywhere else.

If you spot the perfect suit but it doesn't fit quite right (or you already own a suit that needs tailoring), have it tailored right on the spot. The in-store tailor is one of the best in town, and his prices are quite reasonable.

MAP 3: 2401 NE Broadway, 503/284-5939, www.wellsuitedpdx.com; Tues.-Sat. 11am-6pm

VINTAGE AND ANTIQUES

Hollywood Vintage

Hollywood Vintage is one of those places where you enter, start browsing, and eventually start to wonder, "Does this place ever end?" With about 15,000 square feet of vintage clothing, costumes, furniture, vinyl records, and collectibles, there is a lot to see. Hollywood Vintage is also the area's largest retailer of vintage eyewear, with an inventory of over 1,000 frames from the 1920s to today. While shopping, keep an eye out for Robin, the in-house cat, who is likely to be napping on one of the vintage chairs or in a cozy box. He is happy to accept your affection, but don't take his advice about which vintage corduroy jacket to choose; his tastes are a little outdated.

MAP 3: 2757 NE Pacific St., 503/233-1890, www.hollywoodvintage.com; daily 11am-6pm

BOOKS AND MUSIC
Things from Another World

Things from Another World is the retail baby of local comic book giant Dark Horse, so TFAW (as it is affectionately called) has comics in spades, especially graphic novels. But what sets it apart is that TFAW focuses on toys, T-shirts, and other nerdy oddities. You will find games like Pathfinder, Warhammer, and Munchkin, as well as game supplies like boards and dice. If you are looking for a collectible statue, this is the place to stop. It has arguably the largest array of collectible figures in town—some of them quite spectacular and large.

MAP 3: 2916 NE Broadway, 503/284-4693, www.tfaw.com; Mon.-Sat. 11am-7pm, Sun. 11am-6pm

The Title Wave Used Bookstore

Housed in an old Spanish Renaissance revival-style library building, this little book lover's dream is, not coincidentally, run by the Multnomah County Library. Overstock of books, CDs, audiobooks, and magazines from the county's libraries are sent here to be sold at astonishingly low prices. Hardbacks and novels often go for $2 or less. And many items, like magazines and children's books, are less than $1. The store is operated entirely by volunteers, and all the proceeds go to benefit the Multnomah County Libraries. The selection is hit-or-miss. Since the store is filled with castoffs and overstock, you may not have luck finding something specific, but you are very likely to find something you didn't know you were looking for.

They do not keep an inventory of the books available, so be prepared to peruse at length.

MAP 3: 216 NE Knott St., 503/988-5021, www.multcolib.org/library-location/title-wave-used-bookstore; Mon.-Tues. 10am-4pm, Wed.-Sat. 10am-6pm

Turn! Turn! Turn!

Like a great song mash-up, Turn! Turn! Turn! mixes the best parts of having a little boutique shop into one overall experience. Here you will find nostalgia, atmosphere, personality, and beer—well, and records, of course. Turn! has a nice collection of rare and vintage country, kitschy 1960s and 1970s rock, as well as some oddball LPs that have probably been collecting dust in someone's basement. In fact, the basement vibe extends throughout the shop from the old concert posters on the wall to the listening station complete with chairs that look like they were rescued from an old barbershop. There are books to read and/or buy, vintage clothes to peruse, and a menu with local beers, cider, wine, and sandwiches. The shop hosts regular trivia nights as well as live music and comedy.

MAP 3: 8 NE Killingsworth St., 503/284-6019, www.turnturnturnpdx.com; Tues.-Thurs. 4pm-11pm, Fri.-Sat. 4pm-midnight, Sun. 3pm-11pm

GOURMET TREATS
✪ Providore Fine Foods

Providore Fine Foods is a collaborative market and a haven for foodies, chefs, and those wishing to sample the best of the Pacific Northwest's flavors. Several vendors come together in this large space to offer an array of grocery and prepared food items, as well as accoutrements. The anchor vendor is Pastaworks, which offers homemade pastas, a large selection of cheese and charcuterie, as well as fancy olive oils, spices, sauces, crackers, canned goods, flours, and wines. Rubinette Produce Market offers delicious greens, wild mushrooms, and other local produce. And at Flying Fish you can buy fresh seafood including freshly shucked oysters on the half shell, poké, and house-smoked fish boards. Each individual vendor would be worthy of a visit, but together Providore makes a great place to find unique gifts or build a really special picnic or dinner.

MAP 3: 2340 NE Sandy Blvd., 503/232-1010, www.providorefinefoods. com; daily 9:30am-8pm

CHILDREN'S STORES
Bella Stella

This little store has everything you could want in terms of brand-name and locally made clothing, organic slings and accessories, and imaginative toys. It's a fun place to shop for boys if you are tired of fire trucks, action heroes, and bugs. Bella Stella is both a resale and traditional retail store, so you can find new and used merchandise that is hip, bohemian, and affordable. Check out the ecofriendly marriage between cloth and disposable diapers, G-Diapers, or explore the extensive collection of carriers.

MAP 3: 2751 NE Broadway, 503/284-4636, www.bellastellababy.com; Mon.-Thurs. 10am-5pm, Fri.-Sat. 10am-6pm, Sun. 11am-5pm

Grasshopper

Nestled in the midst of artsy Alberta Street, Grasshopper has a nice selection of organic and American-made clothes, funky rain boots, diaper bags, and bibs. It offers a unique collection of playthings that are nontoxic and not found on the shelves of any big-box store. The carefully selected amusing and colorful toys, games, and books are both stimulating to the imagination and wildly collectible.

The all-female staff is very sweet and willing to help you find that special something for a gift—and will even gift-wrap it for free.

MAP 3: 1816 NE Alberta St., 503/335-3131, www.grasshopperstore.com; Sun.-Mon. 10am-5pm, Tues.-Sat. 10am-6pm

Green Bean Books

When schoolteacher Jennifer Green looked at the plethora of beloved children's books she had collected over the years, she didn't pack them up and haul them off to Goodwill. She opened a bookstore specializing in new and used children's books in English and a multitude of other languages. Exploring all the nooks and crannies of this charming Alberta Street shop can be a lot of fun, especially when you discover the custom-made vending machines. One dispenses finger puppets (made by the owner); another offers temporary tattoos. An old gumball machine hands out pom-pom pets, and what looks suspiciously like an old sanitary napkin dispenser is now an "Instant Disguise Machine" that distributes fake beards and mustaches for a quarter.

MAP 3: 1600 NE Alberta St., 503/954-2354, www.greenbeanbookspdx.com; Mon.-Sat. 11am-6pm, Sun. 10am-5pm

Polliwog

This whimsical shop stocks the sort of baby clothes that make almost anyone wish they had a little girl to dress up.

IT'S EASY TO BE GREEN AND CHIC!

According to *Popular Science,* Portland is ranked number one as the greenest city in the world. Half of its power comes from renewable sources; more than a quarter of the workforce commutes by bike, mass transit, or carpool; and recycling is done as a matter of principle, and not as an ecological statement. More and more businesses are following suit by remodeling their buildings or altering their practices and products to embrace the green standard.

Little ones can learn from the start how to leave a smaller carbon footprint at **Polliwog** (page 181). Polliwog is chock-full of organic clothing and environmentally conscious items from the likes of Under the Nile, Egg, and Imps and Elves. It also carries luxuriously smooth bamboo clothing by Kicky Pants, David Fussenegger recycled cotton blankets, nontoxic Natursutten natural rubber pacifiers, and Made in Oregon Earnest Efforts rattles, which are composed of reclaimed wood (don't worry—they're safe).

Similarly, **Pie Footwear** (2916 NE Alberta St., 503/288-1999, www.piefootwear.net; Mon.-Sat. 11am-7pm, Sun. noon-5pm) is saving the earth one step at a time with its smart and stylish shoes that are socially responsible to boot. The store is vegan-friendly and stocks ecoconscious socks, hats, and bags.

Tropical Salvage (8315 SE 13th Ave., 503/233-4309, www.tropicalsalvage.com; daily 10am-6pm) makes some truly amazing furniture out of wood that was salvaged from demolition sites or pulled from landslides, lakes, and rivers. Craftspeople also take old, sometimes diseased wood culled from coffee plantations (or dredged up from centuries-old volcanic eruptions), clean it, cut it, kiln-dry it, and then turn it into some pretty impressive cabinets, tables, beds, dressers, and chairs. Local places like **ECOpdx** (2289 N. Interstate Ave., 503/287-8181, www.ecopdx.com; Tues.-Sat. 11am-6pm) and **Salvage Works** (2024 N. Argyle St., 503/899-0052, www.salvageworkspdx.com; Mon.-Sat. 9am-6pm, Sun. 11am-4pm) sell this salvaged-wood furniture.

If you are the crafty sort, check out **ReClaim It!** (1 N. Killingsworth St., 503/866-7855, www.reclaimitpdx.com; Wed.-Sun. 10am-5pm), a nonprofit arts and reuse retail store that saves would-be trash from the Metro Transfer Station (i.e., dump) and salvages it for people to reimagine or love as is. You will find antique trinkets and furniture, jewelry, and sporting equipment, as well as raw materials like piano keys, carpet samples, or sheets of metal and plastic. Upcyclers and repurposers also love **SCRAP PDX** (1736 SW Alder St., 503/294-0769, www.scrappdx.org; daily 10am-7pm), a nonprofit, donation-based craft reuse shop—and an adventure in imagination. Bottle caps found here might become mosaic art, Scrabble tiles could find their way into necklaces, and old spoons morph into fancy coat hooks. In addition to its varied and ever-changing inventory, SCRAP also provides a number of educational opportunities for people in the community and hosts local reuse-based artists in their gallery.

If you're looking to relax but don't want to fret about the impact your pampering might have on the environment, check out **Blooming Moon Wellness Spa** (1417 N. Shaver St., 971/279-2757, www.bloomingmoonspa.com; Tues.-Sun. 10am-8pm). The spa uses only all-natural products that are never tested on animals, adheres to a recycling and sustainable energy plan, and encourages employees and guests to bike or take the streetcar to the spa. Book a Sore Muscle Relief package (foot bath, acupuncture, and massage) and you just might need to call a taxi to get you home.

The clothes can be a little pricey, but it's worth it if you want to find something unique. Send the kids to play in the back corner while you check out the Glug tees' cute urban chic designs. Service can be a bit aloof sometimes, but this edgier-than-Gap store is full of fun children's clothing, like bright baby hats, striped PJs, and appliquéd onesies, as well as slings, wonderful wooden toys, and shoes.

MAP 3: 234 NE 28th Ave., 503/236-3903, www.polliwogportland.com; Mon.-Sat. 10am-6pm, Sun. 11am-5pm

LOCAL GOODS

Memento

Memento is filled with everything you could possibly want, but nothing you need. On every shelf and wall, you'll find tchotchkes, cards, posters, bags, housewares, wind-up toys, and more—much of it from Pacific Northwest designers and craftspeople. You may not need three different sizes of mirrored disco balls, but you will want them. The same goes for the Virgen de Guadalupe candles, the cardboard blimp, or avenging narwhal play set. This is a terrific spot to find a gift for someone back home as proof-positive that Portland is a very weird place.

MAP 4: 3707 SE Hawthorne Blvd., 503/235-1257, www.mementopdx.com; Sun.-Thurs. 10am-6pm, Fri.-Sat. 10am-7pm

Presents of Mind

Presents of Mind has an eclectic mix of amazing locally made jewelry, bags, and clothes, along with hilarious gag gifts and stationery. It's a fun place to pick up a killer diaper bag or a onesie for the newborn in your life, or a retro apron for a bridal gift, or a yodeling pickle. You never know when you'll need a yodeling pickle, but you will. It also has pretty, elaborately handmade cards, specialty wrapping paper, and premade bows that make the presentation of the gift rival whatever might be inside.

MAP 4: 3633 SE Hawthorne Blvd., 503/230-7740, www.presentsofmind.tv; Sun.-Thurs. 10am-7pm, Fri.-Sat. 10am-8pm

Presents of Mind

GIFTS AND HOME

Cargo

A longtime purveyor of imported artifacts and antiques, Cargo is a veritable treasure trove of trinkets, oddities, jewelry, furniture, decor, and more. This industrial Southeast warehouse is just a few shouting vendors away from being an Asian street market, with baubles and beads adorning statues, colorful displays, and teak furniture stacked high. Cargo specializes in garden statuary, folk art, religious memorabilia, carpets, vibrant glassware, and propaganda art, as well as antique and custom-designed furniture, all with a heavy emphasis on Asian designs. This place is huge, and there is something eye-catching at every angle, so allow yourself time to get lost for a while.

MAP 4: 81 SE Yamhill St., 503/209-8349, www.cargoimportspdx.com; daily 11am-6pm

Cargo

CLOTHING AND ACCESSORIES

Buffalo Exchange

Buffalo Exchange is a great spot to find one-of-a-kind pieces, locally made T-shirts and dresses, as well as secondhand high-end brands like Joe's Jeans, Rock & Republic, Anna Sui, BCBG, Betsey Johnson, and Nicole Miller. The store seems to cater to the young, hipster crowd of Portland, so you are likely to find odd vintage blouses, punky leather pieces, and earthy organic cotton dresses. While there is a second **Buffalo** downtown (1036 W. Burnside St., 503/222-3418), the Hawthorne location is superior, if only because the racks are easier to navigate.

MAP 4: 1420 SE 37th Ave., 503/234-1302, www.buffaloexchange.com; daily 10am-9pm

Duchess Clothier

For stylish men in the market for something custom made, unique, and beautiful, Duchess Clothier is a must.

When it comes to bespoke suits, no one does it better. Duchess takes inspiration from the dandy men of the past using influences from film, literature, and life. From a classic *Mad Men*-style gray suit to a colorful double-breasted ensemble, the options are unlimited. They even do costumes and have created custom designs for a number of famous clients like Nick Cave, Crispin Glover, Lance Bangs, and John Hodgeman.

MAP 4: 2505 SE 11th Ave., 503/281-6648, www.duchessclothier.com; Fri.-Sat. 10am-5pm, by appointment Tues.-Thurs.

Imelda's and Louie's Shoes

Like moths to a flame, Portland shoe addicts keep coming back to Imelda's and Louie's for a fix. The styles here range from functional work shoes to date-night pumps and everything in between—with many pairs boasting buttery leathers or ecofriendly materials. This is a great source of shoes for both men and women. The shoes are expensive but well made, colorful, and beautifully designed. Sizes are sometimes limited due to space, but if you fall in love with something, don't fret. They are often able and more than happy to order a pair in your size.

MAP 4: 3426 SE Hawthorne Blvd., 503/233-7476, www.imeldasandlouies.com; Mon.-Fri. 10am-7pm, Sat. 10am-6pm, Sun. 11am-6pm

Naked City

If style for you means channeling Bettie Page or Elvira, Naked City is the shop for you. This little Belmont store has a plethora of retro, 1940s- and 1950s-style dresses, tops, pencil skirts, swimsuits, and cropped pants for all shapes and sizes. While host to many things, the overall vibe of this store is rockabilly and pinup. You'll find brands like Sourpuss Clothing, Kreepsville 666, and Rock Steady, as well as some locally made jewelry and accessories. Make sure you check out the sale rack outside for some steals on end-of-season items for $10 or less.

MAP 4: 2701 SE Belmont St., 503/239-3837, www.nakedcityclothing.com; Mon.-Sat. 11am-7pm, Sun. noon-6pm

VINTAGE AND ANTIQUES

House of Vintage

House of Vintage is a collective of more than 55 independent dealers all sharing over 13,000 square feet. This place is an absolute maze, but also a wonderful cache of odds and ends. Give yourself plenty of time to explore; you could easily spend hours wandering from room to room trying not to miss anything. Keep looking and you may just find a vintage lunchbox tucked into a curio cabinet, a kitschy table set for dinner with cute melamine dishes, or a diaphanous slip hanging from a

wrought-iron gate. All you have to do is wade through the seemingly endless stacks of clothing, accessories, shoes, memorabilia, housewares, music, furniture, and tchotchkes.

MAP 4: 3315 SE Hawthorne Blvd., 503/236-1991, www.houseofvintage.net; daily 11am-7pm

Noun: A Person's Place for Things

It is easy to miss Noun, unless you are looking for cupcakes as well. This little Belmont boutique shares a space with popular Portland bakery Saint Cupcake. While the cupcakes alone are worth a visit, this shop with the clever name is a wonderfully curated mix of vintage and modern. The buyers for Noun search everywhere for their vintage pieces—estate sales, flea markets, auctions, and even occasionally a dumpster. Modern and locally made pieces are then selected to fit the mood with the other furnishings, art, antiques, and artists' works.

MAP 4: 3300 SE Belmont St., 503/235-0078, www.shopnoun.com; Mon.-Sat. 11am-7pm, Sun. 11am-5pm

BOOKS AND MUSIC

✪ Books with Pictures

Comic book culture is big in Portland, in part thanks to the presence of local publishers like Dark Horse, Image, Ooligan Press, and Oni. However, something has long been missing from the comic book store experience, which can be intimidating or alienating to those who fall outside the assumed demographic. Books with Pictures creates a space where everyone feels comfortable discovering new stories or sharing their passions; this shop is built on inclusivity. So in addition to comic books and graphic novels that one would expect to find at any comics shop worthy of note, owner Katie Proctor is also mindful about maintaining a stock that features titles with female protagonists and protagonists of color.

MAP 4: 1100 SE Division Blvd., Ste. 103, 503/206-4369, http://bookswithpictures. com; Sun.-Tues. 10am-6pm, Wed.-Sat. 10am-8pm

✪ Music Millennium

You know those bumper stickers appealing to everyone to "Keep Portland Weird"? It all started here. What began as a public awareness campaign to keep local businesses alive and boost independent thinking has become a mantra for the Rose City way of life. Music Millennium gets it, and it always has. This independent seller of used and new CDs, DVDs, and vinyl has been a staple since 1969, in part because of its impeccable knowledge and taste, but also because of the constantly evolving selection. Music Millennium holds regular in-store concerts and events and also sells advance tickets to shows at the Doug Fir Lounge.

MAP 4: 3158 E. Burnside St., 503/231-8926, www.musicmillennium.com; Mon.-Sat. 10am-10pm, Sun. 11am-9pm

Excalibur Books and Comics

Back in 1974, Peter Fagnant visited every newsstand between Portland and Salem, buying up every copy of a comic book featuring a new character named Howard the Duck. When he opened his comic book shop, Portlanders soon found out that it was the place to go when you need comics—be they obscure or current. That legacy continues today. It's the oldest comic book shop in town, but Excalibur Books and Comics is still a

favorite stop for true collectors. Boxes upon boxes of back issues sprawl over the floor, and an ever-rotating wall of rare finds can include golden, silver, and modern age back issues. It's a library you can own. Just inside the door you'll see an artist's rendition of a duck pulling the magical sword from its stone. More than forty years later, Excalibur is still aware this is the house that duck built.

MAP 4: 2444 SE Hawthorne Blvd., 503/231-7351, www.excaliburcomicspdx. com; Mon.-Thurs. 11am-8pm, Fri.-Sat. 10am-8pm, Sun. 11am-7pm

Guardian Games

Tucked in the industrial Southeast is a place where "play time" takes on a whole different meaning. It may not look like much from the outside, but Guardian Games is a one-stop shop for gamers of all walks of life. If you like a traditional board game, they have those aplenty, but the real delight is for those who believe gameplay should involve strategy, creativity, and just a little bit of storytelling. Owner Angel May is said to have played her first game of Dungeons and Dragons at age six and was hooked. Since then, she has sought out the best in all things gaming: video games, table top games, card games, and role-playing adventures. Even with a sprawling, multilevel gaming and retail space, there are surprises everywhere you look, like an impressive collection of out-of-print board games, card games, and book sets. The store hosts regular gaming nights, D&D camps, and beer and pizza nights, and even houses an in-store bar.

MAP 4: 345 SE Taylor St., 503/238-4000, www.ggportland.com; Mon.-Sat. 10am-10pm, Sun. noon-8pm

Jackpot Records

This independently owned music store is popular among those seeking indie labels, rock, and metal. The jewel cases are kept behind the counter and CDs are filed with their inserts into plastic sleeves, the color of which denotes whether it is a new or used album. While the method irks some music store purists, who enjoy the "clack clack" of searching the bins, it means you'll find a greater selection thanks to the added space, and it means you can check out the liner notes before you purchase the CD. Make sure you check the outside sale bins, which are occasionally a jackpot for obscure oddities and classic staples.

MAP 4: 3574 SE Hawthorne Blvd., 503/239-7561, www.jackpotrecords.com; Mon.-Sat. 10am-7pm, Sun. 11am-6pm

Powell's Home and Garden

Just two spaces down from Powell's Southeast location is an outpost devoted to books on home and gardening. The cookbook section is fun, well organized, extensive, and inspiring. It's this outpost's specialty, and you'll find over 6,000 cookbooks ranging in subject from vegan to barbecue, Jerusalem to Japan. This branch also has a wide range of books on crafts like knitting, jewelry making, and woodworking and often hosts readings from crafting experts and chefs. This Powell's is also a great place to pick up trinkets and gifts. It has a marvelous collection of candles, garden tools, dishware, tablecloths, and art.

MAP 4: 3747 SE Hawthorne Blvd., 503/228-4651, www.powells.com; Mon.-Sat. 9am-9pm, Sun. 9am-8pm

GOURMET TREATS
Edelweiss

If you have spent any amount of time in Germany, Edelweiss will feel all too familiar to you: the narrow aisles filled with jars of mustard, pickles, and sauerkraut; the candy aisle with European sweets; the brusque, impatient service. Every inch of this store is crammed with sweets, treats, and authentic delicacies, many of which are made on-site, imported, or produced locally in the traditional European style. What's more, it has one of the best collections of imported European beers and wines in town.

Be sure to grab a number as you walk in the door. It gets crowded and the wait can be maddeningly long, but the selection in the deli case makes it all worthwhile. If you are a meat lover, don't be surprised if you get a little dizzy at the sight of all their handmade sausages, house-smoked meats, and house-cured bacon.

MAP 4: 3119 SE 12th Ave., 503/238-4411, www.edelweissdeli.com; Mon.-Sat. 9am-6pm

Food Fight

This store is just one part of what is essentially a vegan strip mall. The veggie-centric grocery is next to Herbivore Clothing Company and Sweet Pea Bakery, both of which share a desire to encourage a life free from the unnecessary use of animal products. Vegans and vegetarians can find everything from vegan health and fitness items to the delicious (locally made) NoFishGoFish soups and grab-and-go vegan nachos. You can also find vegan household products, including shampoos, cleansers, and vegan cookbooks.

MAP 4: 1217 SE Stark St., 503/233-3910, www.foodfightgrocery.com; daily 10am-8pm

CHILDREN'S STORES
Kids at Heart

Kids at Heart is a locally owned shop that specializes in creative and educational toys and games. That means you won't find any mega-blasters or current movie merchandise here, but you will find adorable puppets, plush robots, sticker books, magical costumes, and science kits. The books room has new releases and old favorites for newborns and readers up to young adults. The store is a wee bit on the small side compared to some others in the region, but it seems to make up for its size in judicious selection and knowledgeable service.

MAP 4: 3445 SE Hawthorne Blvd., 503/231-2954, www.kidsathearttoys.com; Mon.-Sat. 10am-7pm, Sun. 10am-6pm

Sellwood and Moreland   Map 5

VINTAGE AND ANTIQUES
Sellwood Antique Collective

This store gathers numerous sellers—typically 10 or more—into one space, which makes for a nice diversity of antiques, collectables, and oddities. Dealers curate their own space, so you can get a pretty good feel for each individual personality. Spaces are updated often, and since whoever is behind the counter likely has a spot here as well, he or she is usually happy to point you toward favorite items in the store.

Map 5: 8027 SE 13th Ave., 503/736-1399; daily 11am-5pm

Sellwood Antique Mall

This two-story antique mall houses over 100 dealers, so you are bound to find something you love, whether antique books, dishes, costume jewelry, art, coins, furniture, or old Disney memorabilia. There is a lot of ground to cover here and a lot of things to see in the well-organized space, so give yourself plenty of time to get a little lost in nostalgia.

Map 5: 7875 SE 13th Ave., 503/389-7670, http://sellwoodantiquemall.com; Sat. noon-5pm

BEAUTY AND WELLNESS
Camamu

This tiny, natural care-focused soap shop has been creating hand-crafted bars for over a decade. Everything in the store and online is made in small batches using no animal fats. With the exception of a couple of products (like the delightful Argan Milk and Honey Soap), everything is certified vegan. They even have a couple of bars designed specifically for dogs, with natural anti-itch and flea-repellent ingredients. The shop is pretty laid-back (they occasionally close up early), but employees are usually able to answer a lot of questions, especially for those with sensitive skin—a specialty of the Camamu folks.

MAP 5: 1229 SE Nehalem St., 503/230-9260, www.camamusoap.com; Tues.-Fri. 10am-5pm, Sat. 10am-3pm

LOCAL GOODS
Land Gallery

This unpretentious multiuse space has a fun upstairs gallery that hosts a new showing every month featuring local artists. Downstairs is a gift shop curated by the Portland-based online gift retailer buyolympia.com, where you can buy locally made tote bags, T-shirts, cards, and art. The company was founded in Olympia, Washington, in 1999 as a means to showcase artist friends and help them distribute their wares to a wider international market. Land Gallery's careful curation extends to its store, so like the upstairs space, it feels like something of a gallery too, and individual items tend to speak volumes about the Pacific Northwest mentality.

MAP 6: 3925 N. Mississippi Ave., 503/451-0689, www.landpdx.com; daily 10am-7pm

PDXchange Fair and Square

PDXChange Fair and Square is a great boutique for finding a gift for someone else or a Pacific Northwest souvenir for yourself. You will find beautiful jewelry, housewares, aprons, bags, quilts, and children's toys. The owners are very excited about supporting local artists and will direct you to some of their favorite pieces. Pick up some colorful handmade scarves or candles from Roman Ruby in scents named after Portland landmarks like the Burnside Bridge (don't worry, the candle smells a lot better than the actual Burnside Bridge). It also features fair-trade products from around the world.

MAP 6: 3916 N. Mississippi Ave., 971/202-2616, www.pdxchange.net; Mon.-Sat. 11am-6pm, Sun. 11am-5pm

GIFTS AND HOME
Paxton Gate

If you're looking to find a little weirdness, look no further than this outpost of San Francisco's Paxton Gate. The shop specializes in taxidermy, plants, fossils, and framed insects. Walls are packed with mounted heads of wildcats, bears, deer, bison, and even a hippopotamus. Real animal and human skulls line the shelves, and glass cases are filled with butterflies preserved forever in pretty frames. Some items are presented in fearsome fashion—capturing the animal as if in a state of attack or terror—while other items are pure whimsy. Even if you're not in the market for a taxidermied mouse wearing a chef's hat or a caterpillar battle scene diorama, it's a fun place to poke around.

MAP 6: 4204 N. Mississippi Ave., 503/719-4508, www.paxtongate.com; daily 11am-7pm

ACCESSORIES
✪ Sock Dreams

If your sock drawer doesn't cause you to giggle, ooh and aah, or at least smile, you need to make a trip to Sock Dreams. A longtime cult favorite on the web, Sock Dreams' brick-and-mortar store houses a colorful collection of toe socks, striped socks, thigh highs, garters, leg warmers, tights, and more. The company's online warehouse, with its dizzying array of socks—a collection so big only the Internet could hold it—is housed off-site.

MAP 6: 3962 N. Mississippi Ave., 503/232-3330, www.sock-dreams.com; daily 11am-6pm

BOOKS AND MUSIC
Bridge City Comics

Ask a comic book enthusiast what his or her favorite shop in town is and Bridge City is likely to rate at the top of the list. Bridge City is bright and open with wide, passable aisles and displays that allow you to see what you are looking for (even if you don't know you are looking for it). The staff is helpful, and never in a sneering, judgmental way. They actually seem happy to help you find whatever it is you are looking for. They have a great kids' section and a wall of new releases from major publishers and local small presses. They even have local, self-published comics. Also, they offer staff picks and recommendations based on previous things you may have read and liked.

MAP 6: 3725 N. Mississippi Ave., 503/282-5484, www.bridgecitycomics.com; Mon., Wed., and Fri.-Sat. 11am-8pm, Tues. and Thurs. 11am-7pm

CD Game Exchange

CD Game Exchange has five locations around the Portland metro area and is a popular stop for collectors of DVDs, video games, LPs, and, yes, even old VHS tapes. The shop pays out cash for used discs and equipment, and it is a common thing for Portlanders looking for a little extra cash to schlep a bag of games and movies here. They price things according to availability, interest, and quality, so it is not uncommon to find more than one copy of that special disc you are looking for. It is an especially great place to pick up DVD box sets of favorite TV shows or classic movies at a fraction of what they would cost online or new. It could also be a great place to cash in on that Buffy box set you have been holding on to for far too long.

If you are looking for something really obscure, employees can check the other stores for availability. If none of the stores have it, they can special order it for an extra fee.

MAP 6: 3719 N. Mississippi Ave., 503/287-0382, www.cdgameexchange. com; Mon.-Thurs. and Sat. 11am-7pm, Fri. 11am-8pm, Sun. 11pm-6pm

GOURMET TREATS
The Meadow

Salt takes on a whole new life at The Meadow, a boutique specializing in gourmet sea salts, with a fine selection of chocolate, hard-to-find wines, bitters, and edible flowers such as apple blossoms and hibiscus. Before you do anything else, buy some of the salted chocolates, which hit the salty, rich, and sweet trifecta. Then, sample some of the alderwood-smoked salt or the Maboroshi plum salt. Ask for some advice on how to use the Vietnamese Pearl *sel gris* (gray salt) or the *sel rose* (pink salt) curing salt, and you'll find that regular table salt is actually pretty harsh. Before you leave, pick up a Himalayan salt plate, a pretty, translucent pink slab quarried straight from

The Meadow

the Himalayan mountains that will revolutionize the way you cook.

MAP 6: 3731 N. Mississippi Ave., 503/228-4633, https://themeadow.com; daily 10am-7pm

CHILDREN'S STORES

Black Wagon

This hip and stylish shop has had a presence online for over a decade, and the flagship store on Mississippi Avenue is an adorable representation of the sort of hip baby chic the company represents. The brick-and-mortar shop is full of fantastic, fashion-forward items for babies and toddlers as well as hand-crafted toys, games, shoes, and a fine selection of books. This is where to shop if you want your kids to look like tiny celebrities. The boutique is well stocked with specific attention to locally made pieces and unique, clever designs.

MAP 6: 3964 N. Mississippi Ave., 503/916-0004, www.blackwagon.com; Mon.-Fri. 11am-7pm, Sat. 10am-7pm, Sun. 10am-5pm

SpielWerk Toys

The name of this store is German for "play work," implying that children have the very important job of playing. For that reason, the objects in this store are designed to engage, develop, and thrill. Instead of simply entertaining kids, the hand-carved, hand-painted, or hand-sewn toys are meant to promote positive brain activity. The store also hosts regular "WerkShops," where young ones can learn how to do imaginative things like build a fairy garden, paint silk scarves, or make their own hula hoops.

MAP 6: 3808 N. Williams Ave., 503/282-2233, www.spielwerktoys.com; Mon.-Sat. 10am-6pm, Sun. 10am-5pm

WHERE TO STAY

Each hotel in this city, whether new or old, embodies some aspect of Portland's identity—the artist, the music buff, the jet-setter, the foodie—so there really is a place for everyone and every taste. The best choice is really a matter of preference.

Caravan: A Tiny House Hotel

Portland is home to a large collection of boutique-style hotels as well as the usual large chain hotel groups—but even many of these offer a peek at the city's distinctive personality. And, of course, you'll find a few funky indie accommodations that are particularly Portlandy.

The greatest concentration of hotels can be found downtown. This is where most of Portland's public transportation systems converge and much of the city's commercial business takes place, as well as in close proximity to many of the city's main attractions. With Portland State University, Oregon Health and Sciences University, and Lewis and Clark College all in the southwest sector of town, downtown hotels are a particularly hot commodity, especially for visiting families and prospective students.

Rates vary a lot by season, with the months between May and October often considered high season. April can be affordable, and the coldest days of the year have usually passed. The same is true of October and November, when the weather is still fairly mild and the rates have dropped. December, January, and February are great times to take advantage of low rates and super-saver specials, but these months usually bring with them the most inclement weather.

HIGHLIGHTS

Hotel Vintage Portland

✪ **BEST PLACE TO STAY WITH FIDO:** Modern and stylish **Hotel Rose** is super dog-friendly. If you didn't bring a pooch, don't worry; the hotel leaves a little stuffed one on the bed for you (page 195).

✪ **BEST PLACE TO SIP AND STAY:** Oenophile darling **Hotel Vintage Portland** has wine-themed rooms and tastings (page 195).

✪ **BEST PLACE TO GET RETRO-CHIC:** At the all-suite **Inn at Northrup Station,** color and whimsy are definitely not in short supply (page 202).

✪ **BEST PLACE TO GIVE GREEN LIVING A TRY:** Each adorable "hotel room" at **Caravan: A Tiny House Hotel** is a self-contained tiny house complete with kitchen, bathroom, electricity, and running water (page 204).

✪ **BEST PLACE TO PARTY ALL NIGHT:** If Studio 54 were a hotel in Portland, it would be the **Jupiter Hotel,** a sleek and modern urban lodge where the parties often spill into the courtyard (page 205).

✪ **BEST PLACE TO EXPLORE PORTLAND'S DARK PAST:** McMenamins **White Eagle Motel** has a titillating, scandalous history rumored to still haunt the premises (page 207).

PRICE KEY

$	Less than $100 per night
$ $	$100-200 per night
$ $ $	More than $200 per night

WHERE TO STAY IF...

YOU WANT TO CHECK OFF YOUR PORTLAND BUCKET LIST:
Stay **downtown,** where you'll find be in close proximity to iconic spots like Voodoo Doughnut, Powell's City of Books, and the *Portlandia* statue.

YOU WANT TO SHOP UNTIL YOU DROP:
Look for accommodations in the **Northwest and Pearl District,** where you'll find locally owned boutiques as well as national retailers.

YOU WANT TO EXPERIENCE THE CITY LIKE A HIP LOCAL:
Head over the river to Portland's **Southeast,** where there is nary a chain in sight and you can mingle with the regulars at indie bars, eateries, and boutiques.

YOU WANT A QUIRKY PORTLAND CRASH PAD:
Stay at one of the **McMenamins** hotels, like the White Eagle, Kennedy School, or Crystal Hotel; the refurbished historical properties come with added touches of trademark whimsy.

YOU WANT TO STAY SLIGHTLY OFF-THE-BEATEN PATH:
Accommodations in **Northeast** and **North Portland** may be a bit farther from the city center, but if you're interested in staying in quieter, leafy neighborhoods, or conversely want to hang in happening 'hoods like the Alberta Arts District, this may be the right choice for you.

ALTERNATIVE LODGING

Various temporary rental options in the city are available via AirBnB, Vacasa, and Vacation Rentals by Owner (VRBO), which offer affordable options for comfortable lodging, especially outside of the downtown area. The greatest concentration of vacation rentals in Portland is centered in the Southeast and inner Northeast neighborhoods where housing shortages have been the highest. Given this, these types of vacation rentals have been controversial. While the city has rules requiring hosts to acquire a permit, live at the residence at least nine months a year, and keep guest stays to a maximum of 30 days, such regulations are hard to track and enforce. Many locals have argued that vacation rentals are consuming available apartments and rooms while both

eating away at the commercial tourism industry and forcing an increase in local rental rates. To combat this, the Portland City Council tacked on two new fees to vacation rentals in 2018. A $4 per night booking fee will go toward housing and homelessness initiatives and a 2 percent fee toward tourism marketing.

If you're looking to stay outside of town near the airport, numerous options line the way on NE Airport Way and NE Cascades Parkway. The **Aloft Portland Airport Hotel** (9920 NE Cascades Pkwy., 503/200-5678, www.starwoodhotels.com/alofthotels; $280-310) is your best bet of these, with modern decor, a 24-hour fitness center, an in-house lounge, and a location just steps away from the MAX transit center, which can whisk you straight to city center.

Downtown

Map 1

WHERE TO STAY

DOWNTOWN

✪ Hotel Rose $$$

Hotel Rose is stylish, colorful, and sleek, and offers easy access to Tom McCall Waterfront Park. In your room, you'll be greeted by Dash, a stuffed husky who is the hospitality mascot. You can purchase the stuffed puppy if you like and a portion of that "adoption fee" goes to animal rescue charities. The hotel is a self-proclaimed "dog-obsessed" venue and happy to provide you with special amenities for your pooch like a bed, water bowl, and treats. For humans, Hotel Rose provides super comfortable, double-duvet European-style bedding (each sleeper gets his or her own comforter), and you'll find free high-speed Wi-Fi, in-room Keurig coffeemakers, and cute pineapple-themed decor throughout. There are even free pineapple cupcakes in the lobby and pineapple-emblazoned beach cruiser bikes that you can borrow.

MAP 1: 50 SW Morrison St., 503/221-0711, www.staypineapple.com

✪ Hotel Vintage Portland $$$

Oenophiles will feel right at home in this boutique hotel, a Kimpton property that offers wine-themed accommodations in a majestic, 1894 downtown building that received a $10 million makeover in 2015. In addition to some graffiti-themed cork art, the hotel has a stylish game room (with billiards and shuffleboard) and a lobby bar appropriately named Bacchus, for the Roman god of wine. Each of the 117 casual yet chic rooms is named

Hotel Rose's mascot Dash will be waiting on your bed to greet you.

Hotel Vintage Portland

after an Oregon winery, and namesake wine partners host a complimentary wine hour at 5pm Thursday-Saturday. The hotel is also committed to being ecofriendly; there are complimentary bicycles to reduce your carbon footprint, and if you decline housekeeping services during your stay, you'll receive a voucher for Il Solito, the attached Italian eatery.

MAP 1: 422 SW Broadway, 503/228-1212, www.vintageplaza.com

The Benson Hotel $$$

Simon Benson, a Portland lumber baron, visionary, and philanthropist (and namesake for the Benson Bubblers drinking fountains), opened The Benson (then The New Oregon Hotel) in 1913. It was a grand spectacle, with a French Second Empire glazed terra-cotta and brick exterior, arched lobby windows, and mansard roof with dormers. The interior was no less grand, with carved Circassian walnut from the forests of Imperial Russia. Over the years, this hotel has seen a number of renovations and expansions, but still maintains remarkable beauty and opulence. The hotel has played host to celebrities, sports figures, and politicians—and has bedded almost every U.S. president since Harry S. Truman.

MAP 1: 309 SW Broadway, 503/228-2000, www.bensonhotel.com

The Benson Hotel

Dossier Hotel $$$

The Dossier Hotel (formerly The Westin) is located right near the heart of downtown. Rooms are fairly spacious and modern, some with pretty spectacular views of the city, particularly if you opt for a corner room. Parking can run you almost $50 a night, so it's best to stick with public transit or walking while staying here—but that's easy to do given its convenient location. Complimentary umbrellas and bicycles are here for you to borrow, and other nice amenities include a range of pillow options, free pet-welcoming kits, and a weekday happy hour with free beer and kombucha.

MAP 1: 750 SW Alder St., 503/294-9000, www.dossierhotel.com

The Duniway $$$

The Duniway Hotel, which is under the Hilton umbrella, is named for Abigail Scott Duniway, an American women's rights advocate and newspaper editor who is remembered for her successful campaign to win the right for women to vote. The hotel received a major renovation in 2017, and the new interior is a lovely mix of traditional and contemporary furnishings with nature-inspired elements. Each of the 327 guest rooms is fairly spacious and comes stocked with a selection of books from Powell's City of Books, espresso machines, and umbrellas to use during your stay. This hotel is also the home to the Chris Cosentino restaurant, Jack Rabbit.

MAP 1: 545 SW Taylor St., 503/553-7000, www3.hilton.com

Embassy Suites Portland Downtown $$$

If you have been to an Embassy Suites before, this one is going to seem just a little bit different. It is housed in the historic 1912 Multnomah Hotel building, one of the largest and most magnificent of its time. In its heyday the Multnomah hosted U.S. presidents, a Romanian queen, Charles Lindbergh—and even Elvis Presley in 1957. John Kennedy gave an impromptu speech here. The building was renovated in 1995 to operate as an Embassy Suites with upscale, all-suite guest rooms, complimentary cooked-to-order breakfasts, and afternoon manager's receptions with free alcoholic and nonalcoholic beverages and appetizers.

MAP 1: 319 SW Pine St., 503/279-9000, www.embassysuites.com

Heathman Hotel $$$

When it comes to luxury, the Heathman is really trying to corner the market. French press coffeepots and electric kettles in every room with Peet's coffee and loose-leaf teas? Complimentary L'Occitane products? MP3-compatible sound systems? Blackout drapes? A menu that lets you choose your own mattress, with options like the oh-so-European featherbed? This historic, elegant hotel is popular for travelers looking to take in a little culture, especially since it is mere steps away from the Portland'5 Centers for the Arts and Portland Art Museum. It has received a lot of attention lately for its featured role in the *Fifty Shades of Grey* books.

MAP 1: 1001 SW Broadway, 503/241-4100, http://portland.heathmanhotel.com

Hotel deLuxe $$$

If you have ever imagined yourself as Bette Davis or Cary Grant, the Hotel deLuxe, at the edge of downtown, has got your number. The former Mallory Hotel, built in 1912, has been carefully restored but still evokes Hollywood's Golden Age. With richly detailed high ceilings, elegant columns, and crystal chandeliers, the hotel has a sophisticated elegance and romantic ambience. Each floor has a different theme based on Old Hollywood personalities, and the rooms come equipped with luxurious amenities and menus that allow you to select your own pillow and even order up a Torah over the Bible if you prefer.

MAP 1: 729 SW 15th Ave., 866/895-2094, www.hoteldeluxeportland.com

Hotel Lucia $$$

Throughout Hotel Lucia you will find Pulitzer Prize-winning photographer David Hume Kennerly's odd and intriguing work. This downtown boutique hotel has 127 smallish guest rooms, each smartly decorated and appointed with pillow-top mattresses, high-thread-count duvets, pillow menus, plush robes, 24-hour room service, Tivoli Bluetooth clock radios, and Lather bath products. One of the hotel's signature features is the "Get It Now" button, which promises to get you anything you desire, from a basic amenity to a grand wish. If you are traveling with a dog, you will find Lucia well equipped to host. The fourth floor is devoted to travelers with four-legged friends.

MAP 1: 400 SW Broadway, 503/225-1717, www.hotellucia.com

Hotel Monaco $$$

This artsy hotel can be a lot of fun if you like art, wine, or free stuff. Every evening there is a wine reception with paints and canvases available (in case you get inspired). Send your shoes out for a complimentary shoeshine or take advantage of the free bike rental to explore the city. Work out in the 24-hour gym or browse the free Internet all night, knowing the morning brings complimentary Starbucks coffee and tea service with free newspapers. If you bring your dog, it gets free spring

Hotel Lucia

water and treats, a bed to sleep in, and "Dispose-a-scoop" bags. Didn't bring your dog? That's okay, Monaco will lend you a goldfish to keep you company (for free).

MAP 1: 506 SW Washington St., 503/222-0001, www.monaco-portland.com

The Mark Spencer Hotel $$$

Central to a number of downtown arts organizations, the Mark Spencer bills itself as Portland's "Hotel to the Arts." In fact, it's the hotel that many visiting artists take up residence in while performing here. Rates are remarkably reasonable given the hotel's proximity to downtown and the Pearl District, and they also give you the opportunity

Hotel Monaco

to "bid your own price." Simply submit a proposed price and they will let you know if they can swing it. If they can't, they'll let you know when that rate might be available or will offer you the best price for the date you would like to come.

MAP 1: 409 SW 11th Ave., 503/224-3293, www.markspencer.com

The Nines $$$

When your car pulls up to The Nines, you may wonder if there has been a mistake. This 331-room luxury hotel occupies the top nine floors of the historic Meier & Frank Building, and Macy's (which purchased the building from Meier & Frank) fills the building's lower five levels. The word of the day at The Nines is "posh," and that goes from valet service to beds that seem to swallow you in a heap of European linens. Interior rooms overlook the atrium—interesting if you like to people-watch but otherwise rather ho-hum. Book an exterior room for views of the city and Pioneer Courthouse Square.

MAP 1: 525 SW Morrison St., 877/229-9995, www.starwoodhotels.com

The Porter Hotel $$$

This luxury hotel is part of Hilton Curio, a collection of small, boutique hotels each with its own distinct character and history. This particular iteration features 297 guest rooms, a library, an indoor pool, a sauna, a steam room, and four dining options, including the Terrane Italian Kitchen and Bar and the Chiosco Pizza Window. There is a spectacular rooftop bar with cozy couches, firepits, and panoramic views of the city, as well as indoor and outdoor seating. The hotel is marketed largely toward business travelers.

MAP 1: 1355 SW 2nd Ave., 503/306-4800, www.curiocollection3.hilton.com

The RiverPlace Hotel $$$

The RiverPlace Hotel is especially suited for business travelers, with a 24-hour business center with all the amenities as well as rooms equipped with complimentary high-speed Internet, a spacious Craftsman-style work desk, and an ergonomic office chair for finishing those big reports. But rooms also boast creature comforts like 37-inch flat-screen TVs, in-room umbrellas, binoculars, yoga mats, Atelier Bloem bath products, plush bathrobes, and coffeemakers. The hotel is right on the waterfront, which is a bit more peaceful than being in the center of downtown and is a great place to jog before you head out to begin your day.

MAP 1: 1510 SW Harbor Way, 503/228-3233, www.riverplacehotel.com

The Sentinel $$$

This historic hotel—known as The Governor Hotel until 2014—was originally built in 1909 as the Seward Hotel, a "hotel of quiet elegance." With its ornate facade complete with art deco gargoyles and an interior that boasts Native American-inspired themes, rustic chandeliers, and rich wood textures, it certainly is elegant. The building was added to the National Register of Historic Places in 1985 and has

The RiverPlace Hotel

Ace Hotel

served as the set for films including Madonna's *Body of Evidence* and *My Own Private Idaho.*
MAP 1: 614 SW 11th Ave., 503/224-1236, www.sentinelhotel.com

Ace Hotel $$

Ace Hotel, edging downtown and the Pearl, has one of the most photographed lobbies in town. Whether for a fashion shoot, headshots, engagement photos, or an impromptu photo op with friends, the lobby reeks of coolness. Friendly and affordable, this art-meets-music hotel is especially popular with creative professionals and international travelers. The rooms are achingly hip—some come with turntables and vintage vinyl records! With enormous murals painted by hot local artists, vintage furniture, claw-foot tubs, flat-screen TVs, and custom-made Pendleton blankets, each room is unique. If you're a light sleeper, bring your earplugs or ask for a room away from the street.

MAP 1: 1022 SW Harvey Milk St., 503/228-2277, www.acehotel.com

Courtyard by Marriott Portland City Center $$

Opened in May 2009, this 256-room Courtyard by Marriott enterprise was all too recently a vacated bank building. But after a major renovation, the hotel is sleek, stylish, and designed to meet LEED gold certification. It's a Marriott with a distinctly Portland twist. All the artwork in the hotel was created by local artists. Paintings of local scenes adorn the hallways and lobby, and each guest room features an original ceramic piece by graduates of the Oregon College of Art and Craft. The hotel offers the regular comforts one would expect of a Marriott, like smoke-free rooms, wireless Internet, business services, complimentary lobby coffee, and valet parking.

MAP 1: 550 SW Oak St., 503/505-5000, www.marriott.com/pdxpr

Crystal Hotel $$

A McMenamins property, the Crystal Hotel has a varied past, having housed everything from a tire shop to a raucous nightclub and bathhouse. These days, the triangular Crystal bears the distinct artistic signature of its owners. The hotel's walls are covered with vibrant murals of the most famous musical acts to play at the hotel's namesake Crystal Ballroom next door, and hand-painted headboards and art panels inspired by the same grace each of the 51 rooms. While most of the rooms are "European-style" (the bathroom is down the hall), there are nine king-bed rooms with private bathrooms. There is a subterranean saltwater soaking pool, a full-service restaurant, and a cozy music venue that hosts live bands, comedy shows, and post-show concerts.

MAP 1: 303 SW 12th Ave., 503/972-2670, www.mcmenamins.com/crystalhotel

Hotel Modera $$

Hotel Modera offers a comfortable and modern place to stay for people visiting Portland State University who want to be downtown but not smack-dab in the middle of it. The beds have pillow-top mattresses, nice linens, and a fur throw that almost makes the whole stay worthwhile. Be sure to use the Tarocco blood orange bath products; they smell so good you'll wish they were edible. There's a business center as well as free Wi-Fi, which works well in the hotel's pretty courtyard. It doesn't have a gym on-site, but you can get complimentary passes to the nearby 24-Hour Fitness.

MAP 1: 515 SW Clay St., 503/484-1084, www.hotelmodera.com

Hotel Modera

Northwest and the Pearl District

Map 2

Canopy Hotel $$$

This hotel under the Hilton banner has 153 rooms in the Pearl District, which is otherwise a little shy on such options. There are filtered water stations and ice makers on each floor, 60-inch HD televisions and espresso machines in each of the rooms, and free Wi-Fi. Guests are also able to pre-check into the hotel and pre-select their ideal room from the hotel map, then check in using their mobile devices and a keyless entry. One great amenity is the grab-and-go breakfast goody bag delivered directly to your room so you can take it with you on your way out, as well as several "thoughtfully themed and priced" foodie bags that can be selected from and are included with the in-room minibar. Rooms are sleek, and the modern decor of the lobby is nice, with inviting lounge areas and cozy spots for reading books.

MAP 2: 425 NW 9th Ave., 971/351-0230, www.canopy3.hilton.com

✪ Inn at Northrup Station $$

This hotel looks unassuming from the outside, but it's not your average hotel. It seems like it was designed by Willy Wonka, right down to the giant glass jars filled with colorful candies adorning the lobby tables. Staff is friendly and energetic, and the entire place feels modern, fun, and trippy. The inn will provide free tickets for the streetcar to downtown and connections farther out. This is an all-suite hotel, and most rooms come with a kitchen—though there are plenty of Alphabet District restaurants nearby. Continental breakfast is free and usually includes pastries, cereal, fruit, bagels, and yogurt. The inn also hosts a number of free events in the lobby, such as movie nights, wine and beer tastings, and Sundae Sundays.

MAP 2: 2025 NW Northrup St., 503/224-0543, www.northrupstation.com

Silver Cloud Inn $$

Although referred to as Silver Cloud Portland–Downtown, this hotel is at the brink of Northwest Portland—about two miles from downtown at the Alphabet District's industrial edge. If you're a light sleeper, ask for a room away from busy Vaughn Street; otherwise, the location is removed from the bustle of the city, yet easily accessible by freeway and about six blocks from the main shopping and dining areas of NW 23rd Avenue. It's an attractive and comfortable place. Silver Cloud has moderately spacious, clean rooms and mini-suites with free Wi-Fi, 42-inch plasma televisions, refrigerators, coffeemakers, and microwaves.

MAP 2: 2426 NW Vaughn St., 503/242-2400, www.silvercloud.com

Portland International Guesthouse $

This sweet little guesthouse in the heart of the Alphabet District is a great place if you're looking to save money but don't want to be far from the bustling heart of the city. With five bed-and-breakfast-style private rooms sharing two full bathrooms, it is a popular place for families who want to stay together. Here you will find free wireless Internet; a sitting room with a fireplace; a kitchen area with free coffee, tea, juice, and cereals in the morning; and Steven and Thomas, two of the nicest hosts in town, who live on-site and are regular travelers themselves.

MAP 2: 2185 NW Flanders St., 503/224-0500, www.pdxguesthouse.com

The Society Hotel

The Society Hotel $

Located in the Old Town/Chinatown neighborhood, which has long been lacking in accommodations, The Society Hotel has a lot going for it, particularly for the traveler on a budget. The hotel-hostel hybrid offers an enormous bunkroom with 24 beds, 24 Euro-style rooms with shared bathrooms, and 12 suites with private bathrooms. Bunkrooms feature triple-decker curtained beds with luggage lockers and gigantic ladders to access each tier. Multiple shared bathrooms are stocked with shower products, a hair dryer, tissue, bamboo bath mats, and hangers to keep your things tidy. Note that the area sees heavy foot traffic from clubgoers and is in close proximity to a number of local shelters and missions.

MAP 2: 203 NW 3rd Ave., 503/445-0444, www.societyhotel.com

Northeast

Map 3

Hotel Eastlund $$$

Answering the call for some much needed lodging near the Oregon Convention Center is Hotel Eastlund. The former Red Lion received a $15 million remodel in 2015 and bears no resemblance to its outdated former self. The new, swanky digs are colorful, modern, and full of amenities that cater to the convention crowd, like a 24-hour business center, posh meeting rooms, and a roof top bar. The rooms are equally stylish and well equipped with Keurig coffeemakers, free Wi-Fi, and electronic "do not disturb" technology.

MAP 3: 1021 NE Grand Ave., 503/235-2100, www.hoteleastlund.com

Hotel Eastlund

Lion and the Rose Victorian Bed & Breakfast Inn $$$

This breathtaking Queen Anne inn sits amid stately Victorian homes in Portland's historic Irvington District. Rooms have a distinctive, romantic flair, like the pretty, sun-drenched, turret-style sitting area in the Lavonna room. Each room has a private bathroom, with the exception of the Avandel, which has a dedicated bathroom and claw-foot soaking tub down the hall. The Lion and the Rose offers two-course breakfasts and light refreshments in the afternoon or evening. If you're traveling with family, you can opt for the Victorian Apartment, which sleeps up to six and has a kitchenette, dining table, bathroom, washer/dryer, wireless Internet, television, and an electric fireplace.

MAP 3: 1810 NE 15th Ave., 503/287-9245, www.lionrose.com

Portland's White House $$$

If you find yourself peeking around the corners to catch a glimpse of the president, don't be surprised. No, POTUS hasn't stayed here, but the mansion does bear more than a passing resemblance to the "official" White House. The grand portico and circular drive are just the beginning. The five guest rooms in the main house and the three in the adjoining

Caravan: A Tiny House Hotel

Carriage House are lavishly and meticulously decorated, each one a grand affair with fabulous linens along with four-poster beds or magnificent canopies. The proprietors go to painstaking lengths to ensure that your stay is superb, so if you like a hands-off approach, either mention it in advance or stay somewhere else.

MAP 3: 1914 NE 22nd Ave., 503/287-7131, www.portlandswhitehouse.com

Kennedy School $$

This elementary school, which was built in 1915, was saved from probable destruction when the McMenamin brothers decided to turn it into a fantastic hotel. Now the old classrooms have been stripped of their desks (but not their chalkboards) in exchange for comfy beds. Work out your kinks playing basketball or dodgeball in the gymnasium. Watch a movie in the old auditorium while sipping beer and noshing on pizza, or take a dip in the soaking pool. If you still feel guilty for nodding off in class, you can always send yourself to the Detention Bar for a little redemption.

MAP 3: 5736 NE 33rd Ave., 503/249-3983, www.kennedyschool.com

✪ Caravan: A Tiny House Hotel $

The tiny house movement is sweeping the world, and this six-home hotel in the heart of the Alberta Arts District offers guests an opportunity to try out the lifestyle. Houses range from 100-200 square feet, and each has its own layout and personality and comes equipped with a small kitchen and bathroom, all with electricity, running water, and plumbing. The neighboring Radio Room restaurant-lounge provides room service. Adding to the overall charm, the homes are assembled around a shared firepit, where guests can gather, roast marshmallows, and occasionally hear some live music by performers brought in by the hotel owners as a special treat.

MAP 3: 5009 NE 11th Ave., 503/288-5225, www.tinyhousehotel.com

STAY STRANGE

In a city that thrives on being unique, it is no surprise there are a number of oddball options where would-be travelers can rest their heads. Cyclists passing through may want to check out **The Friendly Bike Guesthouse** (4039 N. Williams Ave., 503/799-2615, www. friendlybikeguesthouse.com; $36 dorm bed, $76 private room), a hostel-style spot where cyclists are given access to a mechanic stand, bike tools, and secure bike storage.

Or take a walk down memory lane at **Kennedy School** (page 204), a 1915 schoolhouse turned hotel, restaurant, and bar. Guests sleep in converted classrooms where chalkboards still hang on the walls and imbibe adult libations in the Detention Lounge.

If you want to skip the hotel, Portland boasts a number of tiny houses, backyard studios, converted trailers, and funky lofts available for rental. The tiny houses especially are experiencing a boom in popularity. Answering that call is **Caravan: A Tiny House Hotel** (page 204), a gaggle of tiny houses that reside in a former vacant lot with a security fence, a communal firepit, and a lot of charm. You can also find tiny house accommodations at **Tiny Digs** (2646 NE Glisan St., 844/395-8469, www.tinydigshotel.com; $185), a converted car dealership that now boasts seven tiny homes, each with running water, a small kitchen, flushing toilets, and an adorable attached deck.

From September to mid-June, you can arrange to spend the night at the Oregon Zoo with its **ZooSnooze program** (4001 SW Canyon Rd., 503/220-2781, www.oregonzoo.org; $52 pp). It's an opportunity usually seized by schoolchildren, but groups of adults can also make arrangements to bring their camping gear and spend the evening hours touring the zoo, listening to special keeper talks, and engaging in hands-on activities.

Everett Street Guesthouse $

Everett Street Guesthouse is decked out in the style of a true Portlander—elegant, eclectic, and not the least bit pretentious. The Wellfleet Room, for two, and Sophie's Room, a single, are in the main house; the studio cottage is separate and features a kitchenette, tiled shower, washer/dryer, television, wireless Internet, private patio garden, and deck. Breakfast can be added for $10 per person. Everett Street has a three-night minimum for the cottage and a two-night minimum the other rooms. The proprietors require a 50 percent deposit to book and prefer cash or personal checks.

MAP 3: 2306 NE Everett St., 503/230-0211, www.everettstreetguesthouse.com

Southeast   Map 4

Jupiter Next $$$

If you need a little more luxe in your life than the Jupiter Hotel has to offer, check out its swanky sister up the street. It's a great option for people who like the hip, party vibe of the Jupiter and its attached Doug Fir Lounge, but who also want to get a reasonable amount of sleep. The sleek, asymmetrical building houses 67 rooms ranging from basic to XL, which has a king-sized bed, oversized windows, bar, and convertible sofa. In the lobby, you'll find the full-service café and late-night bar, Hey Love, a self-proclaimed "indoor jungle" that features tropical, bold flavors and pretty presentation.

MAP 4: 900 E. Burnside St., 503/230-9200, www.jupiterhotel.com

✪ Jupiter Hotel $$

Oh, the Jupiter Hotel. This inner Southeast hub is the irresistible black sheep of Portland accommodations. Although it provides modern and sleek rooms in which to rest weary heads, the Jupiter is the place to stay if you're less interested in sleeping than in experiencing some of the city's late-night charms. Throw your door open and interact with the other guests, who are likely to be spilling out of their own rooms and partying between the hotel and the attached Doug Fir, a perennially popular bar-lounge and live music venue. There's an indoor fireplace as well as outdoor firepit here, and the attitude is no-frills fun. Those wanting to shake things up can take advantage of Oregon's first-ever 420 hotel package; there's no actual cannabis included, but you do get a vape pen, a munchie kit, and all the details you need to fulfill your adventure.

MAP 4: 800 E. Burnside St., 503/230-9200, www.jupiterhotel.com

Evermore Guesthouse $$

This lovely bed-and-breakfast has five beautifully decorated suites and a studio apartment with a private entrance. Each of the rooms is equipped with its own heat and air-conditioning controls and private bathrooms with claw-foot tubs and showers. The house provides continental breakfast each morning (available when you are ready for it) with goodies like coffee, tea, juice, yogurt, and locally made pastries, bagels, and muffins. It's also within close walking distance to a number of great cafés and restaurants.

MAP 4: 3868 SE Clinton St., 503/206-6509, www.evermoreguesthouse.com

Bluebird Guesthouse $

This quaint and pretty guesthouse has seven guest rooms, each named for a different author: The Gabriel Garcia-Marquez room on the main floor is equipped with a private bath and a claw-foot tub, while the Elliott Smith room is, unsurprisingly, located in the basement. The Bluebird is in Southeast Portland, a healthy walk from the adorable Clinton Street neighborhood and Hawthorne District. The decor combines vintage charm with modern character, lending the place a cozy, at-home feeling that seems miles away from hotel life. Guests are allowed access to the sizable kitchen and refrigerator, with the understanding that they are responsible for their own clean-up. Robes, towels, washcloths, soap, shampoo, and a hair dryer are all provided, and there is an iron and coin-op laundry machine in the basement.

MAP 4: 3517 SE Division St., 503/238-4333, www.bluebirdguesthouse.com

Hawthorne Hostel $

If you prefer a bohemian approach, Hawthorne Hostel might be for you. Located right at the heart of Hawthorne Boulevard, the hostel is actively involved in the community, with potluck brunches every Sunday and summertime open mics or "bike-in" movies in the backyard. The upkeep of the place varies depending on current staff, but everyone is friendly and easygoing. A private room goes for $68-77 a night; a shared dorm space is $27-42. Sheets are included, but you'll need to make your bed every day and strip it when you leave (it's a hostel, remember?), and towels are extra, so it's wise to bring your own. It should be noted that there's a housecat; if you are sensitive to pet fur, you may want to skip this one.

MAP 4: 3031 SE Hawthorne Blvd., 866/447-3031, www.portlandhostel.org

North Portland

Map 6

WHERE TO STAY

✪ White Eagle Motel $

The White Eagle is a McMenamins salvage job with the distinction of having one of the most sordid and storied pasts in Portland history. The legend dates to the early 1900s, when the venue was commonly called "Bucket of Blood." Dock workers and railroad men would stop in for a little pool, cigars, poker, liquor, and, if they played their cards right, a turn in the brothel or opium den upstairs. Numerous violent brawls earned the place its nickname: a prostitute was murdered in a jealous rage, and sailors disappeared in the night only to turn up on a ship and be forced into service. The hotel now rents inexpensive rooms (about $70-95 a night) that are unapologetically modest—and occasionally haunted. It's a fun, cheap way to spend the night in Portland, and you can watch some pretty legendary rock music in the downstairs saloon.

MAP 6: 836 N. Russell St., 503/282-6810, www.mcmenamins.com/whiteeagle

Palms Motor Hotel $

The Palms Motor Hotel is not exactly luxury accommodations, but if you appreciate even a little bit of kitsch, this little dive is calling your name. The neon sign, alive with monkeys and palm trees singing the praises of free HBO and Starz, is one of the most photographed signs in town. For all its tropical silliness, the Palms is a Portland icon. The motel is not all that bad, plus it's right on the MAX's Yellow Line, so access to the rest of the city is steps away. The lime green "honeymoon suite" with Jacuzzi is less than $100 a night— although booking it for your *actual* honeymoon might send you straight into annulment.

MAP 6: 3801 N. Interstate Ave., 503/287-5788, www.palmsmotel.com

TOP EXPERIENCE

DAY TRIPS

One of the great things about Portland is its proximity to some of the Pacific Northwest's most stunning landscapes. Portlanders relish the fact that they're always about an hour away from something spectacularly different than where they are. For visitors, the diversity of landscapes is a bonus as well; with everything so conveniently close, there's no need to choose between mountains or ocean, city or wine country.

Multnomah Falls

The Columbia River Gorge, which begins approximately 20 minutes east of Portland and extends for more than 100 miles, is lush, breathtaking country, with numerous waterfalls, scenic drives, and a plethora of outdoor activities—like hiking, biking, golf, white-water rafting, kayaking, and windsurfing.

Mount Hood, about 50 miles east/southeast of Portland, offers 4,600 acres of skiable terrain and more than 1,200 miles of hiking trails.

About 75 miles to the west, you will find the magnificent Pacific Ocean and a flurry of quaint coastal towns with fun shops and fresh seafood.

A little closer to town (about 25 miles to the southwest) is Oregon wine country, where winemakers grow, age, and bottle some of the best pinot noirs in the world.

PLANNING YOUR TIME

Each of these excursions from Portland are easy day trips by car. Of course, if you have the time to linger for an overnight or weekend, that leaves more time to experience these dramatically different areas.

If you're interested in heading to the Oregon coast, you could pick just one of the northern towns—Astoria, Seaside, Cannon Beach, or Newport— to visit for an easy, focused day trip from Portland. If your heart's set on

HIGHLIGHTS

✪ **BEST PLACE TO FLY A KITE:** At **Cannon Beach,** a blustery day can turn into a whole lot of fun (page 214).

✪ **BEST PLACE TO GET YOUR SQUEAK ON:** At the **Tillamook Cheese Factory,** you can sample some of the finest cheddar in the nation, take a free tour, and purchase some of the infamous squeaky cheese (page 214).

✪ **BEST PHOTO OP:** "Majestic" is perhaps the word most often applied to **Multnomah Falls,** a 620-foot waterfall (page 220).

✪ **BEST PLACE TO SING "ROLL ON, COLUMBIA":** Woody Guthrie wrote his famous song about **Bonneville Dam,** which features a fish hatchery and ladder that Pacific salmon and steelhead pass through on their journey upstream (page 220).

✪ **BEST PLACE TO GO SLEDDING IN THE SUMMER:** There's always a good patch of mountain to ride in the winter months, but in the summer **Mt. Hood Skibowl** has a 300-foot inner-tube course and a 500-foot zip line (page 226).

✪ **BEST PLACE TO SIP A FUTURE STAR: Carlton Winemakers Studio** houses 10 small artisan winemakers who share an ecofriendly space, equipment, and talent for making phenomenal wines (page 234).

✪ **BEST PLACE TO CATCH FLIGHT FEVER:** From a replica of the first plane to the awesome heavy bombers of World War II and Howard Hughes's remarkable *Spruce Goose,* the **Evergreen Aviation and Space Museum** has it all (page 235).

Cannon Beach

Day Trips

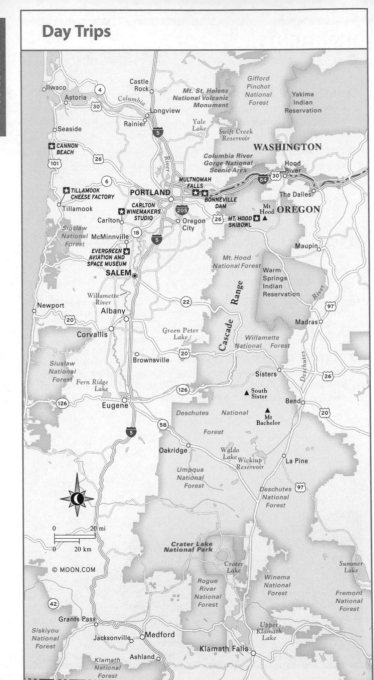

driving Highway 101 down the coast for a stretch, leave early in the day. The drive from Portland to Astoria itself takes a couple of hours, and the drive down the coast from there to Newport takes several, not counting traffic, which can get particularly snarled on summer weekends (though it gives you time to appreciate the scenery).

To the east, the Columbia River Gorge and Mount Hood are considered Portland's backyard. For much of the winter season (particularly Dec.-Mar.), tire chains are a must on your way to Mount Hood, even for vehicles with four-wheel drive.

Wine country is less than an hour's drive from Portland, though it can also clog up with traffic. Your biggest planning to-do for this trip will be figuring out a designated driver.

The Oregon Coast

Oregon has more than 350 miles of coastline, much of it wild, jagged, and beautiful. The water remains fairly chilly (around 45-55°F in most places), and the coastal breeze means cooler climates—but the high basalt rock cliffs, long sandy beaches, and amazing tide pools make it a visitor's paradise.

Along much of the Oregon coastline, you can catch some serious whale-watching, as gray, humpback, and sperm whales migrate south toward Baja during their December pilgrimage from the chilly waters of Alaska. Prime season for whale-watching is between December and March, so coastal hotels with prime spots for viewing book up fast.

ASTORIA
SIGHTS
At the tip-top of the Oregon coastline, you'll find Astoria, a historic spot where Lewis and Clark spent the winter of 1805-1806, holed up at **Fort Clatsop** (92343 Fort Clatsop Rd., Astoria, 503/861-2471, ext. 214, www.nps.gov/lewi; summer daily 9am-6pm, after Labor Day daily 9am-5pm; $3 adults, free for children under 15), which still stands today. The visitors center at Fort Clatsop National Historical Park has an exhibit built in 1955 inspired by the expedition members' journals, as well as an interpretive center, gift shop, and orientation film. In summer months, the center also features ranger-led programs and reenactors in the fort.

Fort Stevens (Fort Stevens State Park, Hammond, 503/861-1470, www.visitftstevens.com; daily generally 10am-6pm; free, $5 car pass) is a former U.S. military installation that guarded the mouth of the Columbia River in the state of Oregon. The structure was built near the end of the U.S. Civil War and named for general and former Washington Territory governor Isaac Stevens. Nowadays, it is a popular campsite and day park with beach access to the famous *Peter Iredale* shipwreck, which ran aground in 1906 and is still visible today.

Astoria has a lot of history for such a small town. In fact, don't be surprised if you recognize a lot of the landscape as you walk through it. This has been the filming locale for movies like *Goonies, Overboard, Short Circuit,*

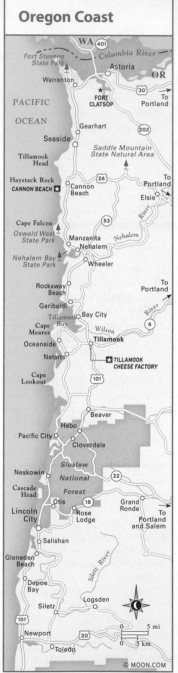

Oregon Coast

The Black Stallion, Kindergarten Cop, Free Willy, Free Willy 2, The Ring, The Ring Two, and *Into the Wild.*

Both fishing and crabbing are popular sports in Astoria. **Astoria Fishing Charters** (503/440-0912, www.astoriafishing.com; $160 adults, $85 crabbing) provides guided trips for salmon, steelhead, sturgeon, and crab at reasonable prices.

RESTAURANTS

A popular dining spot is **Fort George Brewery** (1483 Duane St., 503/325-7468, www.fortgeorgebrewery.com; Mon.-Thurs. 11am-11pm, Fri.-Sat. 11am-midnight, Sun. noon-11pm; $10-20). The huge brewery and pub, which features multiple levels and a pizza kitchen upstairs, was built on the original settlement site of Fort Astoria. It's also the host of the hugely popular Festival of the Dark Arts held during Stout Month in February, which features over 60 unique stouts and some wild entertainment.

The family-owned **Himani Indian Cuisine** (1044 Marine Dr., 503/325-8171, www.himaniic.com; Sun.-Thurs. 11am-3pm and 5pm-9pm, Fri.-Sat. 5pm-9pm; $13-20), is a great spot for comfort food on a budget. The dinner menu features many delicious traditional dishes like naan, curry, biryani, vindaloo, and tandoori, all beautifully executed. Go for the lunch buffet, when you can sample multiple dishes and pay less than most single dinner entrées cost.

WHERE TO STAY

The **Cannery Pier Hotel** (10 Basin St., 888/325-4996, www.cannerypierhotel.com; $209-525), as the name might suggest, sits on what was once the site of Astoria's Union Fisherman's Cooperative Packing Company

Explore tidepools on the Oregon Coast.

Cannery. This boutique hotel rests atop a pier some 600 feet into the river, offering breathtaking views of the passing ships and storms rolling through the mouth of the Columbia.

SEASIDE
SIGHTS

A little farther down the coast, Seaside is one of the most popular tourist destinations on the northern coast. It hosts annual events like the Miss Oregon contest, the Hood to Coast Relay After-Party, and Dorchester Conference, a convention of the Oregon Republican Party.

Just a short walk from Fort Clatsop National Monument is the **Seaside Aquarium** (200 N. Prom, Seaside, 503/738-6211, www.seasideaquarium. com; daily generally 9am-5pm, closing time varies seasonally; adults $8.50, children 6-13 $4.25, seniors $7.25, family $29, children 5 and under free with paid admission), where you can visit starfish, harbor seals, wolf eels, crabs, and other Pacific sea creatures.

You can also find family-fun activities, like the carousel, arcades, miniature golf, bumper cars and boats, tilt-a-twirl, paddleboats, and canoes.

RESTAURANTS

In Seaside, you will find **Pig 'N Pancake** (323 Broadway St., 503/738-7243, www.pignpancake.com; Sun.-Thurs. 6am-9pm, Fri.-Sat. 6am-10pm; $8-15), a rather iconic Northwest greasy spoon. It's been in operation in Seaside since 1961, and the franchise has since expanded to Lincoln City, Cannon Beach, Astoria, Newport, and Portland.

Clam chowder is a must-have at the Oregon coast, and you can find a hearty bowl of it at **Norma's Seafood and Steak** (20 N. Columbia St., 503/738-4331, www.normasseaside. com; daily 10am-9pm; $7-32). If you really dig it, you can take some to go by the pint or the quart. For dessert, check out **Zinger's Ice Cream Parlor** (210 Broadway, 503/738-3939, www.

zingersicecream.com), where every flavor is made from scratch.

HOTELS
Try the **Gilbert Inn** (341 Beach Dr., 503/738-9770, www.gilbertinn.com; $109-229), a comfortable 10-room inn made cozy and romantic by classic Victorian decor. The inn is just one block from the beach and the popular promenade.

Cannon Beach

✪ CANNON BEACH
SIGHTS
Cannon Beach is a handsome coastal town famous for its four-mile-long kite-friendly beach, its galleries and specialty boutiques, and iconic **Haystack Rock,** which rises 235 feet out of the sand and is occasionally accessible by foot during low tide. The city acquired its name in 1846, when a cannon from the U.S. Navy schooner *Shark* washed ashore just north of Arch Cape. Two more appeared in February 2008, having been buried in the sand for about a century and a half. These artifacts and others are on display at the **Cannon Beach History Center and Museum** (1387 S. Spruce St., Cannon Beach, 503/436-9301, www.cbhistory.org; Wed.-Mon. 11am-4pm; free). Late spring is a great time to visit, with the spectacular **Puffin Kite Festival** (www.surfsand.com) in April and the annual **Sandcastle Competition** (www.cannon-beach. net/sandcastle.html) in May or June, depending on the year.

RESTAURANTS
A great place to dine in Cannon Beach is **The Wayfarer** (1190 Pacific Dr., 503/436-1108, www.wayfarer-restaurant.com; daily 8am-9pm; $12-28), where you can find a superb omelet made with whatever is most fresh, like Dungeness crab, bay shrimp, or salmon—or maybe with Rogue Creamery blue cheese and local wild mushrooms.

Like sand in your shoes and windswept hair, **Mo's Clam Chowder** (www.moschowder.com; generally Sun.-Thurs. 11am-8pm, Fri.-Sat. 11am-9pm; $7-15) is synonymous with a trip to the coast, and you can find locations in Cannon Beach, Lincoln City, and Newport. Since 1946, the company has served Mohava "Mo" Niemi's recipe of New England clam chowder, made with locally raised Yaquina Bay oysters.

WHERE TO STAY
The Ocean Lodge (2864 Pacific St., 888/777-4047, www.theoceanlodge. com; $189-379) has spacious and comfortable rooms that have private oceanfront balconies with views of the sea and of Haystack Rock. The lodge is just a short drive from the shops and restaurants of downtown Cannon Beach and very close to great surf breaks as well as hiking and mountain bike trails.

✪ TILLAMOOK CHEESE FACTORY
If you love cheese, the only place you really need to go on your Oregon trip is the **Tillamook Cheese Factory** (4175

Hwy. 101 N., Tillamook, 503/815-1300, www.tillamookcheese.com; mid-June-Labor Day daily 8am-8pm, Labor Day-mid-June daily 8am-6pm; free) in Tillamook. You can tour the facility and find out how it makes its world-class cheddar, plus—best of all—try endless samples of cheeses and buy a scoop of ice cream, selecting from 38 different kinds. An on-site store lets you purchase your favorites at prices far cheaper than online, and the factory even sells its famous "squeaky cheese"—the salty, fresh, and addictive cheddar curds that squeak when you bite into them.

The city of Tillamook is named for a Salish word that means "Land of Many Waters," and it's a popular coastal fishing area today. The seven rivers in Tillamook are abundant with coho salmon and wild steelhead salmon, and the Nestucca, Nehalem, and Tillamook Bays are perhaps the most popular crabbing and clamming areas in the entire Pacific Northwest. Fishing guides like **Lee Darby's Guide Service** (503/351-0547, www.leedarbysfishing.com; $180 full-day trip) can take you out into the churning waters of Tillamook Bay if you want to get your hands on a 30- to 100-pound sturgeon. If you just want to sightsee, charter boats such as **Garibaldi Charters** (503/322-0007,

www.garibaldicharters.com; $40 for 2- to 3-hour tour) can take you out to whale-heavy waters for an up-close and personal look.

NEWPORT
SIGHTS

It's a 2.5- to 3-hour drive from Portland, but if you head over to Newport, you can fill an entire day strolling in the pedestrian-friendly historic Nye Beach district or shopping along the boardwalk—and still sneak in some time on the beach.

The **Oregon Coast Aquarium** (2820 SE Ferry Slip Rd., Newport, 541/867-3474, www.aquarium.org; summer daily 10am-6pm, after Labor Day daily 10am-5pm; $22.95 adults, $19.95 seniors, $19.25 children 13-17, $11.95 for children 3-12, free for children under 3) is the home of more than 500 species of animals in both indoor and outdoor exhibits. Keiko (the whale of *Free Willy* fame) once lived here; when he left, his home was converted into Passages of the Deep, an exhibit that allows visitors to walk through acrylic tunnels surrounded by sharks, rays, and rockfish.

RESTAURANTS

Newport has a number of local favorites, but **Café Mundo** (209 NW Coast Rd., 541/574-8134, www.cafemundo. us; Wed. 11am-8pm, Thurs.-Sat. 11am-10pm, Sun. 10am-3pm; $10-15) tops the list for food, atmosphere, and overall creativity. The menu includes fantastic pastas, sandwiches, salads, and espresso drinks, as well as some great Northwest wines and beers.

For elegant dining, go to **Saffron Salmon** (859 SW Bay Blvd., 541/265-8921, www.saffronsalmon.com; Mon.-Tues. and Thurs. 5pm-8:30pm, Sat.-Sun. 11:30am-2:30pm and

Tillamook Cheese Factory

5pm-8:30pm; $20-28) on a public pier on the west end of Newport's Historic Bayfront. It makes good use out of its proximity to the best seafood in the Northwest by buying direct, which means the salmon you eat for dinner might have been swimming in the Pacific when you woke up.

WHERE TO STAY

Newport has a number of options, but at **Sylvia Beach Hotel** (267 NW Cliff Rd., 541/265-5428, www.sylviabeachhotel.com; $140-245), bookworms will feel right at home. There are no TVs, radios, or phones, but there are a number of books and reading nooks, and each room is decorated in the theme of a particular author, such as Edgar Allan Poe, J. K. Rowling, Amy Tan, J. R. R. Tolkien, and Dr. Seuss.

PRACTICALITIES
INFORMATION AND SERVICES

Before you go, check out the **Oregon Coast Visitors Association** (541/574-2679, http://visittheoregoncoast.com), where you can find advice on where to go and what to do, as well as links to the chamber of commerce and visitors association for each individual city along the coast.

TRANSPORTATION

From I-5, a number of routes will take you to the Oregon Coast. Most are two-lane highways that wind though vast acres of trees, hills, and valleys. To get to the northern part of the coast, you can take Highway 30 along the south banks of the Columbia River through St. Helens and continue on to Astoria.

Another popular route to the Pacific is Highway 26 (sometimes referred to in Portland as the Sunset Highway), which meanders west through Beaverton, Hillsboro, and Banks and continues on to Seaside. Both Highway 30 and Highway 26 connect with Highway 101, which runs north-south parallel to the coastline and passes through most of Oregon's coastal towns. Traffic can drag along Highway 101 on occasion, particularly as you pass through larger towns like Lincoln City. Heading south along 101 makes for a lovely drive with the Pacific Ocean at your constant right, but if you are planning on visiting an area along the central part of the coast, you might be better off finding a more direct route than this pretty but arguably less efficient one.

You can get to the central coast by traveling south down I-5 and heading onto Highway 99 (Portland Rd. East). From there, drive south toward Capitol Street and into downtown Salem. Follow the signs pointing out Highway 22/Ocean Beaches, which will lead you over the Willamette River and out of Salem. Stay on Highway 22 for approximately 25 miles until it intersects with Highway 18, then turn left onto 18 and continue west to the coast. Follow Highway 18 to the Highway 101 junction (about 25 miles), where you can turn south and get to Lincoln City, Depot Bay, and Newport.

Other routes to the coast will inevitably lead you through a series of small towns and blink-and-you-miss-them communities. Once you determine which area of the coast you would like to visit, map your own roundabout route or check with the town's visitors bureau for advice on how to get there.

The Columbia River Gorge

In about an hour or less from Portland, you can find yourself in the heart of the Columbia River Gorge, basking in the rugged natural beauty of the Columbia River, framed by sheer cliffs and majestic mountains. It's a beautiful drive, no matter how deep you get into it. Whether you're heading out to Hood River or just checking out some historical landmarks, you'll find plenty to do. There are countless outdoor adventures (like windsurfing, kiteboarding, rafting, mountain biking, and hiking) for those looking to get an adrenaline fix, but there are also a lot of places to kick back, sip a glass of wine, and enjoy the spectacular view for those who aren't.

SIGHTS
HISTORIC COLUMBIA RIVER HIGHWAY

The Historic Columbia River Highway is a 75-mile stretch of road significant in that it was the first planned scenic highway in the United States. While some sections of the original byway are no longer accessible by car, the stretch that runs from Troutdale to The Dalles provides about a 50-minute detour from the monotony of I-84. Designed to mimic the picturesque winding byways of Europe, the Historic Columbia River Highway takes full advantage of its natural charms, twisting past waterfalls, winding through tunnels, and wandering over bridges. To begin, take exit 17 off I-84. The 24 westernmost miles of the highway begin in

Crown Point and Vista House on the Columbia River Gorge

Columbia River Gorge and Mount Hood

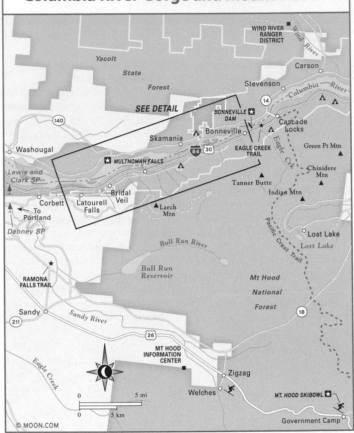

Troutdale and provide access to hiking trails and natural wonders, as well as Crown Point. The road from this point winds in figure eight loops through five miles of waterfalls, including majestic Multnomah Falls. The road here rejoins with I-84 until Mosier, where you can pick up the second leg of the historic highway at exit 74. This is where you will begin to see the drier regions of the Columbia Plateau and Hood River. Be sure to stop at the Rowena Crest vantage point before continuing on to the Columbia Gorge Discovery Center.

Do watch out for occasional road closures as the area continues to rebuild in the aftermath of the 2017 Eagle Creek Fire. It is best to check the **Oregon Department of Transportation** (www.oregon.gov/odot) website before embarking to make sure your trip will not be interrupted.

CROWN POINT AND VISTA HOUSE

You'll know you have arrived at the Columbia River Gorge when you see the unmistakable bluff that is Crown

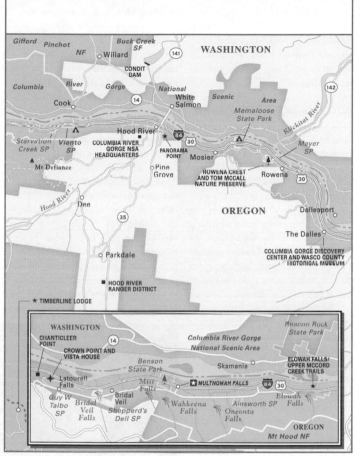

Point, a vantage formed by a 14-million-year-old lava flow that now offers a breathtaking view from 733 feet above the river. The **Vista House Visitors Center** (503/695-2230, www. vistahouse.com; daily 9am-6pm; free), an octagonal stone structure on the Historic Columbia River Highway, was built as a memorial to Oregon pioneers. Its observation deck provides panoramic views that stretch for nearly 30 miles, as well as educational exhibits that relate the history of the area and the building.

Farther up the Historic Columbia River Highway is **Bridal Veil Falls State Park** (www.oregonstateparks. org/park_149.php; free), which can be accessed off I-84 at exit 28. There are two fantastic hiking trails here, the lower of which bears the same name as the park and will take you down to the base of the eponymous falls. The hike is just under one mile round-trip and includes a number of switchbacks. The upper Overlook Trail can be accessed about 20 yards west of the Bridal Veil Falls trailhead. It is a relatively short half-mile loop that will take you to the famous geologic edifice known as the

Pillars of Hercules, a stately pair of basalt towers. Both trails are alive with native flora like trillium, lupine, bead lily, and bleeding heart, all of which are native—but so is poison oak, so stick to the path.

ROOSTER ROCK STATE PARK

Along a beautiful stretch of the Columbia River is one of the largest swimming areas near Portland. **Rooster Rock** (Corbett exit off I-84, 503/695-2261 or 800/551-6949, www.oregonstateparks.org/park_175.php; daily 6am-8pm; $5 per day) also has the distinction of being the country's first officially designated clothing-optional beach. The beach is named for a column of basalt that rises from the Oregon side of the Columbia River Gorge in a natural obelisk; given the lax clothing rules and phallic nature of the rock, the park has acquired some rather unsavory nicknames over the years. Nonetheless, the area is beautiful, and the area of the beach where nudity is allowed is completely separate and not visible from the clothing-required area of the large park. The non-nude area also has two disc golf courses, picnic shelters and tables, and a boat dock. The park is currently managed by Oregon Parks and Recreation and requires a day-use fee for entry.

✪ MULTNOMAH FALLS

There are seemingly more waterfalls in this region than you could count (and it varies by season and rainfall levels), but none is more grand than **Multnomah Falls** (50000 Historic Columbia River Hwy., Scenic Loop Dr., Bridal Veil, 503/695-2376, www.multnomahfallslodge.com; summer daily 8am-8pm, winter Mon.-Thurs. 10am-6pm, Fri. 10am-8pm,

Sat. 8am-8pm, Sun. 8am-6pm; free), which sprouts from an underground spring on Larch Mountain. The falls are a spectacular 620 feet tall and broken into upper and lower courses. The Benson Arch Bridge, which was built in 1914, is a short, steep climb from the parking lot and a popular place for a photo op with the breathtaking falls as a backdrop. Also on the premises is the historic **Multnomah Falls Lodge** (53000 E. Historic Columbia River Hwy., 503/695-2376), which has a **visitors center** (503/695-2372; daily 9am-5pm) as well as a gift shop and restaurant. A trail from the Multnomah Falls Lodge leads to an extensive trail system; ask at the visitors center for more information on accessible hikes as the area continues to recover from the Eagle Creek Fire of 2017.

Multnomah Falls

✪ BONNEVILLE DAM

If anything were going to harness the power of the Columbia River, it had to be the **Bonneville Dam** (70543 NE Herman Loop, 541/374-8344, www.nwp.usace.army.mil; daily 9am-5pm; free), which spans the river and provides the area with power. The first dam powerhouse opened in 1937 in the midst of the Great Depression. The creation of new jobs and the luxury of affordable hydroelectric power

Bonneville Dam

are part of what inspired folk singer Woody Guthrie to write the lines, "Thy power is turning our darkness to dawn. Roll on, Columbia, roll on." But, of course, the sheer command of the dam spoke volumes as well. Both the Oregon and Washington sides of the dam have a visitors center where you can catch a tugboat or barge passing through the locks, or watch salmon, sturgeon, and lamprey as they swim through the fish ladders on their way to spawn. While the visitors center is open year-round, the months between April and September are most abundant with fish.

COLUMBIA GORGE DISCOVERY CENTER

If you are marveling about the wild and mysterious beauty of the Columbia River Gorge, the best place to learn about how it was all created (spoilers—it involves raging floods, volcanoes, and massive landslides) is the **Columbia Gorge Discovery Center** (5000 Discovery Dr., The Dalles, 541/296-8600, www. gorgediscovery.org; daily 9am-5pm; $9 adults, $7 seniors, $6.50 children ages 6-16). This 48,200-square-foot center features exhibits, displays, and videos that bring the rich geological history of the Gorge to life. You will also find an in-depth exhibit on the cargo carried along with Lewis and Clark and their Corps of Discovery, as well as Native American baskets and early American household furnishings and tools. Step outside and tour the 50-acre interpretive trail with a wheelchair-accessible paved path through cottonwoods, willows, cattails, and sedges. Follow the trail around the pond, which provides a home to turtles, ducks, and geese.

SIGHTSEEING TOURS

If you really want to get the lay of the land, book a trip aboard the **Columbia Gorge Sternwheeler** (board at Marine Park at Cascade Locks, 503/224-3900, www. portlandspirit.com; June-Sept.; $20 adults, $12 children) or the historic

Mt. Hood Railroad (110 Railroad Ave., Hood River, 541/386-3556, www.mthoodrr.com; $30-55), both of which allow you to sit back and enjoy the scenery (and, of course, take lots of pictures). If you are looking for something a little more active, Martin's Gorge Tours (877/290-8687, www.martinsgorgetours.com; year-round; $70-100) will take you on a morning hike of one of the area's beautiful waterfalls—a different area for each day of the week. Weekday hikes range from easy to challenging and visit such sights as Ponytail Falls, Horsetail Falls, and the breathtaking Punchbowl Falls. Weekend hikes (which run July-February) take walkers past Latourell Falls and Bridal Veil Falls, and on a picturesque overlook trail that offers some of the best views in the area.

RESTAURANTS

Unless you drive into some of the more populous towns like Hood River or across the state border into Stevenson, Washington, your dining options are fairly limited to either home-style diner fare or romantic, elegant hideaways. If you aren't looking for anything fancy, swing by Tad's Chicken and Dumplins (1325 W. Historic Columbia River Hwy., Troutdale, 503/666-5337, www.tadschicdump.com; Mon.-Fri. 5pm-10pm, Sat. 4pm-10pm, Sun. 4pm-9pm; $15-25), located in Troutdale along the Historic Columbia River Highway. As the name implies, it has a special penchant for comfort food, particularly the eponymous dish; like any roadside diner worth its salt, it does a mean fried chicken, too.

If you'd like a more elegant night out, check out Troutini (101 W. Historic Columbia River Hwy., Troutdale, 503/912-1462, www.troutini.com; Tues.-Thurs.11am-9pm, Fri. 11am-10pm, Sat. 10am-10pm, Sun. 10am-8pm; $16-37), where you'll find French-inspired cuisine and Pacific Northwest favorites like rainbow trout and wild mushrooms.

HOOD RIVER

If you are looking for seafood, 3 Rivers Grill (601 Oak St., 541/386-8883, www.3riversgrill.com; daily 11am-10pm; $12-24) has some of the best in the area. Located on Oak Street in Hood River, the place has a homey feel to it, with a deck area overlooking the river. In addition to some beautiful crab cakes, ceviche, and salmon dishes, it has an award-winning wine selection.

Another master of Northwest cuisine and seafood is Celilo Restaurant and Bar (16 Oak St., 541/386-5710, www.celilorestaurant.com; daily 11:30am-3pm and 5pm-9:30pm; $14-24). It's about as committed to supporting all things local as the sun is to shining, and the result is simple, expertly crafted food. You will want to make a reservation for Celilo (pronounced seh-LIE-low), even if you have a small party, to ensure that you can take your time, and that you will not have to sit at the bar.

As the evening winds down in Hood River, Brian's Pourhouse (606 Oak St., 541/387-4344, www.brianspourhouse.com; Sun.-Thurs. 5pm-10pm, Fri.-Sat. 5pm-11pm; $15-22) is a great spot for a late dinner, or for drinks and appetizers. The small, Colonial-style, white clapboard restaurant has a basement bar that stays open just a wee bit later than many other places in town, and the atmosphere is relaxed and enjoyable.

STEVENSON, WASHINGTON

Just a skip over the river past the Bonneville Dam is Stevenson, on the Washington side of the Gorge. Take I-84 to the Bridge of the Gods, and head east on Route 14 on the other side to find the small town. You'll find a number of popular dining options, not least of which is the Cascade Room (1131 SW Skamania Lodge Way, 800/221-7117, www.skamania.com; Mon.-Thurs. 7am-2pm and 5pm-9pm, Fri.-Sat. 7am-2pm and 5pm-9:30pm, Sun. 9am-2pm and 5pm-9pm; $23-52), a fine dining restaurant housed in Skamania Lodge. Dinners boast such specialties as salmon, smoked pork loin, and roast prime rib of Washington beef, and breakfast and brunch are so good, even the oatmeal is worth writing home about.

For moderately priced burgers, sandwiches, beer, and wine, check out Big River Grill (192 SW 2nd St., 509/427-4888, www.bigrivergrill.us; Mon.-Fri. 11:30am-9:30pm, Sat.-Sun. 8am-11am and 11:30am-9:30pm; $13-26), a popular spot with locals and passers-through that defines its cuisine as "High-End Roadhouse."

A great spot to grab a microbrew and some grub is Walking Man Brewing Company (240 SW 1st St., 509/427-5520, www.walkingmanbrewing.com; Wed.-Fri. 4pm-9pm, Sat. 3pm-9pm, Sun. 3pm-8pm; $10-15). The house-made beers really take center stage here (particularly the Belgian red ale), but the artisan-style pizza isn't bad at all.

RECREATION

KAYAKING

The Columbia River is a favorite spot for lovers of water sports. The Kayak Shed (6 Oak St., 541/386-4286, www.

kayakshed.com) in Hood River can hook you up with all the gear you will need for a wild river adventure. If you are an inexperienced kayaker, Columbia Gorge Kayak School (541/806-4190, www.gorgekayaker.com) offers both group lessons and private instruction. The courses will run you about $50-85. For rafting, try Zoller's Outdoor Odysseys (800/366-2004, www.zooraft.com), which takes passengers on thrill rides down the rapids of the White Salmon (half-day trip, $85-95 per person) and Klickitat (full-day trip, $105 per person).

WINDSURFING

Few sports are more popular in the Gorge than windsurfing. Hood River Waterplay (541/386-9463, www.hoodriverwaterplay.com) offers windsurfing and kiteboarding classes for all levels of experience, plus equipment rentals (starting at $89 per day) and a thorough knowledge of the area—which makes them a great place to get wet, whether you are well versed or just starting out.

FISHING

For fishing, head to Laurance Lake, Drano Lake, Goose Lake, Lost Lake, or the mouth of Eagle Creek, where you won't battle with the currents as you will in the Salmon, Deschutes, and Klickitat Rivers. Or book a guided excursion with Columbia River Fishing Guides (1087 Lewis River Rd., Ste. 206, 360/910-6630, www.columbiariverfishingguide.com; $200 per day), based in Woodland, Washington. Guides will provide you with equipment, and they claim they can guarantee you will catch a sturgeon, steelhead, or salmon.

HIKING

Hiking options abound in the Gorge, especially since it provides access to the **Pacific Crest Trail** (PCT), which extends from the U.S. border with Canada all the way to Mexico. A good spot to access the PCT is the **Herman Creek trailhead**, which provides a challenging but rewarding 16-mile hike up the Benson Plateau. Or, if you are looking for something a bit easier, try the **Latourell Falls trailhead**, an easy two-mile hike past waterfalls, flowers, and streams. You can find detailed hiking plans and maps on **Portland Hiker's Field Guide** (www.portlandhikersfieldguide.org) to prepare you for your trip.

FESTIVALS AND EVENTS
PORTLAND HIGHLAND GAMES

It's not every day that you get to see bagpipes, kilts, and Scottish heavy games all in the same place—at least not on this side of the world. The **Portland Highland Games** (Mount Hood Community College, 26000 SE Stark St., Gresham, www.phga.org; $10-20, free for children under 5) is hosted each year on the third Saturday in July by Mount Hood Community College. Somehow, it manages to bring the Scotsman out in everyone. But it's a lot of fun to don a kilt and slip into a series of bad Mike Myers impressions as you take in world-class Scottish athletic championships, highland dance competitions, traditional Scottish music, the Kilted Mile Race, genealogy workshops, children's activities, traditional wares, and, of course, beer and bangers.

WHERE TO STAY
HOOD RIVER

With arguably one of the best views in the land, **Columbia Gorge Hotel** (4000 Westcliff Dr., 541/386-5566, www.columbiagorgehotel.com; $159-469) was once known as the "Waldorf of the West" and brought in guests like Rudolph Valentino (the lounge is now named after him) and various U.S. presidents.

Adjacent to the historic Columbia Gorge Hotel, **Columbia Cliff Villas** (3880 Westcliff Dr., 866/912-8366, www.columbiacliffvillas.com; $169-895) offers a wide variety of accommodations in 28 privately owned condominiums that range from one to three bedrooms. The condos are great for families because they come equipped with lockout doors, which allow the space to be reconfigured as needed.

For families or those traveling on a budget, **Westcliff Lodge** (4070 Westcliff Dr., 877/386-2992, www.westclifflodge.com; $96-190) has clean, simple, and affordable rooms, many of which have stunning views of the Columbia River. All the rooms have high-speed Wi-Fi, cable TV, a microwave, and a small fridge.

STEVENSON, WASHINGTON

Skamania Lodge (1131 SW Skamania Lodge Way, 509/427-7700, www.skamania.com; $135-389), across the Gorge just outside Stevenson's downtown, also makes use of its beautiful surroundings, sitting proudly on a hill with a commanding view of the river and surrounding hills. The lodge is elegant and peaceful, with grand stone fireplaces, high rustic ceilings, and enormous picture windows.

PRACTICALITIES
INFORMATION AND SERVICES

The **Columbia River Gorge Visitors Association** (www.crgva.org) provides maps and information on events, dining, accommodations, and shopping. It also has a trip planner called *Gorge Guide* with beautiful photos of the area, historical information, and travel tips for regions throughout the Gorge.

TRANSPORTATION

Word to the wise: You will very likely get distracted while driving through the Gorge. With so many viewpoints, historical landmarks, unexpected waterfalls, and surprising panoramas, it's natural to get a bit sidetracked, but that's half the fun. One of the best routes is the Historic Columbia River Highway (exit 17), the first planned scenic highway in the United States. The highway runs past waterfalls (including the majestic Multnomah Falls) and photo stops like Crown Point and the Vista House. You can rejoin I-84 at exit 35, where you can cross over the Bridge of the Gods to the Washington side or continue east to Hood River and access to Mount Hood.

If you are crossing the bridge (which was named after a great Native American legend), you will need to pay a $1 toll. The bridge tollhouse is open 24 hours a day and serves as the emergency relay station for police departments on both sides of the river.

If you continue on to Hood River, which is about 45 minutes from Portland in good traffic, you can pick up the Mt. Hood Scenic Loop, a two-hour drive around the foot of Mount Hood over streams and through lush forests. From here, you can also drive the Fruit Loop, passing a collection of farms, orchards, vineyards, and wineries. There are easy-to-follow maps (which list Fruit Loop farms, attractions, and individual operating hours) available at the Hood River Visitors Center off exit 63 on I-84.

Mount Hood

The Cascade Mountain Range is like no other mountain range in the country. The range is part of the greater Pacific Ring of Fire, which is home to 452 active and inactive volcanoes—where about 90 percent of the world's earthquakes occur. Portland and the Cascade Mountains surrounding it have not seen much volcanic activity since Mount St. Helens blew its top in 1980, but seismologists and scientists are never quick to forget what lurks beneath those luminous peaks and glaciers. Even Mount Hood, which at 11,245 feet is Oregon's tallest peak, is considered a not-quite-dormant volcano. But try telling that to the locals who trek to the mountain all year long to ski and snowboard the 4,600 skiable acres, hike the numerous trails that wind their way through 1,200 miles of forests and wilderness areas, and enjoy the region's pristine rivers and lakes.

Mount Hood

RECREATION
DOWNHILL SKIING
✪ Mt. Hood Skibowl

Mt. Hood Skibowl (87000 E. Hwy. 26, Government Camp, 503/272-3206, www.skibowl.com; Mon.-Tues. 3pm-10pm, Wed.-Thurs. 1pm-10pm, Fri. 9am-11pm, Sat. 8am-11pm, Sun. 8am-10pm; lift ticket $27-76) is one of three major ski resorts on Mount Hood, and America's largest night-skiing area. With the highest lift at 5,027 feet and the base lodge at 3,600 feet, it ranks lowest in elevation but still has some of the steepest terrain on the mountain, with vertical drops of 1,500 feet. There are no high-speed lifts at Skibowl, but that keeps things laid-back and the mountain from getting overly crowded. Avid skiers who travel with beginners will like the diversity of the mountain, from the simpler lower bowl to the upper bowls and backcountry areas for the more experienced. Skibowl is also the closest and least expensive ski destination to Portland, but what really sets this

place apart is that it stays open year-round. When the snow and ice are still months away, Skibowl has an adventure park that offers warm-weather alternatives, such as the Alpine Slide, an epic 300-foot inner-tube slide, a mountain bike park, hiking trails, disc and miniature golf, batting cages, bungee jumping, horseback riding, and zip-line trails.

Timberline Lodge

The beautiful Timberline Lodge (27500 E. Timberline Rd., Timberline Lodge, 503/272-3158, www.timberlinelodge.com; daily 9am-4pm, night skiing Fri.-Sat. 4pm-10pm; lift ticket $47-71) was the picturesque outdoor setting for the 1980 thriller The Shining, but don't worry: All those creepy things happened at a studio far away, and there is no such thing as room 237. Instead of scary ghosts, Timberline is famous for offering year-round resort skiing on the Palmer snowfield at 8,540 feet. Also, Still Creek Basin, Timberline's newest

Timberline Lodge

ungroomed trail nearby. Track fees are inexpensive ($10-39) and you will need a wilderness permit to explore the backcountry, but permits are free and accessible via self-service at the trailhead.

HIKING

Hiking and backpacking are popular pastimes in the Mount Hood area. **Timberline Trail** is one of the best challenging but beautiful hikes. Constructed in the 1930s by the Civilian Conservation Corps, the trail loops near Timberline Lodge and Mount Hood Meadows, but is otherwise surrounded by wilderness. The 40-plus-mile trail has a number of variations depending on where you start and what the season is, but the entire route takes about five or six days to complete. This and many other trails in the region present seasonal hazards that should be researched and prepared for, such as hypothermia, landslides, unstable terrain, and risk of drowning. **Portland Hikers** (www.portlandhikers.org) is a good resource for information on terrain, seasons, and safety tips.

FISHING

If you would like to take in some fishing, there's no better spot to head than **Lost Lake** (www.lostlakeresort.org). On the north side of the mountain, this is a place of quiet serenity where motorboats are never allowed. The best fishing is along the shores, where aquatic insects are most prevalent and the lake's population of rainbow trout and steelhead appear, trying to snatch a meal. There are no fees for using the lake or its surrounding forested areas, but a license is required for anglers over 14 years of age.

network of trails, has eight alpine trails and a lift-served snowshoe and cross-country skiing trail.

Mount Hood Meadows

Finally, with its steep terrain and abundant snowfall, **Mount Hood Meadows** (14040 Hwy. 35, Mount Hood, 503/337-2222, www.skihood.com; Mon.-Tues. 9am-4pm, Wed.-Thurs. and Sun. 9am-9pm, Fri.-Sat. 9am-10pm; lift ticket $12-82) is arguably one of the most popular resorts in Oregon. The 11 chairlifts at Meadows run on 100 percent wind power and provide access to the 2,150 acres of terrain on the southeast flank of Mount Hood. The Cascade Express lift will take you to the highest point at Meadows. At 7,300 feet, it is the access point to a handful of the 85 runs and 1,700 vertical feet of terrain the resort has to offer.

CROSS-COUNTRY SKIING

With the sprawling acreage of the Mount Hood National Forest on hand, there is some great cross-country skiing to be had. **Cooper Spur Mountain Resort** (10755 Cooper Spur Rd., Mount Hood Parkdale, 541/352-7803, www.cooperspur.com; Sat.-Sun. 9am-5pm) has four miles of groomed track and up to 14 miles of

RESTAURANTS
GOVERNMENT CAMP

Mount Hood has a few little gems when it comes to dining, some of them upscale and some of them decidedly not. Government Camp, the community that serves as the gateway for most of the area ski resorts, is a favorite stop on the way to or from the slopes.

Ice Axe Grill (87304 E. Government Camp Loop, 503/272-0102, www. mthoodbrewing.com; Sun.-Thurs. 11am-9pm, Fri.-Sat. 11am-10pm; $10-20) is a traditional pub that also happens to be the home of Mt. Hood Brewing Company. The menu consists of all the fare you would expect from any self-respecting pub, like burgers, sandwiches, salads, pizza, and beer-battered fish. But in a surprising turn from tradition, vegetarian dishes are also available.

Another popular pub is The Ratskeller (88335 E. Government Camp Loop, 503/272-3635, www. ratskellerpizzeria.com; Sun.-Thurs. 11am-10pm, Fri.-Sat. 11am-midnight; $8-10), a casual joint that specializes in pizza. "The Rat," as it is affectionately called, has one side devoted to family dining and another side with a bar, where you will find billiards, live music, and karaoke.

The 24-hour family-style restaurant at Huckleberry Inn (88611 E. Government Camp Loop, 503/272-3325, www.huckleberry-inn.com; daily 24 hours; $8-10) is a great place to stop for breakfast or if you want to treat yourself to a little coffee and pie. The food is homey and hearty here, and for good reason. Stacks of huckleberry pancakes or heaping plates of steak and eggs are sure to fuel you up for a day in the snow.

Feel like dining at 6,000 feet? The views are spectacular from Timberline Lodge, and *Sunset* magazine has named the lodge's Cascade Dining Room (27500 E. Timberline Rd., 503/272-3104, www.timberlinelodge. com; daily 7:30am-10am, noon-2pm, and 6pm-8pm; $16-22) one of the top 10 mountaintop restaurants in the Pacific Northwest and Canada. The Farmers Market Brunch runs every day 11am-3pm and is practically worth the trip itself. Reservations are required for dinner, but breakfast and lunch are more casual and first-come, first-served.

WELCHES

In Welches, the Zig Zag Inn (70162 E. Hwy. 26, 503/622-4779, www. zigzaginn.com; Mon.-Thurs. 10am-9pm, Fri. 10am-10pm, Sat. 7am-10pm, Sun. 7am-9pm; $10-20) feels like what a mountain lodge should feel like, complete with life-sized carved wooden bears and chandeliers made out of antlers. It offers an array of sandwiches, burgers, and rib-sticking dinners, but it's the pizza that's the biggest draw.

The Rendezvous Grill and Taproom (67149 E. Hwy. 26, 503/622-6837, www.thevousgrill.com; daily 11:30am-9pm; $15-20) is perhaps a little more serious, but no less devoted to great food. It is particularly known for desserts but cooks a mean steak Oscar as well.

El Burro Loco (67211 E. Hwy. 26, 503/622-6780, www.burroloco.net; daily 11am-9pm; $8-15) is a bright cantina with inexpensive but tasty food, fresh cocktails, and an extensive collection of microbrews and tequila.

You will find other dining options nearby in the small communities of Brightwood, Rhododendron, and Zig Zag.

WHERE TO STAY
GOVERNMENT CAMP

Accommodations abound up in the mountains, whether you are looking for a cozy cottage or a stately lodge. **Timberline Lodge** (27500 E. Timberline Rd., 503/272-3104, www. timberlinelodge.com; $150-490) is easily one of the most iconic lodgings in Government Camp. Rooms vary from positively dorm-like chalet rooms with bunk beds and bathrooms down the hall to lofty private suites that sleep as many as eight people.

Right next to the Ice Axe Grill and Mt. Hood Brewing Company, **Best Western Mt. Hood Inn** (87450 E. Government Camp Loop, 503/272-3205, www.mthoodinn.com; $129-239) is an affordable way to avoid the big lodge but still be close to all the action. Resembling a hotel more than an inn, Mt. Hood Inn has three room types, from the basic deluxe room to the king spa room, which rents for as little as $179 a night. There's an indoor public Jacuzzi on-site as well, which is nice after you've been hitting the slopes all day.

Collins Lake Resort (88149 E. Creek Ridge Rd., 888/422-4776, www. collinslakeresort.com; $189-469) offers all the luxuries you'd expect from a top-notch resort; its spacious, well-appointed, and comfortable chalets—complete with views of magnificent Collins Lake—really make this a favorite vacation destination. The resort has a number of chalets and lodges available that are great for large groups or families.

WELCHES

In Welches, you will find the beautiful and modern **Resort at the Mountain** (68010 E. Fairway Ave., 503/622-3151, www.theresort.com; $169-569), a premier golf, ski, and meeting resort where you can occasionally hear the bagpipes play as they herald the sunset. The resort was remodeled in 2008 and can now accommodate couples, families, outdoors enthusiasts, meetings, and event groups. It is, of course, popular for its proximity to the slopes, but it also has two restaurants, tennis courts, 27 holes of golf, a heated outdoor swimming pool, and a professional croquet court. Families can stay in the resort's enormous two- and three-bedroom villas, both with a full kitchen and dining room area, laundry facilities, private parking, and private decks. Standard rooms at the Resort at the Mountain can only be oxymoronically described as "basic luxury," with plush memory-foam mattresses, 42-inch plasma HDTVs, terrycloth robes, and environmentally friendly products.

PRACTICALITIES
INFORMATION AND SERVICES

You can find a wealth of up-to-date information about road conditions, snowfall, and weather online. For tips on travel and recreation, check out **Mt. Hood Territory** (www. mthoodterritory.com), which has maps, calendars, and recommendations on everything from activities to lodging. If you plan to take in a little Mother Nature, **Mt. Hood National Forest Headquarters** (www.fs.fed. us/r6/mthood) can provide you with maps, conditions updates, and details on permits and passes. Be sure to check with the **Oregon Department of Transportation** (www.odot.state. or.us/roads) before hitting the road to see if traction devices will be required to make it to your destination. It's also a good idea to check with the

Northwest Weather and Avalanche Center (www.nwac.us) to be sure that conditions are safe, particularly if you plan to venture into the less-groomed areas.

All of the major ski areas have a regularly updated snow report, which will advise you on ski conditions, snow depth, and snowfall, oftentimes providing live webcams of the lifts and slopes. You can visit the **Timberline website** (www.timberlinelodge.com) or call the snow line at 503/222-2211. The same goes for **Mount Hood Meadows** (503/227-7669, www.skihood.com) and **Skibowl** (503/222-2695, www.skibowl.com).

If you plan to hike or explore the backcountry, it's a good idea to rent a Mountain Locator Unit from one of the local mountaineering and outdoor shops or from **Mt. Hood Inn** (503/272-3205, www.mthoodinn.com). The device, which is exclusive to Hood, costs about $5 to rent and is worn on a sash across the chest. When activated, it sends out radio beacons to rescuers, giving them a better chance of finding you in the event of an emergency.

TRANSPORTATION

From Portland, take I-84 East as it passes through some of Oregon's most scenic natural wonders, like the Columbia River Gorge and Multnomah Falls. You can opt to take the Historic Columbia River Highway for a truly spectacular picturesque drive; it will reconnect with I-84 later on. Continue on I-84 to the town of Hood River, where you can visit pretty orchards and vineyards. Next, continue on to Highway 35, where you will soon connect with Highway 26, which passes through Sandy and on to Government Camp.

If conditions are poor, you might be better off skipping the scenic highways and taking the road more traveled. From I-84 East, take exit 16 (Wood Village/SE 242nd) and turn right, through the city of Gresham. Stay on SE 242nd south and turn left onto SE Burnside, which becomes Highway 26 and passes through the small town of Sandy before continuing on to the mountain.

Sno-park permits are required for vehicles almost everywhere, including at the resorts. They are sold through various **Oregon DMV offices** (www.oregon.gov/ODOT/DMV/vehicle/sno_park_permits.shtml) and by permit agents in resorts, sporting goods stores, and other retail outlets. It will cost you about $3 a day or $20 annually.

Oregon Wine Country

If you think the Portland metro area is scenic and green, you'll think Oregon wine country is exceptional. The vineyards of the Willamette Valley are situated between the Coast Range to the west and the Cascades to the east, nestled into a verdant landscape that is fragrant with spruce, fir, and pine.

The wine industry in Oregon is still remarkably young when you consider how much success it has had. It all began when David Lett of Eyrie Vineyards moved to the region in 1965 with some 3,000 clippings and grand intentions to make the most of the Willamette Valley's climate and latitude, which bear a striking resemblance to that of Burgundy, France, pinot noir's ancestral home. Undeterred by his California counterparts, who scoffed at the idea of producing wine in a region that was so cold and wet, Lett planted the first pinot noir grapes in the Northwest, thus sowing the seeds for Oregon's future as a heavyweight in the wine industry.

It wasn't until the late 1970s that people really started to turn their eyes toward what was happening here. Nowadays, the Willamette Valley alone has over 200 wineries and 12,000 acres of grapes, and in these places, artisan winemakers have put Oregon on the international wine map thanks to incomparable vintages and revolutionary practices. According to the **Oregon Wine Board** (www. oregonwine.org), there are 72 grape varieties grown throughout the state,

Willamette Valley

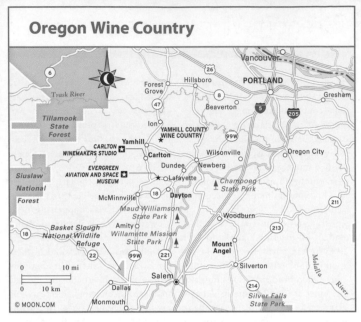

Oregon Wine Country

Vancouver
PORTLAND
Gresham
Forest Grove
Hillsboro
Beaverton
Trask River
Tillamook State Forest
Ion
YAMHILL COUNTY WINE COUNTRY
Wilsonville
Oregon City
CARLTON WINEMAKERS STUDIO
Yamhill
Carlton
Dundee
Newberg
Siuslaw National Forest
EVERGREEN AVIATION AND SPACE MUSEUM
Lafayette
Champoeg State Park
McMinnville
Dayton
Woodburn
Maud Williamson State Park
Amity
Willamette Mission State Park
Mount Angel
Basket Slough National Wildlife Refuge
Silverton
Salem
Dallas
Silver Falls State Park
Monmouth
Medalla River
0   10 mi
0   10 km
© MOON.COM

but only 15 of those varieties make up 97 percent of the vineyards in Oregon. At the top of that list is pinot noir. In fact, this region has been recognized as one of the premier pinot noir-producing areas in the world—which comes as no surprise to the Lett family. Apparently, they knew it all along.

WINERIES

You can just go for tastings ($25-30) or step behind the scenes at **Rex Hill Winery** (30835 N. Hwy. 99W, Newberg, 503/538-0666, www.rexhill.com; daily 10am-5pm) with an in-depth tour of the vineyard, production facilities, and barrel center, where you'll get to taste pinot noir straight from the French oak barrel before heading to a special wine and cheese pairing ($75). The winery also offers complimentary mini tours at 11am each day by reservation.

Adelsheim (16800 NE Calkins Ln., Newberg, 503/538-3652, www.

adelsheim.com; daily 11am-4pm) is a great winery for pinot noir lovers, with several options. You can do wine flights ($15-25) or prearrange a Trek + Taste + Cheese experience, where you'll go on a guided walk through the vineyards and follow it up with a wine and cheese pairing ($95).

In 1974, **Elk Cove Vineyards** (27751 NW Olson Rd., Gaston, 503/985-7760, www.elkcove.com; daily 10am-5pm) became the first winery in the Yamhill-Carlton region to produce a commercial wine. This particular pocket of land is well protected by the Coastal Range, the Chehalem Mountains, and the Dundee Hills, which means slightly drier, more moderate growing conditions perfectly suited for cool-climate grapes like pinot noir. A tasting room flight costs $15.

Check out **Anne Amie** (6580 NE Mineral Springs Rd., Carlton, 503/864-2991, www.anneamie.com; daily

NAVIGATING WINE COUNTRY

As you travel along Highway 99 West from Portland, the first major wine area you'll hit, about 25 miles southwest of the city, is Newberg. The following itinerary starts and ends right off the highway, looping around in counterclockwise fashion.

- Your first stop is on Highway 99 at **Rex Hill Winery,** where you'll find 17 acres of pinot noir grapes and one wee little row of well-attended muscat grapes.

- Another great winery can be found about 8.5 miles away: **Adelsheim** has a tasting room on its 190-acre vineyard at the base of the Chehalem Mountains. Get there by turning right off Highway 99 south of Rex Hill onto NE Benjamin Road, right again onto NE Springbrook Road, and left on NE Bell Road, continuing on as it becomes NE North Valley Road. Make a right onto NE Calkins Lane.

- Continue heading northwest for 13.5 miles into the quiet hamlets of Carlton, Yamhill, and Gaston. Drive via NE North Valley Road, turning left onto NE Flett Road, right onto Highway 47, and left onto NW Olson Road, where you will find **Elk Cove Vineyards.** Founded in 1974, this family-owned winery is known for its classic pinot noir.

- This region is also home to **Carlton Winemakers Studio,** where 10 small-but-savvy vintners work in the same space, each producing some of the region's most remarkable wines. You'll find it by continuing to drive south about 10 miles via NW Olson Road, continuing on as it becomes NW Canyonview Road, turning left onto NW Bishop Scott Road, left again onto NW Pike Road, and right onto Highway 47. Make a right onto W. Johnston Street to N. Scott Street.

- Drive another 5 miles for your next stop, getting back on Highway 47 and turning left on Main Street, following the road until you hit NE Mineral Springs Road, where you'll make a right. Turn left to check out **Anne Amie,** for fine examples of how pinot noir thrives in such a climate.

- Next head southeast about 6.5 miles, following NE Mineral Springs Road, turning left to rejoin Highway 99, and making a left onto NE Sokol Blossor Lane for, fittingly, **Sokol Blosser,** a longtime giant of the Oregon wine industry, where you can soak up the landscape in the picnic area. There are many vineyards in this area and a smattering of excellent restaurants, including the **Joel Palmer House,** so it's a good place to stop and grab a bite to eat.

10am-5pm) or **WillaKenzie** (19143 NE Laughlin Rd., Yamhill, 503/662-3280, www.willakenzie.com; daily 11am-5pm) for pinot noir. In addition to its tasting room, Anne Amie also offers a guided tour by reservation ($30), which includes a reserve tasting and Oregon pinot noir glass. Both wineries offer tasting flights for $15.

Sokol Blosser (5000 NE Sokol Blosser Ln., Dayton, 800/582-6668, www.sokolblosser.com; daily 10am-4pm) is a pioneer in Northwest wine. The Sokol Blosser clan has been a part of the Oregon wine fabric since its first planting in 1971. Years later,

Sokol Blosser is still family-owned and going strong, receiving accolades for both its vintages and its commitment to sustainability. The 72-acre estate vineyards are up in the Dundee Hills, which makes for a lovely picnic spot. Tasting flights start at $20. Tours ($55) are available every Saturday and Sunday by reservation only.

The Four Graces (9605 NE Fox Farm Rd., Dundee, 800/245-2950, www.thefourgraces.com; daily 10am-5pm) is located at the northern entrance to Dundee. When the Black family purchased this 110-acre spot of land in 2003, it was fulfilling a lifelong dream to have a family-owned wine estate. Nowadays, people come from all around to sit in the historic farmhouse and sip extraordinary pinot noir, pinot gris, and pinot blanc. They are an enthusiastic and friendly bunch and more than willing to welcome you into their tasting room, which offers $15 flights. You can also schedule a time to bring a group and meet one-on-one with the tasting room experts, who can explain how the happy trifecta of soil, climate, and topography, combined with meticulous winemaking, makes for outstanding wines.

About nine miles west, in McMinnville, you will find **Eyrie Vineyards** (935 NE 10th Ave., McMinnville, 503/472-6315 or 888/440-4970, www.eyrievineyards. com; Wed.-Sun. noon-5pm), which was founded by David Lett, who is affectionately known as "Papa Pinot." Lett planted the first pinot noir grapes in the Northwest, thus sowing the seeds for Oregon's future as a heavyweight in the wine industry. In 1975, Eyrie Vineyards produced the first pinot noir to successfully vie for recognition alongside the long-recognized pinots of Burgundy, France. With that recognition came the acknowledgment of Oregon as the New World home for pinot noir. The Lett family is still at the helm of Eyrie, and they still produce some of the most respected wines in the region. You can visit the tasting room and sample a discovery flight for $15, which is waived with a $50 purchase.

At **Domaine Drouhin** (6750 NE Breyman Orchards Rd., Dayton, 503/864-2700, www.domainedrouhin. com; daily 11am-4pm), you can sample a flight of five wines for $20. Or, if you really want an inside peek, call ahead and book a tour ($40). Winemaker Véronique Drouhin-Boss uses the Burgundy method, and she comes by it naturally. She is a fourth-generation winemaker who splits her time between Oregon and the other great wine region of the world, Beaune, Burgundy. The tour—a 60-minute walk through the vineyards and the four-story winery—is an exceptional peek into her process, which culminates with comparative tastings between Oregon and Burgundy wines with water and cheese accompaniments.

WINE TOURS

The best way to see wine country is to plan ahead, choose which places you want to see, and then map them out. Or, better yet, leave the driving to someone else and sign up for a tour with the likes of **Beautiful Willamette Tours** (877/868-7295, www.willamettetours.com; $100-175 per person), **EcoTours of Oregon** (888/868-7733, www.ecotours-of-oregon.com; $70-100 per person), or **Wine Tours Northwest** (800/359-1034, www.winetoursnorthwest.com; $139-350 per person). The benefit of opting for a tour is twofold: You do not have to designate your own driver, and you are often allowed to tour places that are otherwise closed to the public.

✪ CARLTON WINEMAKERS STUDIO

If you don't have enough time to tour a bunch of wineries, check out **Carlton Winemakers Studio** (801 N. Scott St., Carlton, 503/852-6100, www. winemakersstudio.com; daily 11am-5pm), where you can sample the wines of several up-and-coming winemakers. The studio is rather like a co-op, in that it allows as many as 10 vintners at a time to share one state-of-the-art, gravity-driven, energy-efficient facility. The concept is a revolutionary way to encourage artisan winemakers to produce ultra-premium wines, while still promoting an ecoconscious, cost-friendly approach. For the consumer, that approach means that the wines produced within the studio have both the pedigree and palate of high-end wines, with the intimacy and price of a mom-and-pop vintner.

SIGHTS

When you need a break from sipping wine, Yamhill County has other things to entertain you. Stop by **Red Ridge Farms** (5510 NE Breyman Orchards Rd., Dayton, 503/864-8502, www.redridgefarms.com; daily 10am-5pm; free), a family-owned herb and specialty plant nursery in Dayton. Nestled in the Red Hills, the farm has more than 300 varieties of herbs and other culinary, medicinal, and landscaping plants, including more than 100 types of lavender. It makes for some really pretty scenery. You can call ahead and have them prepare a picnic for you, or simply wander through the fragrant gardens. While you're there, be sure to browse through the shop filled with hand-crafted items and garden-inspired gifts.

Evergreen Aviation and Space Museum

☉ EVERGREEN AVIATION AND SPACE MUSEUM

The small town of McMinnville is home to the **Evergreen Aviation and Space Museum** (500 NE Captain Michael King Smith Way, McMinnville, 503/434-4180, www.sprucegoose.org; daily 9am-5pm; $27 adults, $24 seniors, $19 for ages 5-16, free for children under 5), the biggest air and space museum west of the Mississippi. It's home to Howard Hughes's H-4 Hercules, a heavy transport aircraft more commonly known as the *Spruce Goose*—a name that Hughes detested. The newest section of the museum, which opened in 2008, has interactive flight simulators that allow you to practice landing the space shuttle, docking a Gemini capsule, or landing the Lunar Excursion Module on the surface of the moon. You can also catch a flick at the 3-D IMAX theater, see a 32,000-pound meteorite, or simply marvel at the amazing collection of military and civilian aircraft, spacecraft, and memorabilia. The museum offers docent-guided tours daily at 11am and 1:30pm.

RESTAURANTS

Nothing goes better with great wine than world-class dining, and this region has plenty of good spots to choose from.

In Newberg, check out the **Painted Lady** (201 S. College St., Newberg, 503-538-3850, www.thepaintedladyrestaurant.com; Wed.-Sun. 5pm-10pm; $60-100), a popular spot for elegant meals and special occasions. The restaurant, which is housed in an old Victorian home, was named for the movement that sought to restore and revitalize Victorian and Edwardian homes by painting them in three or more contrasting colors and highlighting their architectural beauty. Both the menu and the setting seem to embody that ideal of using simple flourishes to highlight what is already there. Dishes are unpretentious, pretty, and well prepared. There's a regular and a vegetarian menu each night, both of which feature a four-course, prix-fixe affair ($60 per person or $100 with wine pairings). In keeping with the elegance of the menu, the service at the Painted Lady is remarkably attentive as well, from offering a napkin to match your pants (thus preventing lint) to brushing the table between courses.

Tina's Restaurant (760 N. Hwy. 99W, Dundee, 503/538-8880, www.tinasdundee.com; Tues.-Thurs. 5pm-9pm, Fri.-Sun. 11:30am-2:30pm and 5pm-9pm; $22-30) takes full advantage of proximity to some of the best wineries in the business, focusing on artisan producers from the Willamette Valley, and typically has about 60 local wines on hand. Wines by the glass are usually about $10-12 and are served in small one-and-a-half-glass carafes. It's a nice touch because it allows you the opportunity to share and sample different wines with different courses. The quiet, 50-seat restaurant serves up rustic French and Northwest cuisine using whatever is locally grown and in season, but it is particularly known for its roasted duck.

At the Joel Palmer House (600 Ferry St., Dayton, 503/864-2995, www.joelpalmerhouse.com; Tues.-Sat. 4:30pm-9:30pm; $29-37), the menu centers almost entirely around Northwest wild mushrooms. Once you have sampled the bounty of chanterelle, portobello, matsutake, and morel mushrooms, you will understand why. Try the Mushroom Madness menu, a prix-fixe meal ($75 per person) that includes six courses of fungus-y goodness.

SHOPS

Shopping in and around McMinnville is also fun, and there are a number of great antiquing stops worth mentioning. Lafayette Schoolhouse Antique Mall (748 Hwy. 99W, Lafayette, 503/864-2720, www.myantiquemall.com; daily 10am-5pm) has more than 100 antiques dealers housed in a 1912 schoolhouse and 1930s-era gymnasium. Also check out the Downtown Historic District and the McMinnville Antiques Mall (334 NE 3rd St., 503/583-1398, www.mcminnvilleantiquemall.com; Sun.-Thurs. 10am-4pm, Fri.-Sat. 10am-5pm), where you will find vintage jewelry, linens, home decor, art, kitchen accessories, and clothing. Also in McMinnville are galleries, restaurants, and independently owned boutiques and shops that specialize in handmade or locally produced items.

WHERE TO STAY

If anything is an indication that Oregon wine country is becoming a destination spot, it is the arrival of the region's first large-scale luxury hotel. The Allison Inn and Spa (2525 Allison Ln., Newberg, 877/294-2525, www.theallison.com; $435 and up) is set on 35 acres of wine country hillside and offers all the amenities necessary for a lavish, romantic stay, such as plush robes, deep soaking tubs, and in-room fireplaces. With 85 guest rooms, including 12 junior suites, seven one-bedroom suites, and a two-bedroom grand suite, The Allison is the largest luxury inn in the area. It also boasts a 15,000-square-foot full-service spa and an 85-seat restaurant that serves Northwest cuisine, wine, and microbrews and provides 24-hour room service for guests.

If you enjoy a simpler bed-and-breakfast, you are in luck. Wine country is ripe with them. **Dundee Manor Bed and Breakfast** (8380 NE Worden Hill Rd., Dundee, 888/262-1133, www.dundeemanor.com; $250), an Edwardian home that sits on five sprawling, manicured acres, comes with a bit more luxury than the average bed-and-breakfast. Guests are treated to a full gourmet breakfast, in-suite snacks, complimentary beverages, fleece robes, fresh flowers, and nightly turn-down service.

In Carlton, the **R.R. Thompson House** (517 N. Kutch St., Carlton, 503/852-6236, www.rrthompsonhouse.com; $160-245) is a good bet. Built in 1936, this bed-and-breakfast features two suites with sitting areas and satellite HDTV, as well as three sunny rooms with private baths and whirlpool tubs. A bonus for the non-morning people: The breakfast room has multiple tables, just in case you are feeling under-caffeinated or antisocial.

Honeymooners and couples looking to get away may want to check out the **Black Walnut Inn** (9600 NE Worden Hill Rd., Dundee, 866/429-4114, www.blackwalnut-inn.com; $265-650), which has been building a reputation as a romance-inducing escape since 2004. Located along the back roads of Dundee, the inn boasts incomparable views of the valley from most of the well-appointed rooms and suites. All of the accommodations here are spacious, cozy, and plush, with decor reminiscent of an Italian villa. Breakfast is a real delight. You may choose from four items each day, all of which are hearty, delicious, and straight from local farms.

Hotel Oregon (310 NE Evans St., McMinnville, 888/472-8427, www.mcmenamins.com; $75-235) is a unique spot to dine or stay thanks to the enterprising McMenamin brothers, who are responsible for 53 properties in Oregon and Washington—including pubs, historic hotels, and movie houses. This particular hotel, which has been around since 1905, has European-style rooms for as little as $75 a night and suites with private bathrooms starting at $115. Hotel Oregon is known for its rooftop bar, which towers over old Main Street and offers a view of the Coastal Range and wine country.

PRACTICALITIES
INFORMATION AND SERVICES

Planning ahead for a trip to wine country is essential, because many wineries have limited hours and even more limited tour options. It's best to pick a few places and map out your day accordingly. A good resource for planning is the **Willamette Valley Visitors Association** (www.oregonwinecountry.org), a nonprofit group that provides travel and tourism information for the entire Willamette Valley region. In addition to having an online calendar of events, it has an interactive trip planner, a breakdown of area wineries, and descriptions of each of the area wine regions.

The **Willamette Valley Wineries Association** (www.willamettewines.com) is another good resource. It oversees more than 150 member wineries and tasting rooms in the valley and provides listings for recommended area restaurants and lodging options. The website also features a map and a link to request a detailed brochure. If you are planning ahead, check out the **Oregon Wine Board** (www.oregonwine.org), which provides extensive looks into the history and horticulture of Oregon wines, notes on sustainability and craftsmanship, and tourism resources. From the website, you can request a comprehensive packet that includes an overview brochure about the industry, maps, and vineyard listings from the Willamette Valley and all over Oregon. There's a small cost, but they will mail the packet to your home so that you can get a head start on mapping out your trip.

TRANSPORTATION

It's not a long stretch of road that separates Portland from the hub of Oregon's Willamette Valley wine region. To get there, take I-5 southbound until you reach exit 289 (Sherwood/Tualatin), or detour through the Champoeg State Heritage Area by continuing south to exit 282A. Follow the signs to Butteville, and from there to Newberg and Highway 99W. Traffic can slow to a crawl as you pass through each of the small cities along the route, particularly during rush hour, so try to avoid traveling that stretch in the early morning or late afternoon.

Getting around Oregon wine country can be a challenge, thanks to rolling hills, gravel roads, and sporadic signage. But there are plenty of maps and tours that can help you navigate. If you are driving yourself, appoint one person as the map checker, who can be on the lookout for driveways and landmarks.

BACKGROUND

The Landscape

GEOGRAPHY

Situated approximately 110 miles from the Pacific Ocean, the city of Portland lies between the Cascade Mountain Range to the east and the Coastal Range to the west. The city, which is the largest in the state and one of the chief cities in the Pacific Northwest, is divided by the Willamette River, which flows into the Columbia River just to the north.

Portland and Mount Hood

The land in the Willamette River Valley is agriculturally productive, and for that reason, it was the desired destination of many pioneers who set out on the Oregon Trail in the 1840s. Although Portland is not often regarded as part of the Willamette Valley basin, it is well within the defining mountain ranges. Much of the area's fertility can be credited to its past, when massive ice dams in the prehistoric Glacial Lake Missoula in Montana repeatedly ruptured, each time flooding through eastern Washington and down through the Columbia River Gorge. It is estimated that during that time, much of the Willamette Valley, including Portland, was under several hundred feet of water—so much that only the West Hills, Mount Tabor, and Mount Scott were visible.

As Portland was beginning to blossom, the logging industry dominated the economy, and around 1847, the city experienced a growth so major that developers decided they needed more roads to encourage trade and to compete with the elder trading post upstream, Oregon City. Unfortunately, they discovered

239

that as they cut down trees to make roads, the labor needed to remove the stumps was stiflingly inadequate, forcing work crews to leave the arboreal remains until workers could address them. To prevent wagon accidents and stumbling, locals began painting the stumps white for visibility, which aided pedestrians in traversing the notoriously muddy landscape and earned the city the nickname Stumptown.

Despite its distance from the waters of the Pacific, Portland has one of the busiest ports on the West Coast, as ocean shipments can reach the city by way of the Columbia and Willamette Rivers. There are also two interstate highways, several freight railways, and rail transit systems that serve the city, and numerous domestic airlines that fly through Portland International Airport.

By car, Portland is only 45 minutes from Salem, the state capital, 1.5 hours from the ski slopes of Mount Hood, two hours from the Pacific Ocean, and about 3.5 hours to Seattle, Washington, or the Great Basin high-desert plateau in Bend, Oregon. But even within the city limits, Mother Nature is rarely more than five minutes or five blocks away. There are a number of botanical gardens, rose gardens, and arboretums; Forest Park, with its 5,000 acres of alder, fir, cottonwood, maple, and yew trees, is the largest wilderness park within a city in the United States.

CLIMATE

The weather in Portland is usually quite mild thanks to the White Mountains to the northwest, which keep snow from reaching the metro area and the temperatures moderate. Fog and rain showers are common, but contrary to popular belief, it doesn't rain all the time. In fact, Portland receives about half of its annual rainfall between November and February. All told, it rains about 36-42 inches per year, with December and January being the wettest months.

The summer months are often mild and pleasant, with temperatures that rarely top 90°F, a climate that often continues into the early months of fall. Winter begins late and usually extends into March, with one or two cold snaps that can last several days.

ANIMALS AND INSECTS

Of course, Oregon is the Beaver State, and while the state mascot is currently under environmental protection, you can still find the beaver in Pacific Northwest streams and rivers, along with its cousins, the muskrat and nutria. Within the city itself you're more likely to see squirrels, chipmunks, raccoons, opossums, frogs, skunks, and the occasional mouse, garter snake, rat, or bat. Step into the wilderness of one of the parks or wildlife refuges and you might see deer, rabbits, otters, turtles, or possibly even a cougar or coyote.

Portland is heaven for bird-watchers, and the city's numerous trees are populated by pigeons, blue jays, swallows, crows, hummingbirds, starlings, thrushes, warblers, woodpeckers, and wrens. When the weather is stormy at the coast, it's not uncommon for seagulls to come inland for a little respite, and when they get a little curious, it is not unusual for owls to set up residency in the rafters of a large building (such as the Oaks Amusement Park carousel) or home.

As far as pests and insects go, Portland is low on the radar. There are, of course, house flies, mosquitoes, honeybees, wasps, ladybugs, butterflies, and moths, all of which are small in comparison to the size they achieve in the southern and northeastern United States. Most of the spiders are harmless, and those that aren't (like the black widow) are extremely rare.

History

LEWIS AND CLARK AND THE EARLY SETTLERS

As Meriwether Lewis and William Clark neared the Pacific Coast goal of their epic expedition across the United States, they were struck by the splendor of the region that would one day become Portland. But long before their journey would begin, Oregon was home to a number of Native American tribes. The mild climate and abundance of fish, game, and wildlife, coupled with the wealth of water sources—not the least of which are the Willamette River and the mighty Columbia—made the Willamette Valley a very rich area

indeed. Native tribes such as the Multnomah and Clackamas based their entire economies and cultures upon the land and the water. Nearby Celilo Falls, for example, was a tribal fishing area on the Columbia River close to what is now the border between Oregon and Washington. This area, called Wynm after the tribe that inhabited it, was a hub of activity for fishing and trading that Lewis and Clark called a "great emporium . . . where all the neighboring nations assemble," until the completion of the nearby Dalles Dam flooded the falls and the neighboring village.

PETTYGROVE AND LOVEJOY'S LEGENDARY COIN TOSS

Portland wouldn't be what it is today if not for the collective $0.26 of Asa Lovejoy and Francis Pettygrove. Back in 1843, a Tennessee pioneer named William Overton and a Massachusetts lawyer named Asa Lovejoy steered their canoe down the Willamette River from Fort Vancouver toward Oregon City and stopped on the banks of what was then known as The Clearing. Knowing that a city would have to be established near the convergence of the Willamette and Columbia Rivers, Overton was certain that establishing a claim on the land would be a lucrative endeavor. Sadly, he lacked

a mural by Richard Haas on the Oregon Historical Society's exterior

241

SYMBOLS OF THE OREGON SPIRIT

- **Animal:** The industrious **American beaver** is right at home in a state known for logging, but the semi-aquatic rodent is considered a pest in some parts of the world.

- **Beverage:** The Oregon dairy industry contributes over $600 million to the state's economy, so it's no surprise that **milk** takes top honors in the beverage department, although there is a push right now to make beer the statewide drink.

- **Bird:** The medium-size blackbird with a distinctive yellow belly is known as the **western meadowlark,** a state symbol shared with Kansas, Nebraska, Wyoming, North Dakota, and Montana. Portland has its own symbolic bird, the **great blue heron,** which can be spotted in some of the wetlands and nature conservatories.

- **Dance:** We all did it in gym class, do-si-do-ing with that awkward kid who had two left feet. But the **square dance** reflects on Oregon's pioneer heritage, and the friendly, spirited nature of it was deemed a part of the Oregon character.

- **Fish:** The **chinook salmon** is born in freshwater and may spend anywhere between one and eight years in the Pacific Ocean before returning to its birth waters to spawn. The fish was a highly valued part of Native American culture.

- **Flower:** The **Oregon grape** is an evergreen shrub with pretty yellow flowers in late spring that form into clusters of purple berries that resemble grapes. They may look tasty, and the birds sure like them, but don't be tempted to try them yourself. While not poisonous, they are extremely tart. Portland's city flower is, of course, the **rose.**

- **Fruit:** Superior growing conditions in the Hood River Valley make it the top **pear**

the $0.25 required to file a land claim. Fortunately for Overton (and all the rest of us), Lovejoy made a deal with him. Lovejoy would pay the fee and in exchange share the 640-acre site with Overton. This suited Overton just fine, and he set about building a homestead on what added up to about 16 blocks of land, but after a year, Overton decided to leave Oregon behind and depart for Texas. So he sold his share of the claim to Pettygrove and the city as we know it began to evolve.

When the founders of this budding city discussed what to name it, however, they hit a snag. Pettygrove wanted to name the city after his hometown of Portland, Maine, and Lovejoy thought it only proper to name it after his home of Boston, Massachusetts. They agreed to flip a coin, and after heads came up two of the three times the penny was tossed, Pettygrove had won. The coin used in

this legendary meeting has come to be known as "the Portland Penny" and is currently on display at the Oregon Historical Society.

PORTLAND'S NOT-SO-PRETTY PAST

As the city grew into a lively port town, so did the traffic of ne'er-do-wells. By the late 19th century, a constant influx of sailors, loggers, sheepherders, ranch hands, and vagabonds meant a growing need for saloons and boardinghouses. Sadly, even the most practical intentions soon fell victim to vice. Brothels and opium dens began to spring up all over town, and visiting them often led to robbery, kidnapping, or death. One notorious tradeswoman of the time was simply known as Sweet Mary. Mary cleverly avoided the usual legalities of owning a brothel by housing hers on a barge that floated to whichever quadrant of the city offered producer in the United States. The Anjou pear, in particular, thrives in the warm, sunny days and crisp, cool nights.

- **Motto:** The Latin phrase *Alis Volat Propriis,* which means "She Flies with Her Own Wings," was adopted in 1854, was replaced about 100 years later, and then readopted in 1967 to reflect the state's independent spirit. Portland has its own motto, **"The City That Works."**

- **Mushroom:** The delicious **Pacific golden chanterelle** is distinguished by its fluted martini glass shape, apricot smell, and mild peppery taste. They commonly grow under pine, beech, or birch trees and can be found from July until the first frosts.

- **Nut:** In 2008, Oregon produced 34,000 tons of **hazelnuts.** These popular nuts are not only quite tasty, they are also a superfood, rich in protein and unsaturated fat with significant amounts of thiamine, vitamin B6, and fiber.

- **Rock:** Similar to geodes, **thunder eggs** are formed within rhyolitic lava flows. They look like plain Jane baseball-shaped rocks on the outside, but once split in half and polished, they reveal pretty layers of agate, jasper, and opal.

- **Song:** The state song, **"Oregon, My Oregon,"** was written for a contest in 1920 by John Andrew Buchanan and Henry Bernard Murtagh. The first verse honors the early settlers and the pioneers of the Oregon Trail. The second praises the natural beauty of the land.

- **Tree:** The hills and parks of Oregon are abundant with **Douglas firs,** the second-tallest conifer in the world (second only to redwoods). The tree commonly lives for 500 years and sometimes as long as 1,000.

the least attention from the law. The police and vice squads couldn't do much about it since her placement on the river meant that she wasn't officially under anyone's jurisdiction.

It was during that time, however, that Portland's more notorious reputation developed, as it came to be known as the "Unheavenly City" or the "Forbidden City." Despite the fact that the United States Constitution had declared slavery illegal, countless intoxicated or naive men came to Portland only to be kidnapped or tricked into captivity and sold into slave labor on merchant ships.

Throughout much of downtown, particularly in Old Town, there is a maze of underground tunnels that were used to trap and transport unsuspecting souls to their doom. There was money in it for the sort of guy who was willing to swindle, drug, or beat his victims into submission—and no one

was more notorious for it than Joseph "Bunco" Kelly. Legend has it that Bunco once swiped a wooden statue from a local cigar shop and sold it to a ship's captain as a drunken sailor. During Prohibition, bars that wanted to allow patrons to drink and gamble moved their operation to the tunnels, which provided some protection from the law, but only served to increase the possibility of capture.

Still to this day, there are hints of Portland's disreputable past, such as trap doors leading to bars, human-sized holding cells, mysterious artifacts, and rumors of ghosts inhabiting the underground tunnels, a veritable warren of deception and despair.

PORTLAND TODAY

Looking around Portland today, you can see that the city is changing, because somehow, the city never lost its pioneering roots or its desire to build

243

or re-create something from nothing. Early efforts in city planning from some of the city's founders ensured that there would always be plenty of green space even in the most urbanized areas. That is why there are big parks, small parks, tree-lined streets, and rooftop gardens all over the city. Some of these spaces are meant for play and some for reflection, but all encompass that need to mix the Pacific Northwest love of nature with a need for growth and progress. Whether it's dogs scampering through the off-leash area of Overlook Park, kids splashing through the fountain at Jamison Square, or a performance of *King Lear* under the trees in Laurelhurst Park, these green spaces are valuable and well used.

The city has also seen quite a bit of urban development of late. In the 1980s, the Pearl District was little more than abandoned warehouses and railroad tracks. Today it's a bustling neighborhood full of world-class restaurants and more galleries than you can shake a paintbrush at. Mississippi Avenue was falling into disrepair before an influx of creative youthful energy turned it into an artsy, eco-focused, and affectionate community. The same can be said for the Alberta Arts District, but perhaps on a much grander scale. Spread throughout the city are neighborhoods that, despite being interconnected, bear a personality and style all their own. In every district, there are funky, unique, and elegant shops, top-notch restaurants, and stylish bars. Getting to all those neighborhoods is a snap, since the transportation system has evolved along with the city—a little more each year, with the streetcar, light rail, and bus system providing yet more car-free access to the metro area. Since the transportation system was built around the idea of urban growth and city planning, it has thus far been a pretty happy marriage.

Cycling is hugely encouraged and supported throughout the city with bike lanes, paths, and parks that often lead to vantage points where, on a clear day, sparkling water and distant mountains are an awesome sight to behold.

The locals, for the most part, are very friendly and willing to point you toward the best cup of coffee, plate of fries, or hamburger in town, but their opinions are likely to vary as much as the weather. One thing is certain, however: Portlanders are all about self-expression, self-sufficiency, and the pursuit of the next best story. It might be about that amazing gnocchi from that shop down the street, the next project we are working on, or that artist we met while touring First Thursday. Every experience seems to be treated as if it is ripe with possibility. That is why chef-owned restaurants are so much more common than franchises, and why you will find them around almost every corner. Almost all of them pride themselves on using local fresh ingredients and tailoring the menu to what's in season.

Government and Economy

GOVERNMENT

The city of Portland leans largely to the left of the political scale. In 2009, there were 341,962 registered voters and 206,412 of those were Democrats. The city as a whole tends to be fairly progressive, with the mayor, four city commissioners, and a city auditor at the helm. In fact, Portland's system of government is one of the few things it is not progressive about as a city. Of all the large cities in the United States, Portland has the last remaining commission form of government. Under the commission structure, the officials elected to represent Portland constitute the legislative body of the city and are, as a group, responsible for taxation, appropriations, ordinances, and other general functions. Each commissioner is assigned a responsibility to one aspect of municipal affairs, like public works, public affairs, or public safety. All city officials, including the mayor, are elected to serve four-year terms, with elections being spaced out every two years so as not to inadvertently fill a council with inexperienced members.

The mayor and city commissioners make up the city council, which carries out its duties in accordance with the laws of the state and the Portland City Code and Charter, and are primarily responsible for making laws that govern the city of Portland. And while the council is accountable for legislative policy and for keeping Portland running like a well-oiled machine, the auditor keeps the council in line with a system of checks and balances. Both city and state law allow Portlanders the right to initiate legislation through the proper processes or even to refer legislation that has passed through city council to a vote of the people.

ECONOMY

Early in its history, Portland's economy was largely dependent on the rivers that flowed through it. The Willamette and Columbia Rivers provided access to the Pacific Ocean, and their deep waters meant that the city was well placed to become a nucleus for logging, farming, and fishing. When the city was selected as the West Coast terminal for the U.S. mailing ship *The Petonia*, it seemed like the city was well on its way to becoming a major part of the nation's economy. But disaster struck in 1873, when a fire reduced 22 downtown blocks and parts of Chinatown to ashes. To add insult to injury, another fire had occurred just eight months earlier when anti-Chinese arsonists set ablaze three city blocks, with a loss estimated at about $2 million. Despite the devastation, the city began to rebuild, this time with only cast iron, brick, and stone. By the turn of the 20th century, the construction of the transcontinental railroad that linked Portland to the East Coast caused the population to swell to 90,000 people.

Today, the city's economy is quite different, and the technology and research industries are leading the pack. In fact, Intel, Providence Health Systems, and Oregon Health and Sciences University are the city's top employers, followed at a distance by Fred Meyer, the Kaiser Foundation, and Legacy Health System. Despite having significant layoffs in the early part of 2009, the health and tech industries continue to dominate the economy for the entire state and the Portland metro area in particular. Even within those fields there has long been a focus on utilizing sustainable practices whenever possible and devising eco-action plans when practices weren't readily available. For a long time, this focus on the environment gave Portlanders a reputation for being tree-hugging hippies, but now that the city is poised to become the leader in green technology and sustainable practices, things are looking even brighter. Cities all over the world are turning to Portland to find out how they can conserve energy and resources without diminishing their way of life.

In the late 2000s, former mayor Sam Adams and the city council made a push to develop a new economic strategy to brand Portland as the nation's most sustainable city; the city's residents followed in stride. The program included economic incentives and training for workers in targeted industries (health, technology, manufacturing), and set up Portland as a "city to watch" in the global green economy.

Local Culture

In 2011, the population of the state of Oregon was estimated at 3,970,239. Of those, about 19 percent lived in Multnomah County—the smallest of Oregon's 36 counties—which encompasses Portland, Gresham, Fairview, Troutdale, Wood Village, and portions of Lake Oswego. In the same year, Portland's population swelled to 619,360, marking a 6 percent increase in the past four years alone, a statistic that outpaced the national average for population growth.

The median age for Portland metro area residents is 35, with 46 percent of the population aged 15-44 and 14 percent of residents over 60. It has been said that Portland is "the whitest city in America," and while the statement is a bit hyperbolic, it is not far off. As of the latest census estimate, the city is about 76 percent Caucasian, 6.3 percent African American, 7.1 percent Asian or Pacific Islander, and 9.4 percent Hispanic.

Portland frequently makes the list of top cities to find single men in a number of online and print publications. This claim is often based less on demographics (which is almost evenly split between men and women), and more on Portland's status as a destination for the youthful creative class. More and more, people are coming to Portland to work and live life outside of the lines. Creative types like artists, chefs, and even engineers and scientists have been lured by the city's tolerant, off-center way of life, and their presence has had a lasting effect on the economy, the lexicon, and the overall personality of the city. The city has long been called a "big small town" because it is easy to meet people and also quite easy to find solitude. People tend to be easygoing, helpful, and more focused on the success of the community than on individual success.

CHINATOWN

Chinese immigrants have been in Portland almost as long as the city founders, and most were brought here to build bridges, tunnels, and railroad beds and to work in the mines, salmon canneries, and textile industries. The numbers in Portland continued to grow each year between 1850 and the early part of the 1880s despite the Chinese Exclusion Act, which was the first federal law to ever be passed banning an ethnic group from entry into the United States based on the fear that they would be an endangerment to the public. In 1885 and 1886, however, the population of Chinese immigrants mushroomed due to the expulsion of immigrants from Seattle, Tacoma, and Olympia in neighboring Washington. At the time, the Pacific Northwest was facing an economic downturn, and the Chinese were blamed for taking jobs away from Americans and driving the average wage down. Although the city of Portland had not yet chosen to expel the Chinese, the immigrants were forced from outer communities into what was essentially a ghetto, an area that was notorious for kidnappings (through the Shanghai Tunnels), opium dens, and brothels. While Chinatown had those less attractive qualities, the neighborhood also had a strong sense of community, with barbershops, grocery stores, schools, and restaurants.

Today, Chinatown residents and property owners are struggling to overcome the neighborhood's reputation as a haven for crime, homelessness, and drug abuse, and they are also struggling to maintain a sense of community. With proposed development that includes large-scale grocery stores and higher-end restaurants, the proponents of Chinatown are eager for the opportunity to clean up the streets but cautious about a development plan that might force out the very families and businesses that have maintained the spirit of Chinatown.

AFRICAN AMERICAN CULTURE

Ask most locals about the earliest recorded history of African American culture in Portland and you are likely to get a variety of answers. What most people don't realize is that there was an African American community that thrived as far back as the early 1900s, near the spot where Union Station still stands today. Job opportunities at the railroads stimulated a small population growth within Portland's African American community. People came from all over the United States, and particularly the South, as part of the Great Migration to work as Pullman porters, Red Caps, cooks, waiters, and shop laborers. The Portland Hotel, which was located at the present site of Pioneer Courthouse Square, was another big draw. More than 70 African American men were brought up from the Carolinas and Georgia to work in the hotel at service positions for what would become a major hub of the city's business and social activity.

Between 1850 and 1900, Portland's African American population increased from about a dozen to 775—not a staggering number, but enough to support two churches, a handful of businesses, and a newspaper. Along with those newcomers came a hardworking sense of spirit and a community alive with barbershops, restaurants, pool halls, haberdasheries, and hotels. On Sundays, the Golden West Hotel, which was owned by an African American man named

P-TOWN CATCHPHRASES

There are so many nicknames for Portland, it's hard to keep track of them all. The city also has a number of catchphrases that are helpful to know so you don't get confused if someone asks you if you have seen "Big Pink."

- **Beervana:** With all the fantastic microbreweries and artisan beermakers in town, this designation makes sense. Portland is a beer lover's heaven.

- **The Benson Bubblers:** Those public drinking fountains you see on the street corners were named for philanthropist Simon Benson. And in case you were wondering, it is safe to drink from them. The water comes from the same municipal source as the rest of the city's drinking water and is not recycled back into the fountain.

- **Big Pink:** This term refers to the 43-story boxy pink building at SW 5th Avenue and Burnside Street.

- **Bridgetown:** Eleven bridges keep Portland cars, buses, bikes, and people moving.

- **Brewery Blocks:** The former site of the Blitz-Weinhard brewery, this Pearl District area is a five-block shopping and professional district that still houses a number of brewpubs.

- **The City of Roses:** The city comes by this nickname naturally. People figured out a long time ago that Portland has the ideal climate for growing roses. It wasn't long before the International Rose Test Garden was established and an annual festival was planned to celebrate this fact.

- **Lake O:** This refers to Lake Oswego, an affluent suburb south of the city.

- **Little Beirut:** Portland has always been pretty blue, politically speaking, and when President George H. W. Bush visited the city in the early 1990s, he was met with so many protesters that he and his staff dubbed the city Little Beirut.

- **NoPo:** This term refers to North Portland. A number of other neighborhoods have tried

W. D. Allen, became a gathering spot of sorts when services at the nearby Mt. Olivet Baptist and Bethel AME churches let out. Dressed in their Sunday best, people would congregate in the Chinese restaurant, Turkish bath, barbershop, gambling room, gymnasium, and ice cream parlor and share stories.

In the early part of the 1900s, the African American community faced less discrimination than it would come to see in later years. In 1906, African American people were allowed to vote and serve as jurors. African American children shared classrooms with Caucasian children, and both sat side-by-side in restaurants. In 1894, Charles Hardin became the first African American man to join the police force, and by 1915, he was the first African American man to be made sheriff's deputy. When work was scarce, many African American men began to explore the opportunity of owning a small business, and in turn began to shop in and patronize only community-owned businesses as a means of economic survival. For many years, it worked. By 1920, 8 percent of Portland's African American community owned or operated their own business, a statistic that was almost unheard of at the time.

But the tide began to turn as more European immigrants began to settle in Portland. Housing discrimination forced most African Americans to adopt this method of nicknaming (SoWa for the South Waterfront, FoPo for Foster-Powell), but NoPo is the only one that has really caught on.

- **PDX:** Yes, it is the airport code for the city, but it is also a well-recognized short-hand epithet.

- **Pill Hill:** This is Oregon Health and Sciences University, which looms above the city in Portland's west hills.

- **Pod:** A group of food carts, oftentimes occupying a whole city block.

- **Puddletown:** With 36-42 inches of rain per year, this name is self-explanatory.

- **Rip City:** Thank basketball announcer Bill Schonely for this nickname. The play-by-play man was known for his creative exclamations during the Trail Blazers games, and this one became a rallying cry for the team and eventually a city moniker.

- **The Schnitz:** Slang for the Arlene Schnitzer Concert Hall.

- **Snob Hill:** This term affectionately refers to Nob Hill, or the shopping districts on NW 21st and NW 23rd Avenues.

- **Stumptown:** This nickname was first meant as an insult when the forested landscape was rapidly stripped to make way for growth. The stumps were not cleared and became hazards when traveling through the mud or dark. Eventually, the stumps were painted white, which made for a scene that rather resembled a graveyard.

- **The Sunset Highway:** A lovely name for the road that jams up bumper-to-bumper during rush hour each weekday, otherwise known as Highway 26 West.

- **Zoobombers:** These daredevils take a weekly wild ride down the hills of Washington Park on kiddie bicycles that they carry with them on the MAX to the Oregon Zoo stop. It is not intended to be an aggressive act, and the Zoobombers are mostly regarded with bemusement. There's a sculpture on the corner of 13th Avenue and West Burnside where the participants stack their bikes with joyful abandon.

to settle near the industrial area on the east side of the Broadway Bridge, where you will now find Memorial Coliseum and the Rose Quarter. The Great Depression, too, was devastating to the African American community. Within a year, most of the African American-owned businesses were forced to close their doors, including the Golden West Hotel. Jobs became even more difficult to come by, with racial tensions rising every day.

Today, little remains of the area that was once so alive with the city's first African American leaders. The Golden West Hotel still stands, but now serves as transitional housing for homeless, mentally ill individuals. The African American community is largely centered in the Albina area, which includes the Boise, Concordia, Eliot, Humboldt, Piedmont, Sabin, Vernon, King, Alberta, and Woodlawn neighborhoods. In many of those neighborhoods, the threat of gentrification has spurred conflict and conversation. The liberal-minded tendencies of Portlanders help a little, but even the best of intentions can have negative results. It's a bit of an uphill battle, but the city and organizations like the Urban League of Portland and National Association for the Advancement of Colored People (NAACP) are doing what they can to preserve the community and promote equality, and encourage a healthy rate of growth and development.

THE LGBT COMMUNITY

The city of Portland has long had an active gay community, and has one of the strongest feminist and lesbian communities in the United States. The history of the community dates back to World War II, when the city received countless traffic in and out of town from lonely soldiers, sailors, and war industry workers away from their families and friends. During that time, though the gay and lesbian community was still fairly closeted, the beer parlors, vaudeville houses, bars, and hotels were willing to look the other way while same-sex curiosities were explored, and thrived. One such spot, the Music Hall, became a popular hangout for lesbians and was known to put on a pretty remarkable drag show. The club received a lot of attention when sin-busting mayor Dorothy McCullough Lee (1949-1953) attacked it most vociferously with liquor license queries and investigations. She did not succeed in shutting the venue down, but did manage to drive the drag act out of town.

At that time, there were gay rights organizations popping up all over the West Coast in major cities like Seattle and San Francisco, but Portland had no such movement toward encouraging pride and establishing rights. In spite of the community's lack of effort, however, gay men and lesbian women continued to flock to the more laissez-faire Portland after being chased out of other cities. In fact, the Portland police department tended to leave suspected gay hangouts alone. When Commissioner Stanley Earl wanted to shut down the Harbor Club in the late 1950s, it was the police who talked him out of it, suggesting that it was better to have homosexuals gathered in one place rather than scattered throughout the city.

Things reached a bit of a boiling point in 1964 when the papers began to run numerous headlines about "homosexual rings" that preyed upon children. Mayor Terry Schrunk was determined to crack down on bars that catered to gay men and lesbians, and formed the Committee for Decent Literature and Films to stop the production of publications that depicted homosexual activity. That summer, an *Oregon Journal* columnist stated to the police that the "unmentionables" were numerous in Portland, and that the number of gay and lesbian bars had inflated from three to ten. He assured the police that some local businessmen promised to take "vigilante action" against them in order to restore the civility of the city. Also that year, the Portland City Council asked the Oregon Liquor Control Commission (OLCC) to revoke the liquor licenses of all the city's suspected gay and lesbian bars. The licenses were revoked but quickly renewed when the OLCC admitted that the bars were operating within the law. After that, the city and the police department were largely unmotivated to continue pressuring the gay and lesbian venues. Throughout the tough periods in the 1960s, Portland still did not have much in the way of activism for the gay and lesbian community, but there was little need for it. Portland was essentially wide open.

The LGBT community in Portland these days is far more active, and the complacency about citywide or nationwide activism seems to have worn off. Organizations like the Portland Area Business Alliance, Basic Rights Oregon, Northwest Gender Alliance, and the Q Center are working overtime to ensure that the city stays "wide open," but smartly so. In 2008, the election of Mayor Sam Adams, the first openly gay mayor of a major American city, sparked a lot of attention and further confirmed Portland as a gay-friendly city.

But there are other reasons why the city is so attractive to the gay community. The city is socially conscious and progressive, with organizations that offer everything from financial to emotional support, HIV/AIDS education and assistance, and networking opportunities and social activities. Portland also offers domestic partnership registration. While Multnomah County made a decision in 2004 to allow such unions, it wasn't until the passage of the Oregon Family Fairness Act in 2007 and its subsequent signing by Governor Kulongoski that the domestic partnership system was made legal by the state of Oregon. Under that ruling, same-sex couples are now allowed to enjoy many of the things that they would have otherwise been denied, like hospital information, mortgage loans, and parental rights.

EDUCATION

Oregon students historically exceed national averages for math and verbal on their Scholastic Aptitude Test (SAT) scores. For dozens of years, Oregon and Washington have held the top two positions among the 23 states that test at least 50 percent of their high school graduates. There are more than 600 schools and 21 districts within the Portland metro area, and a number of secular and religiously affiliated private schools at the primary, secondary, and high school levels.

The Portland metropolitan area is richly endowed with educational resources, including some of the best colleges in the nation. It is a bit of a chicken and egg question because it is hard to define which came first, the prevalence of smart, creative, and educated citizens, or the schools to entice them here. Whatever the cause, Portland boasts a number of colleges, universities, and trade schools. Prominent universities include **Portland State University** (PSU) in the heart of downtown; **Reed College** in Southeast Portland, a private liberal arts college with a distinct reputation for progressive and anti-establishment leanings; **Lewis and Clark College** in Southwest Portland, also a private liberal arts school, whose students are often globally minded, environmentally conscious thinkers; and **Oregon Health and Sciences University** in Southwest Portland, a world-class teaching hospital and research center.

ESSENTIALS

Getting There

AIR

MAX light rail

Portland International Airport, which goes by the call sign PDX, is the number one airport in the state of Oregon. It has direct connections to major airport hubs throughout the United States, plus nonstop international flights to Canada, Japan, Mexico, and the Netherlands. While the airport does have service from some smaller airlines like JetBlue (www.jetblue.com) and Hawaiian Airlines (www.hawaiianair.com), PDX is a major hub for Alaska Airlines and Horizon Air (www.alaskaair.com), and serves as a maintenance facility for Horizon Air. The route between PDX and Seattle-Tacoma International Airport is considered the 19th busiest air route in the world, in terms of flights per week, thanks to a number of travelers who prefer to skip the sometimes slow I-5 crawl (otherwise known as "the slog").

PDX has won a number of awards for its accessibility, courtesy, security, and amenities. Most visitors are pleased with the number of shops, like Brookstone, Powell's Books, and Nike, where they can pick up last-minute supplies or gifts. Stores are not allowed to charge more than their off-site locations would charge, and as always in Oregon, everything is sales-tax free. There are great places to grab a bite to eat or a drink as well. Locals love to stop by Good Dog/Bad Dog, Gustav's Pub & Grill, Laurelwood Brewing Company, or Pizzacato, all of which are favorites in town as well.

AIRPORT TRANSPORTATION

The pickup area for taxis, airport shuttles, parking shuttles, and towncars is located outside baggage claim in the center of the terminal's lower roadway. A few hotels offer complimentary shuttle service to and from the airport, but many are located prohibitively far from the center of the city. However, Portland's light rail system, **MAX** (http://trimet.org/max), picks up at the south end of the terminal, and you can ride straight into the heart of downtown for about $2.50 per person in about 40 minutes. There are plenty of cabs to hail if you prefer to take one in, but cabs are expensive in Portland and will run you about $30 and possibly as much as $70 for the 20 minute trip into town. A towncar service, like **Pacific Cascade** (888/869-6227, www.towncar.com), can be cheaper (about $35-60) if you arrange ahead of time. Just make sure you give them your flight number when you make the reservation so they can track any delays or cancellations. **Lyft** (www.lyft.com) and **Uber** (www.uber.com) also make pickups from PDX at designated areas, Island 1 and Island 2 outside baggage claim, respectively. Prices vary depending on the time of day and availability of drivers, but you can typically get to most places in the city for about $15-30.

CAR RENTAL

All the major national car rental companies have outposts at PDX, so whatever your preference is, you can find it here. If you can wait until you get into town, you can always set up an account with **Zipcar** (503/328-3539, www.zipcar.com) or **Car2go** (www.car2go.com). Both are popular services that stash cars all over the city for temporary usage. With Zipcar, you

reserve the one nearest to you and return it to the same spot when you are done. With Car2go you are limited to Smart Fortwo cars, but you can park the car anywhere inside the Car2go home region (which is most of the city). With both companies, gas and insurance are included.

CAR

From Portland International Airport, head southwest on Airport Way to I-205 South and turn right onto the freeway. Follow I-205 to exit 21B to merge onto I-84 West and US 30 West to Portland.

If you are continuing to downtown Portland, take the I-5 exit on the left that leads to Salem and Beaverton, and keep right as you take the exit marked City Center. Follow the signs to merge onto the Morrison Bridge and into downtown Portland.

TRAIN

Portland's historic **Union Station** (800 NW 6th Ave., 503/273-4865, www.amtrak.com) is served by three Amtrak passenger trains, including three daily departures between Seattle and Portland as well as daily service to Vancouver, British Columbia. The *Amtrak Cascades* travels along the pretty countryside of the Pacific Northwest and British Columbia and offers reclining seats; laptop computer outlets; bicycle, ski, and snowboard racks; and regional food, local wine, and microbrews from the Bistro car.

Amtrak's *Coast Starlight* operates daily, connecting Los Angeles, San Francisco, Portland, and Seattle. This train has both a coach section (with optional at-seat meal service) and sleeping cars, as well as an Arcade Room with a selection of arcade-style video games.

Amtrak's *Empire Builder* takes you through the Lewis and Clark Wilderness, beginning in Portland and heading east to Chicago. Stops along the way include Spokane, Whitefish, Glacier National Park, Minot, Minneapolis, and Milwaukee.

BUS

The **Greyhound bus terminal** (550 NW 6th Ave., 503/243-2361, www. greyhound.com) is next to the Amtrak station at the edge of Old Town. Greyhound offers connecting services all over the United States for reasonable rates, and often combines with Amtrak to reach destinations otherwise unreachable by train. The station is one of many along the I-5 corridor that connects Bellingham, Seattle, Salem, Eugene, and much of California. There are also select affiliate routes that can get you just about anywhere in the United States.

Travelers can also take the Bolt Bus, a sort of young, hip brother of Greyhound that offers super low rates (sometimes less than $20) between Portland and such cities as Eugene, Bellingham and Seattle in Washington, and Vancouver in British Columbia.

Getting Around

Portland is often thought of as a very European city. People here like to walk, bike, and utilize the various systems of public transportation available. In fact, the city as a whole encourages it. Many venues along the MAX or streetcar lines offer discounts to patrons who show their TriMet ticket. Neighborhoods that are particularly bike-heavy (like Mississippi Avenue, Alberta Street, Belmont Street, and Hawthorne Street) are equipped with plenty of bike lanes and places to park and lock up your bike. Most Portland neighborhoods are extremely walkable and have wide, pedestrian-friendly sidewalks with easily recognizable, wheelchair-accessible crosswalks.

The public transportation system in Portland is known for being just about as easy to use and reliable as a system can get. It's a safe, dependable way to get around on the weekdays, but becomes a little more complicated on weekends and holidays as it all but stops running after 2am. So, if you are planning on staying out past last call, be prepared to take a cab or walk. For areas that are particularly congested when it comes to parking (like the Pearl District or NW 23rd), it is best to bike there or ditch your car in a **Smart Park** (www.portlandonline. com/smartpark) lot and use the MAX or streetcar.

PUBLIC TRANSPORTATION
TRIMET BUSES

Nearly all of the **TriMet buses** and some of the **C-TRAN buses** (a system that serves Vancouver, Battleground, Hazel Dell, Camas, and Washougal, Washington) congregate at the transit mall on 5th and 6th Avenues downtown. Buses stop every three to five blocks, with one bus stop location per block. Northbound buses travel along 6th Avenue and southbound buses travel along 5th Avenue. Each bus stop is assigned a Stop ID number, which will be posted on the bus stop sign or on the schedule in the stop's bus shelter. You can use **TriMet's Transit Tracker system** (503/238-7433) by entering the Stop ID number when you call or by texting it to 27299. The system will tell you exactly how long it will be before the next bus arrives.

MAX

Portland is particularly proud of its Metro Area Express, or MAX, system. TriMet and the city of Portland worked to integrate transportation needs with land-use planning to give the city a longer-term model for urban growth, energy resources, and environmental concerns. For this reason, MAX is a popular, affordable, and efficient way to get from place to place in the metro area. The Red Line runs about 25 miles from the Beaverton Transit Center to the Portland International Airport. The Blue Line begins at the Hatfield Government Center in Hillsboro and runs about 33 miles, well into Gresham. The Yellow Line, which is currently the shortest, runs about seven miles from the Portland Expo Center to SW 10th Avenue downtown. The Green Line runs from Clackamas Town Center to Portland State University, and the Orange Line travels from Portland State through inner Southeast to Milwaukie.

THE STREETCAR

The **Portland Streetcar** (www. portlandstreetcar.org) is a little more lightweight than the MAX line but essentially serves the same purpose, which is to connect the various quadrants of town and encourage people to take public transportation instead of cars. Unlike MAX, the streetcar runs with the traffic and must obey signals, so it is obliged to cover shorter distances than its big brother. The streetcar (which arrives about every 12-15 minutes) runs from Legacy Emmanuel Hospital in NW Portland to SW Lowell and Bond at the South Waterfront District and the base of the OHSU Aerial Tram. The streetcar will not automatically stop at every stop, as the MAX does. To indicate your desire to stop, push the yellow strip or the stop button to let the operator know. The fare for the streetcar is the same as MAX or TriMet, and you can use your TriMet ticket or transfer as proof of payment. If you wish to purchase a ticket for the streetcar, you can do so at the fare box on board.

TAXIS AND RIDE-HAILING APPS
BROADWAY CAB AND RADIO CAB

Broadway Cab (503/227-1234, www. broadwaycab.com) and **Radio Cab** (503/227-1212, www.radiocab.net) have been neck and neck for decades in Portland, and very little has changed except that Broadway (in the iconic yellow cab) has added six Toyota hybrids to their fleet of more than 200 cars. It is part of its long-term goal to replace all its cars with vehicles that use sustainable or alternative fuels.

Radio Cab has been driving Portlanders around since 1946, and it is still one of the most popular numbers dialed after last call. If you plan at least 24 hours in advance, you can book your trip online. Radio Cab (the black-and-white tuxedo cabs) has a state-of-the-art system for dispatching, so the response can be pretty quick. Ask your dispatcher for an estimate when you call. As with all the cab companies in Portland, it is best to book a taxi ahead if you are on a schedule.

UBER AND LYFT

The use of these app-based ride hailing programs was fairly controversial when it first was introduced to the city. For a while, city officials even deemed it illegal because it could not be regulated in the same way that commercial cabs could. Since then, trial agreements have been made, and now you can hail a ride from your smartphone for prices that do occasionally give cabs a run for their money. Many locals like to use these programs because the people driving are artists, performers, or just underemployed locals looking to supplement their income.

PDX PEDICAB

If you happen to be downtown or in the Pearl District, **PDX Pedicab** (503/839-5174, www.pdxpedicab.com) may just be your best (and most fun) way to get around. This bike-powered, rickshaw-style vehicle can transport two or three people comfortably (they have canopies and lap blankets) and quickly. You can hail one if you happen to see an empty one, or call dispatch to have one sent. They operate Monday-Friday 10am-midnight and Friday-Saturday 10am-3am. The drivers are fun, knowledgeable, safe, and oftentimes able to tell you a lot about the city. If you're feeling adventurous, you can also book a pedicab tour of Old Town, where you will be given a recorded audio history of the city's most scandalous section.

DRIVING

Driving in Portland can be a bit confusing at first, and it's simpler if you look at a map before you drive so that you can navigate the many one-way streets and sudden on-ramps to bridges and freeways. There is no need to panic. For one thing, even if you get lost, you are still likely to be only a few minutes away from your destination, and if you accidentally land yourself on a bridge or freeway, it is still pretty simple to take the nearest exit and follow the signs back to where you were.

One notable frustration is that once you are in downtown Portland, it is nearly impossible (and often illegal) to make a left turn. To avoid the frustration of going too far and having to backtrack, turn right a few streets early and C-turn yourself back in the right direction.

If you are heading into Southeast Portland and have to pass through or near Ladd's Addition, here's hoping you packed a lunch, because you might be there for a while. This neighborhood is notoriously confusing, so again, consult a map before you drive. Seeing the grid of the area from overhead can make the crazy turns and broken-up streets more navigable.

BIKING AND WALKING

Portlanders love to bike and walk, which may come as a surprise considering the fickle weather in the Pacific Northwest. Even in the winter, cycling remains one of the top methods for locals to commute from place to place. For that reason, the streets (and drivers) tend to be respectful of cyclists and pedestrians.

Downtown, the blocks are approximately half the size of a normal city block, with public art, fountains, and parks scattered throughout the urban areas. In the Pearl District and Northwest, the streets are numbered in one direction (ascending order from the waterfront) and run alphabetically in the other direction using the names of famous Portland historical figures, like Couch, Davis, Everett, Flanders, and so on. Burnside Avenue divides Portland by the north and south, the Willamette River divides the city by the east and west.

Portland has arguably the nation's most progressive support system for bike transportation, thanks to the wide, clearly marked bike lanes on most major commuter routes, municipal bike racks, and access to most bridges. TriMet has created space for bikes to be taken on the MAX trains, and buses are equipped with bike racks on the front, which makes traveling long distances on a bike that much more feasible.

If you prefer to explore on foot, you can pick up a walking map at most downtown hotels, at the **Travel Portland Visitor Information Center** in Pioneer Courthouse Square (701 SW 6th Ave. at Morrison St., www.travelportland.com), and at **Powell's City of Books** (1005 W. Burnside St., www.powells.com). Cyclists will find the **Bicycle Transportation Alliance** (www.bta4bikes.org) and **Bike Portland** (www.bikeportland.org) to be good resources for bike routes, repair shops, and bike-related events.

WHEELCHAIR ACCESS

All of Portland's buses and MAX trains are equipped with lifts, ramps, and accessible seating. The seating near the entrances of both the bus and MAX is reserved as priority seating for seniors and people with disabilities. Both the MAX and the streetcar have a ramp that extends out for easier boarding, and the buses have either a boarding ramp or power lift. Seniors and passengers with disabilities may qualify for the "Honored Citizen" rate of $1 for a two-hour ticket.

Conduct and Customs

UMBRELLAS

The quickest way to mark yourself as a tourist is to pop open an umbrella when it rains. For native Portlanders, a hooded jacket is all you need to ride out the inconsistent weather. Given that the average rainfall in a year is about 36 inches, it may seem like madness not to rely on an umbrella, but there's method in it. For one thing, the rain is often accompanied by a good deal of wind, and an umbrella doesn't fare well in such circumstances. Also, the weather changes so often that you may only need protection from the rain for a few moments before a sun break passes through. Finally, when you have a cell phone in one hand, a latte in the other, and laptop bag on your shoulder, an umbrella just becomes cumbersome.

SHOPPING BAGS

As a means of keeping the city even more environmentally minded, city officials have banned the use of plastic shopping bags within city limits. The ban includes all grocery stores, retailers, and restaurants. Stores can still provide you with a recycled or reusable bag (usually for a fee), but the best thing to do is bring your own bag and consolidate purchases whenever possible. You can buy a reusable bag at all grocery stores, at **Powell's City of Books** (www.powells.com), and at a number of other stores all over the city.

DRINKING SUSTAINABLY

Portlanders love their coffee. While a cup or two of Stumptown a day is not a bad thing, cups, lids, and coffee sleeves add up to a lot of trash—even if it is all made from recycled materials. So bring a travel mug with you and you'll end up fitting right in with the locals. What's more, some places give you a discount on your cup of joe if you bring your own container.

The same is true for bottled water. The tap water in the city comes from the Bull Run Reservoir, one of the purest drinking-water sources in the world. Go ahead and fill up your Nalgene or stainless-steel water bottle right from the tap. Cover your bottle with stickers and people will assume you have lived here all your life.

PUMPING GAS

Self-serve gas fueling is banned in most parts of Oregon. While the state law has been amended to allow self-service for motorcyclists and in some rural parts of the state (with populations of 40,000 or less), in Portland and much of the western part of the state you are still not allowed to pump your own gas; if you try to do so, you could get smacked with a pretty hefty fine.

TIPPING

While always a hotly debated issue, tipping is customary in Portland. For services such as haircuts, manicures, pedicures, and massages, 15-20 percent is acceptable, or 25 percent if extra services or special attention are given. Ten percent or less is appropriate if the services are poor.

Servers in Portland make minimum wage but pay taxes on their tips and must oftentimes share them at the end of the night with kitchen staff, busers, and dishwashers. About 20 percent is standard, or 15 percent if the service is underwhelming. Anything less than that can be construed as insulting, particularly if it is not accompanied by an explanation to the management or the server.

SMOKING

All Portland bars and restaurants are smoke-free. However, you can smoke tobacco 10 feet or more away from any building, which means most sidewalks, parks, and the waterfront are places where it is okay to light up. One notable exception, however, is Pioneer Courthouse Square. Smoking is not allowed on that entire block, and you will be asked to put it out or leave if you don't comply. As far as bars go, there are still places that have smoker-friendly patios and decks. Several bars have expansive patios with outdoor heaters, firepits, and covered seating. More than 50 restaurants and bars in the metro area have heated patios for smoking. If you want an updated list or details on the venues, check out the **Bar Fly** website (www.barflymag.com), which offers reviews and roundups of the bar scene.

Marijuana cannot be smoked in public places, including bars and restaurants.

CITY HOURS

While Portland might seem to be the antithesis of New York, the city isn't exactly sleeping when the sun goes down. If you intend to do some boutique shopping, you'll want to get it done early since most shops close around 6pm or 7pm. Shopping malls and department stores stay open only until 9pm, except during holidays, and most music stores and bookstores stay open until at least 10pm or 11pm. Bars and restaurants are usually bustling around this time, however, because Portlanders tend to be more interested in spending time together and sharing good food than working. The prime dinner hour is 7pm-8pm, but for particularly popular places, it is not uncommon to see a line forming when the venue opens around 5pm. For most venues, things stay busy until about an hour before last call, particularly on the weekends. Bars typically close at 2am.

Travel Tips

WHEN TO GO

Contrary to popular belief, it's not always raining in Portland. In fact, the metro area experiences less average rainfall per year than Atlanta, Birmingham, Houston, Indianapolis, or Seattle. Precipitation tends to come in the form of light drizzle rather than torrential downpour, so locals typically don't let it stop them from doing anything, and travelers may want to follow suit.

Summer (June-Sept.) is a great time to come experience the best of the city, with its open-air markets, gardens, and festivals, as temperatures tend to top out at 80-100°F (27-38°C) and days are often clear and dry. Ski season is often at its height between January and March. If you want to avoid the rainiest season, skip Portland in November, December, and January. But if you don't mind getting a little wet, those months are great times to secure cheap hotel rates and catch seasonal attractions like ZooLights and the festival of new theater works, Fertile Ground Festival.

MAPS AND TOURIST INFORMATION

The best place to find maps and get information on what's happening in and around Portland is at the Travel Portland Visitor Information Center (701 SW 6th Ave. at Morrison St., 503/275-8355, www.travelportland. com) in the center of downtown at Pioneer Courthouse Square. In addition to having a comprehensive calendar of local events, the center offers brochures, maps, and itinerary-planning assistance.

TRAVELING WITH CHILDREN

Portland is a great city for children, and the locals tend to take their kids everywhere they go, from gallery openings to dinners at four-star restaurants. If you would like to take your child along on one of the many art walks in the city, skip First Thursday in the Pearl, which caters more to the over-21 crowd and focuses more on the appreciation of art than it does on frivolity. Instead, opt for Last Thursday on Alberta, where the art tends to spill out onto the street, along with tall-bike riders, performers, stilt walkers, and impromptu parades.

The city is also chock-full of things to do with children that won't bore parents out of their skulls—like the **Oregon Museum of Science and Industry** (www.omsi.edu), the **Oregon Zoo** (www.oregonzoo.org), and the **World Forestry Center** (www.worldforestrycenter.org), which is more fun than the name implies. While you are here, check out **Metro Parent** (www.metro-parent.com) for an updated calendar of family events and tips on what the hottest kid-friendly places are.

SENIOR TRAVELERS

Portland is becoming a particularly popular place for people to retire because it offers the excitement and variety of city life but still retains a sense of small-town charm and security. Seniors also enjoy Portland because the streets, parks, buses, and trains make the city very navigable, which in turn encourages a healthy, active lifestyle that places very little demand on the individual.

TriMet tickets are only $1.25 for those 65 or older (with proof of age); an unlimited monthly pass goes for $28. Many of the local theaters and movie houses offer discounted rates and midweek matinees for seniors.

GAY AND LESBIAN TRAVELERS

Portland has a vibrant and active lesbian/gay/bisexual/transgender (LGBT) community and, in fact, has one of the most active lesbian communities in the United States. *Just Out* (www.justout.com) is the city's free weekly newspaper devoted to

the LGBT community, and it is a great resource for what's happening and where.

In mid-June, Portland celebrates the community with its annual Pride Festival, wherein people from all walks gather along the waterfront for food, drinks, entertainment, and one of the city's most colorful parades (second only to the Grand Floral Parade during the Rose Festival). All told, a number of festivals, arts organizations, and performance groups are particularly popular among the LGBT community. Along with Film Action Oregon, the Portland Lesbian & Gay Film Festival produces an annual showcase of feature, documentary, and short films that are made by, about, or for people in the LGBT community. Another big event, the annual **Red Dress Party** (www.reddresspdx.com), draws thousands of revelers (all of whom are required to wear a red dress) to party all night as a fundraiser for programs that support gay youth, as well as people living with HIV/AIDS and other serious diseases.

There is very little of Portland that is not gay-friendly, and while you won't find a nightlife scene that rivals that of New York or San Francisco, there are plenty of hot spots for lesbians and gay men, whether you prefer to dance all night or share a quiet, romantic meal. A good resource is the **Gay Yellow Pages** (www.pdxgayyellowpages.com), which catalogs gay-owned or gay-friendly restaurants, bars, businesses, and services.

ACCESS FOR TRAVELERS WITH DISABILITIES

Particularly in the former industrial areas, like Old Town and the Pearl

District, Portland has not always been the most accessible city, but things are improving at a rapid pace. The TriMet system is very accessible, with seating, ramps, and lifts on all buses and MAX trains; braille signage at all MAX stations; and ticket machines with both audio and visual instructions. TriMet also has a special service called **LIFT** (503/802-8000), which offers prearranged public transportation service for people who are unable to use buses or MAX due to a disability or disabling health condition. The cost is comparable to that of the regular transit fares.

One way to know if a place is accessible before you go is to check **Where's Lulu** (www.whereslulu.com), a free online database where Portlanders can rate and review places based on their services and accessibility. If you want to know whether or not Bagdad Theater & Pub has wheelchair-friendly tables (it does), you can find out using the search engine. The website also filters for criteria such as whether nearby public transit options exist, whether braille signs are present, and whether aisles and hallways are wide and easy to pass through.

TRAVELING WITH PETS

Many downtown hotels have in-house pet-relations managers and will accommodate your pet at no additional charge. Along with your regular accommodations, some provide food bowls, pet beds, water, treats, and toys for use during your stay, but you can also go all out and book a pet pampering package that includes massage and keepsake gifts.

COMMUNICATIONS AND MEDIA

INTERNET SERVICES

Thanks to the **Personal Telco Project's initiative** (www.personaltelco.net) to provide free Internet access to the city, virtually all of downtown Portland has free Wi-Fi access. You can check the Personal Telco page or **WiFi PDX** (www.wifipdx.com) to find where the hotspots are. Pioneer Courthouse Square is a great spot to pick up free access, and, if you don't mind sitting on a bench or the steps, there are a number of places where you can grab a seat. Another hotspot is in the South Park Blocks, where you can hunker down in the shade or grab a bench. You can always find access at one of the many local coffee shops and at some of the chain coffee stores.

MAIL AND MESSENGER SERVICES

Most downtown hotels offer mail services, but if you need a post office, you can find branches **downtown** (1505 SW 6th Ave.), in the **Pearl District** (715 NW Hoyt St.), and in **Northeast Portland** (815 NE Schuyler St.), just to name a few.

If you need courier service, you have a number of options. **Magpie Messenger Collective** (www.magpiemessenger.com) can deliver anywhere in the greater Portland area for $5-40, depending on distance and urgency. **Rose City Delivery Service** (www.rosecitymessengersvc.com) is another great option. It is a family-owned local business that hires the highest number of women of any company of its kind. The employees are friendly, well informed, and prompt.

Have fun with your pets in Portland.

Traveling with your pooch is easier than you think. Walk down the sidewalk of any Portland neighborhood and one thing is certain: Portlanders love their dogs. Dogs have been unofficially welcomed at restaurant patios and sidewalk cafés for years, but lately, some establishments are taking the needs of their canine customers very seriously.

DOG-FRIENDLY PARKS
When your dogs need to stretch their legs, there are plenty of parks for them to run around and mingle with other dogs. According to Portland Parks & Recreation, however, there are areas for off-leash playtime in 32 Portland parks. Some of the most popular off-leash areas are in **Gabriel Park** (SW 45th and Vermont), **Normandale Park** (NE 57th and Halsey), and **Chimney Park** (9360 N. Columbia Blvd.).

Come summertime in the **North and South Park Blocks** (page 21) and the Pearl District, you will find welcoming bowls of water set near entryways and sidewalk cafés. Frequenters of the Saturday Portland Farmers Market and Portland State University dog owners also appreciate **Shemanski Fountain** (between SW Salmon and Main), a triangular sandstone structure that features three small drinking basins, placed low so that passing dogs can quench their thirst.

RADIO AND TELEVISION
Talk Radio
Portlanders are big fans of National Public Radio's Oregon station, **OPB** (91.5 FM). One of the popular local shows is *LiveWire!*, a one-hour radio variety show recorded in front of a live audience that includes witty speakers, musical performances, and readings. It airs weekly at 7pm.

For talk radio, there's locally owned **KBOO** (90.7 FM), a volunteer-powered, noncommercial, listener-sponsored, full-strength community radio that emphasizes cultural awareness and the arts. On the AM dial, there's **KEX** (1190 AM), a news radio station that airs a number of syndicated shows from the likes of Rush Limbaugh, Dr. Laura Schlessinger, Mike Huckabee, and Dave Ramsey. **KXL Radio** (750 AM) airs the syndicated shows of Bill O'Reilly, Michael Savage, Brian Berger, and Bob Brinker, as well as the locally produced, nationally syndicated show by talk host Lars Larson. **KPAM** (860 AM) is another popular talk radio program that has garnered awards for breaking news coverage, traffic reporting, sports, and overall excellence.

DOG-FRIENDLY EATERIES

Wherever you go, there are many options for bringing your pooch out, especially in the warmer months when many restaurants have open patios. Some restaurants have special items on their menu like in-house baked cookies and cupcakes just for pooches, such as **Cupcake Jones** (page 62) which has a doggy cupcake. Pups (and cats!) love the sweet treats, made fresh daily using oats, nuts, and bananas. **Tin Shed Garden Café** (1438 NE Alberta, 503/288-6966, www.tinshedgardencafe.com) offers a special doggie menu with whimsical items made to order for your best friend.

DOG-FRIENDLY BARS

If you ask most dog owners about their favorite dog-friendly establishments, chances are **Lucky Labrador** (page 106) is at the top of the list. With four area locations, the Lucky Lab brewpubs cater to dog owners' desires to enjoy a pint on the covered patio while spending time with their favorite pooch. Or, you can sip some coffee, wine, or beer at the café inside **Sniff Hotel** (1828 NW Raleigh St., 503/208-2366, www.sniffdoghotel.com), which offers free doggy day care five days a week during its happy hour.

DOG-FRIENDLY HOTELS

When it's time to check in, numerous hotels will roll out the welcome mat for your four-legged friend. **Hotel Rose** (page 195) proclaims itself "dog-obsessed" and happily provides you with special amenities for your pooch like a bed, water bowl, and treats. Each room comes with a stuffed puppy you can opt to purchase, the proceeds of which go toward animal rescue charities. **Hotel deLuxe** (page 197) charges a small fee per day but stocks your room with food and water bowls, a pet bed, a squeaky toy, a bag of treats, and clean-up baggies. Upon check-in, you will also find a personalized note, addressed to your pooch, that outlines the hotel pet policy, offers up a list of things to do that are pet-friendly nearby, and best of all, includes a pet-focused room service menu.

The elegant **Benson Hotel** (page 196) offers a roof overhead for dogs of any size for no extra fee. Call ahead to book, and make sure you advise them that you will be bringing your pet. Your dog will be accommodated with a foam pet bed, collapsible water dish, squeaky toy, and a rawhide chew bone upon arrival. At **The Sentinel** (page 199) your pet will be greeted with a bed and goodie bag, and you will even receive a comprehensive list of pet resources for things you might actually need while visiting, like groomers, dog walkers, veterinarians, and even some crazy-out-there things like pet acupuncturists and psychics.

Another hotel that gets attention for being pet-friendly is the **Hotel Monaco** (page 198) a Kimpton hotel. Dogs are treated like royalty to the extent you allow (and are willing to pay for). You will be greeted with complimentary amenities such as treats, food bowls, water, a mat, a bed, and clean-up bags; you can also set up dog-walking service, pet massage, veterinary services, and grooming.

KPAM has a decidedly conservative propensity and airs popular programs like that of Sean Hannity and local right-wing commentator Victoria Taft. Another noteworthy station is **KPOJ** (620 AM), which was the first Air America affiliate to be owned by Clear Channel Communications. It features non-Air America syndicated host Ed Schultz. Through Schultz, KPOJ was the first station to call its format "progressive talk," a tag that is often used to describe that particular type of liberal-leaning program. Finally, if you're looking for sports, turn to **KXTG** (95.5 FM), an all-sports radio station owned by Paul Allen, who also owns the Portland Trail Blazers.

Music Stations

For classic rock, Portlanders turn to **KGON** (92.3 FM). For a mix of modern and classic rock, go to **KUFO** (101.1 FM), where you will find shock jocks on Wednesdays and head-banging music all day. For alternative rock, the favorite is **KNRK** (94.7 FM), which plays a lot of local musicians, in addition to indie rock and favorites from the 1990s. You can find top 40 hits on **KKRZ** (100.3 FM) and on **The Buzz** (105.1 FM). You'll find acoustic rock, pop, blues, and folk on **KINK** (101.9 FM). There's soul, blues, and rap on **KXJM** (107.5 FM), soft rock on **KKCW** (103.1 FM), and oldies on **KLTH** (106.7 FM). For country music, you can turn to **KUPL** (98.7 FM) and **KWJJ** (95.5 FM); for classical music, turn to **KQAC** (89.9 FM), as well as a number of the aforementioned talk radio stations.

Health and Safety

HOSPITALS AND PHARMACIES

Portland is home to **Oregon Health and Sciences University** (OHSU), which has been recognized several times over by *U.S. News and World Report* as one of the best hospitals in the world and is considered one of the top research and teaching facilities in the United States. OHSU is the place where Gleevec, an anti-cancer medication, was discovered and developed.

This is also the home of **Doernbecher Children's Hospital**, which provides the region's widest range of children's health-care services, serves as the primary center for OHSU pediatric programs, and boasts a kids-only emergency room with a specialized pediatric staff. OHSU and Doernbecher reside in Portland's west hills (affectionately known as Pill Hill) and are easily accessible by car, bus, or aerial tram.

Other notable hospitals in the area are **Legacy Health System** (www.legacyhealth.org) and **Providence** (www.providence.org), both of which have a number of hospitals and clinics around the Portland metro area.

If you have a pet emergency, there's no better place to take your pet than **DoveLewis** (www.dovelewis.org), a clinic that employs board-certified critical care specialists who provide emergency care, observation, and treatment. The clinic is fully equipped and staffed to provide state-of-the-art intensive care medicine around the clock.

You can pick up prescriptions at a number of grocery stores, such as **Safeway** (www.safeway.com) and **Fred Meyer** (www.fredmeyer.com), as well as at drugstores like **Rite Aid** (www.riteaid.com) and **Walgreens** (www.walgreens.com).

EMERGENCY SERVICES

In the case of an emergency, you can reach a dispatcher for police, fire and rescue, and paramedic services by dialing **911** from any phone. To reach the Portland Police Department's nonemergency line, call 503/823-3333.

CRIME AND HARASSMENT

Thanks to the number of walkable streets in Portland, it is relatively safe to be out, even at night, so long as you keep alert and stay in areas where people are congregating.

Of course, every city has crime, but for the most part Portland's rate is relatively low and seems to be centered in outer Northeast, Southeast, and

North Portland (close to the airport and Vancouver, Washington). With the growth of neighborhoods like Mississippi Avenue and the area surrounding the Wonder Ballroom on NE Russell Street, crime has largely been pushed out by the bustling crowds.

In the heart of downtown and on a number of the well-trafficked streets, you will find a lot of homeless people, but they are generally nonconfrontational. If you feel you're in danger, call 911. If you find someone to be of concern, call the **Downtown Clean & Safe Patrol Officers** (503/224-7383), who are very good at dealing with public drunkenness, disorderly behavior, and aggressive street youth.

RESOURCES

Suggested Reading

HISTORY AND GENERAL INFORMATION

Barrett, Alexander. *This Is Portland: The City You've Heard You Should Like.* Portland: Microcosm, 2013. Written by a Vermont transplant to the City of Roses, *This Is Portland* is a commentary on getting to know the oddity that is P-Town. The affectionately critical Barrett explains why you will find so many bars with tater tots. He tells readers whether or not it really rains all the time and explains what the deal is with all the beer, beards, bikes, tattoos, strip clubs, and yard chickens. Regarding the rain, he writes, "Portland is full of cool people. Raincoats are not cool. How do cool people stay cool in the rain? They get really wet, that's how."

Boehmer, Gabriel. *City of Readers: A Book Lover's Guide to Portland.* Portland: Tall Grass Press, 2007. *City of Readers* is a "literary umbrella" that encompasses all things loved and adored by Portland's literati, such as bookstores, libraries, landmarks, lectures, authors, and titles. A self-proclaimed bookworm who got married at Central Library in downtown Portland, Boehmer has compiled a comprehensive directory of the city's bookstores and provides excellent chapters on the authors and titles that have defined the city and the best places to find solitude among many (in other words, great places to read). Borrowing its title from the city's monolithic bookseller, Powell's City of Books, the guide is a love letter to a city where book lovers can read with relish and share with enthusiasm.

Granton, Shawn, and Nate Beaty. *The Zinester's Guide to Portland: A Low/No Budget Guide to Visiting and Living in Portland, Oregon.* Portland: Microcosm, 2014. This locally produced biannual book targets anyone who is looking to experience Portland on the cheap or discover those sometimes hidden gems and hard-to-find happenings. It offers a glimpse into the city's history and local lore, offering up a guide to low- to no-cost bars, bookstores, coffeehouses, restaurants, record stores, video stores, thrift stores, performing arts spaces, and more. Their way is not simply to tell you where you should go but why you want to, and give you the story behind the story whenever possible. The book is illustrated with fantastic line drawings of P-Town landmarks as depicted by the authors and some other notable local artists. It's broken down by the five main P-Town quadrants and the outer neighborhoods, like St. Johns, Kenton, and Sellwood, and also includes a section that will help the reader navigate the city's bus system and bike culture with aplomb.

Lansing, Jewel. *Portland: People, Politics, and Power, 1851-2001*. Corvallis: Oregon State University Press, 2005. This ambitious work covers more than 150 years of Portland's political and economic past, from the days when the excessive logging of a new city in the Pacific Northwest earned it the nickname Stumptown to the 21st century and the bustling, progressive city that we know today (but still occasionally call Stumptown). Lansing served as an elected city auditor, so she knows all too well how the city government works. Lansing's well-researched and lively book gives an insightful account of the mayors of our past, from ambitious Hugh O'Bryant, the city's first mayor, to the savvy and persuasive Vera Katz. Lansing highlights the political, business, and cultural forces that have shaped the city—once a hotbed of corruption and vice—into the cultural metropolis we know today.

Shomler, Steven. *Portland Beer Stories*. Mount Pleasant: Arcadia Publishing, 2015. Portland is a haven for beer lovers, and the men and women who have put the city and the state of Oregon on the map for making some of the world's best beer have some interesting stories. Using his intimate connection to the industry, Shomler takes readers behind the scenes of the process with anecdotes about everything from how popular breweries got started to the life of a beer delivery driver. Shomler is a radio host and organizer for the Spring Beer and Wine Festival, who also wrote a book that gets into the

heads of some of Portland's smallest, most popular businesses, the food carts. It is, not surprisingly, titled *Portland Food Cart Stories.*

Stanford, Phil. *Portland Confidential: Sex, Crime, and Corruption in the Rose City*. Portland: Westwinds Press, 2004. It's no secret that Portland has a few skeletons in its historical closet, and this account of the city's colorful past takes you right into the dark and mysterious heart of it all. Written by former *Portland Tribune* columnist Phil Stanford, the book shows us the Portland of bygone days when prostitution, gambling, and drug running were de rigueur. By the 1950s, underworld kingpin James "Big Jim" Elkins was ruling over the city's vice industry, and just happened to have most of the police force and the local political movers and shakers on his payroll. Loaded with photographs and newspaper clippings of the time, Stanford's book seeks to expose our dirtiest little secrets and show its readers the landmarks that still stand where it all went down.

FICTION AND MEMOIRS

Meloy, Colin. *Wildwood*. New York: Balzar + Bray, 2011. Decemberists front man Colin Meloy has long been known for his creative lyrics and storytelling songs. When Meloy set out to write a novel, he took those same skills and turned his eyes to dark passages of Portland's own Forest Park. He created a whole series of novels about the wonders found within those trees, and the city of Portland plays a strong role in the books.

Palahniuk, Chuck. *Fugitives and Refugees: A Walk in Portland, Oregon.* New York: Crown Publishing, 2011. This book from the author of the best-selling novel *Fight Club* is part travelogue and part memoir as the author reveals some of the city's most interesting (and sometimes terribly unattractive) landmarks, historical moments, and bits of culture. Go behind the doors of sex clubs; learn about the annual rampage of Santas; find out where you can mingle with the dead; and discover the not-so-secret location of Palahniuk's tonsils.

Sampsell, Kevin. *Portland Noir.* New York: Akashic Noir, 2009. A series of short stories from some of the Pacific Northwest's most exceptional writers, *Portland Noir* takes the reader through the underbelly of the Rose City, with stops at the Shanghai Tunnels, Powell's City of Books, Pirate's Cove, Voodoo Doughnut, and many other all-too-familiar places for local readers. This book is a dirty, pretty depiction of the weird, wonderful world otherwise known as the City of Roses. With funny anecdotes of petty mischief, haunting tales of tragedy, and mysterious stories of violence, it's a deliciously dark read.

Vlautin, Willy. *Lean on Pete.* New York: Harper Perennial, 2010. This heartbreaking and beautiful novel from Portland musician and author Willy Vlautin is about a 15-year-old boy who lives and works at a run-down horseracing track in Portland. After he befriends a beat-up old horse named Lean on Pete, the story takes on the rich, mysterious, multilayered tone that made Vlautin such a popular writer and lyricist among his peers.

Internet Resources

INFORMATION AND EVENTS

City of Portland
www.portlandonline.com
This is the official website for the city of Portland, with links to information on current city and state politics, top news stories, and visitor information. Here you will find maps, calendars, and facts about public transportation, city planning, and city services.

Eventful
www.eventful.com/portland
Eventful enables its community of users to discover, promote, share, and create events such as concerts, markets, store openings, political rallies, fundraisers, sporting events, readings, and more.

Geek Portland
www.geekportland.com
This up-to-date and reliable calendar has the dish on all geek-related events happening in and around Portland, from trivia nights to shows and book signings to burlesque.

Oregon Beat
www.oregonbeat.com
Oregon Beat is a weekly calendar with links to exhibits, lectures, festivals, sporting events, tours, performing arts

events, gallery showings, and special food and wine affairs.

PDX Pipeline
www.pdxpipeline.com
PDX Pipeline is a word-of-mouth-fueled website that has up-to-date listings for concerts, festivals, fundraisers, restaurant events, and gallery showings. It does regular promotions through social media and provides links to a number of the city's most popular venues.

Travel Portland
www.travelportland.org
Travel Portland is the city's official visitors association and has a comprehensive website with an events calendar, resources, special offers, historical accounts, and in-depth profiles on what makes the city great. You can also visit the association in person at Pioneer Courthouse Square (503/275-8355), where you can pick up the annual *Travel Portland* magazine, an insider's guide to the city.

NEWS

Just Out
www.justout.com
Just Out is Portland's life and culture biweekly newspaper serving the LGBT community. It has a small web presence and distributes in a number of bars, restaurants, and coffeehouses, as well as in free distribution boxes all over the city.

The Oregonian
www.oregonlive.com
Portland's oldest newspaper is available at newsstands as well as online, with extensive "real-time" news coverage and in-depth reports on sports, entertainment, and local

culture. It publishes a weekly Arts and Entertainment guide on Friday.

Portland Mercury
www.portlandmercury.com
This popular biweekly source for the dish on news, music, art, theater, fashion, and food has an active web presence with a tongue-in-cheek style. You can find print copies of the *Mercury* in white boxes around the city.

Portland Monthly
www.portlandmonthlymag.com
This monthly full-color glossy lifestyle magazine focuses on news and general interests. On the website, you can catch the first few paragraphs of the articles from the most current issue and find comprehensive listings on restaurants, theaters, shops, and galleries.

Portland Tribune
www.portlandtribune.com
The *Tribune* is a free weekly publication published each Thursday and distributed in green boxes on street corners scattered around town. It's best known for its coverage of issues local to Portland and the state of Oregon, as well as its extensive coverage of local high school, college, and professional sports teams, with concentration on the NBA, Pac-10, Big Sky Conference, and West Coast Conference.

Willamette Week
www.wweek.com
The *Willamette Week* is a free alternative weekly that provides savvy, sometimes sardonic coverage of local news, politics, and culture. The website provides extended coverage of the articles that appear in print and offers updated stories, reviews, listings,

calendars, and classifieds. Print copies can be picked up in blue boxes and coffee shops, bars, and restaurants all over the city.

BLOGS

Art Scatter
www.artscatter.com

This blog is an assemblage of articles, essays, and musings about art, storytelling, the performing arts, and life around Portland. The entries come from some of the most educated and innovative minds in the industry, and while it occasionally dips into sessions of navel-gazing, it is still quite a beautiful read.

Beervana
www.beervana.blogspot.com

Beervana (a mash-up of "beer" and "nirvana" and sometimes a nickname for Portland) is a blog devoted to all things beer in Portland and the entire state of Oregon. It's a good resource for information on breweries, bottles, and festivals in a state where beer is taken quite seriously.

Bike Portland
www.bikeportland.org

Bike Portland is an independent, daily news source for Portland's many bike enthusiasts. In addition to posting regular articles about new business, bike-related events, and thought-provoking ideas about a life on wheels, Bike Portland provides the most up-to-date bike-related news, including updates about the accidents that occasionally happen.

Culturephile
www.portlandmonthlymag.com/tags/culturephile

Lisa Randon spent five years running the Ultra PDX blog (www.ultrapdx.com), which showcased art, fashion, music, performance, visual arts, and dance; as the associate editor of *Portland Spaces* magazine, Randon has the pedigree to be called an expert in the field. In August 2009, she started Culturephile, which "chronicles the vibrant world of Portland arts, its movers and makers," and the site is already proving to be a very viable voice on the scene.

Dave Knows Portland
www.portland.daveknows.org

A native Portlander and lover of beer, soccer, basketball, books, pinball, and other such things, Dave maintains a blog that is especially helpful for information on Portland sports (such as Timbers soccer and the Trail Blazers) and any festival that involves beer.

Eater Portland
www.pdx.eater.com

Eater is a nationwide blog with sites devoted to several major cities, and the Portland one is really tuned in to the scene. It's a good resource for news about the food scene in the city, featuring reviews, interviews, "best of" lists, and updates about new restaurant openings and chefs on the move.

Food Carts Portland
www.foodcartsportland.com

This blog is a virtual guidebook on where to find the best food carts and what to eat once you get there. The blog is easily navigated with categories by cuisine type and specific locations, and it provides frequently updated listings of carts with a map to guide you.

Geek in the City
www.geekinthecity.com

Self-proclaimed geek Aaron Duran

rants about all things geeky, dweeby, nerdy, and cool, such as games, comics, movies, music, and pop culture. His website features a geek-centric calendar with links to comic book releases, movie premieres, game nights, and shows. Duran is a freelance writer and media producer who is a regular guest on various Portland radio programs.

PDX Plate
www.pdxplate.com

This gastronomical adventure of a site is both knowledgeable and well-traveled around this fair city. It was gutsy enough to compile a list of 100 things that are must-eats for Portland, and it regularly puts together useful lists on topics such as great late-night dining, recession-proof drinking, and eating local.

Pechluck's Food Adventures
www.pechluck.com

Pechluck Laskey (or Pech, as she is more commonly known) is a popular Portland food blogger in part because of her readability, but also because of her impeccable research and knowledge of the food industry. She is well-respected by the Portland food media and has even been featured in a number of local publications.

Portland Food and Drink
www.portlandfoodanddrink.com

This restaurant review site was born out of a frustration that many venues were receiving overly glowing and not entirely honest reviews. The site rates restaurants on a star system after visiting no fewer than three times. It also has a menu section, where you can view the menus of more than 100 restaurants and bars.

Silicon Florist
www.siliconflorist.com

This blog highlights the websites and startups in the Portland area that might otherwise be missed amid the mighty giants of the Silicon Forest (thus the references to flowers, not trees). Founder Rick Turoczy enthusiastically gives readers news and events straight out of the city's blossoming tech scene.

Urban Honking
www.urbanhonking.com

Urban Honking is a Portland-based hub of more than 80 active bloggers who post articles about everything from writing and visual art to music to movies. UrHo (as it is affectionately called) began as a web magazine and then exploded as its web presence and readership grew. The site now hosts an annual competition, The Ultimate Blogger, which is inspired by reality TV contests, wherein participants engage in challenges and then post the results in their individual blogs.

HISTORY

Kicka** Oregon History
www.orhistory.com

This website is young, hip, and not at all afraid to be a bit brash in its telling of history. It posts regular podcasts and even has frequent events like history-based pub crawls, lectures, and film contests.

Lewis and Clark Trail
www.lewisandclarktrail.com

This comprehensive website details the historic trip that explorers Meriwether Lewis and William Clark made from Pennsylvania to the Pacific Ocean. You can read quotes from their journals about their first glimpse of

Portland and see what remains of their stay in this area.

society's archival collection to tell the story of Oregon.

Oregon Historical Society
www.ohs.org

The Oregon Historical Society (which is also a museum) has studies on its website that offer insight into the history of Portland and the state of Oregon, like the Oregon History Project, which explores the history of the state through the perspectives of the people who helped shape it, and Timeweb, an interactive timeline that uses over 800 records from the

Portland History
www.pdxhistory.com

Portland History is a scrapbook of the past, with vintage postcards and pictures of the city from the earliest days, when pioneers began to make their homes here. You can find pictures of Portland's streetcars of the 1870s, when they were powered by horse, and a number of hotels that were open at the turn of the 20th century that are still in operation today.

Index

Restaurants Index

Nightlife Index

Shops Index

Hotels Index

Photo Credits

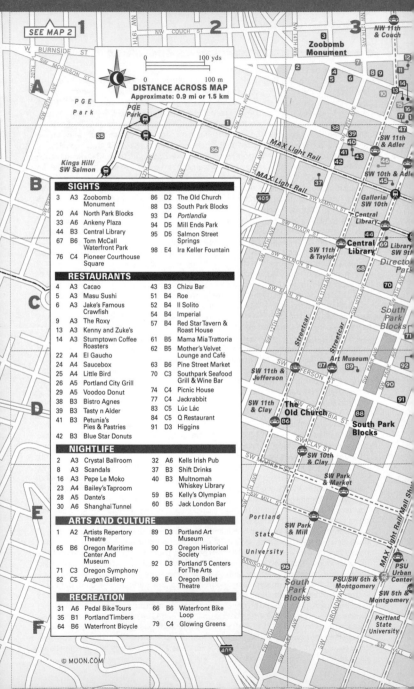

SEE MAP 2

W. BURNSIDE ST
SW MORRISON ST

PGE Park

0   100 yds
0   100 m
DISTANCE ACROSS MAP
Approximate: 0.9 mi or 1.5 km

PGE Park

Kings Hill/
SW Salmon

NW 11th & Couch

Zoobomb Monument

NW 11th & Couch

MAX Light Rail
MAX Light Rail

SW 11th & Adler
SW 10th & Adler

Galleria/SW 10th
Central Library

SW 11th & Taylor

Central Library

Library SW 9th
Directo Park

SW 11th & Jefferson

Art Museum

South Park Blocks

SW 11th & Clay

The Old Church

South Park Blocks

SW 10th & Clay

SW Park & Market

SW Park & Mill

Portland State University

SW Park & Mill

MAX Light Rail/Mall Sh

PSU Urban Center

PSU/SW 6th & Montgomery

SW 5th & Montgomery

Portland State University

SIGHTS
3	A3	Zoobomb Monument
20	A4	North Park Blocks
33	A6	Ankeny Plaza
44	B3	Central Library
67	B6	Tom McCall Waterfront Park
76	C4	Pioneer Courthouse Square
86	D2	The Old Church
88	D3	South Park Blocks
93	D4	*Portlandia*
94	D5	Mill Ends Park
95	D5	Salmon Street Springs
98	E4	Ira Keller Fountain

RESTAURANTS
4	A3	Cacao
5	A3	Masu Sushi
6	A3	Jake's Famous Crawfish
9	A3	The Roxy
13	A3	Kenny and Zuke's
14	A3	Stumptown Coffee Roasters
22	A4	El Gaucho
24	A4	Saucebox
25	A4	Little Bird
26	A5	Portland City Grill
29	A5	Voodoo Donut
38	B3	Bistro Agnes
39	B3	Tasty n Alder
41	B3	Petunia's Pies & Pastries
42	B3	Blue Star Donuts
43	B3	Chizu Bar
51	B4	Roe
52	B4	Il Solito
54	B4	Imperial
57	B4	Red Star Tavern & Roast House
61	B5	Mama Mia Trattoria
62	B5	Mother's Velvet Lounge and Café
63	B6	Pine Street Market
70	C3	Southpark Seafood Grill & Wine Bar
74	C4	Picnic House
77	C4	Jackrabbit
83	C5	Lúc Lác
84	C5	Q Restaurant
91	D3	Higgins

NIGHTLIFE
2	A3	Crystal Ballroom
8	A3	Scandals
16	A3	Pepe Le Moko
23	A4	Bailey's Taproom
28	A5	Dante's
30	A6	Shanghai Tunnel
32	A6	Kells Irish Pub
37	B3	Shift Drinks
40	B3	Multnomah Whiskey Library
59	B5	Kelly's Olympian
60	B5	Jack London Bar

ARTS AND CULTURE
1	A2	Artists Repertory Theatre
65	B6	Oregon Maritime Center And Museum
71	C3	Oregon Symphony
82	C5	Augen Gallery
89	D3	Portland Art Museum
90	D3	Oregon Historical Society
92	D3	Portland'5 Centers For The Arts
99	E4	Oregon Ballet Theatre

RECREATION
31	A6	Pedal Bike Tours
35	B1	Portland Timbers
64	B6	Waterfront Bicycle
66	B6	Waterfront Bike Loop
79	C4	Glowing Greens

© MOON.COM

SEE MAP 2

SEE MAP 3

SEE MAP 4

SHOPS

11	A3	Union Way	49	B4	underU4men
12	A3	Danner	68	C3	Urban Fauna
17	A3	Frances May	69	C3	Crafty Wonderland
18	A3	Rebels and Heroes	73	C4	John Helmer Haberdashery
19	A4	Tender Loving Empire	75	C4	Mario's
34	A6	Portland Saturday Market	81	C5	Pioneer Place Mall
			87	D3	Canoe
45	B3	Boy's Fort	96	E2	Portland Farmers Market at Portland State University
47	B3	Adorn			
48	B4	Finnegan's Toys & Gifts			

HOTELS

7	A3	Crystal Hotel	56	B4	Hotel Monaco
10	A3	The Mark Spencer Hotel	58	B5	Courtyard by Marriott Portland City Center
15	A3	Ace Hotel	72	C4	Heathman Hotel
21	A4	The Benson Hotel	78	C4	The Duniway
27	A5	Embassy Suites Portland Downtown	80	C4	The Nines
36	B2	Hotel deLuxe	85	C5	Hotel Rose
46	B3	The Sentinel	97	E4	Hotel Modera
50	B4	Dossier Hotel	100	E4	The Porter Hotel
53	B4	Hotel Vintage Portland	101	F5	The RiverPlace Hotel
55	B4	Hotel Lucia			

MAP 2

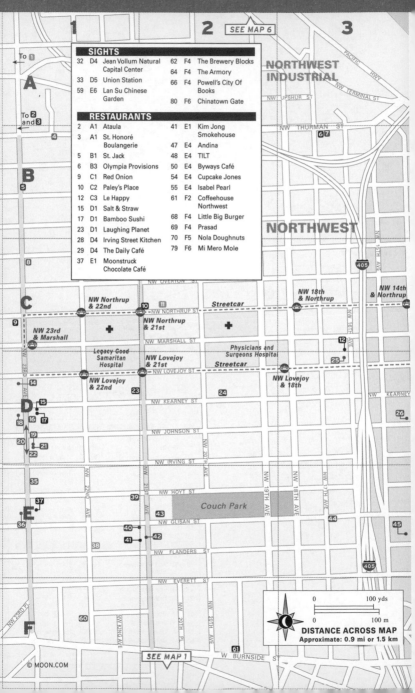

SEE MAP 6

NORTHWEST INDUSTRIAL

NORTHWEST

SIGHTS

32	D4	Jean Vollum Natural Capital Center
33	D5	Union Station
59	E6	Lan Su Chinese Garden
62	F4	The Brewery Blocks
64	F4	The Armory
66	F4	Powell's City Of Books
80	F6	Chinatown Gate

RESTAURANTS

2	A1	Ataula
3	A1	St. Honoré Boulangerie
5	B1	St. Jack
6	B3	Olympia Provisions
9	C1	Red Onion
10	C2	Paley's Place
12	C3	Le Happy
15	D1	Salt & Straw
17	D1	Bamboo Sushi
23	D1	Laughing Planet
28	D4	Irving Street Kitchen
29	D4	The Daily Café
37	E1	Moonstruck Chocolate Café
41	E1	Kim Jong Smokehouse
47	E4	Andina
48	E4	TILT
50	E4	Byways Café
54	E4	Cupcake Jones
55	E4	Isabel Pearl
61	F2	Coffeehouse Northwest
68	F4	Little Big Burger
69	F4	Prasad
70	F5	Nola Doughnuts
79	F6	Mi Mero Mole

NW Northrup & 22nd

NW Northrup & 21st

Streetcar

NW 18th & Northrup

NW 14th & Northrup

NW 23rd & Marshall

Legacy Good Samaritan Hospital

NW Lovejoy & 21st

Physicians and Surgeons Hospital

Streetcar

NW Lovejoy & 22nd

NW Lovejoy & 18th

Couch Park

SEE MAP 1

W BURNSINE ST

0   100 yds

0   100 m

DISTANCE ACROSS MAP
Approximate: 0.9 mi or 1.5 km

© MOON.COM

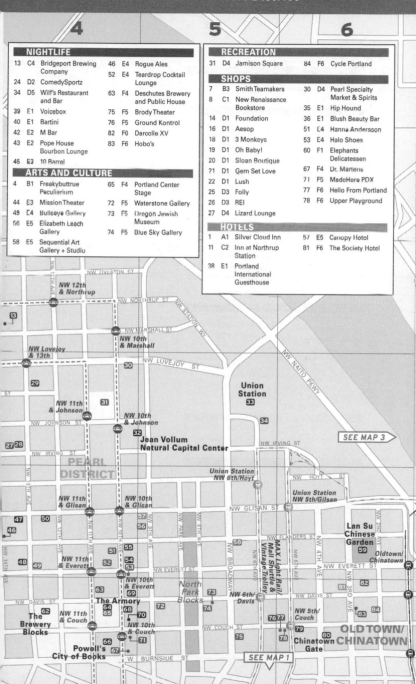

4   **5**   **6**

NIGHTLIFE
13	C4	Bridgeport Brewing Company
24	D2	ComedySportz
34	D5	Wilf's Restaurant and Bar
39	E1	Voicebox
40	E1	Bartini
42	E2	M Bar
43	E2	Pope House Bourbon Lounge
45	E3	10 Barrel
46	E4	Rogue Ales
52	E4	Teardrop Cocktail Lounge
63	F4	Deschutes Brewery and Public House
75	F5	Brody Theater
76	F5	Ground Kontrol
82	F6	Darcelle XV
83	F6	Hobo's

ARTS AND CULTURE
4	B1	Freakybuttrue Peculiarium
44	E3	Mission Theater
49	C4	Bullseye Gallery
56	E5	Elizabeth Leach Gallery
58	E5	Sequential Art Gallery + Studio
65	F4	Portland Center Stage
72	F5	Waterstone Gallery
73	F5	Oregon Jewish Museum
74	F5	Blue Sky Gallery

RECREATION
| 31 | D4 | Jamison Square |

SHOPS
7	B3	Smith Teamakers
8	C1	New Renaissance Bookstore
14	D1	Foundation
16	D1	Aesop
18	D1	3 Monkeys
19	D1	Oh Baby!
20	D1	Sloan Boutique
21	D1	Gem Set Love
22	D1	Lush
25	D3	Folly
26	D3	REI
27	D4	Lizard Lounge
30	D4	Pearl Specialty Market & Spirits
35	E1	Hip Hound
36	E1	Blush Beauty Bar
51	E4	Hanna Andersson
53	E4	Halo Shoes
60	F1	Elephants Delicatessen
67	F4	Dr. Martens
71	F5	MadeHere PDX
77	F6	Hello From Portland
78	F6	Upper Playground
84	F6	Cycle Portland

HOTELS
1	A1	Silver Cloud Inn
11	C2	Inn at Northrup Station
38	E1	Portland International Guesthouse
57	E5	Canopy Hotel
81	F6	The Society Hotel

SEE MAP 6

SIGHTS

46	D5	Beverly Cleary Children's Sculpture Garden

RESTAURANTS

4	A3	PDX Dönerländ
5	A3	Oregon Public House
6	A4	Hat Yai
7	A5	D.O.C.
8	A5	Autentica
9	A5	Beast
14	B3	The Grilled Cheese Grill
16	B4	Swiss Hibiscus
17	B4	Pok Pok Noi
18	B4	Helser's on Alberta
20	A4	Aviary
21	B4	Zilla Saké House
23	B4	Petite Provence
24	B4	Pine State Biscuits
25	A4	Ciao Vito
26	B4	Gumba
27	B4	Fine Goose
30	A5	La Bonita
32	A5	Urdaneta
34	C3	Ned Ludd
35	C4	Verdigris
39	D3	Izakaya Kichinto
41	D3	Toro Bravo
53	E3	Frank's Noodle House
60	E5	Basilisk
65	F4	Pix Patisserie
66	F4	Screen Door
69	F4	Pie Spot
71	F5	Stammtisch
75	F5	Navarre
76	F5	Laurelhurst Market

NIGHTLIFE

2	A3	Curious Comedy
3	A3	Keys Lounge
33	B6	Spare Room
37	C6	Alameda Brewhouse
40	D3	Secret Society Lounge
42	D3	Wonder Ballroom
43	D3	Billy Ray's Neighborhood Bar
49	D6	Laurelwood Brewing Co.
54	E4	Swift Lounge
56	E5	Hale Pele
62	F3	Burnside Brewing Company
64	F3	Noble Rot
68	F4	Pairings
74	F5	Angel Face

ARTS AND CULTURE

10	A5	Kennedy School
13	B3	Portland Playhouse
29	B5	Antler Gallery
31	A5	Guardino Gallery
61	E6	Hollywood Theatre
73	F5	The Laurelhurst

RECREATION

12	B3	Everybody's Bikes
48	D5	Grant Park
50	E2	Portland Winterhawks
51	E3	Portland Trail Blazers

SHOPS

1	A2	Turn! Turn! Turn!
19	B4	Green Bean Books
22	B4	Grasshopper
28	A4	The Pencil Test
36	C6	Amenity Shoes
38	D3	The Title Wave Used Bookstore
47	D6	Popina Swimwear
55	E4	Well Suited
57	E5	Bella Stella
58	E5	Things From Another World
59	E5	Hollywood Vintage
63	F3	Redux
70	F4	Providore Fine Foods
72	F5	Polliwog

HOTELS

11	A5	Kennedy School
15	B3	Caravan: A Tiny House Hotel
44	D4	Lion and the Rose Victorian Bed & Breakfast Inn
45	D4	Portland's White House
52	E3	Hotel Eastlund
67	F4	Everett Street Guesthouse

DISTANCE ACROSS MAP
Approximate: 2.7 mi or 4.3 km

0   500 yds
0   500 m

© MOON.COM

SEE MAP 4

MAP 4

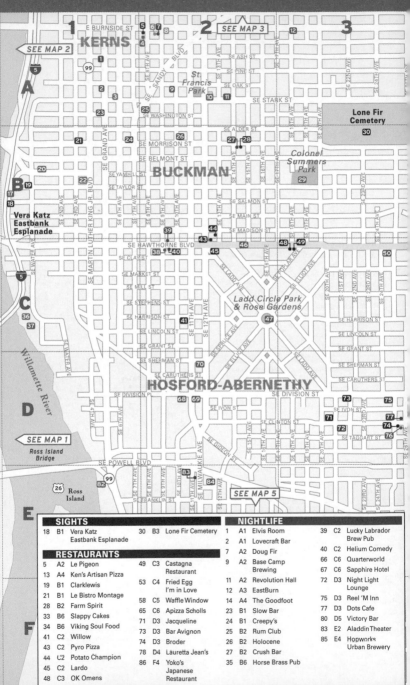

KERNS

SEE MAP 3

St. Francis Park

SEE MAP 2

BUCKMAN

Lone Fir Cemetery

Vera Katz Eastbank Esplanade

Colonel Summers Park

Ladd Circle Park & Rose Gardens

HOSFORD-ABERNETHY

Willamette River

SEE MAP 1

Ross Island Bridge

SEE MAP 5

Ross Island

SIGHTS					
18	B1	Vera Katz Eastbank Esplanade	30	B3	Lone Fir Cemetery

RESTAURANTS					
5	A2	Le Pigeon	49	C3	Castagna Restaurant
13	A4	Ken's Artisan Pizza	53	C4	Fried Egg I'm in Love
19	B1	Clarklewis	58	C5	Waffle Window
21	B1	Le Bistro Montage	65	C6	Apizza Scholls
28	B2	Farm Spirit	71	D3	Jacqueline
33	B6	Slappy Cakes	73	D3	Bar Avignon
34	B6	Viking Soul Food	74	D3	Broder
41	C2	Willow	78	D4	Lauretta Jean's
43	C2	Pyro Pizza	86	F4	Yoko's Japanese Restaurant
44	C2	Potato Champion			
45	C2	Lardo			
48	C3	OK Omens			

NIGHTLIFE					
1	A1	Elvis Room	39	C2	Lucky Labrador Brew Pub
2	A1	Lovecraft Bar	40	C2	Helium Comedy
7	A2	Doug Fir	66	C6	Quarterworld
9	A2	Base Camp Brewing	67	C6	Sapphire Hotel
11	A2	Revolution Hall	72	D3	Night Light Lounge
12	A3	EastBurn	75	D3	Reel 'M Inn
14	A4	The Goodfoot	77	D3	Dots Cafe
23	B1	Slow Bar	80	D5	Victory Bar
24	B1	Creepy's	83	E2	Aladdin Theater
25	B2	Rum Club	85	E4	Hopworks Urban Brewery
26	B2	Holocene			
27	B2	Crush Bar			
35	B6	Horse Brass Pub			

E BURNSIDE ST

LAURELHURST

Laurelhurst Park

SUNNYSIDE

SOUTHEAST

RICHMOND

Sewallcrest
Park

ARTS AND CULTURE		
3	A1	Milagro Theatre
4	A2	Third Rail Repertory Theatre
36	C1	Oregon Museum of Science and Industry
46	C2	Nucleus Portland
59	C5	Do Jump!
63	C5	Bagdad Theater & Pub
76	D3	Clinton Street Theater

RECREATION		
16	A5	Laurelhurst Park
17	B1	Vera Katz Eastbank Esplanade
29	B3	Colonel Summers Park
37	C1	Willamette Jetboat Excursions
38	C2	Clever Cycles
47	C2	Ladd Circle Park & Rose Gardens
70	D2	Pedalounge
82	E1	Springwater Corridor

SHOPS		
10	A2	Food Fight
15	A4	Music Millennium
20	B1	Cargo
22	B1	Guardian Games
31	B4	Naked City
32	B4	Noun: A Person's Place for Things
50	C3	Excalibur Books and Comics
54	C4	House of Vintage
55	C5	Imelda's and Louie's Shoes
56	C5	Kids at Heart
57	C5	Jackpot Records
60	C5	Presents of Mind
61	C5	Buffalo Exchange
62	C5	Memento
64	C5	Powell's Home and Garden
68	D2	Duchess Clothier
69	D2	Books with Pictures
84	E2	Edelweiss

HOTELS		
6	A2	Jupiter Hotel
8	A2	Jupiter Next
52	C4	Hawthorne Hostel
79	D5	Bluebird Guesthouse
81	D5	Evermore Guesthouse

© MOON.COM

DISTANCE ACROSS MAP
Approximate: 3.2 mi or 5.1 km

0   300 yds
0   300 m

SEE MAP 4

1

2

3

Oaks

Hardtack
Island

A

East
Island

SE HAROLD ST

SE ELLIS ST

SE REEDWAY ST

SE 15TH AVE

1

SE KNIGHT ST

SE YUKON ST

SE YUKON ST

SE MARTINS ST

SE CARLTON ST

SE TOLMAN ST

SE TOLMAN ST

SE 13TH AVE

SE HENRY ST

B

Bottom

Willamette River

Springwater Corridor Trail

SE DUKE ST

SE CLAYBOURNE ST

SE CLAYBOURNE ST

SE MILWAUKIE AVE

SE 18TH AVE

3

SE GLENWOOD ST

4

5

6

Wildlife

7

SE BYBEE BLVD

SE 14TH AVE

SE 17TH AVE

C

SE RURAL ST

SE OGDEN ST

SE KNAPP ST

SE KNAPP ST

SE FLAVEL ST

Oaks
Amusement Park

8

SE 11TH AVE

SE REX ST

**SELLWOOD
MORELAND**

Refuge

Oaks Bottom
Wildlife Refuge

9

SE OAKS PARK WAY

SE SELLWOOD BLVD

SE REX ST

SE MALDEN ST

SE MALDEN ST

D

10

SE LAMBERT ST

SE LAMBERT ST

Sellwood
Park

11

SE 13TH AVE

SE BIDWELL ST

SE BIDWELL ST

Sellwood
Riverfront Park

SE 7TH AVE

SE 11TH AVE

12

13

SE LEXINGTON ST

14

SE GRAND AVE

SE MILLER ST

E

15

SE NEHALEM ST

Oaks
Pioneer Park

SE 6TH AVE

SE 7TH AVE

SE 9TH AVE

16

SE SPOKANE ST

17

SE 15TH AVE

SE 16TH AVE

SE 17TH AVE

18

Sellwood
Bridge

SE TACOMA ST

19

SE TENINO ST

21

ARDENWALD

SE UMATILLA ST

20

SE HARNEY ST

F

© MOON.COM

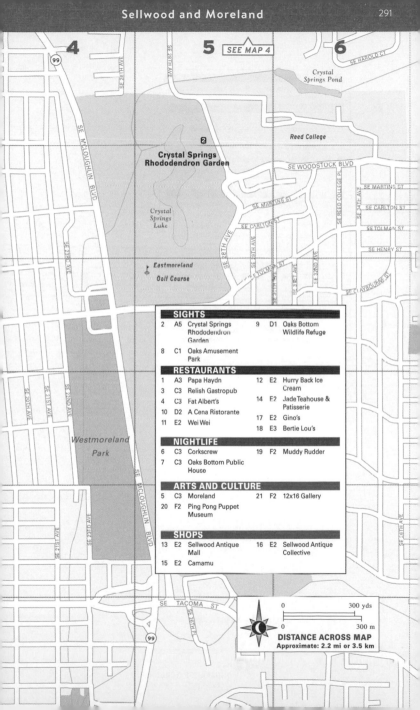

SE HAROLD CT

Crystal
Springs Pond

Reed College

SE WOODSTOCK BLVD

**Crystal Springs
Rhododendron Garden**

SE MARTINS ST

Crystal
Springs
Luke

SE CARLTON ST

SE TOLMAN ST

SE HENRY ST

Eastmoreland
Golf Course

SIGHTS

2	A5	Crystal Springs Rhododendron Garden	9	D1	Oaks Bottom Wildlife Refuge
8	C1	Oaks Amusement Park			

RESTAURANTS

1	A3	Papa Haydn	12	E2	Hurry Back Ice Cream
3	C3	Relish Gastropub	14	E2	Jade Teahouse & Patisserie
4	C3	Fat Albert's	17	E2	Gino's
10	D2	A Cena Ristorante	18	E3	Bertie Lou's
11	E2	Wei Wei			

NIGHTLIFE

6	C3	Corkscrew	19	F2	Muddy Rudder
7	C3	Oaks Bottom Public House			

ARTS AND CULTURE

5	C3	Moreland	21	F2	12x16 Gallery
20	F2	Ping Pong Puppet Museum			

SHOPS

13	E2	Sellwood Antique Mall	16	E2	Sellwood Antique Collective
15	E2	Camamu			

Westmoreland
Park

SE MCLOUGHLIN BLVD

SE TACOMA ST

0		300 yds
0		300 m

DISTANCE ACROSS MAP
Approximate: 2.2 mi or 3.5 km

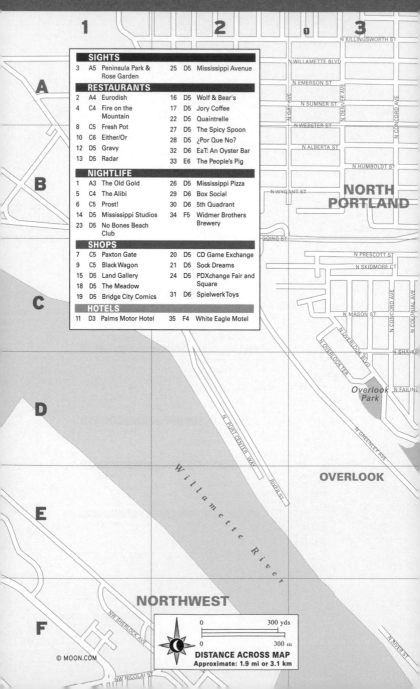

MAP 6

SIGHTS
| 3 | A5 | Peninsula Park & Rose Garden | 25 | D5 | Mississippi Avenue |

RESTAURANTS
2	A4	Eurodish	16	D5	Wolf & Bear's
4	C4	Fire on the Mountain	17	D5	Jory Coffee
8	C5	Fresh Pot	22	D5	Quaintrelle
10	C6	Either/Or	27	D5	The Spicy Spoon
12	D5	Gravy	28	D5	¿Por Que No?
13	D5	Radar	32	D6	EaT: An Oyster Bar
			33	E6	The People's Pig

NIGHTLIFE
1	A3	The Old Gold	26	D5	Mississippi Pizza
5	C4	The Alibi	29	D6	Box Social
6	C5	Prost!	30	D6	5th Quadrant
14	D5	Mississippi Studios	34	F5	Widmer Brothers Brewery
23	D5	No Bones Beach Club			

SHOPS
7	C5	Paxton Gate	20	D5	CD Game Exchange
9	C5	Black Wagon	21	D5	Sock Dreams
15	D5	Land Gallery	24	D5	PDXchange Fair and Square
18	D5	The Meadow	31	D6	Spielwerk Toys
19	D5	Bridge City Comics			

HOTELS
| 11 | D3 | Palms Motor Hotel | 35 | F4 | White Eagle Motel |

© MOON.COM

DISTANCE ACROSS MAP
Approximate: 1.9 mi or 3.1 km

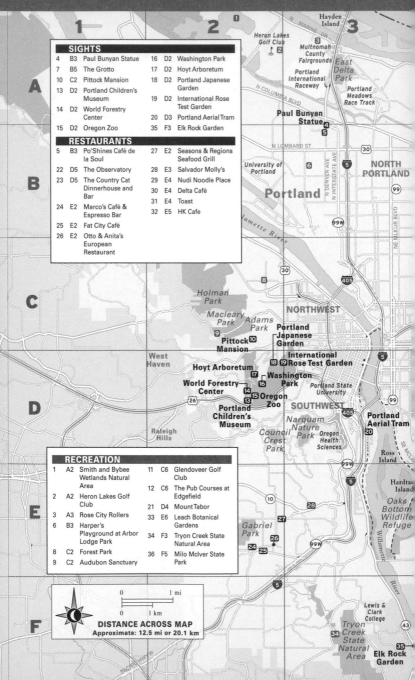

SIGHTS

4	B3	Paul Bunyan Statue	16	D2	Washington Park	
7	B5	The Grotto	17	D2	Hoyt Arboretum	
10	C2	Pittock Mansion	18	D2	Portland Japanese Garden	
13	D2	Portland Children's Museum	19	D2	International Rose Test Garden	
14	D2	World Forestry Center	20	D3	Portland Aerial Tram	
15	D2	Oregon Zoo	35	F3	Elk Rock Garden	

RESTAURANTS

5	B3	Po'Shines Café de la Soul	27	E2	Seasons & Regions Seafood Grill	
22	D5	The Observatory	28	E3	Salvador Molly's	
23	D5	The Country Cat Dinnerhouse and Bar	29	E4	Nudi Noodle Place	
24	E2	Marco's Café & Espresso Bar	30	E4	Delta Café	
25	E2	Fat City Café	31	E4	Toast	
26	E2	Otto & Anita's European Restaurant	32	E5	HK Cafe	

RECREATION

1	A2	Smith and Bybee Wetlands Natural Area	11	C6	Glendoveer Golf Club
2	A2	Heron Lakes Golf Club	12	C6	The Pub Courses at Edgefield
3	A3	Rose City Rollers	21	D4	Mount Tabor
6	B3	Harper's Playground at Arbor Lodge Park	33	E6	Leach Botanical Gardens
8	C2	Forest Park	34	F3	Tryon Creek State Natural Area
9	C2	Audubon Sanctuary	36	F5	Milo McIver State Park

0   1 mi

0   1 km

DISTANCE ACROSS MAP
Approximate: 12.5 mi or 20.1 km

4

5

6

WASHINGTON
OREGON

Columbia River

Lemon
Island

NE MARINE DR

Portland
International
Airport

NE AIRPORT WAY

NE COLUMBIA BLVD

NE 33RD AVE

NE KILLINGSWORTH ST

30

The Grotto
7

NE FREMONT ST

30

NORTHEAST

NE SANDY BLVD

CASCADE HWY

NE BROADWAY

Rose City
Golf Course

84

84

To
12

NE GLISAN ST

11

E BURNSIDE

Laurelhurst
Park

205

SE STARK ST

23
22

SE STARK ST

SE HAWTHORNE BLVD

21

SOUTHEAST

Mt.
Tabor
Park

SE DIVISION ST

SE POWELL BLVD

26

SE 28TH AVE

SE 39TH AVE

SE 52ND AVE

213

32

Lents
Park

SE STEELE ST

31

SE FOSTER RD

SE HAROLD ST

WOODSTOCK

29 30

SE WOODSTOCK BLVD

SE 82ND AVE

33

Reed
College

SE 45TH AVE

MORELAND

Westmoreland
Park

Lincoln
Memorial
Cemetery

SELLWOOD

99

Milwaukie

SE KING RD

224

To
36

39

224

213

205

Linwood

© MOON.COM

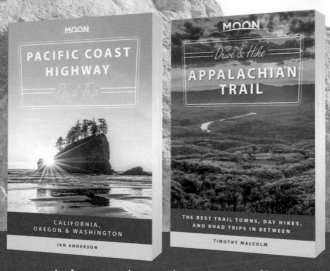

Advice on where to sleep, eat, and explore

Detailed driving directions including mileage and drive times

Itineraries for a range of timelines

MOON

NEW ENGLAND *Road Trip*

BOSTON, ACADIA NATIONAL PARK, WHITE MOUNTAINS, BERKSHIRES, NEWPORT, AND CAPE COD

JEN ROSE SMITH

MOON

PACIFIC NORTHWEST *Road Trip*

SEATTLE, VANCOUVER, VICTORIA, THE OLYMPIC PENINSULA, PORTLAND, THE OREGON COAST & MOUNT RAINIER

ALLISON WILLIAMS

MOON

ROUTE 66 *Road Trip*

JESSICA DUNHAM

MOON

SOUTH FLORIDA & THE KEYS *Road Trip*

WITH MIAMI, WALT DISNEY WORLD, TAMPA & THE EVERGLADES

JASON FERGUSON

MOON

SOUTHWEST *Road Trip*

LAS VEGAS, ZION & BRYCE, MONUMENT VALLEY, SANTA FE & TAOS, AND THE GRAND CANYON

TIM HULL

MOON

VANCOUVER & CANADIAN ROCKIES *Road Trip*

VICTORIA, BANFF, JASPER, CALGARY, THE OKANAGAN, WHISTLER & THE SEA-TO-SKY HIGHWAY

CAROLYN B. HELLER

Explore the city, escape into nature,

or go where the road takes you.....

Gear up for a bucket list vacation

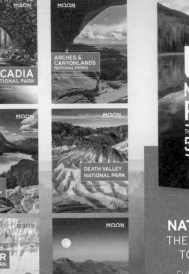

MOON USA
NATIONAL PARKS
THE COMPLETE GUIDE
TO ALL 59 PARKS

Full color · 700 pages
US $24.99 | CAN $32.49

Inside *Moon USA National Parks* find:

· Lists of the best parks for you: Find out where to hike, ski, camp, spot wildlife and more

· Handy resources: planning tips, detailed maps, and full-color photos

· Epic road trips linking multiple parks together

· Spaces to collect each national park's stamp and a fold-out map to chart your adventure